SCHOLARLY RESOURCES FOR CHILDREN AND CHILDHOOD STUDIES

A Research Guide and Annotated Bibliography

Edited by
VIBIANA BOWMAN

The Scarecrow Press, Inc.
Lanham, Maryland • Toronto • Plymouth, UK
2007

SCARECROW PRESS, INC.

Published in the United States of America
by Scarecrow Press, Inc.
A wholly owned subsidary of
The Rowman & Littlefield Publishing Group, Inc.
4501 Forbes Boulevard, Suite 200, Lanham, Maryland 20706
www.scarecrowpress.com

Estover Road
Plymouth PL6 7PY
United Kingdom

British Library Cataloguing in Publication Information Available

Library of Congress Cataloging-in-Publication Data
Scholarly resources for children and childhood studies : a research guide and
annotated bibliography / [edited by] Vibiana Bowman.
    p. cm.
  Includes bibliographical references and index.
  ISBN-13: 978-0-8108-5874-9 (pbk. : alk. paper)
  ISBN-10: 0-8108-5874-6 (pbk. : alk. paper)
  1. Children—Research. 2. Childhood development—Research. 3.
Interdisciplinary research—Methodology. 4. Children—Bibliography. I.
Bowman, Vibiana, 1953–
HQ767.85.S34 2007
305.23072—dc22

                                                                2006030612

∞™ The paper used in this publication meets the minimum requirements of
American National Standard for Information Sciences—Permanence of Paper for
Printed Library Materials, ANSI/NISO Z39.48-1992.
Manufactured in the United States of America.

This book is dedicated to my resource for children and childhood studies—
childhood studies—
my loving husband, Nick, and
my children—Elizabeth, T. K., Anna, Natasha, Michael, and David.

CONTENTS

PREFACE

Dear Reader,

The goal of *Scholarly Resources for Children and Childhood Studies* is to offer you, the student, a guided approach to literature searching in the interdisciplinary field of children and childhood studies (CCS). The contributors to this book are both faculty currently teaching in the area of CCS and academic librarians. The charge given to each contributor was to write a chapter that explained the process of scholarly research in his or her own particular area of expertise to a student unfamiliar with that discipline. Each contributor was to serve as a mentor and to suggest a search strategy, discuss significant concepts and vocabulary, and list the major resources that scholars in that area would be expected to use. Since CCS is an interdisciplinary field, during your course of study you will be doing projects for faculty who are specialists in a variety of disciplines. It was our thought that a resource guide that gave an overview of how scholarly papers are researched and written for those disciplines would be helpful. Thus, this book, which is based on our experiences in producing our own works of scholarly literature as well as our work with undergraduates and graduate students, came to be.

Scholarly Resources for Children and Childhood Studies is not intended as an exhaustive or definitive list of in-print research resources. The creation of such a list would be a Sisyphean task for two reasons: first, any bibliography of resources is essentially outdated once the final manuscript is complete; and second, all sources of scholarly information are potentially relevant to CCS researchers. My collaborators and I, therefore, have chosen to put the emphasis on useful resources and effective research methodologies.

Each chapter is written from a different perspective and uses a different style. The intent of serving as a mentor to you, the interdisciplinary scholar, is the thread that runs through this work to unify it as a whole.

The book is divided into two parts. Part 1, "Defining the Field," provides background information about interdisciplinary study in general and CCS in particular, as well as an outline of basic research practices. A list of recommended websites is also included along with suggested strategies for locating CCS materials. The chapters in part 2, "Research and Resources," include suggested resources from the main disciplines that contribute to CCS and research strategies illustrated with sample searches. Please note, we have made a conscious decision not to include the areas of medicine and law. While these are important areas of inquiry for CCS, the resources and research methodologies are so specialized they could not be compressed into workable chapters for this endeavor. Each area deserves a book of its own and would be worthy research projects for CCS scholars.

If the world of scholarship and intellectual inquiry can be viewed as a large and lively dinner party, CCS scholars are the new guests to the table. They represent the voice of the world's children and the paradigm of childhood—a voice that has not yet had a say at this dinner conversation. Over the next few years, as the field emerges and codifies, there will be lively debates, questions, problems, and wrangling over terms and definitions as scholars attempt to reach a consensus about the field. It is the modest hope of the contributors to this work to help set the table and to guide you to your seat so that you can engage in the conversation.

Cordially,
Vibiana Bowman

I

DEFINING THE FIELD

1

TOWARD A DEFINITION OF CHILDREN AND CHILDHOOD STUDIES

Vibiana Bowman and Laura B. Spencer

IT ISN'T EASY BEING GREEN

This book was not easy to write. Scholarly works, as well as works about scholarship, are usually based on a literary canon, that is, works that have stood the test of time and the scrutiny of the academic community. In the world of academia, children and childhood studies (CCS) is a relative newcomer, and its canon is being built by a group of dedicated scholars. A lack of a well-defined list of canonical works makes it a difficult and humbling experience to write a guide to the literature of the field. Normally in a guide such as this, one gets to be a "dwarf standing on the shoulders of giants."[1] CCS, however, is growing its own giants and we dwarves are scrambling to get a vantage point. So starting with the premise that CCS is a work in progress, and with all due apologies to Kermit the Frog, giants, and dwarves, we begin this discussion on scholarship in CCS.

THE BLIND MEN AND THE ELEPHANT

In this introductory chapter we set the stage for research in the interdisciplinary field of CCS by defining our key terms and concepts. For this endeavor, it is important to be clear about how the term *interdisciplinary* is being used and what one is talking about when referring to *children and childhood studies*. These are terms that are difficult to find a consensus in scholarly literature. So, in the time-honored tradition of using fables to illustrate complicated concepts, we offer the following tale.

3

Long ago the Buddha told this story of "The Blind Men and the Elephant." A raja sent six men, blind from birth, to go observe an elephant. When they returned he asked each in turn to describe the mighty beast. The first blind man had only touched the elephant's head and he answered that the elephant was like a pot. The second man, who had felt the elephant's ear, replied, no—the elephant was like a fan. The third, he who had observed the tusk, said that the beast was like a spear. And so it went with each of the blind men arguing that the elephant was like the only part that he had come into contact with: a tree (the leg), a wall (the side), or a snake (the tail). On and on they quarreled until they came to blows. The Buddha concluded:

> O how they cling and wrangle, some who claim,
> For preacher and monk, the honored name!
> For quarreling, each to his view, they cling.
> Such folk see only one side of a thing.[2]

We use this parable to illustrate the difficulty of writing about a field of interdisciplinary study. Problems abound when it comes to establishing definitions, delineating boundaries, and reaching a consensus about methodology. When approaching an interdisciplinary project, a scholar tends to view that project through the lens of her own discipline. This viewing lens includes many factors and considerations, such as that discipline's vocabulary, constructs, theoretical frameworks, and style of writing. An economist and a literary critic look at the question of adoption from perspectives as different as those of the blind man who held the elephant's trunk to those of the blind man who touched the elephant's leg. While each perception is true, it is only a discrete part of the truth. One must touch all the parts of the elephant, and, perhaps more important, one needs to be aware that such other parts exist in order to arrive at a complete and accurate description. Every discipline provides invaluable contributions to the world community of scholarship. It is the goal of an interdisciplinary endeavor to synthesize those areas of knowledge in order to provide a more complete picture of complex areas of study. In the section that follows, we discuss the problems and promise of the two different approaches to scholarship.

DISCIPLINE AND INTERDISCIPLINE

In "Mending Wall," Robert Frost responds to the proverb "Good fences make good neighbors":

Before I built a wall I'd ask to know
What I was walling in or walling out,
And to whom I was like to give offence.
Something there is that doesn't love a wall,
That wants it down.[3]

The setting of boundaries, the keeping in and keeping out of one thing from another, is as much a part of academic disciplines as it is a part of human relationships. Just as people live in physical communities or neighborhoods, knowledge lives in academic neighborhoods or disciplines. In this discussion, the term *discipline* is used in its broadest sense, that is, as a general field of study: psychology, sociology, anthropology, and so on. Disciplines are a way for scholars to organize information—its creation, analysis, interpretation, and communication—and thus each has its own vocabulary, conventions, style of writing, canon of recognized works, and specific methodology toward addressing scholarly questions. The last part of the twentieth century saw the rise of a different approach to academic inquiry, the interdisciplinary approach, and is represented by areas such as African American studies, American studies, and women's studies. These "interdisciplines" represent the "something" in Frost's poem "that doesn't love a wall." Scholars in these areas jump over boundaries and raid their neighbors' orchards (so to speak) for methods and materials. More simply put, interdisciplinary study draws on all fields of inquiry. Their goal of an "interdiscipline" is to look at research issues from a particular point of view, one that, until the rise of the specific interdiscipline, was underrepresented in the mainstream disciplines. With the rise of the interdisciplinary approach, scholars looking at big-picture issues are discovering that while disciplinary boundaries serve an important and effective means of organizing and creating information, these boundaries can also serve as barriers to scholars outside a field.

In the attempt to overcome the restrictions that accompany a single perspective to a complicated academic inquiry, an interdiscipline runs into difficulties of its own. Scholarly communication requires that some set of terminology, conventions, methodology, writing style, and canon of works must be used. The question arises: Whose? An interdiscipline draws on all pertinent scholarship and will, at least initially, have no conventions unique to itself. When an inquiry leads an interdisciplinary researcher to discipline-specific materials that go beyond his level of expertise, problems arise. While the interdiscipline offers the vantage point of broad vision and broad scholarship, it pays for these advantages by running the risk of compromised focus and methodological messes. It is difficult, if not impossible, for a single researcher to know multiple fields as deeply as his or her own, and it can be difficult to communicate across disciplinary borders. So, while it is refreshing to be not limited to one methodology for studying a chosen phenomenon, that very lack of limits can give rise to scholarly confusion. This tension between depth and specificity versus breadth and big picture is part of the controversy that surrounds the development of interdisciplinary study. The section that follows provides some background information about interdisciplinary endeavors, including the issues that have emerged, problems, and successes.

A VERY BRIEF HISTORY OF
INTERDISCIPLINARY INITIATIVES

At the start of the twentieth century, developed countries had new tools for industry, communication, and transportation. One could argue that the world was beginning to shrink and a nascent global outlook was starting to emerge. World War I inflicted tragic devastation on the world community. As an answer to that devastation, diplomats, scholars, artists, and humanitarians from various fields combined resources and expertise to work on international initiatives, to sponsor culture and peace.[4] By the 1930s, scholars in various disciplines engaged in "modern," that is, postwar, academic inquiry began to find traditional disciplinary boundaries to be limiting and began to form strategies for working around them. The *Oxford English Dictionary* states that the first use of the word *interdisciplinary* was in a 1937 announcement from the Social Science Research Council (SSRC) printed in the *Journal of Educational Sociology*.[5] In this announcement, SSRC offered a postdoctoral research fellowship for "training of an interdisciplinary nature."[6] An earlier use of the term is found in a shorter announcement of an SSRC award in 1933 for "research, training, preferably interdisciplinary in nature" in the journal *Social Forces*.[7]

Interdisciplinary endeavors were spurred on, at least in part, by America's entrance into World War II. As part of the War effort, scholars were pressed into service to understand communities and regions beyond the United States' borders. One such project was the Ethnogeographic Board, created in 1942 and disbanded in 1945. William Duncan Strong, the Board's first director, described the project as "an extra-governmental agency concerned with war and postwar problems in the field of ethnogeography, the study of human and natural resources of world areas, particularly with communities and cultural regions outside the continental United States."[8] The Board, sponsored by the American Council of Learned Societies, the Social Science Research Council, the National Research Council, and the Smithsonian Institution, was charged with helping the war effort through social science research. Social scientists gathered and disseminated information about the "geography, languages, and cultures of non-European theaters of the war, especially Africa, Japan, and Micronesia."[9] According to Strong, "The Ethnogeographic Board, because of its regional approach to human problems in the geographic, biological and social sciences, is interdisciplinary in scope."[10]

Another interdisciplinary initiative that emerged in the 1940s was American studies, an academic approach for studying America as a whole, whose origins can be traced back to the 1920s and 1930s.[11] "In several Eastern universities during the thirties, we can see mounting restlessness with conventional disciplinary boundaries. What gave form to this restlessness was a quest for 'The American Mind.'"[12] The presence and influence of Americans in Europe after World War II were instrumental in the founding of American Studies centers and institutes in European colleges and universities during the late 1940s.[13] Back in the United States, during the same time period, the Carnegie Corporation funded American studies programs in several large colleges and universities "including Brown, Amherst, Minnesota, and the University of Pennsylvania."[14] By the latter part of the 1950s, scholars were debating the merits of this interdiscipline. Henry Nash Smith, as quoted in Maddox, *Locating American Studies*, 1, observed, "The problem of method in American studies arises because the investigation of American culture as a whole does not coincide with the customary field of operations of any established academic discipline."[15]

It can be argued that American studies are now a respected and accepted area of study in the academic community. Currently, there are dozens of college and university undergraduate and graduate American studies programs in the United States and abroad. There are also high school American studies programs throughout the United States.[16] American studies scholars took established boundaries of inquiry and were able to push "those boundaries outward to include objects of study, and methods of study, that reflect more accurately and honestly the varieties of experience in the United States and that can, by their inclusion, decenter the older, monolithic narratives of national history."[17]

While the scholarly community of the 1940s and 1950s was generally supportive of cooperation and communication across disciplines, there were critics of the approach and cautions were raised. In 1958, the journal *An-*

nals of the New York Academy of Sciences examined the trend. D. H. Dabelstein, in "Interdisciplinary Research in Rehabilitation," wrote that "the findings and discussions of the many professions are dispersed among a wide variety of professional publications. No serious effort has been made to bring this literature together to provide a basic body of knowledge or to determine what significance the findings in one profession may have for another profession."[18] The tension between depth versus breadth in scholarship was articulated in the same issue. Dale R. Lindsay, in the essay "Methods and Sources of Stimulating Interdisciplinary Research," wrote, "The solution is not the creation of generalists to displace specialists, but the recognition of the interdependence of disciplines and the willingness to invite expert participation from other fields. There must be a continued effort to maintain and increase the individual's sharp focus upon the details of his primary discipline, coupled with an increased effort to provide him with an awareness of the potential contributions of other disciplines to the solutions he seeks."[19]

Social and political movements in the latter part of the twentieth century gave rise to other interdisciplinary initiatives—ones imbued with political and societal imperatives. African American studies and women's studies programs were initiated by scholars for the purpose of bringing to the academy voices and points of view that had been heretofore unrepresented or underrepresented in the scholarship and canons of various disciplines. As with American studies, the purpose of this interdiscipline was to provide a big-picture, integrated approach to academic inquiry. Politics, power, and voice are all imperatives in the creation of interdisciplinary fields of study, including American studies. "The relationship between politics, power, and American studies is an issue dealt with every day by those who teach about the United States in another country."[20] With African American and women's studies, however, there was an additional impetus—a desire for justice and cultural transformation.

African American studies and women's studies have many points of commonality in their rise as fields of study within the academic community. Both have been instrumental in changing established canon and language used in scholarly communication, and expanding perspectives in scholarship toward multiculturalism and diversity. Scholars in both fields championed the argument that African Americans and women in the United States were disenfranchised and marginalized in politics, the economy, and in society at large. This disenfranchisement extended into academia. Early scholars in these fields argued that the intellectual achievements of African Americans and women were not given proper weight and consideration in the scholarly community. Each program was founded during approximately the same time period. San Francisco State College founded the first black studies program in 1967[21] and San Diego State University founded a women's studies department in 1970.[22] Finally, each field can be termed established and successful. For both African American and women's studies there are graduate and undergraduate programs in colleges and universities throughout the world. In addition, each field has its own body of literature and research created by recognized scholars and writers.

The development of African American and women's studies in the United States each has a long, complicated, and rich history that cannot easily be compressed into a few sentences. For an interesting and concise overview of African American studies, including current issues and challenges in the field, read the "Introduction" to *The Encyclopedia of Black Studies* by Molefi Kente Asante and Ama Mazama.[23] An excellent history of women's studies can be found in *When Women Ask the Questions: Creating Women's Studies in America*.[24] For a more in-depth treatment of the history of interdisciplinary studies, students should read Julie Thompson Klein's *Interdisciplinarity: History, Theory, and Practice*.[25]

As stated previously, interdisciplinary fields of study came to represent a particular perspective in academic inquiry. The field of CCS presents an interesting set of circumstances since, for the most part, unlike women or African Americans, children are not the scholars creating a new area of scholarship. It would, therefore, seem that a particularly important—and somewhat difficult—charge for CCS is to define itself: what perspective does it represent and what, specifically, is it studying?

CHILDHOOD STUDIES: WHOSE CHILDREN? WHOSE CHILDHOOD?

Children, themselves, learn about their world by asking eloquently fundamental questions (such as why is the sky blue). Following this spirit of inquiry, a student of CCS might begin by asking who is a child, what is a child, where is a child, and when is a child?[26] One can begin by an obvious physical description. A child is a young human with a certain physiognomy, expected lifespan, and wants and needs necessary for survival. One can look at a child from a sociological perspective since that child holds memberships in various communities: family, school, and perhaps even work. One can look at the child anthropologically. The child is a *Homo sapiens* and, therefore, has ties and bonds to all humans worldwide, but can be described also by his or her particular time, place, and community. Although it would seem logical that all people share a common understanding of the concept of *child*, since all adults were once children, in an academic endeavor, it can be argued that careful definitions are needed. *Childhood* is an even more complicated concept on which to reach an accord. While all children pass through some form of childhood, *childhood* is a concept that varies across historic time periods and cultures. Its definition includes aspects of law, politics, sociology, economics, and religion. To illustrate the difficulty in reaching a consensus of meaning for these two concepts, *child* and *childhood* are briefly looked at in the context of contemporary American society.

The question What is a child? is currently at the center of America's culture wars. At what point does one become a child with legal rights and protections? Does a human being become a child by the act of being born or are there rights to be accorded to a human from the period between conception and birth? In the United States dozens of states have passed legislation granting legal protections to a child in utero.[27] In 2004, partly as part of a rising political initiative and partly in response to the Laci Peterson murder (Ms. Peterson was pregnant and nearly full-term at the time of the crime), Congress passed the "Unborn Victims of Violence Act," which makes it a federal criminal offense to do harm to an unborn child.[28] According to the American Civil Liberties Union (ACLU), "Because the Act applies to all stages of prenatal development, it is the first federal law to recognize a zygote (fertilized egg), a blastocyst (pre-implantation embryo), an embryo (through week eight of a pregnancy) or a fetus as an independent 'victim' of a crime with legal rights distinct from the woman who has been harmed by a violent criminal act."[29] As evidenced by these controversies, if it is difficult for one country to reach an agreement regarding who or what is a child, and when, how much more difficult is it for a world community of scholars?

The quest for a consensus of definition does not get any easier with the construct of *childhood*. As previously mentioned, the meaning of *childhood* changes across time, place, and culture. The childhood of a modern twelve-year-old, middle-class girl living in the United States differs radically from that of her counterpart in medieval Europe or her contemporary in Sierra Leone. One could begin to construct a definition of childhood by using the chronological age of a person. But, even such an easily established boundary varies greatly in the United States. Various rights, privileges, and restrictions are granted to American citizens from the ages of thirteen to twenty-one depending on where they live. State definitions of the *age of majority* range from eighteen (most states) to twenty-one in Pennsylvania.[30] There are discrepancies within the definition of *age of majority* as to what rights are bestowed. In some states, while eighteen is the age of majority, the legal age for adult activities like purchasing alcohol or tobacco and gambling is twenty-one. In all states except Mississippi, eighteen-year-olds can marry without parental consent. (In Mississippi, parental consent is required for persons under the age of twenty-one.[31]) States also vary on whether a minor has the right to consent to an abortion without parental consent, whether they can sign legal contracts, and the age of criminal responsibility.

There are historical and cultural considerations for the construct of *childhood*. In the Western world, the concept of *childhood* was radically changed by significant sociological phenomena such as the Industrial Revolution, the shift from rural to urban populations, and the rise of the middle class. For example, *teenager* was not part of the English vocabulary until 1941 and, incidentally, the word was coined in the United States.[32] The appearance of this new word reflected a paradigm shift in America regarding the way that young adults were viewed, including expectations regarding educational levels, professional aspirations, income potentials, and personal responsibility. With the coming of the teenager and the rising expectation that children would complete college, childhood grew longer in middle-class America. Again, as with the definition of *child*, the difficulty in constructing a universally agreed-upon definition of *childhood* is apparent. In the United States alone the construct has changed radically in a relatively short time period. The complexity of reaching a consensus regarding these terms is obvious. This complex task is at the heart of CCS and is what makes it such an intriguing academic field.

A WORKING DEFINITION OF CHILDHOOD STUDIES

Undergraduate and graduate programs that award bachelor's and master's degrees in CCS are a recent addition to higher education. It should be noted that the terms *child studies* and *childhood studies* have been used for decades by scholars and researchers in disciplines such as education, psychology, medicine, anthropology, sociology, and social work. CCS can trace its lineage to groundbreaking research on or about children by intellectual giants including Sigmund Freud, Maria Montessori, Jean Piaget, and Margaret Mead. While a definitive work on the history of CCS as an academic discipline is yet to be written, interesting discussions of the development of the field can be found in Mary Jane Kehily's *An Introduction to Childhood*

Studies[33] and in Jean and Richard Mills' *Childhood Studies: A Reader in Perspectives of Childhood.*[34] There is a general agreement that the first CCS programs began in the United Kingdom in the mid-1980s. These programs were "modules" of study within established fields such as education. According to Kehily, dedicated degree programs in childhood studies are a recent development. "The Open University degree for example, began in 2003 and was one of the first in the UK."[35] As in the UK, in the United States there are dozens of children/childhood "modules," minors, or concentrations within the degree programs of academic disciplines. Rutgers University, Camden, New Jersey, is developing the first program in the United States to award degrees (BA through PhD) specifically in CCS. This program is slated to begin in 2007, and other programs in the United States will follow.

What then is *children and childhood studies*? The definition, which follows, is offered as a starting point of discussion; as the field grows and expands so too will the definition.

Children and Childhood Studies (CCS) is an interdisciplinary field of study that centers on questions regarding children and childhood and representations of children and childhood. While CCS scholars utilize all areas of study, as a field CCS chiefly draws upon scholarship in the social sciences (specifically anthropology, economics, history, and sociology), the humanities (especially literature, religion, and the fine arts), and the behavioral sciences (with an emphasis on psychology). The unique perspective that CCS brings to the academic community is an underlying advocacy of children and the issues affecting their lives and well-being. The mission of CCS as a field of scholarship is to utilize all areas of contemporary study to ask the questions, understand the problems, and find the solutions toward improving the quality of childhood experienced by the world's community of children.

Arlene Skolnick in *Rethinking Childhood* invites the reader "to reconsider the concept of childhood itself—to think about the familiar subject in some unfamiliar ways. . . . [M]uch of what we tend to think of as obvious, natural, and universal about childhood may actually be problematic, arbitrary, and shaped by historical and cultural conditions."[36] This quote, taken from a work published in 1976, is telling. It articulates a quest to formulate a complete picture of childhood by drawing upon all pertinent fields of study. It is interesting to contrast Skolnick's quote with another from a later book also titled *Rethinking Childhood* published in 2004. Editors Pufall and Unsworth write,

[A]cademic disciplines nominally dedicated to the study of children tended to organize their empirical and practical work around ill-examined assumptions about children. More critically, they tended to study childhood by segmenting its facets and putting them under the methodological glass of each participating academic discipline, rather than seeing children first as persons and only then looking at the behaviors, social settings, and problems of their subjects."[37]

NOTES

1. Robert Burton, "The Anatomy of Melancholy," *Project Gutenberg*, www.gutenberg.org/files/10800/10800-h/10800-h.htm (accessed December 1, 2005).

2. Randy Wang, *The Blind Men and the Elephant*, www.cs.princeton.edu/~rywang/berkeley/258/parable.html (accessed December 1, 2005). Note: This website includes Mr. Wang's retelling of the classic Buddhist parable from the *Udana* (68–69) part of the collection of sacred Theravada Buddhist texts. This story was also retold by the American poet John Godfrey Saxe (1816–1887) in his poem "The Blind Men and the Elephant."

3. Robert Frost, "The Mending Wall," *North of Boston* (New York: Henry Holt, 1915), 12.

4. Vibiana Bowman and Nensi Brailo, "Protecting Our Shared Cultural Heritage: An Overview of Protocols and Projects," *Visual Resources* 21, no. 1 (March 2005): 7.

5. *Oxford English Dictionary Online*, s.v. "Interdisciplinary," available through subscription, dictionary.oed.com (accessed December 1, 2005).

6. "Research Projects and Methods in Educational Sociology," *Journal of Educational Sociology* 11, no. 4 (December 1937): 249–52.

7. "Announcements," *Social Forces* 11, no. 4 (May 1933): 588.

8. William Duncan Strong, "The Ethnogeographic Board," *Science* (New Series) 96, no. 2495 (23 October 1942): 381–82.

9. Smithsonian Institution Archives, "Ethnogeographic Board (Washington, D.C.)," *Smithsonian Institution Archives—Agency History*, siarchives.si.edu/research/ah00363egb.html (accessed December 1, 2005).

10. Strong, "The Ethnogeographic Board," 382.

11. Paul Giles, "Virtual Americas: The Internationalization of American Studies and the Ideology of Exchange," *American Quarterly* 50, no. 3 (September 1998): 526.

12. Lucy Maddox, ed., *Locating American Studies: The Evolution of a Discipline* (Baltimore: Johns Hopkins University Press, 1999), 177.

13. Allen Davis, "The Politics of American Studies," *American Quarterly* 43, no. 3 (September 1990): 354.

14. Davis, "The Politics of American Studies," 355.

15. Maddox, *Locating American Studies*, 1.

16. American Studies Association, *American Studies Program on the Web*, www
.georgetown.edu/crossroads/programs (accessed December 1, 2005).

17. Maddox, *Locating American Studies*, viii.

18. D. H. Dabelstein, "Interdisciplinary Research in Rehabilitation," *Annals of the New York Academy of Sciences* 74, no. 1 (30 September 1958): 40–44.

19. Dale R. Lindsay, "Methods and Sources of Stimulating Interdisciplinary Research," *Annals of the New York Academy of Sciences* 74, no. 1 (30 September 1958): 45–49.

20. Davis, "The Politics of American Studies," 354.

21. Molefi Kete Asante and Ama Mazama, "Introduction," in *Encyclopedia of Black Studies*, ed. Molefi Kete Asante and Ama Mazama (Thousand Oaks, Calif.: Sage, 2005), xxv.

22. San Diego State University, "Pioneering in Scholarship, Activism, and Internationalism," *San Diego State University: Women's Studies*, www-rohan.sdsu.edu/dept./wsweb (accessed December 1, 2005).

23. Asante and Mazama, *Encyclopedia of Black Studies*, xxv–xxxii.

24. Marilyn Jacoby Boxer, *When Women Ask the Questions: Creating Women's Studies in America* (Baltimore: Johns Hopkins University Press, 1998).

25. Julie Thompson Klein, *Interdisciplinarity: History, Theory, and Practice* (Detroit, Mich.: Wayne State University Press, 1990).

26. Peter B. Pufall and Richard P. Unsworth, *Rethinking Childhood* (New Brunswick, N.J.: Rutgers University Press, 2004), 12–19.

27. ACLU, "President Bush Signs Anti-Choice Measure into Law; ACLU Decries New Law as Undermining Reproductive Rights," *American Civil Liberties Union—Reproductive Freedom*, www.aclu.org//reproductiverights/fetalrights/12572 prs20040401.html (accessed December 1, 2005).

28. ACLU, "President Bush."

29. ACLU, "President Bush."

30. Richard A. Leiter, ed., "Legal Ages," in *National Survey of State Laws* (Detroit, Mich.: Gale Research, 1997), 405–18.

31. Leiter, "Marriage Requirements," in *National Survey of State Laws* (Detroit, Mich.: Gale Research, 1997), 357–62.

32. *Oxford English Dictionary Online*, s.v. "Teenager," available through subscription dictionary.oed.com (accessed December 1, 2005).

33. Mary Jane Kehily, *An Introduction to Childhood Studies* (Oxford, UK: Open University Press, 2004).

34. Jean Mills and Richard Mills, *Childhood Studies: A Reader in Perspectives of Childhood* (London: Routledge, 2000).

35. Mary Jane Kehily, e-mail message to author, December 19, 2005.

36. Arlene Skolnick, ed., "Introduction," *Rethinking Childhood: Perspectives on Development and Society* (Boston: Little, Brown, 1976), 1.

37. Pufall and Unsworth, *Rethinking Childhood*, x.

WORKS CITED

American Civil Liberties Union (ACLU). "President Bush Signs Anti-Choice Measure into Law; ACLU Decries New Law as Undermining Reproductive Rights." *American Civil Liberties Union—Reproductive Freedom.* www.aclu.org//reproductive rights/fetalrights/12572prs20040401.html.

American Studies Association. *American Studies Program on the Web.* www.georgetown .edu/crossroads/programs.

Announcements. *Social Forces* 11, no. 4 (May 1933): 588.

Asante, Molefi Kete, and Ama Mazama. "Introduction." In *Encyclopedia of Black Studies,* edited by Molefi Kete Asante and Ama Mazama. Thousand Oaks, Calif.: Sage, 2005.

Bowman, Vibiana, and Nensi Brailo. "Protecting Our Shared Cultural Heritage: An Overview of Protocols and Projects." *Visual Resources* 21, no. 1 (March 2005): 5–24.

Boxer, Marilyn Jacoby. *When Women Ask the Questions: Creating Women's Studies in America.* Baltimore: Johns Hopkins University Press, 1998.

Burton, Robert. "The Anatomy of Melancholy." *Project Gutenberg.* www.gutenberg.org/files/10800/10800-h/10800-h.htm.

Dabelstein, D. H. "Interdisciplinary Research in Rehabilitation." *Annals of the New York Academy of Sciences* 74, no. 1 (30 September 1958): 40–44.

Davis, Allen. "The Politics of American Studies." *American Quarterly* 43, no. 3 (September 1990): 353–74.

Frost, Robert. "The Mending Wall." In *North of Boston.* New York: Henry Holt, 1915.

Giles, Paul. "Virtual Americas: The Internationalization of American Studies and the Ideology of Exchange." *American Quarterly* 50, no. 3 (September 1998): 523–47.

Kehily, Mary Jane. *An Introduction to Childhood Studies.* Oxford, UK: Open University Press, 2004.

Klein, Julie Thompson. *Interdisciplinarity: History, Theory, and Practice.* Detroit, Mich.: Wayne State University Press, 1990.

Leiter, Richard A., ed. *National Survey of State Laws.* Detroit, Mich.: Gale Research, 1997.

Lindsay, Dale R. "Methods and Sources of Stimulating Interdisciplinary Research." *Annals of the New York Academy of Sciences* 74, no. 1 (September 30, 1958): 45–49.

Maddox, Lucy, ed. *Locating American Studies: The Evolution of a Discipline.* Baltimore: Johns Hopkins University Press, 1999.

Mills, Jean, and Richard Mills. *Childhood Studies: A Reader in Perspectives of Childhood.* London: Routledge, 2000.

Oxford English Dictionary Online. "Interdisciplinary." Available through subscription, dictionary.oed.com.

———. "Teenager." Available through subscription, dictionary.oed.com.

Pufall, Peter B., and Richard P. Unsworth. *Rethinking Childhood*. New Brunswick, N.J.: Rutgers University Press, 2004.

"Research Projects and Methods in Educational Sociology." *Journal of Educational Sociology* 11, no. 4 (December 1937): 249–52.

San Diego State University. "Pioneering in Scholarship, Activism, and Internationalism." *San Diego State University: Women's Studies*. www-rohan.sdsu.edu/dept./wsweb.

Skolnick, Arlene, ed. "Introduction." *Rethinking Childhood: Perspectives on Development and Society*. Boston: Little, Brown, 1976.

Smithsonian Institution Archives. "Ethnogeographic Board (Washington, D.C.)." *Smithsonian Institution Archives—Agency History*. siarchives.si.edu/research/ah00 363egb.html.

Strong, William Duncan. "The Ethnogeographic Board." *Science* (New Series) 96, no. 2495 (23 October 1942): 381–82.

Wang, Randy. *The Blind Men and the Elephant*. www.cs.princeton.edu/~rywang/berkeley/258/parable.html.

2

THE BASICS OF SCHOLARLY RESEARCH AND WRITING

Vibiana Bowman and Ellen Fennick

As stated previously, the goal of this book is to serve as a research guide for students of Children and Childhood Studies (CCS). In chapter 1 we discussed terminology and provided some background information about interdisciplinary studies in general and CCS in particular. In this chapter we focus on the basics of literature searching and scholarly writing. We approach these topics with the specific challenges and needs of the CCS student firmly in mind.

Scholarly writing, that is, literature written by scholars for scholars, is a particular kind of writing style with its own conventions and standards. Expectations of quality in a scholarly paper include good writing (flawless spelling and grammar); clarity of expression; a logical progression of ideas, opinions, and conclusions; and a listing of authoritative and verifiable source materials. While there are differences in style and content among different disciplines, these general expectations hold true throughout the academic community. Scholarly literature usually undergoes a process called peer review. In this process, as the name implies, a scholar's work is reviewed by his peers. Content, style, and the original contribution that the work makes to the *academy* (a term used to describe the academic community at large) are all judged. After careful consideration, the work in question is deemed worthy for publication or is sent back to the author. This editorial process serves a gate-keeping function. It ensures that only quality work finds its way into the literature of a particular field.

Student papers, at both the graduate and undergraduate level, also are a form of scholarly writing. While they do not go through the rigors of peer review, they are critiqued by faculty, who, as participants in the scholarly publishing community, also have high expectations for the content and style of the work that their students produce.

When writing for a community of interdisciplinary scholars and students (such as the readers of this book), it is important to be aware of the vocabulary one uses, namely, to define one's terms and to keep discussions as jargon-free as possible. Note to our readers: in this chapter, in which we are writing about scholarly writing while writing a scholarly work, we are painfully aware of our own shortcomings and feel a bit like Alice at the Mad Hatter's tea party:

> "Then you should say what you mean," the March Hare went on. "I do,"
> Alice hastily replied, "at least—at least I mean what I say—that's the
> same thing, you know." "Not the same thing a bit!" said the Hatter.[1]

We, therefore, attempt to heed our own advice and try to be as clear and concise as possible.

Even a simple term like *research* has different meanings to different types of scholars. *Research* for a history student frequently involves going to original source materials such as letters, diaries, and newspaper accounts of an event from the date that it occurred, and so on. *Research* for an experimental psychologist means designing a project according to accepted scientific procedures. *Research* for a statistician is gathering a set of meaningful statistics used for the analysis of a particular demographic group or a phenomenon. In this chapter, *research* refers to the process of a literature review: gathering information that relates to a particular topic; assessing that information with regard to relevance, timeliness, and accuracy; and using that information in an appropriate and intellectually honest manner. In order to research a topic efficiently and effectively, it helps to understand how scholarly information flows.

Research of scholarly literature is done in the opposite manner by which scholarly literature is created (see figure 2.1). Basically, a work of scholarly literature begins as an original idea, which is then vetted and codified through an incremental and formalized process. An original idea gets circulated informally within a scholar's network (verbally, in writing, or on the Web). Next, the idea/original work goes through the process of peer review (described earlier). The outcome of this process is that the work may be published in a journal or in an edited book or the author may expand the concept to a book-length work. This article or book may be cited by other scholars. Finally, this piece of scholarly literature may find its way into a reference work, and ultimately be considered part of the canon (established literature) of the author's field. This is a very simplified description of a complicated process that varies from discipline to discipline. However,

The Flow of Information

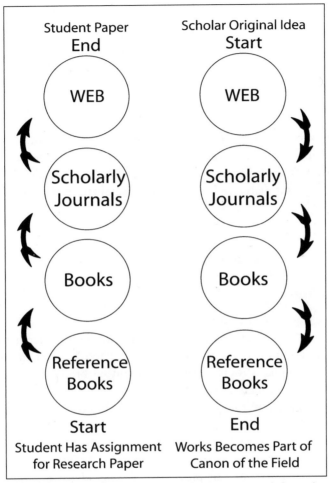

Figure 2.1.   **In the scholarly communication process, information is created through a process of peer review. So for a student, starting from the established canon of a discipline and working backwards is the most efficient way to do a literature search on a topic.**

the general outline serves for understanding the flow, which moves from informal to formal. The most efficient strategy for a student, therefore, is to start with the most codified, formal resource and work backwards, that is, reference resources, books (especially those from a university press), journal articles, and Web resources.

The next section outlines the basics of writing a research paper. Again, while there are variations in different disciplines, the basic process remains the same. The step-by-step procedure that follows is based on an online tutorial, *How to Write a Better Research Paper*, from the Paul Robeson Library, Rutgers University[2] (used with permission of the author and modified for students of CCS). Readers, please note that in this discussion, we mention some resources that may be available only from college and university libraries. Some of these resources are print-based, and therefore require a visit to the library, but others are available online through subscriptions (although very expensive) and, thus, may be available for you to use from home. Such online resources are usually password-protected. For more information about using academic, online, subscription materials check with a reference librarian at your college or university.

SCHOLARLY RESEARCH 101

Select a Topic

Before one begins to research and write, one needs to establish clearly what one wants to write about. A student may be assigned a topic or given a selection of topics by the instructor. There is a certain art to selecting or refining a topic. Ideally, it should be broad enough so that much related information is available, but narrow enough so that the paper has a meaningful focus. The supervising faculty member should always be a student's first recourse for help in establishing an area of research. Next, students should use one of the most important resources available at the library—the reference librarian. As information specialists, reference librarians can provide invaluable advice on the best resources for getting ideas for topics, devising search strategies, and for instruction on how to use research tools.

Some strategies for selecting topics include browsing recent journals to see what the "hot topics" are, looking through reference books and specialized encyclopedias, browsing through the library's new books and recent acquisitions, and using the bibliography provided in a course textbook. The student should then "test drive" the topic. An hour of concentrated searching should deliver enough books and articles to at least get a student started. If not, that student should seek some help with search strategies or with the topic selection process.

Locate Background Information

To research a topic, the student needs to know something about it. For example, a student writing a paper about the impact of Maria Montessori on early childhood education would need to know several basic facts about her in order to track down more in-depth information. When did Montessori live? What where her major accomplishments? What concepts or theories are associated with her? This kind of information is necessary in order to know what keywords or subject headings to use when searching catalogs and indexes.

In general, for a college-level paper, a student would do well to begin with a specialized encyclopedia for the subject area that she is researching. *The Encyclopedia of Early Childhood Education,*[3] for example, would serve for establishing background information about Maria Montessori. Specialized encyclopedias exist for all subjects from art to zoology. Students have access to these as well as other reference materials, whether print or online, through the reference department of their academic libraries. This search for background materials will also help the student to sharpen the focus of her paper and give her an overview of the topic.

Locate Books

Our student investigating Maria Montessori now knows when she lived (1870–1952), what she is famous for (the Montessori Method of education), and some concepts (early childhood development, early childhood education, sensory learning, discovery method).[4] She now needs some books and scholarly journal articles. For books, she can search the catalog, the tool for locating books in the library. Search strategy enters at this point. Our student can use *Montessori* as a keyword, which will locate all books that have any mention of that term in any of the fields for the catalog record for a book. Thus our student will retrieve books written by Montessori, books which have "Montessori" in the title, and books that have *Montessori* as a subject word. Once she retrieves her list of catalog "hits," she can look at the record to see what the exact subject headings are for the search she is doing. Another approach would be for her to use *Montessori* initially as a subject word or as an author search.

Depending on the specificity of the subject of the paper, the student may need to narrow the search results from the catalog. At this point she may need to use Boolean operators, such as *And* and *Or*. *And* is used to narrow results. *Montessori and Piaget* will produce a set of hits that intersects the set of books or articles about Montessori and the set of books or articles about Piaget. That means the hit list will include all books in which both people are mentioned (see figure 2.2). The operator *Or* is used to expand a search. *Montessori or Piaget* will produce a set of results that includes books or articles about either Montessori or Piaget (see figure 2.3). These same Boolean operators are used for creating searches when locating articles in indexes.

Every research project or writing assignment will have its own parameters, guidelines, restrictions, or suggestions for the materials to be used. Frequently, a student will be instructed to use books published by academic presses, that is, by publishing companies affiliated with colleges or universities or publishers who specialize in scholarly materials. This guideline is frequently imposed to steer students away from popular treatments of topics. For example, *Secrets of the Baby Whisperer: How to Calm, Connect, and Communicate with Your Baby*[5] is a popular press book about early childhood. *Theories of Infant Development*[6] would be considered a scholarly work. Again, depending on the topic, the publication date of the work might be of primary importance. Current advances and discoveries will not be reflected in older books.

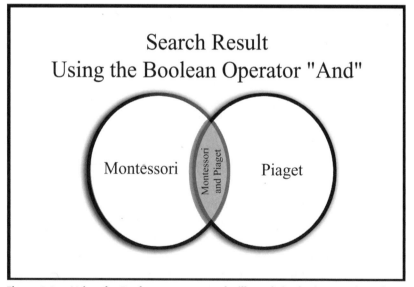

Figure 2.2.   Using the Boolean operator *and* will result in the intersection of two terms. In this case, the search results will include all items that have both the search terms *Montessori* and *Piaget*. *And* limits the number of hits since each hit must have both terms specified in order to be a match.

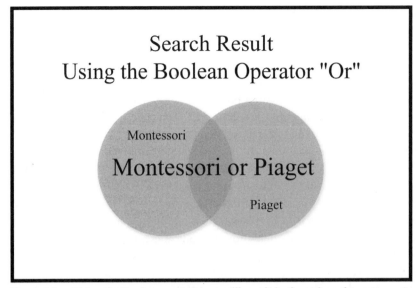

Figure 2.3.   Using the Boolean operator *or* will result in the union of two terms. In this case, the search results will include all items that have either the search term *Montessori* or the search term *Piaget*. Or expands the number of hits since each hit is required to have only one of the two terms specified.

When searching for books, students should ask a reference librarian about interlibrary loans and reciprocal borrowing agreements with other academic and public libraries. A catalog search will only uncover the books that the library owns. To locate all available books on a given topic, a student can use multilibrary catalogs, databases such as Books in Print, and Web resources such as Amazon.com.

Locate Articles

Typically, a book takes one to two years to be researched, written, and published (frequently longer). Thus, many books are outdated by the time the ink dries on the page. A student's next step in the research process is to find updated material from newspaper, magazines (such as *Time, Cosmopolitan,* or *Redbook*), professional and trade journals (*American Libraries, Computer World,* or *Chemical Week*), and scholarly journals (*Child Development, JAMA: Journal of the American Medical Association,* and *Pediatrics*). As with the books, there may be restrictions on the type of periodicals that a student can use as source material for a research project. Often a faculty member will require that students use only scholarly journals.

Scholarly journals differ from popular press magazines in scope and purpose. These periodicals are written by scholars and for scholars; they are not usually found for sale at magazine stands or general retail outlets; they do not sell advertising for consumer goods; and they do not usually have a staff of writers. Scholarly journals are typically published by professional organizations or a scholarly press with a board of editors that decides which articles will be published through a process called peer review. This is a process by which a panel of scholars selects articles for publication. The articles selected are judged on the quality of the research and writing and on the quality of the content. Are the results verifiable? Is the research sound? Does this article contribute something of substance to the academic community?

The finding tool for locating articles in any periodical is an index. Many academic libraries have searchable, online indexes and databases that allow students to access articles from periodical literature. Depending on the subscription that the library has to the indexing and database service, the results will either be full text or bibliographic citations that the student can use to locate the article in a periodical. Most academic libraries subscribe to hundreds of online databases that provide coverage for thousands of periodicals and journals. In part 2 of this book, the student can find suggestions for important databases for specific fields of inquiry.

It is frequently useful to begin a research project by using the full-text, multidisciplinary database for which the college or university has a subscription. EBSCO and ProQuest are two of the largest providers of such databases. A researcher can get a quick overview of scholarly journal literature on a topic by doing a search in such a database, but restricting the results to "peer reviewed" and "full text." The results list produced by such a search will inform the student as to what is the current status of the topic in the scholarly literature. It is also a way of testing out a potential topic to see what kind of materials are available. As with the catalog search for books, a researcher can search using keywords, author, or subject headings (the controlled vocabulary used by the database vendors). Typically, students will use indexes and databases to find articles by topic and therefore will search by a keyword or subject. Again, as with books, it may be necessary to narrow down or expand search results through the use of Boolean operators. Several searches may be necessary before a student gets the exact results that he or she needs. Some databases offer a "Search History," which lists the searches the student has performed and the results that those searches produced. If the database being used does not automatically keep track of searches, it is useful to keep notes on which search terms were used. For example, our student was researching Maria Montessori. She has located background material, found books by and about Montessori, and now wants to locate current information about the Montessori approach. She does a search in her library's full-text database using *Montessori* as a keyword. She restricts her search to "full text" and "peer reviewed." If she retrieves too many results, she may want to limit her search by using *And* and another concept such as methods or development, or she may decide to concentrate on a specific aspect of childhood such as infancy. If our student does not get enough results she may want to open up her search by using a broader concept such as early childhood education, try a different database, or remove the full-text limit for her search.

Remember—for help in locating materials that are not available as full text through the database, for help in creating a search strategy, and for help in using the databases, the student should not hesitate to ask the librarian. If the library does not own a particular journal, the student should ask the librarian about interlibrary loan procedures for accessing articles.

Locate Additional Materials on the World Wide Web

The beauty of the World Wide Web—its accessibility—is also its greatest flaw. The freedom of expression fostered by the free flow of information; the opportunities for musicians, writers, and artists to find an audience for their creative efforts; and business opportunities for small businesses and cottage-industry entrepreneurs that the Internet has made possible are all remarkable. There is a downside, however. There is no editorial control with postings on the Internet, which means that for a large percentage of the content on the Web there is no fact checking and no quality screening. Internet sites truly range from the ridiculous to the sublime, from postings from hate groups to the Vatican home page, from the National Geographic resource material to sites about Elvis and alien abductions. When venturing out on the World Wide Web, students need to make good use of their critical thinking skills in assessing the accuracy, validity, editorial voice, and authenticity of websites. A good rule of thumb is that Web pages produced by educational institutions and government and professional organizations have more weight than websites hosted by public domains. Many academic libraries and departments have pathfinders and lists of suggested Web resources. For example, our student who is researching Maria Montessori may find very useful material at the International Montessori Index (www.montessori.edu/web.html). This page lists an author, it is hosted by an educational organization (signified by the "edu" in the URL), it was recently updated, and shares links with other reputable organizations. When in doubt about the validity of a website, check with a librarian or supervising faculty member.

When using search engines such as Google or Yahoo, researchers can make use of Boolean operators for restricting or widening a search. Most search engines offer help and searching tips for using Boolean operators, truncation symbols (to search on base words and get alternate endings), and for keeping words together as phrases. Google is now offering Google Scholar (scholar.google.com), which limits Google searches to scholarly material. Researchers can also set their preferences so that the search links with their college or university's library catalog. While this service is fairly new and the academic community is debating its pros and cons, students should certainly use it as another information-gathering tool in conjunction with the resources mentioned above.

In conclusion, it is important for students to be able to distinguish the kind of materials that are accessed through the Web. The databases, indexes, catalogs, and e-books available through academic libraries are delivered electronically, but they have print counterparts or are subject to a screening process or editorial review. Most of these materials are part of the "Invisible Web" in that they cannot be accessed though search engines. They are only available through subscription and usually available through the library at a college or university, and as mentioned above, are frequently password-protected. Other materials that are available freely on the Web, be they from educational, professional, or government organizations, or even from individuals, may answer a student's information needs but should be carefully vetted. Chapter 12 of this book goes into detail regarding how to locate and assess relevant CCS materials on the World Wide Web. The author also provides a webography of useful resources and relevant organizations.

INFORMATION LITERACY
AND INTELLECTUAL HONESTY

Information Literacy

In this first decade of the twenty-first century, scholarly information is literally at one's fingertips—only a few mouse clicks away. This electronic environment allows for easy access and dissemination, and a specialist in one field can read cutting-edge research in another field. But what of the skill set that is needed to evaluate the relevancy of the information, analyze its content, and use the information in a meaningful manner according to the conventions of good scholarship? These kinds of critical thinking skills fall under the general paradigm of information literacy. Information literacy is a skill set distinctive from computer literacy. A computer-literate person has the skills necessary to use a computer to complete specific tasks and would include such skills as using the keyboard for typing, creating a document with a word processing program, using the mouse for navigating Web pages, and demonstrating an understanding of the conventions of either a Windows or Macintosh operating system. While these skills are necessary and valuable, they constitute a different skill set than those necessary for information literacy. The Association of College and Research Libraries in association with the American Association for Higher Education has created a set of information literacy standards for colleges and universities.[7] According to these guidelines,

> An information literate individual is able to: determine the extent of information needed; access the needed information effectively and efficiently; evaluate information and its sources critically; incorporate selected information into one's knowledge base; use information effectively to accomplish a specific purpose; understand the economic, legal, and social issues surrounding the use of information, and access and use information ethically and legally.[8]

Intellectual honesty is a cornerstone of good scholarship. The academic community depends on authors and researchers creating clear paper trails in research and writing so that other scholars can verify and build upon the literature that is created and the claims that are made. Unfortunately, in recent years there have been one too many scandals in the academic community—some due to deliberate dishonesty, others due to sloppy scholarship. One of academia's biggest concerns is an apparent rise of plagiarism in papers produced by students as well as by senior scholars and professionals. In the next section we define plagiarism and provide some tips on how to avoid it.

Intellectual Honesty and Plagiarism

A writer is guilty of plagiarism when he or she presents another person's intellectual property as his or her own. While some writers may deliberately and knowingly lift portions of a document (or even an entire document), many inadvertently plagiarize by neglecting to cite sources properly. The list that follows is a quick guide on when and what to cite:

- Established facts, that is, things that are common knowledge, don't need citations. Statements such as "The sky is blue" or "England is in Europe" need not be cited.

- Your own opinion does not need to be cited. For example, "Shakespeare is the greatest dramatist that ever wrote in the English language." If you did not think it up and it is not a historical fact then it needs to be cited.
- Any opinions, criticisms, or items of original research that are not your own need to be cited. This is true whether you use a direct quote or even if you change the wording.
- If you use an idea from an article or a book, even if you reword that idea, you must cite it. Information taken from the World Wide Web needs to be cited just the same as information from an article or a book.
- When in doubt, cite the material. It is good scholarship to do so.
- The original theories, ideas, and research that your professor shares with you in class needs to be cited even if it is not officially published, unless your professor gives you express permission to use it.
- Factual information that comes from research needs to be cited. An example of this would be statistics. "How many people die each year in the United States from a heart attack?" The answer to this is a fact that needs to be cited. Someone had to research it to come up with the answer.[9]

Tools for Intellectual Honesty

In a scholarly paper, at any level, the writer is faced with several tasks. He has to gather together resource materials, that is, the work of scholars who have previously investigated the topic at hand. He reads and synthesizes this material and then infuses his own ideas and opinions into the mix. Finally, he writes—making sure that he properly identifies any intellectual property that isn't his through proper attribution. One can quickly see that the author of this scholarly paper needs several sets of skills involving critical thinking, information gathering, and specialized writing. The task of producing a scholarly paper can appear even more daunting when the work is interdisciplinary in nature—such as a paper in children and childhood studies (CCS). How then does the CCS student begin?

To borrow from Gertrude Stein, good scholarship is good scholarship is good scholarship. There are certain standards and practices that cross all disciplinary lines—intellectual honesty a case in point. A simple way to ensure intellectual honesty is through good record keeping. An excellent guide on the basics of how to manage and document research information is found in the *MLA Handbook for Writers of Research Papers* by Joseph Gibaldi.[10] Gibaldi also provides an informative discussion of plagiarism.

While the Modern Language Association (MLA) style guide is most frequently used by scholars in the humanities, Gibaldi's guidelines have a universality that interdisciplinary scholars will find especially useful.

Standards for good scholarship, including good research, good writing techniques, and the careful use of critical thinking skills, are essential in producing a quality paper. As mentioned above, the MLA guide provides excellent advice for research and the use of critical thinking skills in gathering and assessing materials. Standards for documentation vary depending on the discipline for which one is writing. An interdisciplinary scholar needs to have a working familiarity with the major style guides that provide writers with standardized methods for grammar, punctuation, notes, and bibliographies. In addition to MLA, the most frequently used guides include *The Chicago Manual of Style*[11] and *The Publication Manual of the American Psychological Association*.[12]

THE ART OF WRITING WELL

The mechanics of scholarly writing are important. The practice of standardization in documentation facilitates the communication of ideas; everyone is literally on the same page. Writing style is important as well and is the point at which a student gets to express himself or herself as an individual. In the next section, we discuss the intersection of art and scholarship.

In a nutshell, the best advice for any writing endeavor is to keep the prose simple and clear and to keep the progression of ideas obvious and logical. This is especially true for those writing for a cross-disciplinary perspective. At a recent conference on American popular culture, eminent music critic, author, and a founding editor of *Rolling Stone Magazine*, Michael Lydon, offered some sage advice for fledgling scholars. After first discussing some general considerations on the art of writing about the aesthetics of music, Lydon stated,

> I know that you are writing and working in an academic context, and there is strong pressure that your writing make arguments using the vocabulary of contemporary theory. So what are you supposed to do? We all need to keep our gigs! I say: find the best in those theoretical ideas—but as much as possible: say what you have to say in words that ordinary humans with some education—can understand.[13]

Lydon went on to note that overabstraction and overtheorization remove an academic writer from the reality of what he or she is writing about, loses the interest of the readers, and obscures the truth of the idea that she is trying to convey.[14]

"Clarity, clarity, clarity," write Strunk and White in *The Elements of Style*.[15] This slim volume, the gold standard of writing advice, sets forth rules for simple and elegant writing in a simple and elegant style that is a pleasure to read. A sample from a "list of reminders" included by Strunk and White that would well serve interdisciplinary scholars include the following: do not overwrite; do not overstate, do not explain too much, and be clear.[16] Prolific author Stephen King recommends *The Elements of Style* to novice writers in his excellent book *On Writing*. The King book, part biography and part how-to, is also short, concise, and full of invaluable advice. Like Lydon, and Strunk and White, King emphasizes uncluttered language and a clear, expository style. King is also an advocate of rigorous self-editing. He recommends writing a first draft, almost in a stream-of-consciousness fashion, putting it away, and returning to it after a short time with editing pencil in hand.[17] King suggests that at least 10 percent of all that is first written should be deleted.[18] Never use two words when one will do; go light on the adjectives and adverbs; and never use an obscure word when a simpler one can do the job.[19] Again, all excellent advice for an interdisciplinary student whose work is to be read and critiqued by scholars from various fields.

SOME FINAL THOUGHTS ON RESEARCH AND WRITING IN CCS

Some scholars are talented and elegant writers. Some scholars are diligent, meticulous researchers. Some scholars are both. Clarity of thought, simplicity of expression, careful record keeping, and documentation of sources are all virtues of academic writing—virtues to which even beginning writers can aspire. Strunk and White write that "although there is no substitute for merit in writing, clarity comes closest to being one."[20] While writing is a talent, research is a skill that can be learned. Faculty members and academic librarians are excellent resource people who are willing to share their research skills and advice with students. We encourage our readers to avail themselves of the resource people at their colleges and universities. In part 2 of this book, experts—faculty and librarians in the main disciplines that comprise CCS—will offer help, advice, and suggestions for resources in their areas of expertise.

NOTES

1. Lewis Carroll, *Alice's Adventures in Wonderland*, Project Gutenberg, www.gutenberg.org/dirs/etext97/alice30h.htm (accessed December 1, 2005).

2. Paul Robeson Library Reference Department, Rutgers University Libraries, *How to Write a Better Research Paper*, www.libraries.rutgers.edu/rul/libs/robeson _lib/libres.html (accessed December 1, 2005).

3. Leslie R. Williams and Doris Pronin Fromber, eds., *Encyclopedia of Early Childhood Education* (New York: Garland, 1992).

4. Williams and Fromber, *Encyclopedia of Early Childhood Education*.

5. Tracy Hogg with Melinda Blau, *Secrets of the Baby Whisperer: How to Calm, Connect, and Communicate with Your Baby* (New York: Ballantine, 2001).

6. Gavin Bremner and Alan Slater, eds., *Theories of Infant Development* (Oxford: Blackwell, 2003).

7. Paul Robeson Library, *How to Write*.

8. Association of College and Research Libraries, *Information Literacy*, www.ala.org/ala/acrl/acrlstandards/informationliteracycompetency.htm (accessed December 1, 2005).

9. Vibiana Bowman, "Information about Plagiarism," in Paul Robeson Library Reference Department, Rutgers University Libraries, *How to Write a Better Research Paper*, www.libraries.rutgers.edu/rul/libs/robeson_lib/flash_presents/avoidplag .html (accessed December 1, 2005).

10. Joseph Gibaldi, *MLA Handbook for Writers of Research Papers* (New York: Modern Language Association of America, 2003).

11. University of Chicago Press Staff, *The Chicago Manual of Style* (Chicago: University of Chicago Press, 2003).

12. American Psychological Association, *Publication Manual of the American Psychological Association* (Washington, D.C.: American Psychological Association, 2001).

13. Michael Lydon, "Writing Music Writing" (keynote address, annual meeting of the Mid-Atlantic Popular/American Culture Association, New Brunswick, N.J., November 5, 2005).

14. Lydon, "Writing Music Writing."

15. William Strunk Jr. and E. B. White, *The Elements of Style* (New York: Macmillan, 1979), 79.

16. Strunk and White, *Elements of Style*, 72–79.

17. Stephen King, *On Writing* (New York: Simon & Schuster, 2002), 209–12.

18. King, *On Writing*, 209–12.

19. King, *On Writing*, 124–28.

20. Strunk and White, *Elements of Style*, 79.

WORKS CITED

American Psychological Association. *Publication Manual of the American Psychological Association*. Washington, D.C.: American Psychological Association, 2001.

Association of College and Research Libraries. *Information Literacy*. www.ala.org/ ala/acrl/acrlstandards/informationliteracycompetency.htm

Bowman, Vibiana. "Information about Plagiarism." In *How to Write a Better Research Paper*. Paul Robeson Library Reference Department, Rutgers University Libraries. www.libraries.rutgers.edu/rul/libs/robeson_lib/flash_presents/avoidplag.html

———. "What Is Plagiarism." In *How to Write a Better Research Paper*. Paul Robeson Library Reference Department, Rutgers University Libraries. www.libraries.rutgers.edu/rul/libs/robeson_lib/flash_presents/whatisplag.html

Bremner, Gavin, and Alan Slater, eds. *Theories of Infant Development*. Oxford: Blackwell, 2003.

Carroll, Lewis. *Alice's Adventures in Wonderland*. Project Gutenberg. www.gutenberg.org/dirs/etext97/alice30h.htm

Gibaldi, Joseph. *MLA Handbook for Writers of Research Papers*. New York: Modern Language Association of America, 2003.

Hogg, Tracy, with Melinda Blau. *Secrets of the Baby Whisperer: How to Calm, Connect, and Communicate with Your Baby*. New York: Ballantine, 2001.

King, Stephen. *On Writing*. New York: Simon & Schuster, 2002.

Lydon, Michael. "Writing Music Writing." Keynote address, annual meeting of the Mid-Atlantic Popular/American Culture Association, New Brunswick, N.J, November 5, 2005.

Paul Robeson Library Reference Department. *How to Write a Better Research Paper*. www.libraries.rutgers.edu/rul/libs/robeson_lib/libres.html

Strunk, William, Jr., and E. B. White. *The Elements of Style*. New York: Macmillan, 1979.

University of Chicago Press Staff. *The Chicago Manual of Style*. Chicago: University of Chicago Press, 2003.

Williams, Leslie R., and Doris Pronin Fromber, eds. *Encyclopedia of Early Childhood Education*. New York: Garland, 1992.

II

RESEARCH AND RESOURCES

3

ANTHROPOLOGY

Chip Perkins

One of the main goals of anthropology is to explore and understand other people's cultures and represent them to an audience in such a way as to "make the strange familiar and the familiar strange." This certainly is an adroit goal with any research with young children because when you observe and interact with children, you will quickly discover that they are *very* strange. This is one of the main reasons they fascinate us: they act in strange ways; they make unexpected choices; they get involved in interesting dramas; and they play unique and creative games. Ultimately, children fascinate us because they have a different culture. Since its inception in anthropology, culture has been paradoxically our bread and butter and simultaneously a thorn in our side. This is because culture is a fluid process that is both simple and complex—it exists in our minds as general ideas but takes place in specific actions. Culture is like Oobleck—the mixture of about two parts of cornstarch to one part water—that kids play with in U.S. preschools. It's messy and gooey . . . it's fun for kids and adults alike. But the most interesting aspect of Oobleck is its amazing, contradictory, physical property of being both fluid and solid: when it's fluid it takes on the shape of what you put it in; but it can also be solid—when you apply pressure to it. Particularly, when you put Oobleck in your hand and squeeze it, Oobleck becomes very solid—that is, until you open your hand and try to look at it (or try to show its solidity to someone else) and then it liquefies and can easily escape your grasp. Culture is like Oobleck in the same sorts of ways: it's solid because you can see it by watching other people act; you can "feel" the reality of it by participating in other people's worlds; and as a researcher you make it "solid" by fixing these knowledges into text. However, like Oobleck, culture under other conditions is still fluid: it's hard to nail down the domains of how, when, and where it operates; culture is also ephemeral—it's a process that takes place within and through people . . . and it changes with time. So, like Oobleck, what is held in the hand as solid will eventually turn to mush as you are "showing" its solidity to others. For this reason, culture is a quandary that anthropologists and other scholars have been dealing with and trying to codify, quantify, and qualify for at least a century. The goal of this chapter is to explicate the general tools, methods, and theories of anthropological inquiry that have been useful in locating, exploring, and interrogating culture, with a particular focus on children and childhood.

CHILDREN AND CULTURE

Mind and Practice

There are many domains where culture exists and takes place. However, when we focus on children it is exigent that we understand culture as part of their physical, social, emotional, and mental development. Here, we must recognize that culture lives simultaneously within at least two domains: the mind and action—including both the ideational and real tools that are used in everyday human life.[1] Culture exists as meaning in the mind; people think and learn in categories that are similar to the other people they interact with—this is why thought is culturally contingent and diverse. Only recently have scholars begun seriously to discard the traditional, dualist frame of social versus physical science[2]—culminating in the "nature versus nurture" debates.[3] Recent studies mediating the ground between psychology and anthropology in particular have begun to explore how the human mind and its development, as a unique human feature with significant biological and psychological processes, is patterned in cultural ways.[4] This is because culture organizes cognition through important themes, categories, and actions that particular groups of people value.[5] Here, the development of meaning is a particular area of interest with scholars who work with children. This is because meanings are shared or different not only among individuals of the same culture[6] but also among peoples of different cultures.[7] For a long time, anthropologists have been dealing with a host of problems that surround the notion of cultural transmission[8] coded in anthropological terms of enculturation[9] or cultural acquisition.[10] Anthropologists have also been working to understand the process of adapting to another culture, or acculturation: a process rife with contradictions that cannot be easily quantified.[11] Acculturation, or learning cultural meanings different from those originally acquired, is a particularly important field of research for scholars working in schools because the cultural values of early schooling[12] may vary widely with the diversity of peoples that the schools serve.[13]

What things mean to children, as well as how they learn them, is certainly an important domain of investigation. But culture also takes place through the actions of children in how they manipulate the world. Here, it is important to note that the arena of action anthropologists are interested in is more than simply random activity; they use the notion of practice to index actions that are common, if not habitual, everyday physical and mental behaviors that are structured by and that simultaneously restructure cultural notions.[14] Using the concept of skill is another way that scholars have been working to explore in depth what cultural practices entail as well as how they are learned.[15] Here, some research has begun to uncover that action, like mind, works to make children "attend" to knowledge[16]—or the process of how they learn to focus on specific things and activities that are valued and important for specific cultural contexts.

IDENTITY AND POWER

Cultural practices and skills that children learn and engage in—physical behaviors like lining up, singing songs, and playing as well as other, more "mental" behaviors like literacy and numeracy—not only have an impact on what kids do and how they learn but fundamentally implicate who children are. This is why we need to explore the notion of identity—or how and why people act, who they think they are, as well as how they are perceived by others. Everyone shapes identities with regards to many different aspects of their lives. However, children are simultaneously crafting notions of identity while they are also developing a sense of what their body is socially,[17] how it is meaningful in particular contexts[18] and how it can and should be used as a tool for learning.[19] The most significant and commonly researched social aspects of identity with children that have been investigated are race,[20] class,[21] ethnicity,[22] gender,[23] and to some extent sexuality.[24]

Identity, like culture, is a process that is fluid and very complex: the social aspects of people's identities are rarely singular—race, class, gender, ethnicity, and sexuality often intersect in very important and meaningful ways for people.[25] Identity is also a dual, mutually constructed process—that is, people craft their own identities but are simultaneously identified, or put into culturally significant groups, by other people. This is a very important distinction that needs to be understood in depth by qualitative researchers because the social axes of identity—class, race, ethnicity, and gender in particular—necessarily influence not only the history of childhood at large[26] but also the history of early childhood education and reform.[27] Because social identity works to empower or constrain both privileged and disenfranchised children is also why we need to investigate the nuances of power.

On the one hand, when it comes to power, people have choices and control over shaping who they are. This is because identity is, to a great extent, a performance.[28] However, the process of shaping one's identity also takes place among the larger social fields of power. This is because identity, or who people are and where they are in relationship to other people, is a contested process, because it makes significant distinctions among people in defining commonality, difference,[29] and access to power. But there are certain aspects of identity that are relatively more mutable than others; and people can choose whether or not they want to "pass" as members of other groups, or accommodate to the culture of others.[30] But at the same time, there are other aspects of identity that are more immutable, or so fundamental to people's worlds—the ways they live and understand them—that they cannot be discarded or modified to fit a different culture.

Whether children can modify the performances of their identity— some to the chagrin of their parents as it typifies the disintegration of their home and community culture[31]—or not, schools still operate according to particular cultural norms and practices.[32] And those cultural values, ideas, norms, and practices that are different or even discordant with schools are often not understood or valued—sometimes these different cultural practices and values are even vilified as central to children's school failure.[33] It is here that larger social inequities surrounding identity intersect with school performance, success, and failure. For quite some time now, anthropologists and other scholars have been investigating exactly how the culture of school—that operates with regards to particular values, identities, practices, and norms—facilitates the success of some students while disenfranchising others with regards to their class,[34] race,[35] gender,[36] ethnicity,[37] and language.[38] The failure and success of children with regards to their identity is one of the fundamental ways that social inequity and the larger social structures of racism, sexism, classism and so on are produced. Here, power operates almost beyond children's local identities: kids in school are at the behest of social forces surrounding the ideologies of politics,[39] economy,[40] and governmentality[41]—like standards of school performance and readiness,[42] forms of evaluation like assessment and testing,[43] and even globalization.[44]

This is widely apparent in the fact that even when nonwhite children accommodate to the white, middle-class norms of the school many may still be seen as outside the frame of being "real Americans."[45] Ultimately, schooling is one of many important sites where children's identities are contested. And children have to mediate,[46] submit to, or even resist[47] the many different aspects of this process as they work to find their place in the world.

There is one final aspect of identity that must necessarily be recognized when we work with children, since it is one aspect of our work that is essentially omnipresent: the social axis of age. It is vital that we recognize how age and power intersect to frame children's lives. Children's developing physical, mental, and emotional capacities differ widely among themselves as well as radically with their adult caretakers. For any group activity, children and adults of different ages and capacities are constantly mediating power relationships that significantly enable and constrain their actions and learning.[48] In my own dissertation research, I have realized that the power relationship between teachers and students of preschool and kindergarten classrooms in the U.S. Midwest revolve around the fundamental antimony[49] of choice and creativity or control and curriculum. In the early childhood classrooms in which I work, both of these sides are valued but they operate in a variety of ways according to spatial contexts and identity politics. However, even in play-based, child-centered curricula, children often have to substantially submit to the wants and needs of adults.[50] Here, the way that children are perceived by adults and caretakers is very important to investigate because these perceptions substantially frame local action as well as public policy.[51] This final point is most important for us as researchers: we must not forget the fundamental power relationship of age in our research—we are adults with "grown-up" perceptions of the world studying children with widely different ideas, meanings, values, intentions and practices. Therefore, doing research that attempts to understand and interrogate children's worlds can be difficult; but it can be almost impossible if we don't recognize our own position in this process.

ANTHROPOLOGICAL RESEARCH

Qualitative and Ethnographic

The difference in age between researcher and child is certainly a significant reason that kids appear so strange, but it is also a fundamental reason why it can be substantially problematic to research children. Anthropological investigations involve long-term ethnographic work where the researcher acts as both participant and observer in attempts to understand and represent the quality of an insider's perspective. This can be particularly difficult with children. To some extent, this is due to the nature of childhood: it becomes increasingly difficult to interview a child the younger they are; and because many children have a tendency to treat adults as adults, "going native" in order to understand children's worlds is that more difficult. These "reactive effects of the observer,"[52] or the qualitative version of Heisenberg's Uncertainty Principle, can be a substantial roadblock in working with and understanding kids. But over the past few decades there has been a substantial increase in qualitative research with children. And one of the central themes many of these works share is the novel form of exploration into worthwhile qualitative methods for successfully studying kids.[53] Researchers have new ideas with regards to participant observation[54] and how to become involved in children's worlds as a "nonadult."[55] Other researchers, in the same vein, have begun exploring novel interviewing methods,[56] ways to check validity,[57] and important research sites that are unique to children[58]—physical[59] as well as mental and cultural.[60]

AGENCY AND PERSPECTIVE

Getting an insider perspective also means understanding that children have certain aspects of control and choice in their worlds. As Bowman states in the preface to this text, "CCS scholars represent the voice of the world's children and the paradigm of childhood—a voice that has not had a say at this dinner conversation." One of the main roadblocks in allowing children's worlds to emerge from research is the "adult-centric" focus of theories of development and learning—adults as researchers have difficulty recognizing and eliminating their own bias as adults.[61] One of the most evident aspects of this is what Super and Harkness call the "problem of endpoint."[62] The problem of endpoint has a "vertical" developmental theory bias within it where adults assume that children will eventually turn into them; therefore, everything that children do is placed within the frame as necessarily relating to some eventual, but putative, adult form. Adult-centric research is problematic because it doesn't focus on the child's perspective and their ability to make choices; instead, it focuses on what social and cultural forces, and meanings and practices, are at work to make them adults eventually. Doing research that explores children's perspectives by investigating where, and to what extent, children have self-conscious intentions that inform their choices so that they have agency can help fill this gap.

Exploring the ways in which children's choices work to create novel and unique worlds, ones that aren't necessarily related to adult ones, is one significant way we can allow children to have a voice within the adult research paradigm. Although anthropological works have been interested in understanding children's worlds and cultures, it is only within mainly the last three decades that scholars have begun to directly regard the importance of working toward an insider's perspective, one where children's agency and their point of view is a primary lens in interpreting the process of learning.[63] Some scholars have begun exploring the quality of learning and development as a multifaceted, interactive process[64] where children are substantially involved as participants in the process of meaning making as well as their own development.[65] There are other works that illustrate the strengths of involving child agency in the exploration of child development. First and foremost, some researchers locate the presence of child intentions and motives in interactions[66] even in infants,[67] where young children are involved in power relationships.[68] Focusing on child perspectives and their agency and power also uncovers that children are not just "acquiring" adult competencies but are involved in the production of patterns of interaction as well as their own mind and identities through interaction.[69] Second, other scholars have recognized that learning is a social practice; therefore, the contexts that children value and are involved in are central in understanding what they learn and how they form up their identities.[70] For these reasons, many researchers have begun to explore the range of features, values, meanings, and practices within those spaces of children's worlds that are important to children themselves as contexts for learning.[71] These contexts are important to understand in depth (and from the child's point of view) because cognition takes place in context: the total context shapes thought as well as the process of what is significant about the moment-action that should be learned.[72] In different contexts, different cultural values and practices are indexed and evoked—here, contexts frame how people learn and interpret events by both narrowing the frame of reference and by "pointing to" particular knowledge, values, or practices.[73] In exploring the role and significance of context, many scholars have been recently reinvestigating familiar contexts, like the home–school relationships,[74] children's talk,[75] media,[76] and literacy.[77] At the same time, others have also identified previously overlooked contexts that are commonplace for children, particularly ones where children are free from parental dominion in producing their own identities. Here, some of the most important, more recently investigated contexts are the peer group,[78] the playground,[79] and other "free time" spaces,[80] including artwork,[81] games,[82] as well as aspects of play[83]—particularly, role play.[84] Ultimately, in doing worthwhile, qualitative research with children, as researchers we must utilize methods and theories that look at the diversity of contexts and actions where the creativity and imagination of children intersect with their motivations and intentions to produce important aspects of child agency and identity.

CROSS-CULTURAL APPROACHES
TO CHILDREN AND CHILDHOOD

One of the most valuable insights that anthropologists have made to studies of children and childhood is research that investigates non-Western cultural practices and meanings involving children. By comparing cultural meanings and practices surrounding children between and among cultures around the world, cross-cultural research is valuable because it challenges, critiques, and expands the Western, European theories, models, and methods that have historically framed our fundamental notions of child and childhood.

One of the original, general goals of cross-cultural, anthropological research was to attempt to locate and understand universal concepts about the human experience. This is still a goal today, but it is much more difficult under the watchful eye of postmodern scholars.[85] However, anthropological and cross-cultural research has been relatively productive in amplifying the larger human experience of what it means to be a very young child as a biological, cultural, and social being. A few scholars have discovered some key theoretical frames that help expand Western notions of what it is to be a child as a social, psychological being[86] through exploring aspects of growth and development.[87] By examining the diversity of child behavior and personality among cultures, other scholars have recently reconsidered the role that emotion plays as a central mechanism in the development of the child as a pan-cultural human[88] as well as a specific cultural being.[89] In this way, cross-cultural research has added substantially to the significance of how children's emotions and affect operate in the reproduction of traditional cultural values and meanings[90] or the transmission of novel ones.[91]

Because the central goal of cross-cultural analysis is the comparison of cultures, investigating children in different places in the world fosters the production of universal theories of child and childhood; but it simultaneously lays the foundation for its own demise by supplying a plethora of data that have been used to challenge the Western epistemology surrounding the study of children—particularly in terms of biology,[92] psychology,[93] cognition and learning,[94] as well as language development and socialization.[95]

This challenge goes beyond the notion of the developing child: in describing and comparing the gamut of physical, social, political, and economic realities around the world that necessarily involve children,[96] the Western conceptions of childhood development and personality as social constructs themselves have been substantially challenged.[97] Many of these works illustrate again the adult-centric bias of how kids are researched and perceived, but more important, works like these also indict how adult-centrism fosters the insidious social, economic, and political processes of power that cause violence to children around the world.[98]

At its base, a fundamental goal and method of cross-cultural research with children is a descriptive, qualitative exploration of how children learn larger cultural notions and practices of their particular culture.[99] A related, larger goal is to understand in greater depth how important ideologies of the social structure (like those of class, race, ethnicity, and gender) as well as others of economy and polity are taught and learned to produce the "national character" of certain countries and cultures.[100] In exploring education with young children across cultures, one important early theoretical thread that was useful in this endeavor was simply exploring the definition and distinction between socialization, enculturation, and education.[101] Here, many anthropologists have worked to explore the range of differential practices that mark the difference between modern, formal, institutional schooling[102] and informal, indigenous education with children.[103] In the middle of the twentieth century, an important aspect of these studies illustrated the complexity of the intersection of traditional informal, indigenous education when formal, Western schools supplant it.[104]

One final way that cross-cultural research with children around the world has been worthwhile is that researchers have been able to locate and investigate important and often-overlooked arenas that influence and implicate the local, culturally contingent as well as universal processes of child learning, development, and socialization. Works that explore the social relationships between children and the rest of society have clearly illustrated that the social axes of identity—particularly gender[105] and kinship[106]—are a central part of being and becoming a child cross-culturally. Research in this vein has also explicated the dynamic diversity of relationships that even infants and fetuses can have toward others, living and dead,[107] as they play a substantial role in their own development as a "person" in society.[108] The different ways that children and childhood is conceived in other cultures can be shocking to scholars who are unfamiliar with these ways of being. However, these works are priceless in the study of children and childhood because they have almost unlimited potential to shed light on other undiscovered, yet vital, aspects of social relationships and human development in which children are involved around the world.

As an anthropologist, I cannot stress enough the value of works like these. Anyone working with children should consider anthropological and cross-cultural approaches regarding, at least, their particular interests with kids in order to challenge and amplify their ideas about children and childhood. This is because children are also like Oobleck: they're messy and malleable, often unfathomable; but, under the right conditions, they are also orderly and sensible, and sometimes predictable. The goal of my chapter is to give anyone who works with children—scholars of children or childhood, teachers, parents, and those who make public policy shaping kids' lives, or simply anyone who wants to revel in the worlds of children—the tools and methods of anthropological inquiry so that they may be better equipped to make more sense of the creative worlds that children inhabit.

NOTES

1. James Wertsch, *Mind as Action* (New York: Oxford University Press, 1998).

2. Christina Toren, "Do Babies Have Culture," *Anthropological Quarterly* 77, no. 1 (2004): 167–79.

3. Barbara Rogoff, *The Cultural Nature of Human Development* (Oxford: Oxford University Press, 2003).

4. Pascal Boyer, "Human Cognition and Cultural Evolution," in *Anthropological Theory Today*, ed. Henrietta L. Moore (Malden, Mass.: Polity, 1999), 206–33; Michael Cole, *Cultural Psychology: A Once and Future Discipline* (Cambridge: Harvard University Press, 1996).

5. Frances Christie, "Pedagogic Discourse in the Primary School," *Linguistics and Education* 7 (1995): 122–42; Jacqueline Goodnow, "The Socialization of Cognition: What's Involved?" in *Cultural Psychology: Essays on Comparative Human Development*, ed. James Stigler, Richard Shweder, and Gilbert Herdt (Cambridge, UK: Cambridge University Press, 1990), 260–86; Solon Kimball, "The Transmission of Culture," *Educational Horizons* 43 (1965): 161–86; Hugh Mehan, *Learning Lessons* (Cambridge: Harvard University Press, 1979); James Stigler, Richard Shweder, and Gilbert Herdt, eds., *Cultural Psychology: Essays on Comparative Human Development* (Cambridge, UK: Cambridge University Press, 1990).

6. Deborah Hicks, ed., *Discourse, Learning and Schooling* (New York: Cambridge University Press, 1996); Douglas Hollan, "Constructivist Models of Mind, Contemporary Psychoanalysis, and the Development of Culture Theory," *American Anthropologist* 102, no. 3 (2000): 538–50; Rebecca Kantor, "Creating School Meaning in Preschool Curriculum," *Theory into Practice* 27 (1988): 22–35; Bradd Shore, *Culture in Mind: Cognition, Culture and the Problem of Meaning* (New York: Oxford University Press, 1996).

7. Claudia Strauss and Naomi Quinn, *A Cognitive Theory of Cultural Meaning* (New York: Cambridge University Press, 1997).

8. Judith Friedman Hansen, *Socio-Cultural Perspectives on Human Learning: An Introduction to Educational Anthropology* (Englewood Cliffs, N.J.: Prentice Hall, 1979); George Spindler, "The Transmission of Culture," in *Education and Cultural Process: Anthropological Approaches*, ed. George Spindler (Prospect Heights, Ill.: Waveland, 1997), 375–79; Harry Wolcott, "The Anthropology of Learning," in *Education and Cultural Process: Anthropological Approaches*, ed. George Spindler (Prospect Heights, Ill.: Waveland, 1997), 310–38.

9. Margaret Mead, "Socialization and Enculturation," *Current Anthropology* 4, no. 2 (April 1963): 184–88; Thomas Rhys Williams, *A Borneo Childhood: Enculturation in Dusun Society* (New York: Holt, Reinhart and Winston, 1967).

10. Gustav Jahoda and I. M. Lewis, eds., *Acquiring Culture: Cross-Cultural Studies in Child Development* (London: Crom Helm, 1988).

11. Edward Bruner, "Cultural Transmission and Culture Change," *Southwest Journal of Anthropology* 12 (1956): 191–99; Takie Sugiyama Lebra, "Acculturation Dilemma: The Function of Japanese Moral Values for Americanization," *Council on Anthropology and Education Newsletter* 3, no. 1 (1972): 6–13; Susan Laird Mody, *Cultural Identity in Kindergarten: A Study of Asian Indian Children in New Jersey* (New York: Routledge, Taylor & Francis, 2005).

12. Margaret LeCompte, "The Civilizing of Children: How Young Children Learn to Become Students," *The Journal of Thought* 15 (1980): 105–27.

13. Jo Anne Kleifgen, "Prekindergarten Children's Second Discourse Learning," *Discourse Process* 13 (1990): 225–42; Vera Michalachik, "The Display of Cultural Knowledge in Cultural Transmission: Models of Participation from the Pacific Island of Kosrae," in *Education and Cultural Process: Anthropological Approaches*, ed. George Spindler (Prospect Heights, Ill.: Waveland, 1997), 393–426; Susan Philips, "Participant Structures and Communicative Competence: Warm Springs Children in Community and Classroom," in *Functions of Language in the Classroom*, ed. Courtney Cazden, Vera John, and Dell Hymes (New York: Teachers College Press, 1972), 370–94.

14. Pierre Bourdieu, *Outline of a Theory of Practice* (Cambridge, UK: Cambridge University Press, 1977).

15. Tim Ingold, *The Perception of the Environment: Essays on Livelihood, Dwelling and Skill* (New York: Routledge, 2000).

16. James Gibson, *The Ecological Approach to Visual Perception* (Boston: Houghton Mifflin, 1979); Jane Ritchie and James Ritchie, *Growing Up in Polynesia* (Boston: George Allen & Unwin, 1979).

17. Iris Young, *Throwing Like a Girl and Other Essays in Feminist Philosophy and Social Theory* (Bloomington: Indiana University Press, 1990).

18. Dennis Raymond Bryson, *Socializing the Young: The Role of Foundations, 1923–1941* (Westport, Conn.: Bergin and Garvey, 2002); Margaret Jones and Chris Cunningham, "The Expanding World of Middle Childhood," in *Embodied Geographies: Spaces, Bodies and Rites of Passage*, ed. Elizabeth Teather (New York: Routledge,

1999), 27–42; Jan Nespor, *Tangled Up in School: Politics, Space, Bodies, and Signs in the Education Process* (Mahwah, N.J.: Erlbaum, 1997).

19. Greg Downey, *Learning Capoeira: Lessons in Cunning from an Afro-Brazilian Art* (New York: Oxford University Press, 2005).

20. Shirley Brice Heath, *Ways with Words* (Cambridge, UK: Cambridge University Press, 1983); Sally Lubek, *Sandbox Society: Early Education in Black and White America* (London: Falmer, 1985); Darla Miller, "Infant/Toddler Day Care in High, Middle and Low Socio-economic Settings: An Ethnography of Dialectical Enculturation and Linguistic Code" (unpublished doctoral diss., University of Houston, 1986).

21. Annette Lareau, *Home Advantages* (London: Falmer, 1989); Amanda Lewis and Tyrone A. Foreman, "Contestation or Collaboration? A Comparative Study of Home-School Relations," *Anthropology and Education Quarterly* 33, no. 1 (2002): 60–89.

22. Guadalupe Valdés, *Con Respeto: Bridging the Distance between Culturally Diverse Families and Schools, An Ethnographic Portrait* (New York: Teachers College Press, 1996).

23. Marjorie Harness Goodwin, *He-Said-She-Said* (Bloomington: Indiana University Press, 1994); Barrie Thorne, *Gender Play: Girls and Boys in School* (New Brunswick, N.J.: Rutgers University Press, 1993); Jerri Willett, "Becoming First Graders in an L2: An Ethnographic Study of L2 Socialization," *TESOL Quarterly* 29, no. 3 (1995): 473–503.

24. Margaret Mead, *Coming of Age in Samoa: A Psychological Study of Primitive Youth for Western Civilisation* (New York: Morrow, 1928); Emma Renold, "'Coming Out': Gender, (Hetero)sexuality and the Primary School," *Gender and Education* 12, no. 3 (2000): 309–26.

25. Willett, "Becoming First Graders in an L2." In this section the author examines how the interactional routines of classroom children mutually construct the identities of ESL children and the importance of the intersection between gender and ethnicity. While all ESL children were positioned as outsiders in the class, girls interact in more exclusive and collaborative group work and, therefore, they are able to learn with their female peers and illustrate their competence. Meanwhile, because the gendered interactions of boys involve a larger, competitive group, an ESL boy is not able to work in collaboration and learn from his male peers. For this reason, he was perceived by teachers as incompetent and a problem because they saw him as unable to work independently. This work shows how the micropolitics of identity and identification work to produce larger social relations—particularly, those of school competence and ability.

26. Phillipe Ariès, *Centuries of Childhood: A Social History of Family Life* (New York: Knopf, 1962); Colin Heywood, *A History of Childhood: Children and Childhood in the West from Medieval to Modern Times* (Malden, Mass.: Polity, 2001); Linda Pollock, *Forgotten Children: Parent-Child Relations 1500–1900* (Cambridge, UK: Cambridge University Press, 1983).

27. Barbara Beatty, *Preschool Education in America: The Culture of Young Children from the Colonial Era to the Present* (New Haven, Conn.: Yale University Press, 1995); Marianne Bloch, "Becoming Scientific and Professional: An Historical Perspective on the Aims and Effects of Early Education," in *The Formation of the School Subjects: The Struggle for Creating an American Institution*, ed. Thomas Popkewitz (New York: Falmer, 1987), 25–62; Marvin Lazerson, "Urban Reform and the Schools: Kindergartens in Massachusetts, 1870–1915," *History of Education Quarterly* 11 (1971): 115–38; Margaret O'Brien Steinfels, *Who's Minding the Children? The History and Politics of Child Care in America* (New York: The Free Press, 1986); David Tyack and Larry Cuban, *Tinkering toward Utopia: A Century of Public School Reform* (Cambridge: Harvard University Press, 1995).

28. Judith Butler, *Gender Trouble: Feminism and the Subversion of Identity* (New York: Routledge, 1990).

29. Alma Gottlieb, *Under the Kapok Tree: Identity and Difference in Beng Thought* (Bloomington: Indiana University Press, 1992).

30. Margaret Gibson, "Playing by the Rules," in *Education and Cultural Process: Anthropological Approaches*, ed. George Spindler (Prospect Heights, Ill.: Waveland, 1997), 262–70.

31. Peter Sindell, "Some Discontinuities in the Education of Mistassini Cree Children," in *Education and Cultural Process: Anthropological Approaches*, ed. George Spindler (Prospect Heights, Ill.: Waveland, 1997), 383–92; Carola Suárez-Orozco and Marcelo M. Suárez-Orozco, *Children of Immigration* (Cambridge: Harvard University Press, 2001); Murray Wax and Rosalie Wax, "Great Tradition, Little Tradition, and Formal Education," in *Anthropological Perspectives on Education*, ed. Murray Wax, Stanley Diamond and Fred O. Gearing (New York: Basic Books, 1971), 3–18.

32. Jules Henry, "Attitude Organization in Elementary School Classrooms," in *Education and Culture*, ed. George Spindler (New York: Holt, Rinehart and Winston, 1963), 192–214; Solon Kimball, *Culture and the Educative Process* (New York: Teachers College Press, 1974).

33. William Ryan, *Blaming the Victim* (New York: Vintage Books, 1976).

34. Shirley Brice Heath, "Linguistics and Education," *Annual Review of Anthropology* 13 (1984): 251–74.

35. Robyn Holmes, *How Young Children Perceive Race* (Thousand Oaks, Calif.: Sage, 1995); Lubek, *Sandbox Society*. In this section, by comparing race and class within the institutions of preschool as well as the U.S. Head Start program, Lubek shows how white children are more adequately prepared for public school vs. black children.

36. Myra Sadker and David Sadker, *Failing at Fairness: How America's Schools Cheat Girls* (New York: Scribner, 1994).

37. Jim Cummins, "Empowering Minority Students: A Framework for Intervention," in *Beyond Silenced Voices*, ed. Michelle Weis and Lois Fine (Albany: State University of New York Press, 1997), 101–10; Donna Deyhle, "Navajo Youth and Anglo Racism: Cultural Integrity and Resistance," *Harvard Educational Review* 65,

no. 3 (1995): 403–44; Toni Griego Jones and Mary Lou Fuller, *Teaching Hispanic Children* (Boston: Allyn and Bacon, 2003); Dinah Volk, "Questions in Lessons: Activity Settings in the Homes and School of Two Puerto Rican Kindergartners," *Anthropology and Education Quarterly* 28, no. 1 (1997): 22–49.

38. Eugene Garcia, "Instructional Discourse Style of an 'Effective' First-Grade Teacher in a Hispanic Classroom," *Early Child Development and Care* 38 (1988): 119–32; Muriel Saville-Troike and JoAnne A. Kleifgen, "Scripts for School: Cross-Cultural Communication in the Elementary Classroom," *Text* 6 (1986): 207–21.

39. Lourdes Diaz Soto, ed., *The Politics of Early Childhood Education* (New York: Peter Lang, 2000).

40. Douglas Foley, *Learning Capitalist Culture: Deep in the Heart of Texas* (Philadelphia: Philadelphia University Press, 1996); Shirley Steinberg and Joe Kincheloe, eds., *Kinderculture: The Corporate Construction of Childhood* (Boulder, Colo.: Westview Press, 1997).

41. Jeff Bezemer, *Dealing with Multilingualism in Education: A Case Study of a Dutch Primary School Classroom* (Amsterdam: Askam Academic Publishers, 2003); Valerie Polokow Suransky, *The Erosion of Childhood* (Chicago: University of Chicago Press, 1982).

42. Arnold Gesell, Frances L. Ilg, and Louise Bates Ames, *The Child from Five to Ten* (New York: Harper & Row, 1977); Elizabeth M. Graue, *Ready for What? Constructing Meaning of Readiness for Kindergarten* (Albany: State University of New York Press, 1993); J. Amos Hatch and E. Freeman, "Who's Pushing Whom? Stress and Kindergarten," *Phi Delta Kappan* 70 (1988): 145–48.

43. Aaron V. Cicourel, *Language Use and School Performance* (New York: Academic, 1974).

44. Sharon Stephens, ed., *Children and the Politics of Culture* (Princeton: Princeton University Press, 1995).

45. Mody, *Cultural Identity in Kindergarten*; Ooka Pang and Lilly Cheng, *Struggling to Be Heard: The Unmet Needs of Asian Pacific American Children* (Albany: State University of New York Press, 1998).

46. Deborah Reed-Danahay, *Education and Identity in Rural France: The Politics of Schooling* (New York: Cambridge University Press, 1996).

47. Linda K. Christian-Smith, "Voices of Resistance: Young Women Readers of Romance Fiction," in *Beyond Silenced Voices*, ed. Michelle Weis and Lois Fine (Albany: State University of New York Press, 1993), 169–89; Janice Jipson and Richard T. Johnson, eds., *Resistance and Representation: Rethinking Childhood Education* (New York: Peter Lang Publishing, 2000); Bradley Levinson, Doug Foley, and Dorothy Holland, "The Cultural Production of the Educated Person: An Introduction," in *The Cultural Production of the Educated Person: Critical Ethnographies of Schooling and Local Practice*, ed. Bradley Levinson, Doug Foley, and Dorothy Holland (Albany: State University of New York Press, 1996), 1–34; Shelia Riddell, "Pupils, Resistance and Gender Codes: A Study of Classroom Encounters," *Gender and Education* 1, no. 2 (1989): 83–97.

48. Loren S. Barritt, *An Elementary School in Holland: Experiment in Educational Practice* (Utrecht, Netherlands: International Books, 1996).

49. Jerome Bruner, *The Culture of Education* (Cambridge: Harvard University Press, 1996).

50. Solon Kimball, "Cultural Influences Shaping the Role of the Child," in *Education and Culture*, ed. George Spindler (New York: Holt, Rinehart and Winston, 1963), 268–83; Robin Leavitt, *Power and Emotion in Infant-Toddler Day Care: A Guide to Responsive Caregiving* (Albany: State University of New York Press, 1994).

51. Allison James and Alan Prout, eds., *Constructing and Reconstructing Childhood: Contemporary Issues in the Sociological Study of Childhood* (London: Falmer, 1990); Suransky, *The Erosion of Childhood.*

52. Norman K. Denzin, *The Research Act: A Theoretical Introduction to Sociological Methods*, 3rd ed. (Englewood Cliffs, N.J.: Prentice-Hall, 1970), 174–75.

53. David F. Lancy, *Studying Children and Schools: Qualitative Research Traditions* (Prospect Heights, Ill.: Waveland, 2001).

54. Susan Florio, "Learning How to Go to School: An Ethnography of Interaction in a Kindergarten/First Grade Classroom" (PhD diss., Harvard University, 1978).

55. William A. Corsaro, *Friendship and Peer Culture in the Early Years* (Norwood, N.J.: Ablex, 1985).

56. J. Tamivarra and D. S. Enright, "On Eliciting Information: Dialogues with Child Informants," *Anthropology and Education Quarterly* 17, no. 2 (June 1986): 218–38.

57. Elizabeth M. Graue and Daniel L. Walsh, eds., *Studying Children in Context: Theories, Methods and Ethics* (Thousand Oaks, Calif.: Sage, 1998).

58. J. Amos Hatch, ed., *Qualitative Research in Early Childhood Settings* (Westport, Conn.: Praeger, 1995).

59. Min-Ling Tsai and Georgia Earnest Garcia, "Who's the Boss? How Communicative Competence Is Defined in a Multilingual Preschool Classroom," *Anthropology and Education Quarterly* 31, no. 2 (2000): 230–52.

60. Allan Luke, "Text and Discourse in Education: An Introduction to Critical Discourse Analysis," *Review of Research in Education* 21 (1995): 3–48.

61. Alma Gottlieb, "Where Have All the Babies Gone? Toward an Anthropology of Infants (and Their Caretakers)," *Anthropological Quarterly* 73, no. 3 (2000): 121–32; Mary Ellen Goodman, *The Culture of Childhood: Child's-Eye Views of Society and Culture* (New York: Teachers College Press, 1970).

62. Charles Super and Sara Harkness, eds., *Anthropological Perspectives on Child Development* (San Francisco: Jossey Bass, 1980).

63. William A. Corsaro, *We're Friends, Right? Inside Kids' Culture* (Washington, D.C.: Joseph Henry Press, 2003); Andrew Pollard, *The Social World of the Primary School* (London: Holt, Rinehart and Winston, 1985); Andrew Pollard and Anne Filer, *The Social World of Children's Learning: Case Studies of Children from Four to Seven* (London: Cassel, 1996); Stuart Reifel, "Children's Thinking about Their Early Education Experiences," *Theory into Practice* 27, no. 1 (1988): 62–66.

64. Lev Vygotsky, *Mind in Society: The Development of Higher Psychological Processes* (Cambridge: Harvard University Press, 1978).

65. Mariane Hedegaard, *Learning and Child Development: A Cultural-Historical Study* (Aarhus, Denmark: Aarhus University Press, 2002); Jean Lave and Etienne Wenger, *Situated Learning: Legitimate Peripheral Participation* (Cambridge, UK: Cambridge University Press, 1991).

66. Jenny Cook-Gumperz, William A. Corsaro, and Jürgen Streeck, eds., *Children's Worlds and Children's Language* (New York: Mouton de Gruyter, 1986); Sara Harkness and Charles Super, "The Cultural Construction of Child Development: A Framework for the Socialization of Affect," *Ethos* 11, no. 4 (1980): 221–32.

67. Elinor Ochs and Bambi Schieffelin, *Acquiring Conversational Competence* (Boston: Routledge and Kegan Paul, 1983).

68. Liz Jones and Tony Brown, "Reading the Nursery Classroom: A Foucauldian Perspective," *Qualitative Studies in Education* 11, no. 6 (2001): 713–25; Debra Skinner, Donna Bryant, Jennifer Coffman, and Frances Campbell, "Creating Risk and Promise: Children's and Teachers' Co-Constructions in the Cultural World of Kindergarten, *The Elementary School Journal* 98, no. 4 (March 1998): 297–310.

69. Paul Reisman, *First Find Your Child a Good Mother: The Construction of Self in Two African Communities* (New Brunswick, N.J.: Rutgers University Press, 1992).

70. Allison James, *Childhood Identities: Self and Social Relationships in the Experience of the Child* (Edinburgh: Edinburgh University Press, 1993); Lave and Wenger, *Situated Learning*; Stigler et al, *Cultural Psychology*.

71. Cook-Gumperz et al., *Children's Worlds and Children's Language*; Jenny Cook-Gumperz and John Gumperz, "Context in Children's Speech," in *The Development of Communication: Social and Pragmatic Factors in Language Acquisition*, ed. Natalie Waterson and Catherine Snow (London: Wiley, 1978), 55–73; Evelyn Jacobs, "Context and Cognition: Implications for Educational Innovators and Anthropologists," *Anthropology and Education Quarterly* 28, no. 1 (March 1997): 3–21.

72. Super and Harkness, eds., *Anthropological Perspectives on Child Development*.

73. Jenny Cook-Gumperz and William A. Corsaro, "The Socio-Ecological Constraints on Children's Communicative Strategies," in *Papers on Language and Context*, ed. Jenny Cook-Gumperz and John Gumperz (Berkeley, Calif.: Language Behavior Research Laboratory, 1976), 29–35; Sylvia Scribner and Michael Cole, *The Psychology of Literacy* (Cambridge: Harvard University Press, 1981).

74. Rosalind Edwards, ed., *Children, Home and School: Regulation, Autonomy or Connection* (London: Routledge and Falmer, 2002); Luis C. Moll, Cathy Amanti, Deborah Neff, and Norma Gonzalez, "Funds of Knowledge for Teaching: Using a Qualitative Approach to Connect Homes and Classrooms," *Theory into Practice* 31, no. 2 (1992): 132–41; Denny Taylor, "The (Con)Textual Worlds of Childhood: An Interpretive Approach to Alternative Dimensions of Experience," in *Home and School: Early Language and Reading*, ed. Bryant Fillion, Carolyn N. Hedley, and Emily C. Di Martino (Norwood, N.J.: Ablex, 1987), 93–107.

75. John Dore, "Children's Conversations," in *Handbook of Discourse Analysis*, vol. 3, *Discourse and Dialogue*, ed. Teun van Djik (San Diego, Calif.: Academic, 1985), 47–66; Susan M. Hoyle and Carolyn Temple Adger, eds., *Kids Talk: Strategic Language Use in Later Childhood* (New York: Oxford University Press, 1998); Harvey Sacks, "On the Analyzability of Stories by Children," in *Directions in Sociolinguistics: The Ethnography of Communication*, ed. John J. Gumperz and Dell Hymes (Chicago: Holt, Rinehart and Winston, 1972), 325–45.

76. Anne Haas Dyson, "Coach Bombay's Kids Learn to Write: Children's Appropriation of Media Material for School Literacy," *Research in the Teaching of English* 33, no. 4 (May 1999): 367–402; Neil Postman, *The Disappearance of Childhood* (New York: Delacorte, 1981); Joseph Tobin, *"Good Guys Don't Wear Hats": Children's Talk about the Media* (New York: Teachers College Press, 2000).

77. Kathryn Au, "Participant Structure in a Reading Lesson with Hawaiian Children: Analysis of a Culturally Appropriate Instruction/Event," *Anthropology and Education Quarterly* 11, no. 2 (June 1980): 91–115; Bernardo Ferdman, "Literacy and Cultural Identity," *Harvard Educational Review* 60, no. 2 (1990): 181–204; Eve Gregory, Susi Long, and Dinah Volk, eds., *Many Pathways to Literacy: Young Children Learning with Siblings, Grandparents, Peers and Communities* (New York: Routledge Falmer, Taylor & Francis, 2004); Kathleen Holland, David Bloome, and Judith Solsken, eds., *Alternative Perspectives in Assessing Children's Language and Literacy* (Norwood, N.J.: Ablex, 1994); Cynthia Lewis, *Literary Practices as Social Acts: Power, Status, and Cultural Norms in the Classroom* (Mahwah, N.J.: Erlbaum, 2001).

78. Sofia Avgitidou, "Peer Culture and Friendship Relationships as Contexts for the Development of Young Children's Pro-social Behaviour," *International Journal of Early Years* 9, no. 2 (June 2001): 145–52; Corsaro, *Friendship and Peer Culture in the Early Years*.

79. Bronwyn Davies, *Life in the Classroom and Playground: The Accounts of Primary School Children* (London: Routledge and Kegan Paul, 1982); Nespor, *Tangled up in School*.

80. Peter Blatchford, *Social Life in Schools: Pupils' Experience of Breaktime and Recess from 7 to 16 Years* (Bristol, Pa: Falmer, Taylor and Francis, 1998).

81. Jacqueline Goodnow and A. Burns, *Home and School: Child's-Eye Views* (Sydney: Allyn and Unwin, 1985).

82. Luigia Camaioni, "From Early Interaction Patterns to Language Acquisition: Which Continuity?" in *Children's Worlds and Children's Language*, ed. Jenny Cook-Gumperz, William A. Corsaro, and Jürgen Streeck (New York: Mouton de Gruyter, 1986), 69–82.

83. L. R. Goldman, *Child's Play: Myth, Mimesis and Make-Believe* (New York: Berg, 1998); Nancy King, "Play: The Kindergartener's Perspective," *The Elementary School Journal* 80 (1979): 81–87; Donna M. Lanclos, *At Play in Belfast: Children's Folklore and Identities in Northern Ireland* (New Brunswick, N.J.: Rutgers University Press, 2003); Jane P. Perry, *Outdoor Play: Teaching Strategies with Young Children* (New York: Teachers College Press, 2001); Olivia Saracho and Bernard Spodek, eds.,

Multiple Perspectives on Play in Early Childhood Education (Albany: State University of New York Press, 1998).

84. Corsaro, *Friendship and Peer Culture*; David Fernie, "Becoming a Student: Messages from First Settings," *Theory into Practice* 27 (1988): 3–10; Becky Reimer, "When the Playground Enters the Classroom," in *Children on Playgrounds: Research Perspectives and Applications*, ed. Craig Hart (Albany: State University of New York Press, 1993), 316–43.

85. Goodman, *The Culture of Childhood*.

86. Beatrice Whiting, ed., *Six Cultures: Studies of Child Rearing* (New York: Wiley, 1963); John Whiting and Irvin L. Child, *Child Training and Personality: A Cross-cultural Study* (New York: Yale University Press, 1953).

87. C. W. M. Hart, "Contrasts between Prepubertal and Postpubertal Education," in *Education and Cultural Process: Anthropological Approaches*, ed. George Spindler (Prospect Heights, Ill.: Waveland, 1997), 362–82.

88. Sara Harkness and Philip Kilbride, "Introduction: The Socialization of Affect," *Ethos* 11, no. 4 (1983): 215–20.

89. Jean Briggs, *Inuit Morality Play: The Emotional Education of a Three-Year-Old* (New Haven, Conn.: Yale University Press, 1998).

90. Dorothy Eggan, "Instruction and Affect in Hopi Cultural Continuity," in *Education and Cultural Process: Anthropological Approaches*, ed. George Spindler (Prospect Heights, Ill.: Waveland, 1997), 339–61; Kimball, "The Transmission of Culture"; Elinor Ochs, "Indexicality and Socialization," in *Cultural Psychology: Essays on Comparative Human Development*, ed. James Stigler, Richard Shweder, and Gilbert Herdt (Cambridge, UK: Cambridge University Press, 1990), 296–320; Strauss and Quinn, *A Cognitive Theory of Cultural Meaning*.

91. Helen Morton, *Becoming Tongan: An Ethnography of Childhood* (Honolulu: University of Hawaii Press, 1996).

92. Cole, *Cultural Psychology*.

93. Jahoda and Lewis, eds. *Acquiring Culture*; Super and Harkness, eds., *Anthropological Perspectives on Child Development*.

94. Jean Lave, "Mathematics Learning in Japanese, Chinese, and American Classrooms," in *Cultural Psychology: Essays on Comparative Human Development*, ed. James Stigler, Richard Shweder, and Gilbert Herdt (Cambridge, UK: Cambridge University Press, 1990), 321–56; Rogoff, *The Cultural Nature of Human Development*.

95. Elinor Ochs and Bambi Schieffelin, "Language Acquisition and Socialization: Three Developmental Stories and Their Implications," in *Culture Theory: Essays in Mind, Self and Emotion*, ed. Richard A. Shweder and Robert LeVine (Cambridge, UK: Cambridge University Press, 1984), 276–320; Bambi Schieffelin, *The Give and Take of Everyday Life: Language Socialization of Kaluli Children* (New York: Cambridge University Press, 1990).

96. Beth Blue Swadener, with Margaret Kabiru and Anne Njenga, *Does the Village Still Raise the Child? A Collaborative Study of Changing Child-Rearing and Early Education in Kenya* (Albany: State University of New York Press, 2000).

97. Goodman, *The Culture of Childhood*; Reisman, *First Find Your Child a Good Mother*; Radhika Viruru, *Early Childhood Education: Postcolonial Perspectives from India* (New Delhi: Sage, 2001).

98. Catherine Panter-Brick and Malcolm T. Smith, eds., *Abandoned Children* (Cambridge, UK: Cambridge University Press, 2000); Karen Riley, *Schools behind Barbed Wire: The Untold Story of Wartime Internment and the Children of Arrested Enemy Aliens* (Lanham, Md.: Rowman & Littlefield, 2002); Nancy Scheper-Hughes and Carolyn Sargent, eds., *Small Wars: The Cultural Politics of Childhood* (Berkeley: University of California Press, 1998).

99. Mariko Fujita and Toshiyuki Sano "Day Care Teachers and Children in the United States and Japan: Ethnography, Reflexive Interviewing and Cultural Dialogue," in *Education and Cultural Process: Anthropological Approaches*, ed. George Spindler (Prospect Heights, Ill.: Waveland, 1997), 430–35; Mariko Fujita Sano and Toshiyuki Sano, *Life in Riverfront: A Midwestern Town Seen through Japanese Eyes* (Philadelphia: Harcourt, Brace College, 2001).

100. Robin Alexander, *Culture and Pedagogy: International Comparisons in Primary Education* (Malden, Mass.: Blackwell, 2001); Kathryn Anderson-Levitt, *Teaching Cultures: Knowledge for Teaching First Grade in France and the United States* (Creskill, N.J.: Hampton, 2002); Catherine Lewis, *Educating Hearts and Minds: Reflections on Japanese Preschool and Elementary Education* (New York: Cambridge University Press, 1995); Joesph Tobin, D. Y. H. Wu, and D. H. Davidson, *Preschool in Three Cultures: Japan, China, and the United States* (New Haven, Conn.: Yale University Press, 1989); Roberta Wollons, ed., *Kindergartens and Cultures: The Global Diffusion of an Idea* (New Haven, Conn.: Yale University Press, 2000).

101. Mead, "Socialization and Enculturation"; Melville Herskovitz, *Man and His Works* (New York: Knopf, 1956).

102. Jack Goody, *The Domestication of the Savage Mind* (Cambridge, UK: Cambridge University Press, 1977); Walter Ong, *Orality and Literacy: The Technologizing of the World* (New York: Routledge, 1982).

103. Raymond Firth, "Education in Tikopia," in *From Child to Adult: Studies in the Anthropology of Education*, ed. John Middleton (New York: Natural History Press, 1970), 75–90; David F. Lancy, "Becoming a Blacksmith in Gbarngasuakwelle," *Anthropology and Education Quarterly* 11, no. 4 (1980): 266–74; Margaret Mead, *Growing Up in New Guinea* (New York: Morrow, 1930); Margaret Mead and Martha Wolfenstein, *Childhood in Contemporary Cultures* (Chicago: Chicago University Press, 1955); John Whiting, *Becoming a Kwoma: Teaching and Learning in a New Guinea Tribe* (New Haven, Conn.: Yale University Press, 1941).

104. Nat J. Colletta, *American Schools for the Natives of Ponape: A Study of Education and Culture Change in Micronesia* (Honolulu: University Press of Hawaii, East-West Center, 1980); Alan Peshkin, "Kanuri Schoolchildren: Education and Social Mobilization in Nigeria," in *Case Studies in Education and Culture*, ed. George Spindler and Louise Spindler (Chicago: Holt, Rinehart and Winston, 1972), 82–110; Harry F. Wolcott, *A Kwakiutl Village and School* (Prospect Heights, Ill.: Waveland, 1967).

105. Super and Harkness, eds., *Anthropological Perspectives on Child Development*; Christine Tanz, "Introduction: Gender Differences in the Langauge of Children," in *Language, Gender, and Sex in Comparative Perspective*, ed. Susan Philips, Susan Steele, and Christine Tanz (New York: Cambridge University Press, 1987), 163–77.

106. Mead, *Coming of Age in Samoa*; Ritchie and Ritchie, *Growing Up in Polynesia*; Schieffelin, *The Give and Take of Everyday Life: Language Socialization of Kaluli Children*.

107. Alma Gottlieb, *The Afterlife Is Where We Come From: The Culture of Infancy in West Africa* (Chicago: University of Chicago Press, 2003).

108. Beth Conklin and Lynn Morgan, "Babies, Bodies, and the Production of Personhood in North America and a Native Amazonian Society," *Ethos* 24, no. 4 (1996): 657–94; Judy DeLoache and Alma Gottlieb, *A World of Babies: Imagined Childcare Guides for Seven Societies* (Cambridge, UK: Cambridge University Press, 2000).

WORKS CITED

Alexander, Robin. *Culture and Pedagogy: International Comparisons in Primary Education*. Malden, Mass.: Blackwell, 2001.

This lengthy work examines how social and historical structures as well as cultural processes regarding the ideals and values of educational and governmental policy mutually intersect and implicate the ideals and practices of primary school pedagogy in five nations (the United States, the United Kingdom, India, Russia, and France). This work is impressive because it examines the structural aspects of policy and pedagogy as well as the local schools', teachers', and students' actions and conceptions of these processes through ethnographic analysis. This work shows the similarity in public policy and pedagogy that all five nations share due to their similar histories of mass, public schooling for democratic ideals. This work also highlights the diversity of pedagogical forms that implicate their specific historical, social, cultural, and political ideals.

Anderson-Levitt, Kathryn. *Teaching Cultures: Knowledge for Teaching First Grade in France and the United States*. Creskill, N.J.: Hampton, 2002.

The author illustrates, through ethnographic and historical analysis of reading instruction in French and U.S. first-grade classrooms, how cultural differences as well as notions of transnationality are formed.

Ariès, Philippe. *Centuries of Childhood: A Social History of Family Life*. New York: Knopf, 1962.

As a germinal work exploring the history of childhood in the West from the seventeenth century to the present, this work illustrates the changing nature of what childhood meant. By focusing on what parents thought about children (or the sentiments approach), the author argues that childhood was "discovered" differently at different times with different meanings. Aries shows that a key moment in the "discovery" of childhood occurred when institutionalized education and notions of the educated person gained favor—at this point childhood was conceived as distinct from adulthood. The author also shows how middle-class elitist notions of family worked with schooling to maintain boundaries and distinctions between them and the poor.

Au, Kathryn. "Participant Structure in a Reading Lesson with Hawaiian Children: Analysis of a Culturally Appropriate Instruction/Event." *Anthropology and Education Quarterly* 11, no. 2 (June 1980): 91–115.

The author argues for more culturally appropriate contexts for learning by showing that Hawaiian children participated more in reading events that reflected their own "native" peer group communicative style of talk-narrative or story-talk.

Avgitidou, Sofia. "Peer Culture and Friendship Relationships as Contexts for the Development of Young Children's Pro-social Behaviour." *International Journal of Early Years* 9, no. 2 (June 2001): 145–52.

Through research with Greek kindergarteners' peer groups, the author shows how "pro-social behavior" in friendships are formed and become meaningful. The author illustrates this process by focusing on the day-to-day maintenance and negotiation of friendships in the key childhood contexts of shared experiences, beliefs, and intentions.

Barritt, Loren S. *An Elementary School in Holland: Experiment in Educational Practice.* Utrecht, Netherlands: International Books, 1996.

The author uses a phenomenological approach to understand how the everyday lives of many different actors in a Dutch elementary school affect the processes of schooling. A central theme in this work is the notion of classroom conflict and control as well as the significance of children's agency in their complicity or resistance toward the teacher's and school's goals. This work is useful as a cross-cultural work because the author details the culturally diverse ways that Dutch educators perceive, understand, and negotiate aspects of control.

Beatty, Barbara. *Preschool Education in America: The Culture of Young Children from the Colonial Era to the Present.* New Haven, Conn.: Yale University Press, 1995.

This is an excellent feminist history of preschools in the United States from the 1820s to the 1990s. This work is very comprehensive: the author uses great detail in describing the constant vacillation in the United States toward more or less publicly funded preschools. In just as much detail, the author also explicates the complex ideological interplay of gender and class in the consistent marginalization of U.S. preschools.

Bezemer, Jeff. *Dealing with Multilingualism in Education: A Case Study of a Dutch Primary School Classroom.* Amsterdam: Askam Academic, 2003.

The author examines the implementation and inconsistencies of second-language learning of seven-year-old immigrants in Dutch schools. The work illustrates how the ideology of language homogenization operated to undervalue "other language" use and practices as well as subvert the larger curriculum of second-language learning.

Blatchford, Peter. *Social Life in Schools: Pupils' Experience of Breaktime and Recess from 7 to 16 Years*. Bristol, Pa: Falmer, Taylor and Francis, 1998.

Blatchford explores the many spaces that are within schools but are outside the context (and rules) of the classroom. Through his interviews with seven- to sixteen-year-olds he particularly investigates the notion, norms, and rules regarding friendship and the ideas surrounding "growing up." This work is novel because the author focuses upon the often ubiquitous agonistic "play" in school interactions (like bullying, teasing, and fighting).

Bloch, Marianne. "Becoming Scientific and Professional: An Historical Perspective on the Aims and Effects of Early Education." In *The Formation of the School Subjects: The Struggle for Creating an American Institution*, edited by Thomas Popkewitz, 25–62. New York: Falmer, 1987.

The author traces the history of early childhood education in the United States from the early eighteenth century into the middle of the twentieth century—discussing Sunday schools, infant schools, as well as the primary and nursery school movements. Bloch shows that key aspects of identity (namely, class, race, culture, and ethnicity) were central in crafting the many different forms of curricula of early child care. A central theme in the totality of this process is that schools and public policy focused on institutionalizing and normalizing young children through the use of science, family, morality, and values in order to create specific types of school subjects that legitimized certain forms of knowledge, society, and polity.

Bourdieu, Pierre. *Outline of a Theory of Practice*. Cambridge, UK: Cambridge University Press, 1977.

This is a germinal work for anthropologists and other social scientists interested in the social nature of practice. Bourdieu illustrates how culturally important actions are simultaneously products and producers of culture and history. The author illustrates how interpersonal relations are embodied and internalized. The totality of this system is what Bourdieu calls the habitus. The habitus is central in understanding the production of inequality in society—for habitus differs among people and is reproduced according to these differences. And, when it comes to social class, the difference in habitus between classes (particularly, rich and poor) is a fundamental way in which people maintain key distinctions and ultimately boundaries to social power, wealth, and privilege.

Boyer, Pascal. "Human Cognition and Cultural Evolution." In *Anthropological Theory Today*, edited by Henrietta L. Moore, 206–33. Malden, Mass.: Polity, 1999.

In this heady piece, the author argues that humans possess an "intuitive ontology" of domain-specific cognitive principles (like number, human, animal, and artifact) that temper the expectations and learnings of the experienced world. These principles, and the expectations they mold, are formed very early and seem to change little into adulthood. Because cultural concepts are based on these principles, there are limits on the range of variation for meanings among cultures. The author also discusses how these principles fit into the much larger process of cultural evolution.

Briggs, Jean. *Inuit Morality Play: The Emotional Education of a Three-Year-Old.* New Haven, Conn.: Yale University Press, 1998.

By studying the child-rearing techniques and development of a very young Inuit child, the author illustrates that social drama (play, teasing, fighting) is a chaotic, yet fecund, source of cultural meanings and practices that assist children in their emotional development. The author argues that we must investigate and understand the centrality of emotion in child development in order to more fully understand the multiple, mutable, contradictory, and ambiguous nature of culture.

Bruner, Edward. "Cultural Transmission and Culture Change." *Southwest Journal of Anthropology* 12 (1956): 191–99.

Working with the Mandan-Hidatsa of North Dakota, the author poses the "Early Learning Hypothesis" that what is learned first and earliest is more resistant to change because it is most dependent on original cultural meanings. For this reason, acculturation to a new culture's practices and meanings is more difficult because later aspects of culture are more readily discarded or resisted.

Bruner, Jerome. *The Culture of Education.* Cambridge: Harvard University Press, 1996.

This is an outstanding book regarding the cultural politics of education. Bruner shows through history and detailed qualitative work that education revolves around a continuum of key, mutual cultural contradictions—what he calls antimonies—of seemingly opposing, polar values both of which are necessary for education. For this reason, understanding, valuing, and validating both poles of these antimonies are necessary in order to effectively teach our children equitably. Some important antimonies that have framed our notions of education throughout time are talent-centered/meritocratic ideals vs. tool-centered/culturally contextual ones; the value of local, particularized knowledge vs. universal and standardized knowledge; and the tension between individual and intrapersonal learning vs. group and interpersonal learning. Bruner clearly shows that at different times, for different reasons, certain poles of these antimonies gain favor and substantially impact schooling and public policy.

Bryson, Dennis Raymond. *Socializing the Young: The Role of Foundations, 1923–1941.* Westport, Conn.: Bergin and Garvey, 2002.

The author uses a Foucauldian analysis to investigate how philanthropic organization of this time interacted with schools, other governmental bodies, as well as with social scientists to normalize children's bodies to socialization of particular social norms for the goal of greater social control. Bryson traces the details of how all these actors worked together, with a consistent focus on governing children's bodies in the contexts of both schools as well as family–child relationships, in order to produce a governmentality of the larger social body where education could transform culture toward state and national ideals.

Butler, Judith. *Gender Trouble: Feminism and the Subversion of Identity.* New York: Routledge, 1990.

By focusing on how people are gendered beings that are always incomplete and in process, the author shows that gender is actually a performance—here, the author contends that the body is a cultural product that people are always in the process of making. These performances are produced by larger social ideas, practices, and discourses that many people share, but through their physicality and materiality these performances simultaneously reproduce and transform those larger social ideas, practices, and discourses about gender and identity.

Camaioni, Luigia. "From Early Interaction Patterns to Language Acquisition: Which Continuity?" In *Children's Worlds and Children's Language*, edited by Jenny Cook-Gumperz, William A. Corsaro, and Jürgen Streeck, 69–82. New York: Mouton de Gruyter, 1986.

By watching mother–infant interactions, the author shows how mothers use games as conventions for teaching first words. The author traces the substantial continuity through games that facilitates the move from the prelinguistic to the linguistic.

Christian-Smith, Linda K. "Voices of Resistance: Young Women Readers of Romance Fiction." In *Beyond Silenced Voices*, edited by Michelle Weis and Lois Fine, 169–89. Albany: State University of New York Press, 1993.

In their reading of romance texts, young, white, black, and Asian middle-class as well as working-class women use the many ideological threads that exist in the United States regarding the continuing struggle over women's place in the world. The author shows that through this process, young women come to grips with realities of women today, sometimes reproducing traditional gender identities and sometimes refashioning them—particularly, when it comes to the links between beauty and consumption.

Christie, Frances. "Pedagogic Discourse in the Primary School." *Linguistics and Education* 7 (1995): 122–42.

The author connects discourse and learning by showing how pedagogical discourse works to construct a range of subjectivities that students can use to form school identities. These subjectivities operate around specific principles as well as value systems that implicate culturally appropriate actions and meanings in school. The author does this by illustrating how learning is built incrementally through exposure to the pedagogic discourse that has two registers (or a style of talk that indexes and accompanies specific situations): one register for relating the goals, rules, and sequence of the activity and another that "points to" the actual knowledge being taught.

Cicourel, Aaron V. *Language Use and School Performance*. New York: Academic, 1974.

The author focuses on the relationships among assessment, testing, as well as ranking and tracking of schools and how this whole process relates to larger society. He discusses the gap that exists between the qualitative assessment of teachers and the quantitative assessment of objective tests because the detailed, local interpretation of students' abilities to negotiate normative rules, contexts, and interpretive frames through language use and acquisition is not used in assessment.

Cole, Michael. *Cultural Psychology: A Once and Future Discipline*. Cambridge: Harvard University Press, 1996.

The author marries the social and biological fields within the science of mind (particularly, American and developmental psychology, anthropology and the cultural—historical science of Vygotsky). He does this by investigating how the general features of psychology and biology are mediated by society in the shaping of individual human minds. Cole also explores the simultaneous construction of ideal culture and the physical, material one by linking cultural artifacts to the purposes that they are put within context. In chapter 7 of this work, the author works to thread culture into the ontogenetic development of the child as well as the phylogenetic development of humans through time. The author shows how the physical, biological structures and development of the child's body promotes, mediates and constrains culturally mediated action and artifacts.

Colletta, Nat J. *American Schools for the Natives of Ponape: A Study of Education and Culture Change in Micronesia.* Honolulu: University Press of Hawaii, East-West Center, 1980.

This is an ethnographic account of how American schools substantially change the cultural values and meanings of people. The young children that are the first to enter U.S. schools are confronted with a substantially different reality from the one their parents are familiar with. Within this process of culture change, the author illustrates that the children's perceptions of history and its link to social control is very important for them in mediating their identity as Ponapean or American.

Conklin, Beth, and Lynn Morgan. "Babies, Bodies, and the Production of Personhood in North America and a Native Amazonian Society." *Ethos* 24, no. 4 (1996): 657–94.

The authors describe a cross-cultural exploration of the notion of the developing fetus in the United States and the Wari of Brazil. This work does a good job tracing the central models of infant, development, and personhood in the United States, where there is a focus on the materiality of being; autonomous notions of nurturance and growth; biological models; and the dyadic individual–society dichotomy omnipresent in U.S. society. In comparison, the Wari notions of the body and personhood revolve around the notion of social exchanges and power relationships.

Cook-Gumperz, Jenny, and John Gumperz. "Context in Children's Speech." In *The Development of Communication: Social and Pragmatic Factors in Language Acquisition,* edited by Natalie Waterson and Catherine Snow, 55–73. London: Wiley, 1978.

The authors show that the presuppositions that both speakers and hearers use to interpret communication are renegotiated in the course of the context of conversation. Here, children rely both on their background knowledge as well as on their understandings of the conventions of context. The authors illustrate that it is important to recognize that the total context is not simply a set of fixed rules but instead more fluid, guiding principles that moderate or change expectations with regards to social outcomes, goals, and interests.

Cook-Gumperz, Jenny, and William A. Corsaro. "The Socio-Ecological Constraints on Children's Communicative Strategies." In *Papers on Language and Context,* edited by Jenny Cook-Gumperz and John Gumperz, 29–35. Berkeley, Calif.: Language Behavior Research Laboratory, 1976.

The authors show how nursery school is an ecological space where certain verbal and nonverbal activities become associated with spatial subdivisions. That is, certain locations in the classroom become regularly used for play while others are used within the more formal boundaries of games. The intersection between space and these conventionalized activities influences the nature of talk as well as the interpretation of what is said. This then fosters the larger conventions of rules and talk, which are fully understood only by those consistently involved in those spaces-contexts.

Cook-Gumperz, Jenny, William A. Corsaro, and Jürgen Streeck, eds. *Children's Worlds and Children's Language.* New York: Mouton de Gruyter, 1986.

This work traces the links between language acquisition and socialization in naturalistic settings. The central focus is to investigate the interactive communicative competence of children and how they use their competence intentionally to learn—this central theme is a coherent critique of functionalist, linear models of development. The chapters involve a host of discourse analyses, from microanalytical conversation analysis to larger sociolinguistic analysis of learning in context.

Corsaro, William A. *Friendship and Peer Culture in the Early Years.* Norwood, N.J.: Ablex, 1985.

As a germinal work that qualified some of the first key features of children's culture, such as the importance of routines in play and friendship, this is an excellent and vital work. Methodologically, Corsaro discovered the "reactive strategy/role," where the researcher investigates the role of adults so they are able to not act like one—a very fruitful strategy in getting involved in kids' worlds in more childlike ways. The author traces important links between role-play and significant cultural values like sex and gender roles as well as adult roles.

———. *We're Friends, Right? Inside Kids' Culture.* Washington, D.C.: Joseph Henry Press, 2003.

Based on over three decades of his work in Italian and U.S. preschools, as well as in the Head Start program in the United States, the author discusses the fascinating intersection between children's worlds and those of adults—focusing on a range of important contexts like peer group play as well as the effect of researchers' perceptions and interpretations. Power and agency are at the heart of this book, in that Corsaro shows how children are constantly working to position their own interests, ideas, and actions within these schooling contexts. And they often do this by appropriating and transforming important aspects from adults' worlds into their own in attempts to "manipulate" adults for their creative concerns.

Cummins, Jim. "Empowering Minority Students: A Framework for Intervention." In *Beyond Silenced Voices,* edited by Michelle Weis and Lois Fine, 101–10. Albany: State University of New York Press, 1997.

This is an excellent piece that illustrates that educational reform for minority students is unsuccessful because the larger, inequitable cultural, class, race, and ethnic relationships between teachers and students as well as schools and communities have remained essentially unchanged in the structure of schools and society. Cummins asserts that we need to change our policies to revolve around the fact that successful minorities are those that are positively oriented to *both* their own cultures as well as the school's culture—one where minorities do not perceive themselves as inferior and alienated from both their own cultural values or the larger cultural values of the United States. Cummins discusses the details of a Spanish-only preschool program (Carpinteria in California) that actually works in preparing children and parents better for kindergarten vs. bilingual programs that are assimilationist (being focused toward learning English as soon as possible).

Davies, Bronwyn. *Life in the Classroom and Playground: The Accounts of Primary School Children*. London: Routledge and Kegan Paul, 1982.

By comparing the classroom to the playground, as well as kids' culture to adults' culture, the author defines some important foundations for research with kids, as well as rules of these children's peer culture. The author shows that although friendship is fragile and characterized by fighting—leading to the need for more dynamic interpersonal relationships—this strangely serves to maintain the order of kids' total worlds. Here, the author explores their shared worldview and shows that it is organized by three main rules: reciprocity; "discoverable facticity," or the belief in one correct interpretation; and the plasticity of character.

DeLoache, Judy, and Alma Gottlieb. *A World of Babies: Imagined Childcare Guides for Seven Societies*. Cambridge, UK: Cambridge University Press, 2000.

The authors discuss seven different cultures from the point of view of a fictitious author writing in the style of a child care manual. This work is tempered with expert ethnographic narratives that focus on the cultural diversity of ideas and practices surrounding "babyhood" from pregnancy and notions of the fetus to the upbringing and development of children. The authors' overall goal is to illustrate that the child and childhood is shaped substantially by the social context of cultural meanings and practices. This work is particularly useful as an introductory look, or database, regarding child care practices and notions of childhood around the world for scholars unfamiliar with its diversity of forms.

Denzin, Norman K. *The Research Act: A Theoretical Introduction to Sociological Methods*. 3rd ed. Englewood Cliffs, N.J.: Prentice-Hall, 1970.

Although not specifically about research with children, this is still an excellent resource for qualitative methods. It is especially worthwhile in its discussion of collecting good data and methods of checking the validity of research findings.

Deyhle, Donna. "Navajo Youth and Anglo Racism: Cultural Integrity and Resistance." *Harvard Educational Review* 65, no. 3 (1995): 403–44.

The author illustrates the range of white, racist representations surrounding Navajo children in U.S. public schools. She argues that this fosters a substantial cultural divide between Navajo students' home and school lives and is a central reason that Navajo students fail. For this reason, the author asserts that Navajo experiences of racial and cultural warfare must be placed at the center of explaining and understanding their educational success or failure. The author bolsters this claim by showing that most successful Navajo students are those who have a firm background in their Navajo families.

Dore, John. "Children's Conversations." In *Handbook of Discourse Analysis*, vol. 3, *Discourse and Dialogue*, edited by Teun van Djik, 47–66. San Diego, Calif.: Academic, 1985.

The author shows that contexts, meanings, and conversational competence shifts according to a child's age. This is due to four important factors as a child gets older: a child's social membership changes; they are accountable in different ways; the functions of language vary according to these differences in accountability; and this influences the meanings of words. The author traces this transforming process by explicating the nature of context, meaning, and communication from infants to school-aged children.

Downey, Greg. *Learning Capoeira: Lessons in Cunning from an Afro-Brazilian Art.* New York: Oxford University Press, 2005.

Although not specifically about children, this book is essential for anyone interested in exploring the links between learning, action, perception, and the body. This is because the author phenomenologically describes how knowledge, perception, and practices are learned with and through the body. He describes in thick detail people's perspectives and notions of their body as they are developing their skills within the martial art form of Capoeira. The author illustrates how learning Capoeira is part and parcel of learning a novel set of habits, perceptions, and comportment so that individuals will perceive and act differently in the everyday world. This book is an excellent read, full of detailed, interesting examples that clearly illustrate the theoretical claims the author is making.

Dyson, Anne Haas. "Coach Bombay's Kids Learn to Write: Children's Appropriation of Media Material for School Literacy." *Research in the Teaching of English* 33, no. 4 (May 1999): 367–402.

Through ethnographic work in a first-grade classroom, the author traces how kids use media texts to interact in peer literacy events as well as academic ones. Dyson illustrates the diversity and hybridity of media texts (particularly, sports) as very early foundations for literacy acts and interpretations.

Edwards, Rosalind, ed. *Children, Home and School: Regulation, Autonomy or Connection.* London: Routledge and Falmer, 2002.

Although this work involves many different authors, utilizing a host of different methods in many different countries, it consistently focuses on the voices of children as central to the methodology of qualitatively understanding their worlds. In many places, this work investigates the tensions, contradictions, and gaps that exist between home and school as well as between children and adults. This work is particularly useful in understanding how children are perceived, understood, and regulated as "autonomous or connected" in their intersection at numerous locales (spatial and discursive) with adults.

Eggan, Dorothy. "Instruction and Affect in Hopi Cultural Continuity." In *Education and Cultural Process: Anthropological Approaches*, edited by George Spindler, 339–61. Prospect Heights, Ill.: Waveland, 1997.

Originally published in 1956 as part of the "culture and personality" tradition in anthropology, the author describes how Hopi systems of affect are central to the transmission of culture and education of children. The author shows that the Hopi traditional cultural model was so strong that many children were able to fend off the forced indoctrination in U.S. schools—in particular, parents and other kin used fear as a mode of social control and taught modes of anxiety displacement so their children would be able to both understand what makes a "good Hopi" as well as resist white-schooled practices and meanings. Eggan also illustrates that the use of affective elements is not cordoned only to children: they are used by everyone throughout people's life cycles in order to constantly refashion and recondition people to core values.

Ferdman, Bernardo. "Literacy and Cultural Identity." *Harvard Educational Review* 60, no. 2 (1990): 181–204.

Ferdman investigates the importance that cultural diversity plays in influencing the learning of literacy by individuals from both a social and psychological perspective. The author illustrates that literacy is a form of socialization contingent on particular cultural contexts. Here, cultural identity mediates the process of becoming literate as well as the types of literacy behaviors children engage in because a person's cultural perspective of self as well as their culturally relevant relationships to others changes with and through literacy.

Fernie, David. "Becoming a Student: Messages from First Settings." *Theory into Practice* 27 (1988): 3–10.

Fernie traces the transformation and development of the student role from preschool to kindergarten. That is, the central role for the preschooler is the student-player, whereas the central role for the kindergartener is the student-worker. The author argues that in the move from preschool to kindergarten, play is transformed into work.

Firth, Raymond. "Education in Tikopia." In *From Child to Adult: Studies in the Anthropology of Education*, edited by John Middleton, 75–90. New York: Natural History Press, 1970.

Originally published in 1936, this work shows that traditional education is necessarily, pragmatically linked to the family and society in the everyday world. The author illustrates this by focusing on how punishment and obedience teaches good manners through social disapproval. In this context, formal lessons are scarce; people develop as individuals through daily interactions and activities at the developmental level they are able.

Florio, Susan. "Learning How to Go to School: An Ethnography of Interaction in a Kindergarten/First Grade Classroom." PhD diss., Harvard University, 1978.

Florio represents the importance of context, situated meaning, and face-to-face negotiation in the production and learning of participant structures—which are the rules, obligations, and interpretations for different early classroom contexts. The author shows that understanding the contextual cues that "cue up" the different participant structures (and rules for action and interpretation they frame) are essential for understanding what is to be learned and how it is to be learned.

Foley, Douglas. *Learning Capitalist Culture: Deep in the Heart of Texas*. Philadelphia: Philadelphia University Press, 1996.

Although not specifically about early childhood education, this work is very enlightening when it comes to the intersection of culture, politics, and economy. This is because it examines the ways in which white U.S. citizens and Mexican American immigrants learn the materialistic culture that is competitive, individualistic, and unegalitarian and which turns people into commodities or objects. This process has corrosive effects on people's lives. This work also investigates the history of this process keying into the fact that cultural politics are actually class politics. The author explicates this by showing how school performance and ideology fits with white, middle-class ideology that both objectifies people and socializes them to reproduce the endemic violence of classism and racism within capitalism.

Fujita, Mariko, and Toshiyuki Sano. "Day Care Teachers and Children in the United States and Japan: Ethnography, Reflexive Interviewing and Cultural Dialogue." In *Education and Cultural Process: Anthropological Approaches*, edited by George Spindler, 430–35. Prospect Heights, Ill.: Waveland, 1997.

This is a fascinating work because it engages Japanese and U.S. preschool teachers' voices in what the authors call "cultural dialogues." Here, teachers from the two cultures watch video about the other culture's child care practices and dialogue about the comparisons between this and their own practices. Within these "cultural dialogues," teachers become reflexive about their pivotal concerns of the other and then contrast them with what they find disturbing in their own schools. The authors and teachers in this dialogue deal with central, yet different, cultural notions like control/strictness, child safety, play, teacher–child interaction, dependence, independence and individualism, as well as the "nature" of the child.

Garcia, Eugene. "Instructional Discourse Style of an 'Effective' First-Grade Teacher in an Hispanic Classroom." *Early Child Development and Care* 38 (1988): 119–32.

The author illustrates through first-grade Mexican American peer interactions that these kids have exceptionally developed linguistic abilities. However, their linguistic ability and capacity is not understood, legitimized, or utilized by teachers because the teacher–child interaction, with its focus on turn taking, doesn't allow these kids the same opportunity or context for these linguistic skills.

Gesell, Arnold, Frances L. Ilg, and Louise Bates Ames. *The Child from Five to Ten*. New York: Harper & Row, 1977.

This work explores the history of early schooling in the United States by focusing on the tension surrounding child maturity (both developmental and chronological) as it relates to readiness for school. The authors show how at different historical periods different "growth gradients"—along the axes of behavior, maturity, motor, hygiene, motion, fears, sex, interpersonal relations, play, school, ethics, and philosophy—were given legitimacy and primacy, fostering novel cultural practices, tools, and products that were the most rational within the realm of schooling and child socialization at that time.

Gibson, James. *The Ecological Approach to Visual Perception.* Boston: Houghton Mifflin, 1979.

This is an important work in the field of Environmental and Ecological Psychology. The author illustrates how humans shape the world and their perceptions of it over time by "handing down" important frames or contexts for perception that filter or select for certain learning, actions, and perceptions. Ideas central to a culture or society are not reproduced via a wholesale delivery of important information and ideas over time. Instead, people learn about what's important in their world through what the author calls an "education of attention" that frames perception and action in such ways that important ideas, values, and practices are called attention to, focused on, and then learned.

Gibson, Margaret. "Playing by the Rules." In *Education and Cultural Process: Anthropological Approaches,* edited by George Spindler, 262–70. Prospect Heights, Ill.: Waveland, 1997.

Through her decades of ethnographic work with Punjabi Sikh immigrants in California, the author illustrates that these children acculturate (what the author calls "accommodate") to the dominant values of the school without assimilating completely into U.S. society or becoming "Americanized." This is because that they are discriminated against in school and the larger society, as well as because that they are warned by their families about this process. The author argues that schools need to account for the specific relationship between the dominant group and the immigrant group in order to understand the mutual processes of accommodation, assimiliation, or resistance to dominant cultural ideals by focusing on three main aspects: the cultural preferences of the group (e.g., notions and goals of education, interest in assimilation to U.S. values), the historical context of settlement in their host society (i.e., voluntary or involuntary immigrants), and the specific group's response to current dominant and institutional values (particularly, discrimination and racism).

Goldman, L. R. *Child's Play: Myth, Mimesis and Make-Believe.* New York: Berg, 1998.

The author investigates the range of children's play in Papua New Guinea and shows how kids creatively modify their physical, social, and symbolic environment to create "make-believe" worlds. This book focuses on mimesis, or forms of imitation, where normative identities, roles, and social structures are toyed with and manipulated, often in chaotic ways. Here, children work to find their own links between their experiences as child and the social normative, or adult, forms of the world. This book is important for anyone who is interested in exploring the range and significance of creativity from a cross-cultural perspective.

Goodman, Mary Ellen. *The Culture of Childhood: Child's-Eye Views of Society and Culture*. New York: Teachers College Press, 1970.

Because this cross-cultural work illustrates the variety of childhood from many societies around the world, it clearly illustrates that there are few behavioral universals of childhood (i.e., many aspects of culture are malleable and context dependent). This work is interesting because it involves both children and adult perspectives—ripe ground for misinterpretation on either side. By showing the variety and diversity of meanings and practices surrounding childhood, this work demonstrates how few universals actually exist about childhood and being a child. The author illustrates that we have two culturally contingent assumptions that underlie our notions of childhood (particularly when it comes to pedagogy). First, we believe in the necessary links between chronological age and developmental stages. Second, we suffer from an "underestimation fallacy" of children, believing that they are sufficiently unable to deal with their own lives on their own terms. The author argues that this is why in the United States, children are perceived as senseless, confused, and irrational.

Goodnow, Jacqueline. "The Socialization of Cognition: What's Involved?" In *Cultural Psychology: Essays on Comparative Human Development*, edited by James Stigler, Richard Shweder, and Gilbert Herdt, 260–86. Cambridge, UK: Cambridge University Press, 1990.

This work is particularly insightful in how kids learn what's valued in a culture very early. Goodnow investigates how culture guides learning through the socialization of skills, strategies, and values in cognition. The author shows how kids learn how to evaluate the process of learning by asserting that a sense of audience, or who wants and values what, is of central importance—this is why cognitive performance can vary due to audience (or context).

Goodnow, Jacqueline, and A. Burns. *Home and School: Child's-Eye Views*. Sydney: Allyn and Unwin, 1985.

Through empirical, qualitative research on young children, the authors investigate children's perspectives about the domains of school and home. This work is particularly valuable in examining how artwork is interesting and engaging to preschool kids because art allows them to explore a variety of productions—where their interests and values are more readily accepted by adults.

Goodwin, Marjorie Harness. *He-Said-She-Said*. Bloomington: Indiana University Press, 1994.

This is a fascinating work that deals with early-grade-school black children and how their different face-to-face communicative interactions provide for their social organization and identities. Goodwin traces the intersection of identity and talk and how both mutually produce each other. By focusing on participant frameworks, the author shows how speech is a key resource for accomplishing social organization: by aligning participants to each other in certain ways and by depicting or characterizing participants in certain ways. This work argues against stereotypical gender roles and speech patterns by showing how black girls' talk is powerful and involves both cooperation and competition.

Goody, Jack. *The Domestication of the Savage Mind*. Cambridge, UK: Cambridge University Press, 1977.

As part of the "Great Divide" or "Grand Dichotomy" theory distinguishing between preliterate, oral, or traditional societies and literate or modern ones, the author asserts there are key universal processes that occur with and through the development of communicative technology via literacy. That is, literacy fosters certain modes of thought—cognition, objectivity, and abstractness—as well as particular social institutions (individualism and larger, more complex bureaucracies) that are distinctively modern.

Gottlieb, Alma. *The Afterlife Is Where We Come From: The Culture of Infancy in West Africa*. Chicago: University of Chicago Press, 2003.

This ethnographic account of the Beng of the Ivory Coast explores the centrality of cosmology with regards to child care, child development, and the notion of the infant. The author shows in great detail how religious worldview—particularly the cosmology linking the living and the dead, as well as important rituals and practices that work to keep the infant safe, healthy, and alive—is put into practice as infants are brought into important relationships with both alive and dead kin and affines.

———. *Under the Kapok Tree: Identity and Difference in Beng Thought*. Bloomington: Indiana University Press, 1992.

Working with the Beng of Africa, the author illustrates that, in many different aspects of life, identity wavers between the exclusivity and incorporation of difference. Difference and identity exist side by side, in many thematic, contradictory fashions as alternative models about how to organize society and how to think about that organization. This sticky combination of difference and identity and the many contradictions between them is central in understanding larger notions of how people think of themselves as members of distinct groups.

———. "Where Have All the Babies Gone? Toward an Anthropology of Infants (and Their Caretakers)." *Anthropological Quarterly* 73, no. 3 (2000): 121–32.

The author discusses many reasons that infants have been ignored or elided from anthropological research and the discussion of culture—due to the biases of adults, parents, and gender as well as for philosophical, scientific, political, and economic reasons. The author argues that we reconceive our notions of the infant as dependent by focusing specifically upon the independence and agency of infants, while simultaneously exploring how different cultures perceive infants to be dependent or independent in different ways for different reasons, in looking at an "anthropology of infants themselves" (127).

Graue, Elizabeth M. *Ready for What? Constructing Meaning of Readiness for Kindergarten*. Albany: State University of New York Press, 1993.

This work examines how the social construction of readiness is central in understanding the process and curricula of early childhood education programs. The author deals with three demographically different school communities in the same school district and how they differ in their construction of readiness along the axes of class, race, and ethnicity.

Graue, Elizabeth M., and Daniel L. Walsh, eds. *Studying Children in Context: Theories, Methods and Ethics*. Thousand Oaks, Calif.: Sage, 1998.

This edited volume is a key work due to the involvement of many important and well-known childhood researchers. Besides an important introductory discussion on the history and theories of childhood research, the different chapters also have useful suggestions for methods as well as ways to check the validity of research. This compilation is also very easy to read: the chapters are well organized and well written, and all have fascinating anecdotes; the narratives by the many authors discuss important issues, concerns, and questions relevant to the field of childhood studies.

Gregory, Eve, Susi Long, and Dinah Volk, eds. *Many Pathways to Literacy: Young Children Learning with Siblings, Grandparents, Peers and Communities*. New York: Routledge Falmer, Taylor & Francis Group, 2004.

By exploring a host of different communities like African and Asian Americans, Latinos as well as Native Americans, this collection explores how the significant social relationships among family, peers and many others in outside-school spaces are significant contexts for learning language and literacy for young children. This investigation shows how children become literate in a variety of ways that are not often recognized, valued, and utilized by schools—because they aren't like the prescribed curricula of schools.

Hansen, Judith Friedman. *Socio-Cultural Perspectives on Human Learning: An Introduction to Educational Anthropology*. Englewood Cliffs, N.J.: Prentice Hall, 1979.

This work examines the centrality of education and learning in the processes of enculturation and cultural transmission. Hansen discusses "transmission theory" in depth, asserting that the organization of transmission expresses key cultural values that are largely implicit within that structure. The author illustrates that knowledge is very diverse even within a culture. Hansen further argues that cultures are themselves multicultural owing to the different knowledge, values, practices, and ideas that exist within and among people of "a culture."

Harkness, Sara, and Philip Kilbride. "Introduction: The Socialization of Affect." *Ethos* 11, no. 4 (1983): 215–20.

This work discusses the contemporary position of psychological anthropology in switching its emphasis from personality to intellectual functioning and cognition. Here, a central goal is to find links between the universal, biological aspects of affect/emotion as products of human evolution and the experiential, phenomenological, relativistic factors of particular cultural contexts. The authors argue that key methodological and philosophical concerns are, how to make correct judgments about the meaning of emotional expression in various cultural contexts, how to uncover the links between the socialization of affect, and the more general patterns of child rearing. As a further note, this whole issue of *Ethos* is devoted to the socialization of affect.

Harkness, Sara, and Charles Super. "The Cultural Construction of Child Development: A Framework for the Socialization of Affect." *Ethos* 11, no. 4 (1980): 221–32.

Through cross-cultural investigation of child development, the authors show the importance of understanding context—particularly, the setting, as well as the expectations and behaviors of children—in exploring the cultural construction of child development or how children acquire culture.

Hart, C. W. M. "Contrasts between Prepubertal and Postpubertal Education." In *Education and Cultural Process: Anthropological Approaches*, edited by George Spindler, 362–82. Prospect Heights, Ill.: Waveland, 1997.

Originally published in 1955, this work finds commonality regarding the structures and processes of pre- and postpubertal education in "primitive societies" around the world. The author shows that prepubertal education tends toward being highly variable, taught in or near the home with intimates, where everyday knowledge is utilized—this is where children learn their personality. Postpubertal education, on the other hand, is much more standardized—taking place in a novel context/environment (which often is sacred and can be rife with traumatic experiences), learned among strangers, and focused on adult knowledge. Here, one learns aspects of citizenship, society, and history.

Hatch, J. Amos, ed. *Qualitative Research in Early Childhood Settings*. Westport, Conn.: Praeger, 1995.

This is an excellent reader for synthetic discussion of qualitative research with very young children. Because of the wide variety of contributors, this work has an immense number of sources to assist scholars at any level doing qualitative research with very young children. The many authors cover a range of topics, including child socialization, peer culture, child care, preschool, and kindergarten. This work also illustrates the importance of poststructuralism in teaching, learning, and researching in CCS, for some chapters deal with the cultural politics and pedagogy of early childhood education (as well as teaching early childhood education to others) and explore the significance of the global politics of early childhood education as well as childcare.

Hatch, J. Amos, and E. Freeman. "Who's Pushing Whom? Stress and Kindergarten." *Phi Delta Kappan* 70 (1988): 145–48.

The authors illustrate how the concerns with academic standards, and the resulting change in curricula toward standards, conflict with the wishes and philosophies of child-centered teachers.

Heath, Shirley Brice. *Ways with Words*. Cambridge, UK: Cambridge University Press, 1983.

This is a germinal work that illustrates in detail the diversity of meanings and practices among class and race, homes and schools. Heath shows how black and white working-class communities and white, middle-class communities have different oral and written communicative practices (ways of speaking as well as literacy events) that have different social, interactional, pragmatic and educative uses. The gamut of these meanings and practices have substantial impact on language socialization, cultural meanings, and behavior—that is, they substantially impact children's identities and ability to succeed in schooling (because the school culture is much closer to white and middle-class meanings and practices).

———. "Linguistics and Education." *Annual Review of Anthropology* 13 (1984): 251–74.

In this very synthetic review of linguistics, discourse, communication, and interaction in schools, the author explicates how research and public policy (beginning in the 1960s and peaking in the 1970s focused on language use and language acquisition/socialization) affected schools. She shows how school testing and performance was structured by research in middle-class homes with a focus on the middle-class mother–child interaction, which ultimately favored middle-class, white, mainstream families while depriving others. She goes on to illustrate how this process was essential to the larger cultural politics of "cultural deficiency," "culture of poverty," and "disadvantaged children" that blamed kids' failures in school on their home environment.

Hedegaard, Mariane. *Learning and Child Development: A Cultural-Historical Study.* Aarhus, Denmark: Aarhus University Press, 2002.

Through her close participation and observation of fourth- and fifth-graders in Danish schools and society, the author explores the changing notions of child development, practices, and meaning systems. The author works to move beyond a Vygotskyian approach by intersecting psychology with anthropology through focusing specifically upon the children's perspectives as participants in their interactions and learnings with adults. In this way, she focuses on the symbolic aspect of knowledge, distinguishing between different forms of knowledge (social, empirical, narrative, and theoretical), in order to explicate how all work to scaffold a child's development and cognition.

Henry, Jules. "Attitude Organization in Elementary School Classrooms." In *Education and Culture*, edited by George Spindler, 192–214. New York: Holt, Rinehart and Winston, 1963.

The author explicates the key values that underline the main practices as well as attitudes that are taught in early schooling in the United States. He also shows that these values mirror and help reproduce the larger national culture, which is centered around the culture of the middle class.

Herskovitz, Melville. *Man and His Works.* New York: Knopf, 1956.

This early, functionalist account makes key distinctions between education and socialization. Education subsumes the appropriation of the individual for institutional, adult socialization—notions of role, status, and the division of labor. Meanwhile, socialization is focused more on the notion of moral and ethical codes that regard the specific cultural values implicated in gender, kinship, power et al.

Heywood, Colin. *A History of Childhood: Children and Childhood in the West from Medieval to Modern Times.* Malden, Mass.: Polity, 2001.

This work is a postmodern response to Aires (1962) and other child historians that attempt to construct "grand narratives" surrounding the notion of childhood through time. By focusing on the interaction of children with adults, society, and key institutions, the author illustrates that central themes and antimonies surrounding childhood (like notions of depravity/innocence, nature/nuture, independence/dependence, and age, sex, and gender) continually appear in different eras as well as among different social and political groups (like, classes, religions, and philosophies). The author asserts that it is the way in which these themes are developed, legitimized, and used for child care and socialization that should mark different historical eras as well as different social groups.

Hicks, Deborah, ed. *Discourse, Learning and Schooling*. New York: Cambridge University Press, 1996.

The contributions to this work focus on how language and cognitive development are interwoven. Through a range of methods—like face-to-face interactions, curricular or schooling discourses, and larger community–social discourses—this work illustrates how discourse (or patterns of communication and action) mediates learning in social context. An important theme in this work is how the "unruliness" or multiplicity and diversity of discourses in school operate to organize social experiences and activities that become important contexts for thinking and learning in certain ways.

Hollan, Douglas. "Constructivist Models of Mind, Contemporary Psychoanalysis, and the Development of Culture Theory." *American Anthropologist* 102, no. 3 (2000): 538–50.

Through person-centered ethnography, the author argues that since culture is fluid and complex, investigations into culture must also regard the same complexity/fluidity regarding psychology (even with highly conventional models of action).

Holland, Kathleen, David Bloome, and Judith Solsken, eds. *Alternative Perspectives in Assessing Children's Language and Literacy*. Norwood, N.J.: Ablex, 1994.

An important work in understanding that assessment of children's work with language and literacy, in any fashion, inherently relies upon context because the variety of meanings and practices are contingent upon context. Through anthropological, sociolinguistic and psycholinguistic research, the contributors illustrate a need to perceive and engage assessment from many, alternative perspectives.

Holmes, Robyn. *How Young Children Perceive Race*. Thousand Oaks, Calif.: Sage, 1995.

This work is useful regarding the cultural politics of race and ethnicity regarding identity because the author clearly explicates the whole diversity of ways that very young children identify themselves and others as raced/ethnic due to their skin color.

Hoyle, Susan M., and Carolyn Temple Adger, eds. *Kids Talk: Strategic Language Use in Later Childhood*. New York: Oxford University Press, 1998.

This collection of thirteen chapters divided into arenas of communication—friends, school, and work—explores how older (seven- to eighteen-year-old) children's talk implicates and interacts with their continual development. The contributions are largely focused upon U.S. children, with one author drawing upon African children.

Ingold, Tim. *The Perception of the Environment: Essays on Livelihood, Dwelling and Skill.* New York: Routledge, 2000.

This text reexamines the relationship of cultural entities like knowledge, education, and learning to people's lives and actions, the world around them, and the way people perceive the world. The author argues that we need a more relational model in investigating how ideas and actions are embedded in everyday life and relationships and how these things simultaneously form and are formed by our perceptions. To illustrate this point the author draws upon a host of interesting scientific fields (like biology, ecology, history, physics, and even chaos theory) and shows how they necessarily intersect and interrelate (e.g., how biology, ecology, and history intersect with plant and animal domestication).

Jacobs, Evelyn. "Context and Cognition: Implications for Educational Innovators and Anthropologists." *Anthropology and Education Quarterly* 28, no. 1 (March 1997): 3–21.

This is an important work when it comes to understanding a more developed notion of context in education. The author shows that context is "obdurate and malleable, emergent and stable" by explicating the substantial domains of context located in a variety of social spaces (e.g., institutions), social interactions and practices (e.g., apprenticeships or face-to-face interactions), as well as in social meanings, values, and goals. Jacobs argues for a more valid and valued notion of context and its intersection with learning by exploring the dialectical relationship between activity and context—because activity is socially constructed by motive.

Jahoda, Gustav, and I. M. Lewis, eds. *Acquiring Culture: Cross-Cultural Studies in Child Development.* London: Crom Helm, 1988.

A central theme in this collection is a critique of Western models of socialization and development. The many contributions illustrate the need to understand the process of cognitive growth by looking at local cultural understandings of personality, self, and development through each group's "indigenous psychology." That is, to understand human development, researchers need to locate and explore what meanings are culturally exigent and how they are dealt with—in particular, sex role differentiation, the tensions between individuality and interdependence, notions of status and rank, and kinship. This work also has an annotated bibliography regarding ethnographies of childhood of the time.

James, Allison. *Childhood Identities: Self and Social Relationships in the Experience of the Child.* Edinburgh: Edinburgh University Press, 1993.

This work illustrates how, in early primary school, kids learn how to classify themselves and others as either "belonging" or as "outsiders" based on bodily appearance and performance (particularly, via stereotypes). James also investigates how kids balance the tension between conformity, individuality, equality, and competition from the ages of three to nine as they are developing their own identities.

James, Allison, and Alan Prout, eds. *Constructing and Reconstructing Childhood: Contemporary Issues in the Sociological Study of Childhood.* London: Falmer, 1990.

The contributions to this work interrogate the ideologies that surround childhood and they explore two important themes. First, that ideologies regarding family, home, and domesticity position children in ways that simultaneously elide adult power while also working to position children as passive bodies and minds. Second, they explore the domain of national and international ideologies to illustrate that the notion of childhood is used by privileged, empowered countries to legitimize the political and economic depravity of poorer countries.

Jipson, Janice, and Richard T. Johnson, eds. *Resistance and Representation: Rethinking Childhood Education.* New York: Lang, 2000.

This edited volume, which draws from a host of research done in the United States, Pacific Islands, Canada, and Australia, works to rethink contemporary theories of resistance in early childhood education by looking at the intersection of children, curriculum, teachers, and the larger society. The authors do this through ethnographic work that substantially draws on indigenous perspectives as well as their own (known as autoethnography). Many of these works take a critical look at the theoretical assumptions and outcomes of a child-centered, progressive, early childhood education in non-Western contexts.

Jones, Liz, and Tony Brown. "Reading the Nursery Classroom: A Foucauldian Perspective." *Qualitative Studies in Education* 11, no. 6 (2001): 713–25.

In a Foucauldian analysis of discourse, practice, and power, the authors show how children in a nursery classroom use particular "regimes of power" (or those larger social fields of power relationships) in order to produce, maintain, and manipulate power relations that foster particular subject positions beyond the normal practices that are central in early school settings. This work is also useful for two other reasons: its discussion of Foucault's notions of discursive power is relatively easy to understand; and it is packed full of sources about primary schooling in this vein.

Jones, Margaret, and Chris Cunningham, "The Expanding World of Middle Childhood." In *Embodied Geographies: Spaces, Bodies and Rites of Passage*, edited by Elizabeth Teather, 27–42. New York: Routledge, 1999.

The authors explore how different genders use a diversity of urban spaces differently for play. This work shows the importance of exploring how different contexts are linked to different notions and uses of the body in constructing the range of different subjectivities within gender identities.

Jones, Toni Griego, and Mary Lou Fuller. *Teaching Hispanic Children.* Boston: Allyn and Bacon, 2003.

Through their work with Hispanic populations as well as with teachers in U.S. schools, these authors argue that to change the popular, stereotypical belief that Hispanic children degrade the quality of classrooms and schools, teachers need to more fully understand Hispanic children, families, and communities as well as their own perceptions of them. The authors assert that a key aspect to this process is self-reflection by teachers in order for them to change their perceptions and curricula. For this purpose, this work focuses on teacher's perceptions and practices and provides an in-depth investigation about the diverse range of Hispanic cultural practices and meanings in the United States.

Kantor, Rebecca. "Creating School Meaning in Preschool Curriculum." *Theory into Practice* 27 (1988): 22–35.

Through ethnographic and discourse analysis, the author shows how the rules of preschool and its central meanings move from more fluid and negotiable ones to more restricted and established ones over the course of the year. In particular, meanings move toward the teachers' and schooling goals for interaction. This work is good because it shows how both teachers and students work to "move on" to more complex interactional issues regarding the structure and rules of circle time where there is less opportunity for development of social meanings and more development toward the institutional meanings and goals that are organized around work. As a further note, the whole volume of this issue is dedicated to qualitative methods surrounding becoming a student in early schooling.

Kimball, Solon. "Cultural Influences Shaping the Role of the Child." In *Education and Culture*, edited by George Spindler, 268–83. New York: Holt, Rinehart and Winston, 1963.

In this early work, the author asserts that we should be concerned with the conditions that affect the larger process of education and cultural transmission. This is because culture and environment frame the early production of discrimination and categorizations that then become foundations for later learning. Solon argues that early childhood is when individuals learn to be culturally acquisitive in developing discriminatory categories through the processes of affect and ethos. The author illustrates that in the United States the central cultural role of children is the preparation for the status of adulthood. This is because adults see that children cannot simply grow up on their own; instead they must be directed in significant ways. Solon argues that we value the "forced abandonment of childhood," focusing on the earlier and earlier maturation of children, which is motivated by our cultural commitment to change, flexibility, and adaptability.

———. *Culture and the Educative Process: An Anthropological Perspective.* New York: Teachers College Press, 1974.

The author traces the historical cultural politics of U.S. schools and uncovers that the central American cultural values that operate in schooling are middle-class ones like competition, violence, the need for certain types of accomplishments in the world, individualism, atomism, belief that change and progress are inevitable, and perpetual optimism. Solon also illustrates how culture is fundamental in education and, therefore, argues that U.S. schools need change to be more continuous with home and community experiences.

———. "The Transmission of Culture." *Educational Horizons* 43 (1965): 161–86.

Kimball argues that the processes of affect and ethos foster discriminatory categories that frame how children learn to be culturally acquisitive.

King, Nancy. "Play: The Kindergartener's Perspective." *The Elementary School Journal* 80 (1979): 81–87.

The author shows that a focus on child perspectives can be very enlightening in looking at how kindergarteners distinguish between play and work. Here, the author illustrates that pleasure is not a salient feature defining and distinguishing between work and play; instead the conception of choice and voluntary or involuntary participation frames this distinction (where play is chosen and work is required). More important, kindergarteners also recognize that teachers value work over play; they also know how play transforms into work when it is impinged upon by teachers.

Kleifgen, JoAnne. "Prekindergarten Children's Second Discourse Learning." *Discourse Process* 13 (1990): 225–42.

This is a fascinating piece because the author shows that learning the important schooling discourses, practices and their meanings has more to do with age and maturity than native language ability. That is, non-English-speaking children that were three to four years old were just as proficient at learning the important, interactive structures of schooling as native English speakers.

Lanclos, Donna M. *At Play in Belfast: Children's Folklore and Identities in Northern Ireland*. New Brunswick, N.J.: Rutgers University Press, 2003.

In tracing the intersection between folklore, play, and the production of identities, the author shows how children's play is distinct from the adult world and a place for liberation as well as resistance. One of the novel and contradictory aspects of this work is the way in which the author investigates how people understand and use religious symbols and ideas to make key distinctions about identities—particulary the difference between Protestants and Catholics as well as those between children and adults.

Lancy, David F. "Becoming a Blacksmith in Gbarngasuakwelle." *Anthropology and Education Quarterly* 11, no. 4 (1980): 266–74.

Focusing on the apprenticeship of blacksmiths in West Africa, the author uncovers the failure of simple typologies that contrast formal schooling and informal schooling. The author shows that the formal/informal learning dichotomy cannot be equated with institutional/noninstitutional learning. He does this by illustrating that there are three key social roles that are involved in becoming a blacksmith—each involves different practices, meanings, and motives. And these three roles, all of which must be learned to be a blacksmith, are learned in a diversity of formal and informal ways.

———. *Studying Children and Schools: Qualitative Research Traditions*. Prospect Heights, Ill: Waveland, 2001.

This work is particularly useful for its in-depth discussion of the gamut of historical and methodological practices of qualitative research worthwhile for researching children. From an anthropological perspective, this piece is particularly useful in explicating the need for increased research reliability and validity through multiple, cross-cultural perspectives.

Lareau, Annette. *Home Advantages*. London: Falmer, 1989.

This is a key work that illustrates the advantages that children from white, middle-class families have over other children in school. White, middle-class children are at an advantage in their ability to perform at school owing to the wealth of privileges (economic and cultural) their home life gives them. This work illustrates how these children are privileged in school due to the concordance that public schools have with white, middle-class family structure, values, meanings and practices.

Lave, Jean. "Mathematics Learning in Japanese, Chinese, and American Classrooms." In *Cultural Psychology: Essays on Comparative Human Development*, edited by James Stigler, Richard Shweder, and Gilbert Herdt, 321–56. Cambridge, UK: Cambridge University Press, 1990.

By looking at the process of learning math in three different cultural contexts, the author asserts that there are two different theories of learning that are foundations for educatory practices and meanings across cultures. First, there is the culture of acquisition, where practices of teaching and transmission are primary over learning and internalizing culture. This model dominates in Western schools that are focused on context-free, logical, top–down models of learning, where the accumulation of facts requires teaching. Second, there is learning in practice, situated in pedagogy-like apprenticeships, where notions of learning and understanding are culturally contingent—that is, what is learned is pragmatically attached to the forms of knowledge and practice from where it is gleaned.

Lave, Jean, and Etienne Wenger. *Situated Learning: Legitimate Peripheral Participation*. Cambridge, UK: Cambridge University Press, 1991.

Although not specifically about children, this work is important because it discusses learning as a social practice. Lave and Wenger illustrate that learning is structured by the participation of the subject and the practices they engage in. The authors also de-center the notion of learning by showing that it takes place among a variety of sources and in ways in which the subject becomes involved slowly and peripherally, from neophyte/apprentice to expert with skills.

Lazerson, Marvin. "Urban Reform and the Schools: Kindergartens in Massachusetts, 1870–1915." *History of Education Quarterly* 11 (1971): 115–38.

The author discusses the many dimensions of change in kindergartens at the turn of the twentieth century. Lazerson illustrates that the rise of public concern with the urban poor fostered a need for more control of institutions like schools. Here, kindergartens moved from a philosophy and curriculum that was child-centered to one that was centered on the goals of society. In this way, kindergartens became much more formalized by focusing largely on academic preparation while they simultaneously became public institutions.

Leavitt, Robin. *Power and Emotion in Infant-Toddler Day Care: A Guide to Responsive Caregiving*. Albany: State University of New York Press, 1994.

This is a very harsh critique of what some children go through in early child care environments that are organized by custodial, curricular routines where play is not a central ideal and practice. The author shows that this process fosters emotional disengagement of caregivers and fragments the relations between teacher and children. This is because caregivers replace children's perspectives, interests, and interpretations of the environment with their own. Leavitt asserts "responsive caregiving" must understand and value the daily experiences and perspectives of the children; the relationships between family, the teacher, and the school; and also the caregiver's ideals and perspectives.

Lebra, Takie Sugiyama, "Acculturation Dilemma: The Function of Japanese Moral Values for Americanization." *Council on Anthropology and Education Newsletter* 3, no. 1 (1972): 6–13.

Lebra argues for an alternative model of acculturation—integrating linear and nonlinear models—by showing both the similarities and contradictions between Japanese and American meanings. The author illustrates how Japanese values of social accommodation fit with historical ideals of Americanization; however, once this occurs American norms don't further facilitate Japanese values of interdependence.

LeCompte, Margaret. "The Civilizing of Children: How Young Children Learn to Become Students." *The Journal of Thought* 15 (1980): 105–27.

The author shows how kindergarten involves a "hidden curriculum" of values and activities that relate to the larger value system of the U.S. economy. In particular, the author shows how cognitive activities and actions that are focused on task orientation and task completion scaffold economic values of submitting to authority and managing impulse control—important dispositions for children who will eventually be adult workers.

Levinson, Bradley, Doug Foley, and Dorothy Holland. "The Cultural Production of the Educated Person: An Introduction," In *The Cultural Production of the Educated Person: Critical Ethnographies of Schooling and Local Practice*, edited by Bradley Levinson, Doug Foley, and Dorothy Holland, 1–34. Albany: State University of New York Press, 1996.

As the introduction to this edited text, the authors illustrate that the host of meanings and practices that are produced in the school, peer group, home, community, and society at large are the milieu that will frame a child's acceptance, resistance, or rejection to school. The authors assert that we need to understand in more detail the tension among individual agency and local culture within the larger discursive and ideological fields of power that are present in social structures, institutions, and history.

Lewis, Amanda, and Tyrone A. Foreman. "Contestation or Collaboration? A Comparative Study of Home-School Relations." *Anthropology and Education Quarterly* 33, no. 1 (2002): 60–89.

The authors trace the range of shared and contested spaces and practices by looking at the home–school relationship and the nature of parental involvement in an upper-middle-class and a working-class public school. The authors show that the school–parent relationship is inherently influenced by class. This is because the upper-middle-class school viewed themselves as primarily professionals that saw parents as clients or consumers of their school and its knowledge. This fostered substantial problems in creating a cooperative relationship between school, staff, and parents because the school, as the patron of knowledge, wanted to limit parental participation to their concerns and goals; therefore, they resisted parental involvement they could not control. Meanwhile, the working-class school that needed the assistance of parents for fiduciary reasons perceived parents as partners instead of clients or consumers; therefore, it had no closed doors and conflict was something to be negotiated through accommodation and cooperation.

Lewis, Catherine. *Educating Hearts and Minds: Reflections on Japanese Preschool and Elementary Education.* New York: Cambridge University Press, 1995.

Lewis investigates the central values and practices that are at work in Japanese preschool and kindergarten classrooms. This work shows how schooling produces notions of ethics and morality, with a particular focus on becoming a responsible member of your society and class. This work is particularly useful in its comparisons to U.S. schools because it shows how certain practices valued in the United States—like free time, play, language use, and language socialization—are utilized in Japan as well but produce their own distinctive meanings, practices, and discourses.

Lewis, Cynthia. *Literary Practices as Social Acts: Power, Status, and Cultural Norms in the Classroom.* Mahwah, N.J.: Erlbaum, 2001.

By exploring four different literacy practices in fifth-grade classrooms in the United States, Lewis shows that the range of meanings given to literacies is, above all, a social act and, therefore, is implicated in processes of power along the social axes of gender, race, and class.

Lubek, Sally. *Sandbox Society: Early Education in Black and White America.* London: Falmer, 1985.

The author compares race and class within the institutions of U.S. preschools as well as the U.S. Head Start program. In Head Start, black children are surrounded by an environment that is culturally continuous with their home and community experiences where the needs of the group, or collectivity and expression, are emphasized. Meanwhile, white, middle-class preschoolers live in a different environment where the individualistic perspective is stressed through their work with multiple, changing tools and spaces. Lubek argues that Head Start doesn't adequately prepare black children for public school because of the discontinuity of values and practices they face when they enter it.

Luke, Allan. "Text and Discourse in Education: An Introduction to Critical Discourse Analysis." *Review of Research in Education* 21 (1995): 3–48.

Luke discusses the importance of investigating the language socialization of very young children, with a particular focus on interrogating how categories of difference are constructed. He clearly illustrates that it is the construction and adoption of these categories that begin to structure children's minds in culturally significant ways that filter in and out meaningful ideas and knowledge that lead to success (or failure) in learning.

Mead, Margaret. *Coming of Age in Samoa: A Psychological Study of Primitive Youth for Western Civilisation*. New York: Morrow, 1928.

This is a germinal anthropological work dealing with enculturation or how the child grows into the cultured adult (with a focus on adolescence). The author shows that enculturation occurs in everyday responsibilities that are graded by age and gender. Mead shows how culture creates personality: an argument that debunked biological, universal theories regarding sexuality, promiscuity, and their relationship to adolescence.

———. *Growing Up in New Guinea.* New York: Morrow, 1930.

The author traces the development of New Guinea children from preschool age to preadolescence. She shows the informal ways that young children learn the different forms of culture that are appropriate for the different age groups. Mead illustrates that there is substantial cultural discontinuity throughout this process; however, social notions and actions revolving around the themes of shame, punishment, and competition are very important.

———. "Socialization and Enculturation." *Current Anthropology* 4, no. 2 (April 1963): 184–88.

This piece traces the history of ideas surrounding the socialization and enculturation of the larger, national character of people through practices like child rearing and training.

Mead, Margaret, and Martha Wolfenstein. *Childhood in Contemporary Cultures.* Chicago: Chicago University Press, 1955.

This is a collection of more than twenty articles from many geographic contexts that discusses the diversity and range of formal and informal education around the world. The strength of this collection lies in its rich data collection involving a host of qualitative methods—many of which focus on child-centered data.

Mehan, Hugh. *Learning Lessons*. Cambridge: Harvard University Press, 1979.

This is a germinal work that illustrates through discourse analysis how classroom lessons as "sequentially and hierarchically organized events" structure the interaction and learning of students (172). The author shows in detail how competence regarding classroom meaning and practice is the integration of academic knowledge with interactional and conversational skills that guides the students.

Michalachik, Vera. "The Display of Cultural Knowledge in Cultural Transmission: Models of Participation from the Pacific Island of Kosrae." In *Education and Cultural Process: Anthropological Approaches*, edited by George Spindler, 393–426. Prospect Heights, Ill.: Waveland, 1997.

This is an excellent work that shows the fluidity and diversity of contexts, process and meanings involved in cultural transmission. The author focuses on "knowledge displays" to locate how culture is transmitted along three main axes: context, official knowledge, and the consequences of that knowledge. The author examines knowledge displays in three distinct contexts—church, school, and home. And, through investigating the consequences of knowledge, the author comes to two significant conclusions: first, that the contexts of church and home, which are just as important as school as contexts for learning about the world, are substantially different from the U.S. schools; second, that schools more commonly stratify children through the "official knowledge" of standards (not concordant with much of home and church) into groups with differential access to power and privilege. Here, schools are not a panacea where all children are given opportunities. In this way, official knowledge is hegemonic by setting the standards for evaluation in other contexts—particularly, the U.S. and international economy.

Miller, Darla. "Infant/Toddler Day Care in High, Middle and Low Socio-economic Settings: An Ethnography of Dialectical Enculturation and Linguistic Code." Unpublished doctoral diss., University of Houston, 1986.

The author examines how race and class is produced in three different infant-toddler schools by exploring the different linguistic codes that vary among them. The school with black children works toward a school-oriented routine of attention and obedience through a curriculum that is teacher-centered. Working-class white children are socialized to play-oriented activities and goals through cooperation and a child-centered curriculum. However, both working-class white and black children learn a restricted code that is contingent on their specific classroom context, which produces a hierarchy where kids have less control. Meanwhile, the world of the upper-middle-class school relies upon a literal and elaborated code (particularly, through the process of children "using their words") that teaches children how to be independent and view the world as an egalitarian one.

Mody, Susan Laird. *Cultural Identity in Kindergarten: A Study of Asian Indian Children in New Jersey*. New York: Routledge, Taylor & Francis Group, 2005.

By studying Asian Indian children in U.S. preschools, this book explores the identity formation that occurs during the acculturation from the more interdependent nature of Asian Indian family life to the individualist white, middle-class public context of schools. The author investigates how this occurs through a range of children's activities (including play, talk, and narratives). In regards to ethnicity and class, this work is interesting because although Asian Indian children's identities and interactions are concordant with teacher–school goals in important ways, these children and their families are still perceived by white, middle-class identified teachers as separate. That is, teachers perceive them as a "model minority" that is distinctly (and some times represented pejoratively) different from white Americans. This process is part and parcel of the larger social and economic divisions and distinctions that exist among Asian Indian identities and white American identities in the United States.

Moll, Luis C., Cathy Amanti, Deborah Neff, and Norma Gonzalez. "Funds of Knowledge for Teaching: Using a Qualitative Approach to Connect Homes and Classrooms." *Theory into Practice* 31, no. 2 (1992): 132–41.

In this work, these authors worked with teachers as coresearchers in a multi-dimensional research process involving ethnographic analysis of house dynamics,

classroom practices, and after-school study groups in investigating the relationship between Mexican American families' cultures and the culture of the teachers and schools. This piece discusses "how to develop innovations in teaching that
draw upon the knowledge and skills found in local households."

Morton, Helen. *Becoming Tongan: An Ethnography of Childhood*. Honolulu: University of Hawaii Press, 1996.

This ethnopsychological work focuses on how knowledge is acquired in the
context of emotional dispositions encountered in everyday lives. In particular,
desire, joy, and anger are central to the process of learning how to be clever and
learning how to manipulate rules (as well as other people) for one's own advantage. The author shows that this process is implicated even with babies, since
adults perceive them to be clever or foolish in their actions and treat them ac-
cordingly—fostering relative joy or frustration. This work also discusses other
important sites of learning (like language socialization) as well as the centrality of
education in culture change.

Nespor, Jan. *Tangled Up in School: Politics, Space, Bodies, and Signs in the Education
Process*. Mahwah, N.J.: Erlbaum, 1997.

This is an excellent work that shows how children's bodies, as their primary
tool for mediating the world, are replaced with other cultural tools like language,
literacy, and other forms of communication through the process of schooling.
The author's long-term research focuses on fourth- and fifth-graders from a
working-class neighborhood and investigates how the many different parties
(teachers, parents, administrators) and spaces (school as well as off-campus) interact to help shape bodies "as children" as well as by gender, race, and class. The
author investigates how the many different spaces inside and outside of schools
are involved in the production of student bodies.

Ochs, Elinor. "Indexicality and Socialization." In *Cultural Psychology: Essays on Comparative Human Development*, edited by James Stigler, Richard Shweder, and
Gilbert Herdt, 296–320. Cambridge, UK: Cambridge University Press, 1990.

This work examines the key relationships among discourse, indexicality, and
sociocultural knowledge. Indexicality in discourse and practice is the action of
indexing or pragmatically "pointing to" the presence of certain sociocultural
meanings, phenomena, or context. Ochs asserts that the indexicality of affect is
central in how children acquire culturally relevant and legitimate categories of
what people can or cannot know and what domains and types of knowledge are
valued most.

Ochs, Elinor, and Bambi Schieffelin. *Acquiring Conversational Competence*. Boston:
Routledge and Kegan Paul, 1983.

From infants, to toddlers, to preschoolers, these authors investigate how very
young children are competent speakers that are pragmatically oriented to the
world and control communication for their own motives. The authors use a variety of discourse analysis techniques (speech act theory, pragmatics, ethnography of communication, etc.) focused upon child–child as well as child–adult

interactions to illustrate the complexity of children's communicative competence. This is another work that gives substance to the critique of linear developmental psychology and psycholinguistic models as well as the Piagetian egocentric theory of communication.

———. "Language Acquisition and Socialization: Three Developmental Stories and Their Implications." In *Culture Theory: Essays in Mind, Self and Emotion*, edited by Richard A. Shweder and Robert LeVine, 276–320. Cambridge, UK: Cambridge University Press, 1984.

By looking at the specific connections between language acquisition, socialization, and development in three different cultures, the authors critique Western theories of language and child development that rely on specific Western ideals—particularly, notions of individuality. They do this by illustrating that not all cultures adapt the world toward the child. This is an important work because it regards a coherent challenge toward many theories of child development (particularly, Piagetian).

Ong, Walter. *Orality and Literacy: The Technologizing of the World*. New York: Routledge, 1982.

This work can be considered a touchstone of the "Great Divide" theory that distinguishes between literate and preliterate societies. The author focuses on describing the differences in the "mentality" or consciousness due to the material aspects of sound and orality versus those of text and writing. He argues that the two models are incommensurable, and once the shift from sound to space occurs, written text takes over oral history in concept and practice.

Pang, Ooka, and Lilly Cheng. *Struggling to Be Heard: The Unmet Needs of Asian Pacific American Children*. Albany: State University of New York Press, 1998.

This is a critical look at both the experiences of Asian Pacific Americans in the United States and the sticky, limiting cultural politics they have to negotiate. The book focuses upon the concerns that Asian Pacific Americans have as a neglected model minority and the pressures they negotiate in the United States as they are not fully able to assimilate as "Americans."

Panter-Brick, Catherine, and Malcolm T. Smith, eds. *Abandoned Children*. Cambridge, UK: Cambridge University Press, 2000.

The contributions to this work challenge the dominant notions of "abandoned children" posing that this notion conceals more than it reveals by stigmatizing and dehumanizing children. The authors give detailed descriptions and discussions of how children in many different countries are and have become abandoned due to political and economic factors and forces (e.g., war, poverty, orphanhood). In this way, this collection works to challenge the notion of childhood itself, by illustrating how we produce it through discourse with economic, social, and political ramifications and power implications.

Perry, Jane P. *Outdoor Play: Teaching Strategies with Young Children*. New York: Teachers College Press, 2001.

By researching the play that occurs in extra-classroom spaces with four- and five-year-old children, the author investigates kid's culture, particularly through the range of mediation strategies that peers use with each other as well as with teachers (here the author also discusses teacher's cultures). This piece is particularly useful regarding in-depth qualitative methods for working on the playground. This is an excellent book about the intricacies and value of kids play: through rigorous analysis and interpretation, the author makes a strong case in favor of more play for kids in school, giving good suggestions for policy as well.

Peshkin, Alan. "Kanuri Schoolchildren: Education and Social Mobilization in Nigeria." In *Case Studies in Education and Culture*, edited by George Spindler and Louise Spindler, 82–110. Chicago: Holt, Rinehart and Winston, 1972.

The author uses historical data and ethnographic research with Nigerian children to show the development of a "generation gap" between school children and their kin when Kanuri children enter European, institutionalized schools. The author not only shows the process of identity change—particularly, gender roles as well as economic and occupational interests—but also how the rural values of Nigerian traditional life are transformed toward more modern ones.

Philips, Susan. "Participant Structures and Communicative Competence: Warm Springs Children in Community and Classroom." In *Functions of Language in the Classroom*, edited by Courtney Cazden, Vera John, and Dell Hymes, 370–94. New York: Teachers College Press, 1972.

This is one of the earliest sociolinguistic explanations of the difference in "participant structures" that operate between Native American children and schools that fosters kids' failure. This is because Native American kids' cultural traditions of communication and conceptions of context do not fit the school's unfamiliar and threatening social frameworks for participation. That is, the difference between home and school "participant structures" produce different communicative competencies that work against Native American children's success.

Pollard, Andrew. *The Social World of the Primary School*. London: Holt, Rinehart and Winston, 1985.

The author examines the everyday actions, rituals, and perspectives of both teachers and students in a British Primary school. He focuses this work on how teacher–student relationships are formed in the context of notions of teaching and learning and poses that individual personalities, identities, and motives do substantial work in creating the classroom context and environment.

Pollard, Andrew, and Anne Filer. *The Social World of Children's Learning: Case Studies of Children from Four to Seven*. London: Cassel, 1996.

The authors concentrate this work on five children's narratives engaging their own perspectives and notions about their schooling, development, social identities, and social relationships as they grow from four to seven years old in a public school. The authors use these data, amplified with narratives of teachers and parents as well, to illustrate the symbolic and social construction of school success as part of the network of social relationships in which all actors in school are embedded.

Pollock, Linda. *Forgotten Children: Parent–Child Relations 1500–1900*. Cambridge, UK: Cambridge University Press, 1983.

Drawing on the "sentiments approach" that attempts to understand what parents thought of children, this work responds to Ariès (1962) and argues that a concept of childhood existed before the seventeenth century. The author shows that Europeans were clearly aware of differences and developmental stages of children that distinguished them from adults. Pollock also asserts that different notions of childhood existed in the past but since these concepts have little in common with the modern, Western notion of childhood, scholars have missed or ignored them.

Postman, Neil. *The Disappearance of Childhood.* New York: Delacorte, 1981.

The author focuses on how the history of mass-literacy (the printing press, television, movies, and music) has reconstructed the social notion of childhood. Today, childhood is no longer as temporary a state where one learns to critically "read the world" but is, instead, disappearing because children are prematurely pushed into adulthood.

Reed-Danahay, Deborah. *Education and Identity in Rural France: The Politics of Schooling.* New York: Cambridge University Press, 1996.

This ethnographic work explores how rural families in France have particular strategies of education that both resist and accommodate to national ideologies. The author shows how local, rural identity—linked more to kin, gender, age, and class—has coexisted alongside the national identity and influenced the processes of schooling, politics, economy, as well as childhood socialization.

Reifel, Stuart. "Children's Thinking about Their Early Education Experiences." *Theory into Practice* 27, no. 1 (1988): 62–66.

The author examines kindergartener's experiences about the order and structure of kindergarten by looking at scripts that inform their actions and meanings. The author shows that even children who are not as successful in adapting to the novel context of kindergarten still understand the scripts that kindergarten operates around.

Reimer, Becky. "When the Playground Enters the Classroom." In *Children on Playgrounds: Research Perspectives and Applications,* edited by Craig Hart, 316–43. Albany: State University of New York Press, 1993.

This work illustrates how the cognitive and symbolic ordering process of gender and friendship that structure children's chase games are transformed into classroom reading and writing activities.

Reisman, Paul. *First Find Your Child a Good Mother: The Construction of Self in Two African Communities.* New Brunswick, N.J.: Rutgers University Press, 1992.

By comparing child development in Africa to that in the United States, the author argues for a more general theory of personality formation: one that regards "the relations between self, personality, and society for all situations." Reisman illustrates the importance of exploring and understanding the overall social system of relations and relationships in forming individuals' identities and personalities. In this way, the author also illustrates that the person himself or herself is "a process of meaning making" where the sense of "connectedness" to others, particularly close relatives, is crucial to understand how children develop personality and identity more synthetically.

Renold, Emma. "'Coming out': Gender, (Hetero)sexuality and the Primary School." *Gender and Education* 12, no. 3 (2000): 309–26.

The author shows how masculinity and femininity for young adolescents is ultimately embedded in presupposed, compulsory heterosexuality that students must position themselves within or be labeled an outsider (i.e., homosexual). The author also illustrates that performances that are highly sexualized are actually more about producing and maintaining gender boundaries than about actual sexual practices per se.

Riddell, Sheila. "Pupils, Resistance and Gender Codes: A Study of Classroom Encounters." *Gender and Education* 1, no. 2 (1989): 83–97.

This is a fascinating piece that illustrates that in the process of their resistance to and subversion of stereotypical gender norms, through the manipulation of traditional gender codes, students don't substantially challenge or subvert these codes. Instead, this process works to reproduce and reinforce the status quo.

Riley, Karen. *Schools behind Barbed Wire: The Untold Story of Wartime Internment and the Children of Arrested Enemy Aliens.* Lanham, Md.: Rowman & Littlefield, 2002.

Through archival and oral histories, this work explores how the children of German, Japanese, and Latin American descent in the United States were treated and educated in the Crystal City Family Internment Camp of southwest Texas during World War II. This work is "cross-cultural" in tone because the U.S. government, in complicity with some of the prisoners involved, worked to set up three different schools to accord to these different types of people, their educatory needs, their language and learning styles, as well as their ideological and political interests. The author also focuses upon the cultural politics of the time in how governmental motives positioned people as "outside" the frame of being American (which then led to their imprisonment). The author also shows how these schools worked in particular ways to subvert the process of becoming culturally German and Japanese to further the U.S. goals of "Americanization."

Ritchie, Jane, and James Ritchie. *Growing Up in Polynesia.* Boston: George Allen & Unwin, 1979.

This is a very excellent, detailed, ethnographic piece that describes how Polynesian kids develop from infants to adolescents. This work is important because it illustrates clear, yet different, cultural boundaries that exist between infant, child, adolescent and adult—which is clearly marked by rites of passage. This work also shows how notions of kinship operate beyond the social domain of family (blood or affine)—that is, meanings and practices of kinship are a very important context that affect development and learning with everyone in society. In chapter 6 on the development of Polynesian children, the authors argue for an ecological approach for understanding development through the socialization of attention. The authors show how this process takes place in adult–infant interactions, where caregivers limit the context of lexical development. In ways like this, the authors pose that the education of attention occurs through the promotion of noticing affordances (or bits of animate and inanimate ecological environment that can give the creature advantages/disadvantages). The attention to affordances frames perceptual differences that are a foundation for later learning in distinctive ways.

Rogoff, Barbara. *The Cultural Nature of Human Development.* Oxford: Oxford University Press, 2003.

The author draws upon years of work by developmental psychologists and anthropologists to show that the nature of cognitive development is both biological and cultural. Rogoff illustrates both the human commonalities of development—the universal and local aspects of social and cultural development—as well as the uniqueness of the individual in the process of their own cultural development. The author rethinks the notion of learning as accumulating ideas and abilities and instead shows that learning occurs through the everyday social interactions among people where many are involved in the "guided participation" of each other. In guided participation, people "share" the action and learning at whatever level they are adept in that particular moment/context.

Ryan, William. *Blaming the Victim.* New York: Vintage Books, 1976.

This book uncovers the many insidious ways that white, racist ideology operates in the United States to blame nonwhite people for the many structural inequities they suffer. Chapter 2, "Savage Discovery in Schools: The Folklore of Cultural Deprivation," deals with the racial inequities of schools in their practices and values that are then legitimized with the discourses of culture of poverty and cultural deprivation.

Sacks, Harvey. "On the Analyzability of Stories by Children." In *Directions in Sociolinguistics: The Ethnography of Communication,* edited by John J. Gumperz and Dell Hymes, 325–45. Chicago: Holt, Rinehart and Winston, 1972.

Through ethnomethodological analysis of children's stories, the author shows the cultural assumptions and norms that frame children's worlds. Sacks shows that even very young children (kids approaching three years of age) can tell "stories" that not only rely on culturally appropriate categories but also follow the "structure" and rules of stories at large. This work is useful for discursive and communicative methods by showing some key links between discourse and knowledge/development.

Sadker, Myra, and David Sadker. *Failing at Fairness: How America's Schools Cheat Girls.* New York: Scribner, 1994.

This work illustrates the host of contemporary as well as historical ways that girls are disadvantaged in U.S. schools. The authors show that one of the main aspects of this problem is the ubiquitous and very persistent sexist attitudes and actions that undermine girls' self-confidence and abilities. Even teachers that believe in equity and fairness and think they are being fair to girls are shown still discriminating against females in numerous ways.

Sano, Mariko Fujita, and Toshiyuki Sano. *Life in Riverfront: A Midwestern Town Seen through Japanese Eyes.* Philadelphia: Harcourt, Brace College, 2001.

Chapter 8 of this in-depth ethnography of U.S. culture from the point of view of two Japanese scholars deals with their participatory observation in both a preschool and a senior center. The authors compare both sites in the United States to their experiences in Japan, with a focus on the prevalence and use of talk. In this chapter, the authors show how cultural values of group identification, cooperation, and equality are produced alongside the seemingly contradictory ones of voluntary choice and self-reliance. The authors argue that becoming an adult is produced against the notion of "babies." For this reason, "growing up" is understood as becoming independent through the ownership and control of things that should be shared.

Saracho, Olivia, and Bernard Spodek, eds. *Multiple Perspectives on Play in Early Childhood Education.* Albany: State University of New York Press, 1998.

This lengthy collection deals with the host of theories and their applications that link play to learning and development. The contributions discuss the intersection between play and learning at many different domains—for example, different types of play (social and nonsocial); children's conception and use of symbolic meanings; child narratives; and the intricate intersection between play, literacy, and assessment. A central theoretical concern in this collection is the expansion of theories and notions of play beyond structurally informed theories of play and development (particularly, Piaget). Anyone who investigates play in their research with young children will find something of use in this work.

Saville-Troike, Muriel, and JoAnne A. Kleifgen. "Scripts for School: Cross-Cultural Communication in the Elementary Classroom." *Text* 6 (1986): 207–21.

The authors show the cultural discontinuity between U.S. schools and many different international families and their children. In general, U.S. schools are less rigid when it comes to authority, control, and rules; the child-oriented curriculum of many schools can be very disorienting for parents and children as well as foster roadblocks for cross-cultural communication.

Scheper-Hughes, Nancy, and Carolyn Sargent, eds. *Small Wars: The Cultural Politics of Childhood.* Berkeley: University of California Press, 1998.

The collections in this work all regard the diversity of cultural practices around the world where children's bodies and lives are "fought over." In this vein, the contributors deal with comparing cultural notions surrounding the unborn fetus (e.g., in vitro fertilization, abortion, surrogacy, and maternal health care) as well as infants and children who are subjected to violent circumstances like physical, sexual, and drug abuse as well as war, poverty, and hunger. Because these works consistently deal with the themes of control and violence, this text is useful in exploring key ethical ideas and battles surrounding children where culture and politics collide.

Schieffelin, Bambi. *The Give and Take of Everyday Life: Language Socialization of Kaluli Children.* New York: Cambridge University Press, 1990.

Based on her ethnographic work in New Guinea, the author illustrates how the socialization of language is a central part of the larger socialization of the child toward cultural norms and relationships. Schieffelin illustrates in detail how particular kinship and gender terms, as well as how they are learned and used in practice, structure the culturally specific social relationships among different kin and the genders.

Scribner, Sylvia, and Michael Cole. *The Psychology of Literacy*. Cambridge: Harvard University Press, 1981.

This is a germinal work that deflated the "great divide" theorists' claims that literacy autonomously and universally causes an increase in intellectual ability. By comparing schooled literacy to a nonschooled literacy in numerous cultures, the authors show that certain cognitive tasks—assumed to be products of literacy—are more the result of schooling as a set of practices in context. This book is a vital precursor for cultural psychology that shows the vital links between culture and cognition.

Shore, Bradd. *Culture in Mind: Cognition, Culture and the Problem of Meaning*. New York: Oxford University Press, 1996.

Shore takes a dialectical approach in order to integrate and explicate the relationship between the individual mind and the larger group processes of thought (or institutional culture) at the level of meaning making. The author shows through some interesting examples that every cultural meaning and model has two distinct moments of birth: one public and conventional and the other a subjective appropriation and integration of the conventional form by a particular person.

Sindell, Peter. "Some Discontinuities in the Education of Mistassini Cree Children." In *Education and Cultural Process: Anthropological Approaches*, edited by George Spindler, 383–92. Prospect Heights, Ill.: Waveland, 1997.

There is great cultural discontinuity between Cree children's family, home, and community lives and the mainstream school that is organized around white, middle-class values and practices that they attend. The Cree children find it more and more difficult to participate in their parents' lives as they attend these schools. This is because they learn to be dependent, competitive, and openly aggressive—dispositions that are not central in Cree life.

Skinner, Debra, Donna Bryant, Jennifer Coffman, and Frances Campbell. "Creating Risk and Promise: Children's and Teachers' Co-Constructions in the Cultural World of Kindergarten." *The Elementary School Journal* 98, no. 4 (March 1998): 297–310.

The authors illustrate the order of discourse surrounding notions of student "risk" and "promise" by following the transition of twenty-one former Head Start children into kindergarten in U.S. public schools. This work illustrates that children actively work with teachers in producing the notions and practices that are central in the process of school failure or success. This work also clearly shows how the discourse-practices that position students on the path of being successful or a failure is an often nefarious process that exists even in very early schooling. For this reason, they locate many ways that children position themselves as being at "promise" and give suggestions for teachers, and others, in how to foster success with students that get placed on the path to failure.

Soto, Lourdes Diaz, ed. *The Politics of Early Childhood Education*. New York: Lang, 2000.

This collection works to challenge the fundamental beliefs surrounding childhood and development, particularly in how they relate to social policy. These works explore the many different contemporary and historical sites—like media, Head Start, family/community, child research and public policy—where dominant meanings and representations of knowledge foster the inequitable status quo and the cultural supremacy of the privileged.

Spindler, George. "The Transmission of Culture." In *Education and Cultural Process: Anthropological Approaches*, edited by George Spindler, 375–79. Prospect Heights, Ill.: Waveland, 1997.

The author illustrates that education across cultures is patterned in at least three important ways to foster cultural transmission: first, cultural continuity or a smooth progression in learning one's culture; second, cultural discontinuity, where life is radically altered in order to transmit key aspects of culture (usually accompanied by ritual); third, there is cultural compression, where many cultural meanings and responsibilities are compressed into a short period of time, usually through new rules to change and limit behavior (often accompanied by high drama and ritual). The author also discusses the problems regarding the wide discontinuity that exists between non-Western cultures and "modern" Western forms of education and schooling.

Steinberg, Shirley, and Joe Kincheloe, eds. *Kinderculture: The Corporate Construction of Childhood*. Boulder, Colo.: Westview, 1997.

The works in this collection revolve around a postmodern, cultural studies approach to the construction of childhood that focuses on the impact of media—not as a one-sided or linear force but as a salient part of the symbolic environment—as a central aspect of children's pedagogy. These works illustrate and critique the power and impact that corporations have in shaping and defining children's experience by focusing on an ideology of consumption—where redemption, security, and joy are acquired through consumption. This collection is both enlightening and fun to read because it deals with culture industry icons like Disney, popular toys and television shows, as well as commercials.

Steinfels, Margaret O'Brien. *Who's Minding the Children? The History and Politics of Child Care in America*. New York: The Free Press, 1986.

The author shows that child care and early education stemmed from two distinct forms: care as part of child and public welfare due to urbanization (which was later transformed into programs like Head Start); and the production of kindergartens and nursery schools by largely the middle-upper classes for their own privileges and needs.

Stephens, Sharon, ed. *Children and the Politics of Culture*. Princeton: Princeton University Press, 1995.

A central theme in this collection is how children are co-opted by the state for international, political, and economic interests (viz., capitalism) due to the many changing social relationships of globalization.

Stigler, James, Richard Shweder, and Gilbert Herdt, eds. *Cultural Psychology: Essays on Comparative Human Development*. Cambridge, UK: Cambridge University Press, 1990.

This edited volume frames the goals and boundaries of Cultural Psychology. The many contributions in this book examine how culture frames cognition through social interaction, social practice, language development, and schooling as well as through the acquisition and socialization of cultural values and norms. These chapters work together to conclude that there are two fundamental, often mutual, processes of cognitive development underlying acquisition of culture: first, messages about cultural values and norms are directly or implicitly coded or referenced in everyday life and through everyday routines; second, social knowledges and skills linked to identities can account for and scaffold cultural acquisition of norms and values while also subverting them.

Strauss, Claudia, and Naomi Quinn. *A Cognitive Theory of Cultural Meaning*. New York: Cambridge University Press, 1997.

The authors locate meaning making within both the intrapersonal and the internal by focusing on the notions of motivation, durability (both historical and individual), thematicity, and sharedness in meanings as well as schemas. Strauss and Quinn marry the intrapersonal being and actions with internal, psychological processes (like schemas, understandings, motivations) and link these to the extrapersonal worlds of social behavior and environment. They illustrate that cultural meanings arise in people by becoming both shared and internalized in social interactions, and those meanings, which are thematic and connected to many other aspects of culture, are fundamental in child socialization.

Suárez-Orozco, Carola, and Marcelo M. Suárez-Orozco. *Children of Immigration*. Cambridge: Harvard University Press, 2001.

Through their work with immigrant families in the United States, the authors give an impressive account of the range of significant social contexts and experiences that immigrants, as well as members of the dominant society, negotiate and live with in this cultural borderland. Although the authors show how gender roles and family relationships (viz., the parent–child relationship) are commonly transformed in this process, the authors simultaneously illustrate how immigrant children and families also resist other aspects of U.S. society, culture, and schools. This bolsters their claim that immigrants do not necessarily have to surrender their culture and identities in order to become American. This point is supported by the fact that school children craft "transcultural identities" by retaining key aspects of their parents' culture while adopting some aspects of the dominant society. In such ways, these immigrants do better than both those that actively resist acculturation as well as those that discard their heritage in adopting the U.S. culture.

Super, Charles, and Sara Harkness, eds. *Anthropological Perspectives on Child Development*. San Francisco: Jossey Bass, 1980.

In illustrating the importance of understanding and interpreting cultural meanings and practices in context, the authors show that the Western theories that dominate child development are teleological because they are oriented toward a specific end point of becoming adult (59–60). This work illustrates the need for cross-cultural perspectives and theories informed by cross-cultural research, particularly in the field of psychology, if we want to construct worthwhile theories of child development and socialization. A central theme throughout these collections is the importance of context in development—the authors illustrate that there is little intrinsic to the experience itself that is meaningful; you cannot isolate or remove behavior from context because it deprives it of its contingent meaning. This collection shows that much of the contemporary scientific theories of developmental psychology are problematic not only because they are based on monocultural studies but also because they have emerged from a white, American sociocultural context, or what the authors call the "folk psychology" of the American middle class.

Suransky, Valerie Polokow. *The Erosion of Childhood.* Chicago: University of Chicago Press, 1982.

A harsh critique of preschools that are run for profit and where bureaucratic rationality dominates to the point that children do not get the care and love that they require. The author does a good job advancing her main argument that U.S. preschools are pushing the development of children too fast, what she labels as the "hurried child." The author shows that adults see kids as incompetent, meaningless participants, if not victims, who don't contribute anything worthwhile to our society.

Swadener, Beth Blue, with Margaret Kabiru and Anne Njenga. *Does the Village Still Raise the Child? A Collaborative Study of Changing Child-Rearing and Early Education in Kenya.* Albany: State University of New York Press, 2000.

Using a host of methods interrogating local knowledge, as well as national and public policy, the authors trace important political, economic, and social changes over the past twenty years in Kenya that have influenced local community practices of child rearing. The authors work against the ideological discourses and practices of colonialism, dependency, and "othering" that are widespread in contexts like these by showing how people in their everyday lives deal with the explosion of meanings in the postcolonial world.

Tamivarra, J., and D. S. Enright. "On Eliciting Information: Dialogues with Child Informants." *Anthropology and Education Quarterly* 17, no. 2 (June 1986): 218–38.

This is an excellent article for methodological suggestions and ideas for interview techniques with child informants, in the United States at least. This is particularly useful for either beginner researchers or anybody who is beginning to work with young children.

Tanz, Christine. "Introduction: Gender Differences in the Langauge of Children." In *Language, Gender, and Sex in Comparative Perspective*, edited by Susan Philips, Susan Steele, and Christine Tanz, 162–77. New York: Cambridge University Press, 1987.

Through studying communicative competence and discourse analysis (particularly, speech acts), the author shows that as children develop communicative competence they organize and structure language around cultural meanings and behaviors in terms of larger social norms, practices, and discourse—not simply just according to language and linguistic factors. The author shows the diversity of language use that is linked to behavioral differences associated with gender, and asserts it is very hard to pose generalities about this process.

Taylor, Denny. "The (Con)Textual Worlds of Childhood: An Interpretive Approach to Alternative Dimensions of Experience." In *Home and School: Early Language and Reading*, edited by Bryant Fillion, Carolyn N. Hedley, and Emily C. Di Martino, 93–107. Norwood, N.J.: Ablex, 1987.

The author discusses the importance of working to interpret the experiences and the worlds that children live in as contexts for understanding their actions and meanings. Taylor illustrates that children's interpretive frameworks often regard very minute details that occur in or around the context of the home—for this reason, we need to understand in detail the meanings children have about their home environments as significant contexts for school learning.

Thorne, Barrie. *Gender Play: Girls and Boys in School*. New Brunswick, N.J.: Rutgers University Press, 1993.

This is a fascinating work that shows in depth how young children craft gender identities. Thorne examines the variation within and between gender groups focusing on the importance of children's collective, interactive, and innovative play. In this way, the author illustrates that gender identities are produced through collective interactions of "borderwork" and "crossing" that draw on significant meanings and actions, which then strengthen boundaries between and within the genders. The author shows that we shouldn't take gender for granted: gender needs to be examined much more closely, since it is just as much about differences between groups as about the differences within them.

Tobin, Joseph. *"Good Guys Don't Wear Hats": Children's Talk about the Media*. New York: Teachers College Press, 2000.

This work focuses on how to understand children's talk in terms of their consumption and perceptions of media texts. This work is useful for both understanding methods that deal with children's talk as well as in investigating the host of theoretical traditions that link contextually contingent children's talk—as well as their contextual, local meanings—to the more general effects and implications of media in children's lives. Through detailed method and interpretation, this work is useful because it shows a worthwhile attempt in explicating the links between specific data or event and general theory or effect.

Tobin, Joseph, D. Y. H. Wu, and D. H. Davidson. *Preschool in Three Cultures: Japan, China, and the United States*. New Haven, Conn.: Yale University Press, 1989.

By focusing on the shift in all these societies from kin- or family-based child rearing to institutionalized group care, the authors show how the rise in preschools and pedagogy in each society fits with their larger social, ideological and cultural interests. Among all three types of early childhood education, the authors trace important themes and tensions throughout the pedagogy of very young children that are important for all nations involved (notions like dependence–independence; academics vs. creativity; language dominance; family and parental involvement; gender roles; and the place of preschool in making a social, political, and economic body). This is an excellent work for its discussion of the intersection among history, policy, and pedagogy that is founded in detailed, qualitative work, allowing for an excellent in-depth comparison among the three cultures.

Toren, Christina. "Do Babies Have Culture?" *Anthropological Quarterly* 77, no. 1 (2004): 167–79.

At the end of this lengthy, in-depth, review of Alma Gottlieb's book *The Afterlife Is Where We Come From: The Culture of Infancy in West Africa*, the author critiques the all-encompassing, self-evident notion of culture represented in works like this. The author asserts that we must be much more reflective about the conception and, more important, the production of culture as an academic construct so it is not simply the misleading qualitative/social counterpart to more positivistic models of biology or psychology. Toren poses that to do this, we must reflect on how we ourselves produce culture in essentializing, taken-for-granted ways through the processes of researching, investigating, understanding, and representing others; therefore, for worthwhile ethnography we must also regard "ethnographic analysis of its ontogeny."

Tsai, Min-Ling, and Georgia Earnest Garcia. "Who's the Boss? How Communicative Competence Is Defined in a Multilingual Preschool Classroom." *Anthropology and Education Quarterly* 31, no. 2 (2000): 230–52.

This article discusses the importance of investigating multiple sites as well as using multiple methods in understanding the complexity of children's worlds when it comes to effective communication according to school and adult standards.

Tyack, David, and Larry Cuban. *Tinkering toward Utopia: A Century of Public School Reform.* Cambridge: Harvard University Press, 1995.

The authors examine the history of public school reforms in the United States from the turn of the nineteenth century into the 1990s by focusing on particular key reform events during this time (e.g., the progressive school movement in the 1920s–1930s, the 1950s reform toward school equity, the right-wing reform toward accountability in the 1980s and 1990s). This work examines how reform in each era influenced the total range of public schooling from kindergarten to high school. Tyack and Cuban show that although reform is a complex, chaotic process, most U.S. school reforms share certain aspects and themes: policy talk, policy action, and actual implementation. Here, most of the reform takes place in the discursive space of policy talk where little rhetoric gets transformed into action, and when it is implemented it is usually additive instead of transformative.

Valdés, Guadalupe. Con Respeto: *Bridging the Distance between Culturally Diverse Families and Schools, An Ethnographic Portrait.* New York: Teachers College Press, 1996.

This is a rich account of the difference in context between Mexican American families and communities and U.S. public schools. The author traces the diversity of many important cultural meanings surrounding family, children, school, success, and learning that vary substantially between Mexican Americans and the schools they attend. Valdés shows that the differences between these two contexts are substantial sources for miscommunication among teachers, students, and families. It is the difference between these contexts that must be considered seriously when working on policy to "fix the problem" of immigrant families.

Viruru, Radhika. *Early Childhood Education: Postcolonial Perspectives from India.* New Delhi: Sage, 2001.

Through work with a preschool in an Indian city, the author critiques dominant Western discourses surrounding childhood and early childhood education. This work is a useful text for a discussion of methods in researching children since the author deals with her own research problems, questions, and concerns in this process.

Volk, Dinah. "Questions in Lessons: Activity Settings in the Homes and School of Two Puerto Rican Kindergartners." *Anthropology and Education Quarterly* 28, no. 1 (1997): 22–49.

Ethnographic research focused on two Puerto Rican kindergarteners, their schooling as well as their home settings, this work explicates the continuities and discontinuities between the contexts of kindergarten and home. The key discontinuities the author uncovers between school and home are as follows: teachers assume children are unprepared for school (which affects the way they treat the children); teacher's roles and their power relationships to parents and children is complex and confusing for both parties; and Puerto Rican parents don't understand and value the use of play in school.

Vygotsky, Lev. *Mind in Society: The Development of Higher Psychological Processes.* Cambridge: Harvard University Press, 1978.

A germinal piece that begins to integrate developmental psychology within the context of cultural systems and history. Like the title says, Vygotsky begins the groundwork for locating important theories of mind and society with the actual links among both.

Wax, Murray, and Rosalie Wax. "Great Tradition, Little Tradition, and Formal Education." In *Anthropological Perspectives on Education*, edited by Murray Wax, Stanley Diamond, and Fred O. Gearing, 3–18. New York: Basic Books, 1971.

In their long-term work with the Ogala Sioux, the authors show how Sioux children are schooled toward the middle-class cultural values of the United Sates. The authors use this work to make a larger argument about the power and politics of U.S. assimilationist schooling where there is substantial cultural and educational conflict between the "great tradition" of the middle class and the "little tradition" of folk communities. Here, one of the worst aspects of schooling is that children from "little traditions" are perceived and treated as deficient, ignorant, and uncivilized.

Wertsch, James. *Mind as Action*. New York: Oxford University Press, 1998.

  The author states that the goal of sociocultural analysis is to find a way to "live in the middle," at the irreducible tension between agent and the mediational means (25). Both mind and action are located in and at "mediational means" through the use of "cultural tools" (physical as well as mental). Here, the individual is inseparable from both social action and thought that is contingent on culture and history (and therefore is also part and parcel of the processes of culture and history). This work is full of many enlightening examples that illustrate this argument—that physical and mental tools are inseparable in the ways that humans mediate the world in a variety of diverse and similar ways.

Whiting, Beatrice, ed. *Six Cultures: Studies of Child Rearing*. New York: Wiley, 1963.

  This work both amplifies and challenges earlier, cross-cultural works regarding child rearing by explicating the substantial diversity and variability in notions of child development, child care, and parenting techniques around the world. The authors ask similar questions in six different cultural contexts to get at the "subsystem replication" of social maintenance systems like economy, polity, and other social institutions. In challenging earlier, generalist theories, this work asserts that distinctive child-rearing practices that lead to child personality form around psychological notions—like dependence, nurturance, and egoistic dominance—that are learned in different contexts where behaviors are "normal" or common. This collection shows that it is these contexts that impact development and not some universal psychology.

Whiting, John. *Becoming a Kwoma: Teaching and Learning in a New Guinea Tribe*. New Haven, Conn.: Yale University Press, 1941.

  Working with New Guinea indigenous forms of education, the author recognizes the notion of becoming-as-learning as a significant cross-cultural theory of learning that is not recognized within Western "teaching models." The author illustrates the intersection of learning and becoming a person (or growing up) by focusing on the basic, cross-cultural conditions of habit formation as a socializing agent.

Whiting, John, and Irvin L. Child. *Child Training and Personality: A Cross-Cultural Study*. New York: Yale University Press, 1953.

  This impressive effort in comparative studies looked across cultures to locate psychological and developmental generalities about how personality is molded by its members as part of a causal chain from child rearing to adult personality. In this top–down and linear model of socialization, the authors attempt to relate how child training practices like child fixation, weaning, toilet training, and other adult-imposed practices regarding independence and isolation produce adult personality. The authors focus on how cultural customs and habits function as socialization mechanisms that maintain social systems (like economy, polity, and institutions) but also impact child training as well as personality (focusing on notions of affect like aggression, fear, fixation, guilt). Both of these aspects work in conjunction to produce the "projective systems" that are important for specific cultures (particularly, religion, magic, and art).

Willett, Jerri. "Becoming First Graders in an L2: An Ethnograhpic Study of L2 Socialization." *TESOL Quarterly* 29, no. 3 (1995): 473–503.

The author shows how a first-grade classroom is constructed as a highly gendered space by all the parties involved. The author examines the micropolitics of gender identities by examining a host of interactional routines like adult–child work, peer group work, and individual work. Through the intersection of these routines, the class was split into highly gendered groups where boys produced identities through competition in the total, public classroom space while the girls produced identities through collaboration that fostered more exclusive, smaller groups.

Williams, Thomas Rhys. *A Borneo Childhood: Enculturation in Dusun Society.* New York: Holt, Reinhart and Winston, 1967.

This is another early anthropological work that explores enculturation from a child's perspective and point of view. The author traces enculturation to traditional Dusun culture as well as enculturation to newly acquired aspects of Dusun society through interaction with Westerners.

Wolcott, Harry. "The Anthropology of Learning." In *Education and Cultural Process: Anthropological Approaches*, edited by George Spindler, 310–38. Prospect Heights, Ill.: Waveland, 1997.

Originally published in 1982, the author calls for an anthropology of learning by focusing on the critical role of "attention" in the process of cultural transmission.

———. *A Kwakiutil Village and School.* Prospect Heights, Ill.: Waveland, 1967.

The author investigates the fallout of mutual oppositions that arise when two different education systems intersect—the informal, indigenous one of the Kwakiutil, and the formal, Western institutional one. Interestingly enough, the children are the ones that are disinterested in schooling; meanwhile their parents ideologically realize that schooling is one of the only avenues for opportunity.

Wollons, Roberta, ed. *Kindergartens and Cultures: The Global Diffusion of an Idea.* New Haven, Conn.: Yale University Press, 2000.

This book traces the expansion of the ideas and practices of kindergarten around the globe in time and space. A central theme in this book is how the philosophies, theories, and practices surrounding kindergarten both shaped cultural changes around the world while also being consistently reshaped in different cultural contexts to suit the needs of local communities; national ideological, economic, and political needs; as well as international needs. This work is fascinating because it shows the power of kindergarten as an intellectual, academic, and philosophical phenomenon that has spread around the globe, yet this phenomenon was consistently in motion, under constant transformation and reformation to meet different local and national interests and motives.

Young, Iris. *Throwing Like a Girl and Other Essays in Feminist Philosophy and Social Theory*. Bloomington: Indiana University Press, 1990.

Through a phenomenological investigation of her own development of a feminine comportment, the author discusses what it is that keeps her female body (and the female body in general) feminine. She focuses on the inhibited intentionality and "discontinuous unity" that frames female bodies due to their contradictory position in U.S. society as well as their ubiquitous objectification.

4

ART

Sara Harrington

Perhaps the most famous and most oft-represented child in the history of Western art is the infant Christ. Pictured most frequently with his mother, the Virgin Mary, the innumerable Madonna and Child artworks spanning the Christian period mark an important transition in visual representations of childhood. Most medieval and Byzantine images of the infant Christ show him as a small-scale adult. This infant Christ possesses a perfectly proportioned, seemingly adult body represented in miniature, and exhibits mature gestures and stoic facial expressions. During the Renaissance, artists made an imaginative leap, which, perhaps ironically, resulted in their portraying the infant Christ more realistically. Artists began to represent the infant Christ as the child that he was, complete with a head proportionally larger than his body, rolls of baby fat, and wispy tufts of hair. This infant Christ was often shown in an affectionate embrace and tender exchange with his mother, the Virgin Mary.

This transition in the representation of the infant Christ, so visible in painting, testified to a larger shift in the cultural understanding of childhood itself. Childhood came to be understood as a special phase in the life cycle—children were not simply considered miniature adults. Rather, childhood was to be studied, delineated, and even celebrated. Philippe Ariès's landmark work, translated into English as *Centuries of Childhood: A Social History of Family Life*, traces the iconography of the family (including images of children) between the fourteenth and seventeenth centuries as seen through representations of the trades, the months of the year, family portraits, and other subjects.[1] Ariès wrote that such iconography was largely nonexistent in the Middle Ages, originating in the fifteenth and sixteenth centuries, and culminating in the seventeenth century. Ariès concluded that this "iconography enables us to follow the rise of a new concept of the family. The concept is new but not the family."[2] Recent scholars have complicated Ariès's work and his conclusions, reclaiming the importance of childhood in earlier periods, including the Middle Ages, from myriad scholarly perspectives.[3]

The study of the paradigm of childhood has been a neglected subject in traditional art historical research, although the theme has garnered some scholarly attention in the field.[4] Art historical research draws on a variety of methodologies, including visual analysis, a close study of the artist's biography, an examination of the social history of the period in which an image was created, and the application of theoretical constructs to an image. While some scholars have adopted a survey approach to the study of representations of children in art—in other words, examining images of children across different chronological and stylistic periods in art history—others have focused closely on the images of children within a particular art historical stylistic period.

Art historical research has its own specific challenges. Art historians must consider both textual and visual sources of information. It is the centrality of the image that defines art history, but it is the balance between visual and textual research that marks the most nuanced scholarly efforts. While art history has harnessed technological advances to further disciplinary work, many research materials nonetheless remain in print format only. While the citations for sources are increasingly accessed via electronic catalogs and electronic indexes, these citations may refer to a print original unavailable in electronic format. Therefore, the art historian must move fluidly between electronic and print sources and develop research expertise in both formats. While some disciplines value recent scholarship more highly than earlier work, art history places an equal value on both the most recent scholarship and retrospective materials. Indeed, the competent researcher must possess a working knowledge of cutting-edge scholarship and retrospective materials, as well as the bibliographic chain that links the two. This highlights yet another important aspect of art historical research: the significance of primary source material, or documentation emerging from the period under study. Current art historical research is marked by its interdisciplinary nature. Art historians, in studying, learning, and writing about an image, make use of a wide body of scholarship, drawn not only from the field of art history, but from history, anthropology, sociology, psychology, literary criticism, women's studies, and many other disciplines.

A SAMPLE SEARCH

There are many types of searches for art historical information. Three broad types of searches include a search for information about an artist (e.g., Berthe Morisot), about a specific work of art (e.g., information about Morisot's painting *The Cradle* of 1872), and information about a particular subject or theme in art (e.g., artists' representations of children). This chapter explores the last of these three types of research, pursuing a sample search for information about representations of children and childhood in nineteenth-century French painting. This search locates sources that examine the history of childhood as a cultural concept in the fine arts during the nineteenth century in France, as seen through the imagery of the period. In some ways, this type of research is among the most challenging in the discipline of art history because it is deductive by nature. The researcher must move from the subject or theme he or she is examining, to the identities of the artists who were engaged with this theme or subject, to the art works of the period that depicted the theme or subject.

This chapter uses a sample search about representations of children in nineteenth-century French art in order to develop a summary checklist of resources in the discipline of art history that might be useful to Children and Childhood Studies (CCS) researchers. This chapter assumes that while the CCS student and scholar is an expert in his or her own field, he or she may have little familiarity with the field of art history, and this chapter therefore is geared toward the novice art historical researcher. I adopt a dual approach, discussing both the bibliographic tools and research sources of utility to CCS scholars in the field of art history. I examine useful reference works, catalogs, indexes, books, periodical articles, Web resources, and other materials. I then discuss some strategies for drafting art historical research. The chapter concludes with an alphabetical, annotated bibliography of useful sources for CCS throughout the history of art.

REFERENCE WORKS

It is often useful to begin the research process with the consultation of reference works. In the case of art history, reference sources serve multiple purposes, including outlining an artist's biography and *oeuvre* (or body of work), discussing the meaning and significance of a canonical work of art, describing different art practices and techniques, tracing the use of particular themes in the history of art, and providing background information on many other subjects within the field. Since CCS is a relatively new focus within art history, traditional art history reference sources do not devote attention to the theme. It is therefore necessary to begin consulting reference sources not under the heading of "children" or "childhood," but rather under the heading of the country and/or time period the researcher is examining, in the case of this sample search, the art of France during the nineteenth century.

The Dictionary of Art (commonly known in the field simply as *Grove*, after the publisher) is a foundational source in the field of art history.[5] *The Dictionary of Art* includes comprehensive articles on a multitude of subjects, including the art of the nations of the world. For the sample search I consulted the article entitled "France." Since this entry is a very lengthy article of over 150 pages, I examined the article's table of contents in order to determine which sections of the article cover the time period and media of interest, namely, painting in the nineteenth century. Looking through the table of contents, I can see that it will be helpful to consult chapter 3, entitled "Painting and the Graphic Arts," section 5, "c. 1814–c. 1914."[6]

The sections of *The Dictionary of Art* article on France that I consulted do not directly address representations of childhood during the nineteenth century. However, at this early stage of research, the kind of information I am looking for includes the art historical issues that marked the time period, the major artists working in the period, and their thematic preoccupations. Two parts of *The Dictionary of Art* article proved particularly useful: "Part 4: Realism and Modern Life" and "Part 5: Development and Influence of Impressionism." During mid– to late–nineteenth century, French Realist and Impressionist artists decisively turned away from mythological and historical subjects to focus on scenes of everyday life, sometimes known as *genre* scenes. I can surmise that some of these scenes might have included family life and images of children. The prominent Realist and Impressionist artists working during the period included Gustave Courbet, Jean-François Millet, Edouard Manet, Auguste Renoir, Claude Monet, and others. I can return to these stylistic periods and specific artists later as I continue to look for information, just as I can consult the bibliography at the end of each section of *The Dictionary of Art* article: all three provide potential avenues for further research.

The *Guide to the Literature of Art History* and the *Guide to the Literature of Art History 2* serve as important reference sources in the field.[7] (The second *Guide*, published twenty-five years after the first, is an expansion and update of the original.) Both volumes are particularly helpful for the sample search because they are organized by country and media. The sections on French painting include an annotated bibliography of authoritative monographs on nineteenth-century French art in both French and English.

It is also important to determine if any of the reference works in the field of CCS examine art images in any depth. While many of these reference works include historical rather than art historical information, there is one prominent exception. *The Encyclopedia of Children and Childhood: In History and Society* includes an extensive and well-illustrated article entitled "Images of Childhood." This article traces representations of children from the fifteenth century through the present day. The article includes a long section on nineteenth-century imagery, with a focus on French painting and a full account of the artists who painted children. The text of this article on the imagery of childhood, along with its comprehensive bibliography, makes it an invaluable source.[8]

BOOKS

The emphasis on monographic literature found in both editions of the *Guide to the Literature of Art History* is appropriate, for books are of paramount importance to art historical research. It makes sense to begin any search for books with a search of the researcher's University library online public access catalog. (It is unlikely that most public libraries will own sufficient art historical research materials for CCS researchers.) It is helpful to take a two-pronged approach, using both keyword and subject searches in the sample search for information about representations of childhood in nineteenth-century French art. A keyword search begins with crafting search terms. For the sample search, it may be useful to try the following keywords: *children and art* or *childhood and art* or, more broadly still, *child$ and art*, where the dollar sign ($) stands for the catalog's truncation symbol, and the search would retrieve results that contain the terms *child* (with any suffix) and *art*. I conducted a keyword search for children and art in my University's online public access catalog. The search returned 557 hits, far too many for me to review.[9] I tried a narrower keyword search, using the terms *child? and art and France*, which produced five hits, but I found that none of the hits were useful.

Moving from a keyword search to a search employing Library of Congress Subject Headings (LCSH) produces more exact results. When an online catalog specifies a subject search, the term *subject* refers specifically to an established Library of Congress Subject Heading. There are at least three Library of Congress Subject Headings of use to CCS researchers in art:

"Childhood in art," "Children in art," and "Children—Pictorial works."[10] The subject search "Children in art" in my local University's catalog produces twenty hits, several of which, judging by the titles, are directly relevant to the sample search, including Robert Rosenblum's *The Romantic Child: From Runge to Sendak* and Bruce Hooton's *Mother and Child in Modern Art.*[11]

Since the specialized study of children and childhood in the history of art is a relatively new area of research, there are few monographs devoted entirely to the topic. The annotated bibliography appended below includes a longer list of relevant titles (including those that examine representations of childhood in specific periods of art history). Some of the more valuable art historical research takes an analytic and scholarly (rather than merely descriptive) approach to the imagery of children and childhood. Anne Higonnet's book *Pictures of Innocence:The History and Crisis of Ideal Childhood* is an important contribution to the literature on representations of children in art. Before concentrating on and problematizing modern photography of children, Higonnet explains in detail the development of images of what she calls Romantic childhood, which concentrate on, in her words, "not the child's age, but an age of childhood,"—at once seemingly innocent, natural, and timeless.[12]

While the use of Library of Congress Subject Headings can often deliver more targeted results, it can sometimes be difficult to determine which Library of Congress of Subject Headings are most useful for a search. There are several ways to find suitable Library of Congress Subject Headings. The first involves using keyword searches to find a monographic record that the researcher finds highly relevant to the search. The researcher can then use the Library of Congress Subject Headings applied to the original record to find other books cataloged under the same subject heading(s). In many catalogs, the Library of Congress Subject Headings are hyperlinked, allowing the researcher to click through lists of books with shared Library of Congress Subject Headings. Another option is to visit the Library of Congress Authorities page at authorities.loc.gov.[13] Clicking on "Search Authorities" allows the researcher to search through lists of Library of Congress Subject Headings, choose those authorized headings that might be useful, and employ the subject heading in later catalog searches. (The research can also consult the five-volume print copy of the *Library of Congress Subject Headings,* see note 10.) A comprehensive search for literature would likely lead the researcher beyond his or her local catalog to multilibrary online catalogs, such as *OCLC's Worldcat* or the *RLG Union Catalog.* Such catalogs, which contain the bibliographic records of the online library catalogs of

universities, institutes, and other organizations in North America and beyond, can serve as unparalled sources for monographic information. Many
university online catalogs are freely accessible. Multilibrary catalogs and indexes, which I discuss later in this chapter, are proprietary databases. It is in-
effectual to conduct broad keyword searches in such catalogs because multilibrary catalogs can contain millions of records, and keyword searches will
likely return too many results for the researcher to carefully and comfort-
ably review. A multilibrary catalog search is more likely to be successful with
a well-defined subject search by a Library of Congress Subject Heading.

I searched the *RLG Union Catalog* with a subject search using the Library of Congress Subject Heading "Children in art." To my surprise, 582
hits were returned. This was too large a set for me to review, so I wanted
to refine my search in order to narrow my results list. I then conducted an
advanced search in the *RLG Union Catalog*, using the Library of Congress
Subject Heading "Children in art," and the keyword *France*. This search
produced a much more manageable and highly relevant results set of 32
hits, including PhD dissertations, books, and exhibitions catalogs. A few of
the results I deem useful are books in a foreign language, such as an older
exhibition catalog in French entitled *L'Enfant dans le Dessin du XVe au XIXe
siecles* (*Children in Drawing from the Fifteenth through Nineteenth Centuries*).[14]
While it is helpful to have reading knowledge of French to use these titles,
it is not strictly necessary because even an examination of the images illustrated in such texts might be useful.[15] There are a number of additional useful techniques to find relevant monographs, which involve launching off
from the useful monographs one has already located. Anne Higonnet's text
is important for my sample search, and I can use Higonnet's text to find
other useful resources in three distinct ways. First, I can make note of the
subject headings applied to Higonnet's book: "Children in art," "Children—Pictorial works," and "Innocence (Psychology)." I was already aware
of the first two subject headings, and the third is not of interest to me.
However, it is always possible that I would have found an additional Library
of Congress Subject Heading of potential utility. I can also record the call
number at which the book was cataloged (N7640), and browse the library
shelves to see if there might be other useful books in this call number
range.[16] I can return to the online catalogs I already searched, and using
Higonnet's full name as the term in a search by author, I can determine if
she authored any other relevant texts that might be of use. Higonnet also
authored two books on the artist Berthe Morisot: *Berthe Morisot* (published
in 1990) and *Berthe Morisot's Images of Women* (published in 1992).[17] This
process, called backward and forward chaining, uncovers work published by

the same author both earlier and later. Operating on the principle that scholars often author more than one book on the same or related subjects, it is possible to uncover other useful sources. I can also consult the "Notes and Sources" section of Higonnet's book, which is extensive, and contains many potential sources that will prove useful to my search.[18] Higonnet's book does not contain a stand-alone bibliography, but it is often helpful to consult both the footnotes or endnotes and the bibliography of an especially useful text.

I would also like to concentrate on reviewing illustrations of paintings to examine how children were represented in nineteenth-century French art. I can consult both general survey texts that span the history of art, and survey texts that explore nineteenth-century art specifically. The best-known English-language art history survey texts are H. W. Janson's *History of Art* and Gardner's *Art through the Ages*.[19] Survey texts specific to the nineteenth century include Robert Rosenblum and H. W. Janson's *19th Century Art*, Lorenz Eitner's *An Outline of Nineteenth Century Painting* and Stephen F. Eisenman's *Nineteenth Century Art: A Critical History*.[20] Coupling what I have learned from the survey texts with the information I gathered from *The Dictionary of Art*, I can identify nineteenth-century French artists who painted children, a list that includes Gustave Courbet, Jean-François Millet, Berthe Morisot, and Auguste Renoir, among other painters. Mary Cassatt, an American artist who studied, lived, and painted in France, and who is often discussed with the French Impressionists, also painted images of children.

I want to return to my university's online catalog to find books about the individual artists. Monographs known as *catalogue raisonnés* and exhibition catalogs are particularly helpful at this stage. *Catalogue raisonnés* include all of an artist's known *oeuvre*, while exhibition catalogs are the monographs that accompany an exhibition of an artist's work. Using the artist's name as a keyword, I can locate numerous monographs on each artist.[21] Scanning these monographs, I can now ascertain specific titles of paintings of children, such as Gustave Courbet's *Stonebreakers* (1850), Jean-François Millet's *The Knitting Lesson II* (c. 1860), Berthe Morisot's *The Cradle* (1872), Mary Cassatt's *Portrait of a Little Girl* (1878), and Auguste Renoir's *Madame Georges Charpentier and Her Children* (1878), to name just a few examples.[22] Even a cursory review of this developing body of imagery begins to suggest a number of questions, such as, Who was the audience for these paintings? Why do women painters seem more preoccupied with mothers and children than their male counterparts? How do these images differ from eighteenth-century genre scenes, or scenes of everyday life? What do scenes of the nineteenth-century domestic interior tell us? How do scenes of working-class children differ from representations of bourgeois children?

PERIODICALS AND SCHOLARLY JOURNALS

Periodical literature (or journal literature—I use the two terms interchangeably) is an important source of scholarship for art historians. In many cases, areas of recent emphasis in the discipline will be examined in periodical scholarship before becoming published in extended format in monographic literature. Most art historical periodical scholarship is published in peer-reviewed periodicals. There are a number of key art history journals in the English language, including the *Art Bulletin*, *Art History*, and *Art Journal*, to name just three of the major journals that cover the entire field. There are also many journals that are focused on specific periods of art history. There is a list of art history journals in the *Guide to the Literature of Art History 2*.[23] It is often helpful to browse or scan the art history journals within the researcher's area of interest. This type of browsing or scanning can accomplish a few different ends. Browsing recently published issues of peer-reviewed art history journals can often point to the newest areas of scholarship in the field. Many journals include comprehensive reviews of important recently published monographs. The *Art Bulletin* includes both a list of "books received" (for potential review) and a subject list of in-process and completed doctoral dissertations in the field.

Thus, browsing current journals can be a helpful exercise, but searching indexes to find exact periodical citations on the topic of interest is a more expeditious way to locate useful periodical literature. There are a large number of art history indexes. It may be most appropriate to begin any search with a few of the general art history indexes: *Wilson Art Full Text*, *Wilson Art Abstracts Back File*, *Art Bibliographies Modern*, *The Bibliography of the History of Art*, and *Avery Index to Architectural Periodicals* (which, as its name suggests, is limited to architectural information). Many of the indexes have different interfaces, a complicating factor that can make the search process confusing. Therefore, before beginning to search the indexes, it is helpful to develop search strategies in advance. It is often useful to begin searching indexes with keyword searches. It is necessary to develop a number of synonymous keywords, since any one keyword or keyword combination may not produce useful results. For my sample search on representations of childhood in the art of nineteenth-century France, I have developed search strategies that include the keywords *children* or *childhood and France*. I am not employing *art* as a search word because I am searching within art-related indexes, and therefore I assume that the theme art is implied in the search itself.

I have chosen the index *The Bibliography of the History of Art* for my sample search. After reading the description, I know that *The Bibliography of the History of Art* covers the time period of interest, extensively indexes materials on European art, and is comprehensive in its indexing not only of periodicals but of chapters in books, dissertations, conference proceedings, and other materials. For my first search, I try a combination keyword search using the terms *child? and France and nineteenth century*, where the question mark (?) is the truncation symbol recognized by the index. This search produces two hits, which are helpful, but I was hoping to review a longer list. The keyword search *child? and France* produces 439 hits, and after paging through a few screens, I realize that this is more than I want to review. In an attempt to come up with a manageable results list, I decide to conduct an advanced search using the title word *child?* and the keyword *France*. This search produces sixty-five hits—a reasonable number to review. Among these results I see two gems, a lengthy article entitled "Images of Instruction and Delight: Illustrations in Nineteenth-Century French Children's Literature," in a lesser-known periodical that I would not have discovered in any other way, and a chapter entitled "Children's Studies and the Romantic Child," in the book *Constructions of Childhood between Rousseau and Freud*.[24] I have seen this book title before, having come across it in my search for monographs. Coming across an individual chapter title here confirms for me that it is a text worthy of close examination.

My search of *The Bibliography of the History of Art* has proven useful. But it would be a mistake for me to stop here in my search for periodical literature. Indeed, I advocate searching as many indexes as possible. While many of the art indexes will return overlapping results, there will be some unique results that make searching a wide variety of indexes worthwhile.[25] In addition, it is worthwhile to search the *Bibliography of the History of Art* and the other art indexes with multiple search strategies. I want to keep track of both my search results and my search strategies, for two reasons: so that I can keep a record of where I searched for information, and so that I can reuse those search terms that elicited the best results during the search process. Multiple searches of a variety of indexes with a range of search strategies (by keyword, by subject, by title word, and using advanced searches combining keyword and title word) as well as the development of synonymous keywords both help to circumnavigate the common problem many researchers face of finding too few or, alternately, too many results when searching indexes.

Art history research has become increasingly interdisciplinary, and it is therefore necessary to search indexes that cover periodical literature outside the field of art history. In the case of the sample search on images of children in nineteenth-century French painting, I believe it would be particularly useful to search history indexes. The historical background on childhood in nineteenth-century France is pertinent to any discussion of imagery. In addition to searching the art indexes I listed above, I will search a variety of indexes outside the field of art history. In addition to the historical insights, I would be interested in the disciplinary perspective of literature, for example. For the sample search, I will search the index ABC-CLIO *Historical Abstracts*. A search using the keywords *child* and france and art* produced twenty relevant hits, including a dissertation (*Growing Up with 'Modernité': Representations of Childhood and Adolescence in French Painting, 1848–1886*) and a journal article ("Images et Representations Figurées du Petit Enfant") that I did not see represented in the art indexes.[26]

Since the vast majority of these indexes are proprietary and thus subscription-based, in the case of any search, the periodical literature the researcher finds depends in part on the indexes available to that researcher at his or her local institution. I suggest reviewing the full list of electronic indexes available at the researcher's local institution, and searching a significant number of the indexes that may contain citations germane to the subject of the search. The researcher's efforts early in the research process must be to cast the net as widely as possible in order to be exposed to the broadest cross section of potentially relevant literature.

Occasionally, the search for relevant periodical literature occurs in a sort of reverse process. This is the case when the researcher knows of a highly relevant journal by name, and wishes to determine if that journal has published articles on the search subject. In this instance, it is helpful to consult *Ulrich's International Periodical Directory*. If the researcher finds the periodical title in Ulrich's, he or she can then see which indexes cover the periodical. Then, the research can return to the index and, using an advanced search, conduct a keyword search for articles in the periodical in question.

WEB RESOURCES

In the development and use of freely available Web-based resources, art history is a discipline in transition. Lois Swan Jones's *Art Information and the Internet* is an excellent reference source to introduce the researcher to the kinds of art information available on the Web. Swan Jones exhaustively reviews the types of electronic information available on the Web, and how to locate such information.[27] There are many reputable freely available Web resources in the field of art history, some of which include peer-reviewed content. Many of these resources include material limited to a specific stylistic period, rather than covering the whole field of art history. In the field of contemporary art, for example, the Web contains information unavailable in any other medium. In addition, the Web often points to print resources in the field that might not have been located in the course of the literature search. I advocate searching for Web-based information for all research projects. It is necessary, however, to very carefully review the sites to determine if the information is accurate and useful. However, if the research project results in a term paper or thesis, it is vital to ascertain the professor's position on the use of Web resources. The best way to know the professor's position is to ask directly.

It is often possible to locate reputable freely available Web resources through an advanced search using the researcher's preferred search engine. An advanced search allows the researcher to search by domain (eliminating commercial sites, if desired), to limit results by language, and to limit results to recently updated pages. I conducted an advanced search with Google, using the keywords *nineteenth-century French painting childhood* and limited my results to pages in English updated during the past year. Scanning through the first couple of pages of results, and then looking through the Web pages themselves, I see two possible websites of interest: a site describing a recent Nineteenth Century Studies Association conference that included a session entitled "Representing Childhood in Nineteenth-Century Painting," and an interview with James Steward, curator of the exhibition *The New Child*, and author of the accompanying exhibition catalog that I came across in my search for monographs.[28] The Nineteenth Century Studies Association website includes only a program, rather than the full text of the papers given in the session. The speakers and their institutional affiliations are listed, however, and I can follow up by conducting author searches in my University catalog, or perhaps even by e-mailing the author directly to inquire about the paper. The website with the interview is exceedingly interesting, as it gives a great deal of background on the curator's research and work in the development of the exhibition and subsequent catalog.

While there are many proprietary image databases, there are, as most researchers know, an enormous number of images on the Web. Searching for images on the Web is somewhat different that searching for text-based materials on the Web. Google has an image search that scans the Web and returns a large number of fine art and other imagery. It is crucially important to be cognizant of copyright and of image rights when searching for imagery on the Web. Images of works of art (those owned in private collections as well as those in art museum or other collections) cannot be reproduced on Web pages or in publications without written permission. (Most larger museums have a link on their website for those researchers who wish to request permission to reproduce a work of art held in the museum's collection.) There are several websites, such as *Art Images for College Teaching*, that include images cleared for educational use; other sites, including the *Archival Research Catalog of the National Archives*, *American Memory from the Library of Congress*, and the *New York Public Library's Mid-Manhattan Picture Collection Online*, include digitized imagery cleared for use in the public domain.[29] It is important, of course, to carefully read the text of the website for information on the legal and appropriate use of any images contained therein.

While it can be difficult to locate Web resources, it can be equally challenging to evaluate them. There are many criteria against which to measure the validity and utility of Web resources.[30] Much evaluation takes place "on the fly," while the researcher is surfing the Web for and through various websites. When I am reading and reviewing the content of a website, I mentally move through a process of initial evaluation during which I try to ask myself the same questions about the website that I would ask and answer when compiling a bibliographic citation for a book. The main elements of a book citation include the book's author, title, publication location, publisher, and date. Transposing these questions to information found on the Web results in the following basic questions about a website:

Who is the author of this site?

If this site has a title, what is it, or what would it be?

Who publishes, or hosts, this site on the Web? Is the publisher/host different from the author?

When was the site "published" on the Web? How frequently is the site updated?

These questions lead me to consider larger issues that help me decide whether or not the Web resource is reputable and worthwhile to cite in my research. While I am answering these questions for myself, they also help me form a cogent rationale of why I decided to use the Web resource in question, in the event that a reader, professor, or editor should ask me. Some of the larger evaluative questions include the following:

What credentials does the author possess that makes him or her a reputable source on this subject?

Is the information I have learned from this source consistent with other reputable sources on the subject?

If the site is commercially sponsored, what stake does the sponsor have in the subject?

Does this site include relatively recent scholarship? If the scholarship is dated, does that affect its validity?

Information on the Web is in a constant state of flux. It is this relative instability that makes the evaluation itself a constantly evolving process. It is therefore mandatory to carefully evaluate and fully cite any Web source that the researcher does decide to employ based on the context in which the researcher found the information, and based on the context in which the researcher will use the information. [31]

WRITING ART HISTORICAL RESEARCH

Every scholar has a personal system for compiling research and writing drafts that is developed over years of scholarly practice. The phase of research discussed in this chapter, which includes using bibliographic tools to locate sources and gathering bibliography, is but the first step in a long research process. My personal research process involves compiling bibliography; reading the accumulated research; taking notes on what I have read; making notes on the connections I see in the research; creating a working outline of my thesis and argument; writing a rough draft; editing and revising the rough draft into a second, more polished draft; and then concluding with a final, refined editing process before sharing my work with an outside reader. There are many books that discuss the process of research. Art historians can consult the most recent edition of the *Chicago Manual of Style*, the bibliographic manual used in the field of art history for compiling footnotes or endnotes and bibliography.[32] I mention here just two of the many useful texts that provide solutions to the research and writing challenges faced by scholars. The classic text *The Craft of Research* addresses all of the constituent parts of the research process, including conducting research, writing a draft, and moving through the revision process.[33] Eviatar Zerubavel's *The Clockwork Muse: A Practical Guide to Writing Theses, Dissertations, and Books* helps the writer combat the terror of the blank page.[34] Zerubavel's work disabuses the researcher of the notion that he or she needs to wait for the creative muse to arrive in order to write; the author proposes a time management system for generating written drafts based on the construction of a detailed outline.

While these texts address the challenges faced by all researchers and writers, art historians also must write quite specifically and directly about the images they use in their research. Often, for scholars who have not been trained to analyze images, it is difficult to describe a work's subject and composition, to discuss nuances of line and color, and to move beyond such descriptions to an analysis that helps to support and advance the scholar's argument. Both Sylvan Barnet's *A Short Guide to Writing about Art* and Henry Sayre's *Writing about Art* address how to craft a cogent visual analysis of a work of art and how to integrate such an analysis with other research and writing.[35] Scholars from another discipline may struggle to find the words to analyze a work of art, and it is therefore helpful at the writing stage for the outside researcher to familiarize himself or herself with the tools that lend a command of the language of the art historical discipline.[36] It is a truism that the hardest part of any research project is getting started, for it is perhaps equally difficult to maintain momentum throughout the research process. This chapter discusses some of the many bibliographic tools and sources in the field of art history that may prove useful to the researcher in CCS. While some resources may be useful to one researcher but not another, all researchers share the need to search, to read, to reconsider, and to reflect. Keeping a detailed record of the research pathway, and carefully compiling and recording bibliography, mitigates the risk of inadvertent plagiarism and greatly eases the drafting process. A one-on-one consultation with a subject librarian may be helpful in order to ferret out specific or little-known sources suited to a particular topic. In the research process, connections are forged, not uncovered. It is the unique nature of each research inquiry that makes it challenging and, ultimately, rewarding. For while the research process leads to insights gained for the researcher alone, it is the written product that results in knowledge shared, which is the ultimate goal of the academic enterprise.

A SELECTIVE ANNOTATED BIBLIOGRAPHY OF SOURCES ON CHILDREN AND CHILDHOOD STUDIES IN THE HISTORY OF ART

(*This bibliography is limited to materials in the English language.*)
Autin Graz, Marie-Christine. *Children in Painting.* Milan: Skira, 2002.
    This visual survey of representations of children in painting is organized by country. While the paintings are described more than analyzed, the works illustrated are drawn from a wide range of imagery and are reproduced entirely in

color and often in large scale. This text therefore serves as an important source for the CCS scholar who wishes to review a range of art history imagery including children.

Beaumont, Lesley. "The Social Status and Artistic Presentation of 'Adolescence' in Fifth Century Athens." In *Children and Material Culture*, edited by Joanna Sofaer Derevenski, 39–50. London: Routledge, 2000.

Beaumont traces the iconography of adolescence in fifth-century Athenian art. The author, while acknowledging *adolescence* to be a relative term, is particularly concerned with the differing representations of girls and boys in the art of the period. Beaumont concludes by outlining the strategies artists employed to represent this ambiguous stage between childhood and adulthood.

Brown, Marilyn R. "Images of Childhood." In *Encyclopedia of Children and Childhood in History and Society*, edited by Paula S. Fass, 449–63. New York: Thomson Gale, 2004.

Brown's essay traces representations of children in the history of art between 1400 and the present. The essay focuses largely on the imagery of the modern period, delineating, among other issues, the differences in the representations of children of both genders, and of various classes. The article presents comprehensive and important introduction to the subject that is both amply illustrated and includes a comprehensive bibliography.

Brown, Marilyn R., ed. *Picturing Children: Constructions of Childhood between Rousseau and Freud*. Aldershot, UK: Ashgate, 2002.

This volume of essays examines images of children in eighteenth- through twentieth-century art from a variety of perspectives. The essays include thoughtful, scholarly examinations of the construction of childhood in artists' biographies, representations of girlhood in Impressionism, images of childhood in Victorian fairy painting, the photography of children and childhood, an examination of the concept of the Romantic child, and other subjects. The text concludes with an extensive bibliography.

Higonnet, Anne. *Pictures of Innocence: The History and Crisis of Ideal Childhood*. London: Thames and Hudson, 1998.

Higonnet's text analyzes contemporary photographs of children in the context of modern American society. In the course of this analysis she employs images taken from so-called art photography as well as from the wider visual culture. In this sense, Higonnet's work is at the forefront of the analytical work being done in the field of visual culture studies. While the author's work focuses on the modern period, she includes a thoroughgoing scholarly history of how the modern understanding of childhood developed.

Jasin, Gabriela. "'De nos Ambitieux, Vous Etes le Symbole': Aspects of Childhood in Eighteenth-Century French Art." PhD diss., Rutgers, The State University of New Jersey, 2003.

This dissertation examines eighteenth-century French images of children in the context of new Enlightenment ideas about the nature of childhood and the primacy of education and recreation in the formation of children. The author closely examines images of the education of both boys and girls as well as images of children at play.

King, Marian. *A Gallery of Mothers and Their Children*. Philadelphia: Lippincott, 1958.

The author has assembled a brief survey of paintings of children in Western art spanning the early sixteenth to early twentieth centuries and held in the collection of the National Gallery in Washington, D.C. Each work is accompanied by a brief description, which is factual rather than interpretative. Although the illustrations are reproduced entirely in black and white, the striking immediacy of the paintings, many of which are portraits of children in which the gaze of the sitter meets that of the viewer, remains vivid.

Klein, Anita E. *Child Life in Greek Art*. New York: Columbia University Press, 1932.

While some scholars argue that the modern understanding of childhood began after the medieval period, the numerous representations of children in Greek art argue for an earlier cultural delineation and understanding of childhood. Klein's early work catalogs representations of childhood in Greek art in a variety of themes, including toys, pets, and games; school; punishment; sickness and death; and other subjects as represented in a variety of media. The volume includes brief chapters describing the theme and is fully illustrated with examples of each artwork discussed.

Macquoid, Percy. *Four Hundred Years of Children's Costume from the Great Masters: 1400–1800*. London: Medici Society, 1923.

Macquoid's text traces the history of children's costume in the work of well-known artists between the fifteenth and nineteenth centuries. As Macquoid correctly notes, only the children of the wealthy would have been represented to any great degree in most of the art of the centuries under consideration. However, given that the children represented are members of the upper classes, their costumes are often elaborate, and the attention given to the costume by the artist, sometimes at the expense of the expression or figure of the child, is notable.

Ni, Ming-Tsuey. "The Construction of Childhood Space as Represented in Victorian Art." PhD diss., University of Louisville, 2002.

This dissertation examines childhood in British art of the Victorian period. The author employs both historical and psychoanalytic approaches in the analysis of the art under question. Given the importance of childhood to the Victorians, this dissertation considers a wide variety of imagery which may be unknown to many viewers.

Reed, Laurel. "Art, Life, Charm and Titian's Portrait of Clarissa Strozzi." In *Childhood in the Middle Ages and the Renaissance: The Results of a Paradigm Shift in the History of Mentality*, edited by Albrecht Classen, 355–71. Berlin: Walter de Gruyter, 2005.

Reed positions Titian's well-known portrait of two-year-old Clarissa Strozzi against Philippe Ariès's interpretation of the meaning of childhood in the sixteenth century. Since portraits of this kind were rare in the period, Reed examines the strategies Titian employed to portray his subject, and explains what the contemporary audience would have read in the portrait.

Rosenblum, Robert. *The Romantic Child: From Runge to Sendak*. New York: Thames and Hudson, 1989.

Rosenblum's discussion of the Romantic child focuses on the work of the nineteenth-century German artist Otto Runge. After briefly discussing the Enlightenment ancestry of Runge's ideas about childhood, Rosenblum analyzes a number of Runge works featuring children. The author concludes with an examination of the work of the illustrator Maurice Sendak, who himself studied Runge's *oeuvre*.

Schorsch, Anita. *Images of Childhood: An Illustrated Social History*. New York: Mayflower Books, 1979.

Anita Schorsch's *Images of Childhood: An Illustrated Social History* includes representations of children throughout the history of art divided into the following categories: children within the family, children at play, children learning, children at work, and images of good and bad children. Schorsch's text covers both painting and lesser-known graphic work, such as prints, that represented the children of the working classes, conspicuously absent in so-called high art.

Spies, Werner. *Picasso's World of Children*. Translated by John William Gabriel. New York: Prestel, 1994.

Spies's text attempts to sets Picasso's images of children against the background of his larger *oeuvre*. The text takes a mostly chronological approach, tracing the images of children across the course of Picasso's extended career, and through the pluralistic styles with which the artist experimented. The text is extensively illustrated, and includes many of Picasso's lesser-known images of children.

Steward, James Christen. *The New Child: British Art and the Origins of Modern Childhood, 1730–1830*. Berkeley: University Art Museum and Pacific Film Archive, 1995.

This text is the catalog that accompanied the traveling exhibition *The New Child* organized by the University Art Museum at the University of California at Berkeley in 1995. The exhibition and the text explore the constructions and representations of childhood in Georgian Britain. The catalog constitutes a major scholarly contribution to art historical studies of children and childhood in its depth and breadth, with chapters examining the role of the Georgian family, child's play, the intersection of children and class, and other subjects. The text includes a full checklist of the works included in the exhibition and an extensive bibliography.

Uzzi, Jeannine Diddle. *Children in the Visual Arts of Imperial Rome*. New York: Cambridge University Press, 2005.

Uzzi's text, which emerges from her doctoral dissertation, examines imagery of children in the art of imperial Rome. She focuses on the gulf between the representation of Roman and non-Roman children in a variety of media, including coins, mosaics, sculpture in the round, tondo portraits, and funerary monuments.

While Roman children are shown in peaceful scenes designed to speed their acculturation in their roles in Roman society, non-Roman children are shown as submissive figures, or worse, as victims of violence. Uzzi carefully lays out her source material and methodology. Her observations are drawn from an examination of both well- and lesser-known works of art.

Wicks, Ann Barrott, ed. *Children in Chinese Art.* Honolulu: University of Hawaii Press, 2002.

This edited volume includes a range of essays on children in Chinese art of different dynasties in a wide variety of media. The volume is profusely illustrated and contains a glossary of Chinese characters as well as an extensive bibliography.

NOTES

1. Philippe Ariès, *Centuries of Childhood: A Social History of Family Life*, trans. Robert Baldick (New York: Vintage Books, 1962).

2. Ariès, *Centuries of Childhood*, 353, 363.

3. See the entire text of, and in particular, Albrecht Classen's introduction, "Philippe Ariès and the Consequences: History of Childhood, Family Relations, and Personal Emotions: Where Do We Stand Today?" in *Childhood in the Middle Ages and the Renaissance: The Results of a Paradigm Shift in the History of Mentality*, ed. Albrecht Classen (New York: Walter de Gruyter, 2005), 1–65.

4. Anne Higonnet, *Pictures of Innocence: The History and Crisis of Ideal Childhood* (London: Thames and Hudson, 1998), 13. In the introduction to her book, Higonnet writes, "my own academic field dismisses the subject of the child as being trivial and sentimental, good only for second-rate minds and perhaps for women."

5. Jane Turner, ed., *The Dictionary of Art* (New York: Grove Dictionaries, 1996).

6. Jon Whiteley, "France, III, 5(vi): Painting and Graphic Arts, c. 1814-1914," in *The Dictionary of Art*, ed. Jane Turner (New York: Grove Dictionaries, 1996), 542–49.

7. Etta Arntzen and Robert Rainwater, *Guide to the Literature of Art History* (Chicago: American Library Association, 1980), 303–6; Max Marmor and Alex Ross, *Guide to the Literature of Art History 2* (Chicago: American Library Association, 2005), 409–15.

8. Marilyn R. Brown, "Images of Childhood," in *Encyclopedia of Children and Childhood: In History and Society*, vol. 2, ed. Paula S. Fass (New York: Thomson Gale, 2004), 449–63.

9. IRIS: Rutgers University Libraries' Information System (2005), www.libraries.rutgers.edu (accessed November 30, 2005).

10. Library of Congress, Cataloging Policy and Support Office, Library Services, *Library of Congress Subject Headings*, vol. 1A–1C, 28th ed. (Washington, D.C.: Cataloging Distribution Service, 2005), 1247, 1250, 1254.

11. Bruce Hooton and Nina N. Kaiden, eds., *Mother and Child in Modern Art* (New York: Duell, Sloan and Pearce, 1964); Robert Rosenblum, *The Romantic Child: From Runge to Sendak* (New York: Thames and Hudson, 1989).

12. Higonnet, *Pictures of Innocence*. Higonnet's work acknowledges Rosenblum's work on Romantic childhood.

13. Library of Congress, "Library of Congress Authorities" (2005), authorities.loc.gov (accessed November 30, 2005).

14. RLG's Eureka RLG Union Catalog (accessed November 30, 2005). *L'Enfant dans le Dessin du XVe au XIXe Siècles* (Paris: Musée du Louvre, 1957).

15. Since imagery forms an important part of my potential research materials, using extensively illustrated foreign language materials is entirely appropriate. For advanced researchers, it may be helpful to consult the national library catalog of the country whose art the researcher is studying. In the case of France, I could consult the online catalog of the Bibliothèque Nationale de France, called BN OPALE PLUS, at www.bnf.fr. When consulting a national library catalog, it is helpful to remember that it is necessary to be able to read the language of the country whose catalog you are accessing, and to recognize that for countries other than the United States, the Library of Congress Subject Headings are not used.

16. The Library of Congress Subject Headings map to specific call number ranges, but it is often easier to move from a title one already has than to find the call number ranges that apply to specific subject headings.

17. Anne Higonnet, *Berthe Morisot* (New York: Harper & Row, 1990); Anne Higonnet, *Berthe Morisot's Images of Women* (Cambridge: Harvard University Press, 1992).

18. Anne Higonnet, "Notes and Sources," in *Pictures of Innocence: The History and Crisis of Ideal Childhood* (London: Thames and Hudson, 1998), 227–42.

19. Frederick Hartt, *Art: A History of Painting, Sculpture, Architecture*, 4th ed. (New York: Abrams, 1993); Marilyn Stokstad, *Art History*, rev. ed. (New York: Abrams, 1999); H. W. Janson and Anthony F. Janson, *History of Art*, 5th ed. (New York: Abrams, 1995); Fred S. Kleiner and Christin J. Mamiya, *Gardner's Art through the Ages*, 12th ed. (Belmont, Calif.: Thomson/Wadsworth, 2005).

20. Stephen F. Eisenman, *Nineteenth Century Art: A Critical History*, 2nd ed. (New York: Thames and Hudson, 2002); Lorenz Eitner, *An Outline of 19th Century European Painting: From David through Cézanne* (New York: Harper & Row, 1987); Robert Rosenblum and H. W. Janson, *19th-Century Art*, rev. ed. (Upper Saddle River, N.J.: Prentice Hall, 2005).

21. Some useful monographs on the individual artists that emerged through keyword searches on the artist's name include Sarah Faunce and Linda Nochlin, *Courbet Reconsidered* (Brooklyn, N.Y.: Brooklyn Museum of Art, 1988); Michael Fried, *Courbet's Realism* (Chicago: University of Chicago Press, 1990); Alexandra R. Murphy, *Jean-François Millet* (Boston: Museum of Fine Arts, 1984); in addition to Higonnet's work on Morisot, Kathleen Adler and Tamar Garb, *Berthe Morisot* (Oxford: Phaidon, 1987); Colin B. Bailey, *Renoir's Portraits: Impressions of an Age* (New

Haven: Yale University Press, 1997); Judith A. Barter, *Mary Cassatt: Modern Woman* (Chicago: The Art Institute of Chicago, 1998).

22. The full citations for these paintings are: Mary Cassatt, *Portrait of a Little Girl*, 1878, oil on canvas, 89.5 × 129.8 cm (Washington, D.C.: National Gallery of Art); Gustave Courbet, *Stonebreakers*, 1850 (destroyed); Jean-François Millet, *The Knitting Lesson II*, c. 1860, oil on panel, 15⅞ × 12⅜ in. (Boston: Museum of Fine Arts); Berthe Morisot, *The Cradle*, 1872, oil on canvas, 22 × 18⅛ in. (Paris: Musée d'Orsay); Auguste Renoir, *Madame Georges Charpentier and her Children*, 1878, 153.7 × 190.2 cm (New York: The Metropolitan Museum of Art).

23. Max Marmor and Alex Ross, *Guide to the Literature of Art History 2* (Chicago: American Library Association, 2005), 654–91.

24. Penny Brown, "Images of Instruction and Delight: Illustrations in Nineteenth-Century French Children's Literature," *Bulletin of the John Rylands University Library of Manchester* 81, no. 3 (1999): 385–415; George Dimock, "Children's Studies and the Romantic Child," in *Constructions of Childhood between Rousseau and Freud*, ed. Marilyn R. Brown (Aldershot, UK: Ashgate), 189–99.

25. For a discussion of such overlap in art indexes, see Tony White, "Journal Title Overlap Study of Four Major Online Art Indexes," *Art Documentation* 24, no. 1 (2005): 26–28.

26. Anna Green, "Growing Up with 'Modernité': Representations of Childhood and Adolescence in French Painting, 1848-1886" (PhD diss., Open University, 2003); Marie-France Morel, "Images et Representations Figurées du Petit Enfant: Pour une Problématique Renouvelée de l'Histoire de l'Enfance (XVe-XIXe Siècles)," *Mélanges de l'Ecole Française de Rome* 109, no. 1 (1997): 465–83.

27. Lois Swan Jones, *Art Information and the Internet: How to Find It, How to Use It* (Phoenix: Oryx, 1999).

28. Nineteenth Century Studies Association, "Infantuation: Childhood, Youth & Nineteenth-Century Culture, 26th Annual Conference 2005 Program" (2005), www.msu.edu/~floyd/ncsa/2005_program.htm (accessed December 1, 2005); "Interview with New Child Curator: An Interview with Curator James Steward" (May 1995), www.bampfa.berkeley.edu/exhibits/newchild/ncinterview.html (accessed December 1, 2005).

29. See the following websites for more information: *Art Images for College Teaching (AICT)* (arthis.cla.umn.edu/aict/html), *Archival Research Catalog of the National Archives* (www.archives.gov/research/index.html), *American Memory from the Library of Congress* (memory.loc.giv/ammem), *New York Public Library Mid-Manhattan Library Picture Collection Online* (digital.nypl.org/mmpco).

30. See, for a relatively early example, Jim Kapoun, "Teaching Undergrads WEB Evaluation: A Guide for Library Instruction," *C&RL News* 59, no. 7 (July/August 1998).

31. See, e.g., Xia Li and Nancy B. Crane, *Electronic Styles: A Handbook for Citing Electronic Information*, 2nd ed. (Medford, N.J.: Information Today, 1996); Marie L. Radford, Susan B. Barnes, and Linda R. Barr, *Web Research: Selecting, Evaluating, and Citing*, 2nd ed. (Boston: Pearson/Allyn and Bacon, 2006).

32. *The Chicago Manual of Style*, 15th ed. (Chicago: The University of Chicago Press, 2003).

33. Wayne C. Booth, Gregory G. Colomb, and Joseph M. Williams, *The Craft of Research*, 2nd ed. (Chicago: University of Chicago Press, 2003).

34. Eviatar Zerubavel, *The Clockwork Muse: A Practical Guide to Writing Theses, Dissertations, and Books* (Cambridge: Harvard University Press, 1999).

35. Sylvan Barnet, *A Short Guide to Writing about Art* (Boston: Little, Brown); Henry M. Sayre, *Writing about Art*, 3rd ed. (Upper Saddle River, N.J: Prentice Hall, 1999).

36. E.g., James Hall, *Dictionary of Subjects and Symbols in Art* (New York: Harper & Row, 1979); Robert Nelson and Richard Shiff, eds., *Critical Terms for Art History* (Chicago: University of Chicago Press, 1996).

WORKS CITED

Adler, Kathleen, and Tamar Garb. *Berthe Morisot*. Oxford: Phaidon, 1987.

Ariès, Philippe. *Centuries of Childhood: A Social History of Family Life*. Translated by Robert Baldick. New York: Vintage, 1962.

Arntzen, Etta, and Robert Rainwater. *Guide to the Literature of Art History*. Chicago: American Library Association, 1980.

Bailey, Colin B. *Renoir's Portraits: Impressions of an Age*. New Haven, N.J.: Yale University Press, 1997.

Barnet, Sylvan. *A Short Guide to Writing about Art*. 6th ed. New York: Longman, 2000.

Barter, Judith A. *Mary Cassatt: Modern Woman*. Chicago: The Art Institute of Chicago, 1998.

Booth, Wayne C., Gregory G. Colomb, and Joseph M. Williams. *The Craft of Research*. 2nd ed. Chicago: University of Chicago Press, 2003.

Brown, Marilyn R. "Images of Childhood." In *Encyclopedia of Children and Childhood: In History and Society*. Vol. 2. Edited by Paula S. Fass, 449–63. New York: Thomson Gale, 2004.

Brown, Penny, "Images of Instruction and Delight: Illustrations in Nineteenth-Century French Children's Literature," *Bulletin of the John Rylands University Library of Manchester* 81, no. 3 (1999): 385–415.

The Chicago Manual of Style. 15th ed. Chicago: The University of Chicago Press, 2003.

Classen, Albrecht, ed. *Childhood in the Middle Ages and the Renaissance: The Results of a Paradigm Shift in the History of Mentality*. Berlin: Walter de Gruyter, 2005.

Dimock, George. "Children's Studies and the Romantic Child." In *Constructions of Childhood between Rousseau and Freud*. Edited by Marilyn R. Brown. Aldershot, UK: Ashgate.

Eisenman, Stephen. *Nineteenth Century Art: A Critical History*. 2nd ed. New York: Thames and Hudson, 2002.

Eitner, Lorenz. *An Outline of 19th Century European Painting: From David through Cézanne*. New York: Harper & Row, 1987.

Faunce, Sarah, and Linda Nochlin. *Courbet Reconsidered*. Brooklyn, N.Y.: Brooklyn Museum of Art, 1988.

Fried, Michael. *Courbet's Realism*. Chicago: University of Chicago Press, 1990.

Green, Anna. "Growing Up with 'Modernité': Representations of Childhood and Adolescence in French Painting, 1848–1886." PhD diss., Open University, 2003.

Hall, James. *Dictionary of Subjects and Symbols in Art*. New York: Harper & Row, 1979.

Hartt, Frederick. *Art: A History of Painting, Sculpture, Architecture*. 4th ed. New York: Abrams, 1993.

Higonnet, Anne. *Berthe Morisot*. New York: Harper & Row, 1990.

———. *Berthe Morisot's Images of Women*. Cambridge: Harvard University Press, 1992.

———. "Notes and Sources." In *Pictures of Innocence: The History and Crisis of Ideal Childhood*, 227–42. London: Thames and Hudson, 1998.

———. *Pictures of Innocence: The History and Crisis of Ideal Childhood*. London: Thames and Hudson, 1998.

Hooton, Bruce, and Nina N. Kaiden, eds. *Mother and Child in Modern Art*. New York: Duell, Sloan and Pearce, 1964.

"Interview with New Child Curator: An Interview with Curator James Steward" (May 1995). www.bampfa.berkeley.edu/exhibits/newchild/ncinterview.html

IRIS: Rutgers University Libraries' Information System (2005). www.libraries.rutgers.edu (accessed November 30, 2005).

Janson, H. W., and Anthony F. Janson. *History of Art*. 5th ed. New York: Abrams, 1995.

Jones, Lois Swan. *Art Information and the Internet: How to Find It, How to Use It*. Phoenix: Oryx, 1999.

Kapoun, Jim. "Teaching Undergrads WEB Evaluation: A Guide for Library Instruction." *C&RL News* 59, no. 7 (July/August 1998), 522–23.

Kleiner, Fred S., and Christin J. Mamiya. *Gardner's Art through the Ages*. 12th ed. Belmont, Calif.: Thomson/Wadsworth, 2005.

L'Enfant dans le Dessin du XVe au XIXe Siècles. Paris: Musée du Louvre, 1957.

Li, Xia, and Nancy B. Crane. *Electronic Styles: A Handbook for Citing Electronic Information*. 2nd ed. Medford, N.J.: Information Today, 1996.

Library of Congress. "Library of Congress Authorities." authorities.loc.gov.

Library of Congress, Cataloging Policy and Support Office, Library Services. *Library of Congress Subject Headings*. Vol. 1A–C, 28th ed. Washington, D.C.: Cataloging Distribution Service, 2005.

Marmor, Max, and Alex Ross. *Guide to the Literature of Art History 2*. Chicago: American Library Association, 2005.

Morel, Marie-France. "Images et Representations Figurées du Petit Enfant: Pour une Problématique Renouvelée de l'Histoire de l'Enfance (XVe-XIXe Siècles)." *Mélanges de l'Ecole Française de Rome* 109, no. 1 (1997): 465–83.

Murphy, Alexandra R. *Jean-François Millet*. Boston: Museum of Fine Arts, 1984.

Nelson, Robert, and Richard Shiff, eds. *Critical Terms for Art History*. Chicago: University of Chicago Press, 1996.

Nineteenth Century Studies Association. "Infantuation: Childhood, Youth & Nineteenth-Century Culture." 26th Annual Conference 2005 Program. www.msu.edu/~floyd/ncsa/2005_program.htm

Radford, Marie L., Susan B. Barnes, and Linda R. Barr. *Web Research: Selecting, Evaluating, and Citing*. 2nd ed. Boston: Pearson/Allyn and Bacon, 2006.

Rosenblum, Robert. *The Romantic Child: From Runge to Sendak*. New York: Thames and Hudson, 1989.

Rosenblum, Robert, and H. W. Janson. *19th-Century Art*. Rev. and updated ed. Upper Saddle River, N.J.: Prentice Hall, 2005.

Sayre, Henry M. *Writing about Art*. 3rd ed. Upper Saddle River, N.J.: Prentice Hall, 1999.

Stokstad, Marilyn. *Art History*. Rev. ed. New York: Abrams, 1999.

Turner, Jane, ed. *The Dictionary of Art*. New York: Grove Dictionaries, 1996.

White, Tony. "Journal Title Overlap Study of Four Major Online Art Indexes." *Art Documentation* 24, no. 1 (2005): 26–28.

Whiteley, Jon. "France, III, 5(vi): Painting and Graphic Arts, c. 1814–1914." In *The Dictionary of Art*, edited by Jane Turner, 542–49. New York: Grove Dictionaries, 1996.

Zerubavel, Eviatar. *The Clockwork Muse: A Practical Guide to Writing Theses, Dissertations, and Books*. Cambridge: Harvard University Press, 1999.

5

BUSINESS AND ECONOMICS

Theodora T. Haynes

How does early entry into the workforce affect the development of aspects of childhood? Is child labor essential to the successful functioning of economic life in developing nations? Topics such as these are of research interest to Children and Childhood Studies scholars. To properly answer these research questions, a scholar needs to initiate a cross-disciplinary literature search and include resources from sociology, anthropology, and political science. Such a scholar also needs to investigate scholarly literature in business and economics. This chapter is intended as a guide for research in those last two fields.

As a business librarian in an academic library for over twenty years, I have helped students with numerous research projects, including searches for historical data, international statistics, and trends and issues in business and economics. It is often difficult to navigate the myriad of information resources such as those produced by the Federal government and governmental agencies (e.g., the Department of Labor), nongovernmental organizations (e.g., the International Labor Organization or the World Bank), and international organizations (e.g., the International Monetary Fund or the United Nations). When one adds scholarly information from colleges and universities, think tanks, foundations, and scholarly presses and journals, the task can seem very daunting indeed.

In this chapter, I make a few assumptions about the reader. I assume that you, the reader, are, first, starting a cross-disciplinary research project with an emphasis on a topic relating to children/childhood as related to the fields of either business or economics; second, I assume that you are not a business or economics major and are, therefore, unfamiliar with the major research tools associated with those fields; third, I assume that you could use a guide. To illustrate both the process and how the resources are used, I explore a sample topic, that of child labor.

With these assumptions in mind, let us begin with a few definitions.

DEFINITIONS

What Is Economics?

According to economist David Hyman, "The discipline of economics is concerned with the use of available productive resources in a society to satisfy what often are conflicting desires and demands. Economics is concerned with choices: with evaluating and selecting among alternatives, realizing that each time we make a choice we also forgo an opportunity."[1] But as Baumol and Blinder note,

> Economics has something of a split personality. Although clearly the most rigorous of the social sciences, it nevertheless looks decidedly more "social" than "scientific" when compared with, say, physics. An economist must be a jack of several trades, borrowing modes of investigation from numerous fields.[2]

The field of economics includes both theoretical and applied research. Both create models to explain and predict human behavior related to value and production. They rely heavily on statistical data to test the models. Much of the economic study of children focuses on the cost of having them or the cost of not having them. Because most children do not generate income, studies of their economic impact looks either at the cost of their existence (of raising or supporting them) as in countries of the North, or at their participation in the labor force before the age of fourteen or sixteen, as in many countries of the South.[3] One definition of economics that seems most apt for studies of the economic impact of child labor is that proposed by James Buchanan, "that the 'public' nature of economics makes its end product the implementation of laws/politics that influence behavior in such a way as 'to allow people to produce more effectively the goods and services that they themselves value.'"[4]

In countries of the South, in spite of attitudes in countries of the North toward child labor, many children do work after the age of seven to ten. In these countries of the South, children twelve to thirteen years old in the workforce can often provide more income for a family than an adult of fifty. Forbidding this practice has vast impact on the children's economic welfare, their families' welfare, and the economy of the regions and countries as a whole. Nonetheless, allowing child labor has implications for the health and education of the children. Negative health effects and little education (a time trade-off, as well as an economic one) means that the future of these children and their surrounding groups is often poor. Thus studies of child labor overlap into education, health, demography, country politics and policies. This kind of study relies heavily on international statistical gathering to evaluate results quantitatively or to construct models that can reliably predict effects and outcomes of policy decisions.

A SAMPLE SEARCH AND SEARCH STRATEGY

Developing a Thesis or Research Question

In order to develop a thesis or research question it helps to start with general sources that provide background information. This type of source—a specialized encyclopedia or a handbook on the topic—will offer many different perspectives on a topic and allow you to explore the various aspects of the topic, as well as help you decide what the most interesting issues are for your research. Once you have decided on the aspect of the issue you want to explore, you can make a list of questions you want to answer about that issue.

Creating a Search Strategy for a Literature Search

These questions will help you formulate the search strategy, deciding on the most useful type of information and therefore the best sources to use to get the information. If, for instance, you want to explore the relationship of mandatory education on whether children work, you will want to find answers to questions like how much money can a child earn in various industries in his or her home country; how necessary is this income to his or her survival; if the child's home country institutes mandatory education, and indeed provides it, what are the effects on the child and his or her living unit (family, street gang, community) if the child no longer works in order to attend school as the law requires. You will need to find statistical data on the income, and on the effect of a decline in that income. You will need to look for the effect of the implementation of mandatory education in other countries in articles on the topic. You will also want articles and statistics on whether mandatory education does cause a decrease in the number of working children. So you will want to use many of the resources that follow.

SUGGESTED RESOURCES

Reference Materials

For definitions of and background information on child labor I start with an encyclopedia. A specialized one works well, such as the *Encyclopedia of Children and Childhood: In History and Society*. Starting with its index leads you to fourteen articles on child labor. The bibliographies for each of these articles help me develop a list of core sources, which I then expand by scanning the bibliographies of books and journal articles that I find using the bibliographies in each of these core sources, and the tools below.

The *Encyclopedia of Children and Childhood* contains a definition of child labor, in the article "Child Labor in the West," as "employment of children who are less than a specific legal age."[5] Other essays, on countries like Brazil and regions like Latin America, have vital information to provide the researcher with needed grounding in the topic, and with cultural and historical contexts for the issue in all areas of the world.[6] The article on "Economics and Children in Western Societies" provided me with a historical picture of the phases of the centuries-long shift from children-as-family-wage-earners crucial to the survival of the family, especially in rural communities, and as they still are in many countries of the South, to the "priceless child"[7] of modern suburbia in countries of the North, in whom the adults invest for their children's future with no hope of repayment within the parents' lifetimes. This is a process that I know modern countries of the North are hoping to encourage or force in poorer developing nations of the South, but I could not put the pieces together easily until I read this essay. Finding it reinforced my belief in the value of browsing widely to benefit fully from serendipity—finding tidbits and pieces to help you understand a narrow problem because you have started by surveying the broad issue.

The entry on globalization describes the conflict between the priorities of large multinational corporations, which employ low-wage workers, namely children, and groups looking out for the long-term welfare of children, who would rather see children forbidden from working for the sake of their health and have them enrolled in mandatory free educational programs because that is the surest method for ensuring that children do not work. At the same time, this entry delineates the simultaneously merging interests of these same multinationals and their hiring of children with the interests of the poor families and the governments of their impoverished countries in having as much income generated as possible to help support the poor individuals, and to help pay down the international debts that their countries owe to wealthier nations and international organizations like the World Bank.[8] Sometimes the effect of differences between the nongovernmental organizations, international organizations, multinational corporations, and various countries' governments on the poverty-stricken people reminds one of the peasants in *Pillars of the Earth* who simply try to survive the random rampaging of errant knights and their pillaging of the habitat of the poor residents.[9]

Handbooks and Research Guides

Handbooks on research methods are another reference type useful for those starting out in a field of study. Handbooks usually provide an overview of the field or topic, by including chapters or essays on various aspects of the subject, and bringing the reader up to date on research in the field. The most relevant for child labor would seem to be the *Handbook of Labor Economics* by Orley Ashelfelter and David E. Card, one of a large current series titled *Handbooks in Economics* from Elsevier. However, while this three-volume set has essays on seemingly every aspect of labor economics, it has very little to say about child labor by comparison with other topics.

Research guides for fields of study are also useful places to start. For a research guide on economics, the best source now seems to be college, university, and other scholarly websites. The American Economics Association sponsors one of the best. Referred to as RFE, it is Resources for Economists on the Internet (rfe.org). This includes links to a variety of information related to economics, data sources and university departments. Another is Internet Resources for Economists (www.oswego.edu/~economic/econweb.htm).

One with a different arrangement is WebEc (www.helsinki.fi/WebEc), which has an Economics Data section, as well as a section on Labor and Demographics. However the site is no longer being updated.

A Sampling of Recommended Books

Once you are well grounded in the large issues, you need to find books to provide the details of the issues. These books will help you to fill in the gaps in your knowledge of the issue, as well as start to provide enough detail to allow you to focus on a narrower topic that you want to explore thoroughly, so that you can formulate a hypothesis you can substantiate. To most effectively search library catalogs, use the subject headings as well as searching by keyword. The Library of Congress subject heading for child labor is just that: Child Labor. This brings up hundreds of titles in a major university catalog or in OCLC's WorldCat. Do not forget that British-spelling alternatives for words (like *labour*) also need to be searched, especially if you are using keyword rather than subject heading searching. Another phrase that occurs frequently in the literature on child labor is *working children*, but this only works as a search term when you are doing keyword anywhere searching, especially in the abstracts. Examples of the types of books you will find from various publishers are as follows:

Cigno, Alessandro, and Furio C. Rosati. *The Economics of Child Labour.* Oxford, UK: Oxford University Press, 2005.

   In this university press publication, the author presents a model he is developing to explain many factors related to child labor: how families decide whether their children will work, whether the children will be educated, and the effect of international trade on the size of the child labor market. Then the author tests the model on empirical data from several countries.

Fassa, Anaclaudia Gastal, International Programme on the Elimination of Child Labour, and International Labour Organization. *Health Benefits of Eliminating Child Labour: Research Paper in Conjunction with the ILO-IPEC Study on the Costs and Benefits of the Elimination of Child Labour.* ILO/IPEC Working Paper. Geneva: International Labour Organization, International Programme on the Elimination of Child Labour, 2003.

   This international organization's publication argues that more education, especially for parents, leads to better health for children, and that education for children is the best alternative to and controller of child labor, which means it also leads to better health outcomes for the children. This surveys the health risks in industries employing many children. It also includes statistics compiled by the World Bank and the International Labor Organization.

Hecht, Tobias. *At Home in the Street: Street Children of Northeast Brazil.* Cambridge, UK: Cambridge University Press, 1998.

   This example of a detailed study of street children in some cities in Brazil is by an authority on the subject, cited by many other researchers on child labor.

Hobbs, Sandy, Jim McKechnie, and Michael Lavalette. *Child Labor: A World History Companion.* Santa Barbara, Calif.: ABC-CLIO, 1999.

   This is an encyclopedia dedicated to this specific topic, from a scholarly press, which includes movements, activists, industries, jobs, countries and issues related to child labor around the world.

Liebel, Manfred. *A Will of Their Own: Cross-Cultural Perspectives on Working Children*. London: Zed Books; Distributed in the USA by Palgrave Macmillan, 2004.

From another scholarly press, this time British, this book articulates the opinions of working children themselves about their situations and lives.

Penn, Helen. *Unequal Childhoods: Young Children's Lives in Poor Countries*. London: Routledge, 2005.

Penn examines the effects of globalization on child labor in four countries: Kazakhstan, Swaziland, India, and Brazil. The author distinguishes between northern and southern countries, rather than developed Western and developing countries, and covers the interactions between them, especially related to child labor expectations, and explores the consequences of globalization on this young labor force.

Schmitz, Cathryne L., Elizabeth KimJin Traver, and Desi Larson. *Child Labor: A Global View*. Westport, Conn.: Greenwood, 2004.

These authors examine child labor in 15 countries, including the United States, which reports no child labor but shows a different picture if one looks closely. Each essay includes a profile of the country, a history of child labor, the current political, social, and public policy situations, and the future of child labor in each country.

Seabrook, Jeremy. *Children of Other Worlds: Exploitation in the Global Market*. London: Pluto, 2001.

Published by a progressive press, this book compares child laborers in nineteenth-century industrial Britain with those in present-day Bangladesh.

Finding Articles in Scholarly Journals

As you narrow and focus your topic you will want more specific and up-to-date resources. A good resource to use for searching these is indexes to journal articles. If you are interested in more information about the justification of corporations for continuing to hire children in a global employment market, you could next look for journal articles. For ones more likely to be written from the viewpoint of the companies, the best periodical index to use is EBSCO's *Business Source Premier* or ProQuest's *ABI/Inform*. These both index many popular and trade magazines as well as hundreds of scholarly academic journals. The indexing will cover many periodicals written for and read by corporate people. These will include many written to support ethical business practices, to share in-depth research on best-business practices, and to evaluate current trends in business thinking. The thesaurus of terms makes it easy to verify that child labor is the subject heading used in an index as well as in library catalogs. Examples of articles from these business indexes are listed as follows:

"ILO Conference Debates Global Employment Issues." *European Industrial Relations Review*, no. 380 (September 2005): 32–34.

This summarizes the annual conference of the UN ILO, May–June 2005, which, among other issues, proposed action on youth employment to make it practical while protecting young workers' rights.

Clement, Douglas. "Why Johnny Can't Work." *Region (Federal Reserve Bank of Minneapolis)* 19, no. 2 (June 2005): 32–40.

Discusses a theory of economists, which explores societal decisions about whether to encourage or forbid children in the labor force.

Dehejia, Rajeev H., and Roberta Gatti. "Child Labor: The Role of Financial Development and Income Variability across Countries." *Economic Development & Cultural Change* 53, no. 4 (July 2005): 913–32.

This cross-country study evaluates whether, over a thirty-five-year period, child labor has diminished as a result of economic growth and what is the best intervention policy with regard to child labor in the event of market failure.

French, J. Lawrence, and Richard E. Wokutch. "Child Workers, Globalization, and International Business Ethics: A Case Study in Brazil's Export-oriented Shoe Industry." *Business Ethics Quarterly* 15, no. 4 (October 2005): 615–40.

An examination of the shoe industry in Brazil and its employment of children, where local employers and children view their labor as benign, while the U.S. government sees it as hazardous to children and unfair to U.S. producers. It concludes that the removal of hazards from the industry may be ethically superior to removing child labor.

Kis-Katos, Krisztina, and Günther G. Schulze. "Regulation of Child Labour." *Economic Affairs* 25, no. 3 (September 2005): 24–30.

This is a discussion of employment of children in developing countries concluding that it is better for policies to address the causes of child labor than to try to regulate it.

Munilla, Linda S. and Morgan P. Miles. "The Corporate Social Responsibility Continuum as a Component of Stakeholder Theory." *Business & Society Review* 110, no. 4 (2005): 371–87.

This examines the impact of various corporate social responsibility issues, including child labor, on the development of corporate policy.

Schrage, Elliot J., and Anthony P. Ewing. "The Cocoa Industry and Child Labour." *Journal of Corporate Citizenship*, no. 18 (2005): 99–112.

This reviews the exposure of child labor in the cocoa industry and evaluates the strength of the industry's executives' various responses.

Watson, Elaine. "Chocolate firms act to give cocoa trade an ethical face." *Food Manufacture* 80, no. 8 (August 2005): 11.

This trade magazine describes a certification scheme that is being funded by the cocoa industry to provide a guarantee to consumers that the worst forms of child labor in the industry have not been used.

If you are more interested in the broad economic implications of child labor by big business in poor countries, a more fruitful periodical index would be *EconLit*, which covers the scholarly journals and working papers in the field of economics. *EconLit* is the electronic version of the indexing originally done for *JEL: Journal of Economic Literature*. This indexing includes a classification scheme, which economic researchers carry over into many other works they produce, such as the series *Handbooks in Economics* published by Elsevier that includes the *Handbook of Labor Economics*. Each entry therein includes a JEL classification code, useful for those in the know. J820 covers articles on "Labor Standards: National and International: Labor Force Composition" (child labor, prison labor, bonded labor, immigrant labor, migrant workers, and racial and gender discrimination). You can find this JEL classification scheme online at http://www.econlit.org/subject_descriptors.html#J. *EconLit* indexes articles in 750 journals, books reviewed in JEL, and working papers included in *RePEc Project: Research Papers in Economics*, with links to the full text of many of the working papers. These articles and papers demonstrate the importance of statistics to economic research and methodology. Besides searching by the JEL classification J820 you can also search using keywords like *child labor*, either of which turns up studies like the following:

Ali Khan, Rana Ejaz. "Children in Different Activities: Child Schooling and Child Labour." *Pakistan Development Review* 42, no. 2 (Summer 2003): 137–60.
     Based on analysis of data from two areas of Pakistan, this article finds that the education of the parents, especially of the mother, as well as whether the child is female, encourages schooling over labor by children. Other school-supporting determinants are family assets, small family size, and urban rather than rural location.
Basu, Kaushik, and Zafiris Tzannatos. "The Global Child Labor Problem: What Do We Know and What Can We Do?" *World Bank Economic Review* 17, no. 2 (2003): 147–73.
     In view of the global nature and concern with child labor, this examines our empirical and theoretical understanding of the problem. A review of recent literature, this also discusses broad policy implications.
Becchetti, Leonardo, and Giovanni Trovato. "The Determinants of Child Labour: The Role of Primary Product Specialization." *Labour* 19, no. 2 (June 2005): 237–71.
     This paper tests a model that demonstrates the complexity of modeling of household decision making in a global market.
Genicot, Garance. "Malnutrition and Child Labor." *Scandinavian Journal of Economics* 107, no. 1 (March 2005): 83–102.
     The author explains that because of intrahousehold altruism, where an increase in income of one family member means an increase in consumption by all members of the family, a strategy of employers to keep the productivity benefits

of increased pay to parents is to hire the children as well, which accounts for the higher incidence of family labor in poor societies.

Krueger, Dirk, and Jessica Tjornhom Donohue. "On the Distributional Consequences of Child Labor Legislation." *International Economic Review* 46, no. 3 (August 2005): 785–815.

This model shows that asset-wealthy households lose from government intervention to prevent child labor, high-wage workers benefit most from a ban on child labor, and low-wage workers benefit most from free education for children, with substantial welfare gains.

Mookerjee, Rajen, and Annalisa Orlandi. "Multinational Corporations and Child Labor." *Global Economic Review* 33, no. 4 (2004): 1–13.

This forty-country sample shows that the impact of multinational corporations' (MNCs') presence on child labor incidence is beneficial, probably because of MNC pressure on host country subcontractors, on governments, and on labor markets in general.

Vasavi, A. R., and Archana Mehendale. "Out-of-School Children: Contexts and Experiences of Education Deprivation." *Journal of Educational Planning & Administration* 17, no. 1 (January 2003): 69–84.

This examines reasons for out-of-school children, the causes and conditions, and what should be done to alleviate the problem.

Statistical Sources

As demonstrated in the previous articles on economics research, statistics provide the backbone and underpinning for developing models to predict how decisions will be made, and for testing whether theory, when applied, works as expected.

Statistical resources abound, although to get the data on children is often more difficult. International statistics are usually gathered by international organizations like the United Nations and its many divisions, for example, UNICEF. The UN Convention on the Rights of the Child 1989 created broad interest in the study of children. One segment of the convention strove to eliminate child labor. Even though the United States has not ratified this convention, the U.S. Department of Labor has gathered statistics to measure the extent of the problem and any progress made toward that end. Many of these statistical sources are now available from the U.S. Department of Labor's Bureau of International Labor Affairs and its office of the International Child Labor Program, online, free of charge at www.dol.gov/ilab. Some of the same and others are also in print and available in large research libraries. Examples of some of these print statistical resources are as follows:

Kaul, Chandrika. *Statistical Handbook on the World's Children*. Westport, Conn.: Oryx, 2002.

This includes statistics on education, health, family and social environment, dangers, as well as economic data on poverty, working age, children's workplaces, and the size of the child workforce, distribution of child labor, and youth unemployment. These statistics are pulled from a wide array of sources, like the World Bank's World Development Indicators and the ILO.

Every Child Counts: New Global Estimates on Child Labour. Geneva: International Labour Office, April, 2002 (www.dol.gov/ilab).
This report details number of children by age group, gender, region, and hazardous nature of the work, with comparison to the ILO data from six years earlier.

Statistical data available on the Web is extensive, and can be found by searching through the major economics research guide sites for data sources (see section above on Handbooks and Research Guides), and by culling through the sites of the organizations concerned with children (see article on Web resources for Children and Childhood Studies in this volume), and sites on labor in general.

Finding Resources on the Internet

Searching the World Wide Web for additional resources can also be useful, although one must be cautious of the source of the information and be careful to evaluate a site's accuracy and point of view for bias. Google and its offshoot, Google Scholar, for example, may return very different products. Also, links that are brought up in such searches may not be current, particularly relevant, or easily accessible. I would recommend students use "known" and "authoritative" Web sources. For example a major site that is useful specifically for child labor is Labordoc (labordoc.ilo.org). This is the catalog of the ILO, which includes books, reports, articles, and working papers, all related to labor. It includes links to any full text available free, and necessary citation data for finding items or requesting them from elsewhere via interlibrary loan. *Child labor* as a search term brings up over 10,000 items, so you would be wise to combine that with a narrower aspect of your research topic like *education* or *cocoa industry*.

Please see chapters 11 and 12 in this book that discuss U.S. government resources and World Wide Web resources. Also consult any Web guides that are available at your college or university library.

NOTES

1. David N. Hyman, *Microeconomics*, 3rd ed. (Burr Ridge, Ill.: Irwin, 1994), 9.
2. William J. Baumol and Alan S. Blinder, *Macroeconomics: Principles and Policy*, 7th ed. (Fort Worth, Tex: Dryden, 1998), 8.

3. Helen Penn, *Unequal Childhoods:Young Children's Lives in Poor Countries* (London: Routledge, 2005), 187.

4. Steven G. Medema and Warren J. Samuels, *Foundations of Research in Economics: How Do Economists Do Economics?* (Cheltenham, UK: Edward Elgar, 1996), 261.

5. Ellen Schrumpf, "Child Labor in the West," in *Encyclopedia of Children and Childhood: In History and Society*, ed. Paula S. Fass (New York: Macmillan Reference, 2004), 159.

6. Ana Cristina Dubeux Dourado and Tobias Hecht, "Brazil," and Elizabeth Anne Kuznesof, "Latin America: Overview," in *Encyclopedia of Children and Childhood: In History and Society*, ed. Paula S. Fass (New York: Macmillan Reference, 2004), 114–17 and 530–32.

7. Gary Cross, "Economics and Children in Western Societies," in *Encyclopedia of Children and Childhood: In History and Society*, ed. Paula S. Fass (New York: Macmillan Reference, 2004), 300.

8. Mark Hunter, "Globalization," in *Encyclopedia of Children and Childhood: In History and Society*, ed. Paula S. Fass (New York: Macmillan Reference, 2004), 390–92.

9. Ken Follett, *Pillars of the Earth* (New York: Morrow, 1989), 27.

WORKS CITED

Baumol, William J., and Alan S. Blinder. *Macroeconomics: Principles and Policy*. 7th ed. Fort Worth, Tex.: Dryden, 1998.

Dourado, Ana Cristina Dubeux, and Tobias Hecht. "Brazil." In *Encyclopedia of Children and Childhood: In History and Society*, edited by Paula S. Fass, 114–17. New York: Macmillan Reference, 2004.

Follett, Ken. *The Pillars of the Earth*. New York: Morrow, 1989.

Hunter, Mark. "Globalization." In *Encyclopedia of Children and Childhood: In History and Society*, edited by Paula S. Fass, 390–92. New York: Macmillan Reference, 2004.

Hyman, David N. *Microeconomics*. 3rd ed. Burr Ridge, Ill.: Irwin, 1994.

Kuznesof, Elizabeth Anne. "Latin America: Overview." In *Encyclopedia of Children and Childhood: In History and Society*, edited by Paula S. Fass, 530–32. New York: Macmillan Reference, 2004.

Levine, Gary, and Gary Cross. "Economics and Children in Western Societies." In *Encyclopedia of Children and Childhood: In History and Society*, edited by Paula S. Fass, 295–302. New York: Macmillan Reference, 2004.

Medema, Steven G., and Warren J. Samuels, eds. *Foundations of Research in Economics: How Do Economists Do Economics?* Cheltenham, UK: Edward Elgar, 1996.

Penn, Helen. *Unequal Childhoods:Young Children's Lives in Poor Countries*. London: Routledge, 2005.

Schrumpf, Ellen. "Child Labor in the West." In *Encyclopedia of Children and Childhood: In History and Society*, edited by Paula S. Fass, 159–62. New York: Macmillan Reference, 2004.

6

EDUCATION

Amy L. Masko

Education is an interdisciplinary field, combining theories and ideas from psychology, sociology, philosophy, linguistics, and the content disciplines (science, math, history, English, etc.). The nature of learning and teaching are so complex that new knowledge is continually being integrated into and challenging previous knowledge from these various disciplines as well as from the interdisciplinary perspective of educational scholars to further inform the field.

Because of the field's inherent complexity, as well as the variability of research participants, educational research sometimes produces contradictory findings;[1] in many cases new knowledge opposes previous knowledge, and concurrent studies may yield conflicting findings. For example, there are studies that provide competing evidence of the effectiveness of placing children in ability groups and tracked classes. There is research that supports this pedagogy[2] and research that challenges it.[3] Educational research is not foolproof primarily because no human scientific research is foolproof. Research participants, in this case children and teachers, are highly variable. Children's learning is variable, so some children may excel in ability groups and others may thrive in heterogeneous groups. One way that researchers try to control for variability among participants is by employing consistent research methods when conducting research. However, even highly controlled scientific laboratories and carefully crafted scientific measures cannot control for the variability of human beings, which is another reason that educational research is sometimes contradictory. The problem of contradiction between research findings

> is not a problem unique to education or the social sciences. Economists battle over whether lowering taxes stimulates the economy more than it

increases deficits, and each side offers evidence. In medicine, cancer researchers give competing interpretations of studies on the efficacy of different kinds of mastectomies, and therefore of the value of alternative treatments.[4]

It is also important to note that sometimes "research accumulates slowly, and what may seem contradictory now may coalesce in time."[5] For these reasons, I caution you to recognize that research in our field is messy. There is no one best way to teach every child, just as there is no one way that every child learns best. As teachers and researchers, we make informed decisions about how best to teach children, and our decisions are based in large part on educational research.

There is a further complication to educational research, another ingredient that increases the potential for contradiction: Not only are human beings variable, but scholars conduct research within certain theoretical frameworks and through their own predispositions of how they view the world. Researchers, of course, collect and analyze data as objectively as possible, but we need to recognize that they work through their own lens. That lens may be supplied by their disciplinary field (e.g., psychology) or by a specific ideology to which the researcher subscribes (e.g., progressivism, postmodernism, feminism). Researchers make judgments about their findings that they hope will inform the field. However, it is the responsibility of the consumer of educational research (policy makers, teachers, administrators) to make reasoned judgments, as well. We need to be critical consumers of research and make our best judgments about how to most effectively educate children. We also need to recognize that those judgments can—and should—change as new knowledge continues to inform the field.

In the next section I discuss the purpose and process of educational research and describe quantitative and qualitative methodologies. Having an awareness of various research methodologies can help us interpret, evaluate, and apply the results of educational research. Finally, I include a list of scholarly texts that address important developments, both historical and current, in the field of education.

OVERVIEW OF SCHOLARLY WRITING IN EDUCATION

Educational research adds to our knowledge about issues on several different levels and often in multiple ways. According to Creswell,[6] educational research has three foundational purposes: (1) to add to knowledge about educational issues, (2) to improve practice, and (3) to inform policy. The following example shows how research on the best way to teach children to read meets these three purposes. It is important to note that reading methods are complex, but are presented here in a concise—perhaps over-simplified—form in order to demonstrate how educational research has informed the field in theory, practice, and policy.

Through multiple research studies, we have reached a general agreement in the field[7] that the interactive model (also known as the balanced literacy approach), which teaches children comprehension and phonics skills through literature-rich environments, is likely to be the most effective and most efficient way to teach reading. Prior to this general agreement, there was what has been dubbed the "reading wars" in education. In the 1980s the whole language approach, which teaches children to read through exposing children to literature-rich environments and focusing on comprehension of text over phonics instruction, was very popular. This method, along with the phonics-first approach, which teaches children to read through letter–sound correspondence, was the matter of the so-called reading wars. Whole language is a student-centered progressive method for teaching reading, while the phonics-first approach is teacher-centered and would be classified within the traditional paradigm of education. Research exists to support each of these two dichotomous methods of teaching reading, as does research that challenges these methods.[8] Collectively, these research studies have demonstrated that some children thrive in progressive whole language classrooms and some children best learn to read through traditional phonics instruction.

> Since children differ in their motivations, interests, and backgrounds, and learn at different speeds in different subjects, there will never be a victory for either progressive or traditional teaching and learning. The fact is that no single best way for teachers to teach or children to learn can fit all situations. Both traditional and progressive ways of teaching and learning need to be part of a school's approach to children.[9]

Because there is sound research that supports and challenges each of these methods of teaching reading, a third, hybrid model—the balanced literacy approach—is currently touted as a best practice and most commonly used in classrooms today. As Cuban states, "Smart teachers and principals have carefully constructed hybrid classrooms and schools that reflect the diversities of children."[10] Balanced literacy is an example of a hybrid method.

These changes in the way that schools teach reading are reflective of the research conducted to investigate these models. In this example, research added knowledge about educational issues and teachers used this information to improve their practice. Now, let us examine how this same research informed policy decisions.

In 1983 when the whole language approach was very common, the official definition of reading adopted by the Michigan Department of Education was, "Reading is the process of constructing meaning through the dynamic interaction among the reader's existing knowledge, the information suggested by the written language, and the context of the reading situation."[11] You can see how this definition was influenced by whole language philosophy. The reader's existing knowledge is at the forefront of the definition, placing its value over anything else, which is consistent with whole language values. Over two decades later, this is still the official definition of reading in Michigan, but the manner in which reading is taught in schools has changed. The state standards call for more emphasis on phonics instruction as a skill and process to help children to decode unknown words. This reflects the trend in Michigan classrooms to teach reading using the interactive model, which supports direct phonics instruction within the context of a literature-rich curriculum.

Currently, there is general agreement in the field of education about how best to teach reading, and this is reflected in both practice and policy. However, this does not mean that research into teaching reading has come to a halt, nor should it. Scholars continue to conduct research to evaluate the effectiveness of the interactive model, and many are still studying and perfecting whole language and phonics-first methods. There has also been more nuanced research that has examined reading and writing instruction within certain learning contexts, such as with English language learners[12] or with African American pupils.[13] Delpit challenged the more progressive approach of whole language from the perspective of traditional African American teachers through her ethnographic research.[14] Her research prompted further studies to examine the cultural contexts of learning, which further informed the field and brought about changes in practice. The transactional model of reading instruction is an elaboration of the interactive model (balanced literacy) in that it teaches reading through both comprehension and phonics, but it also takes into consideration the social and situational context of the reader.[15] The situational context of the learner can include their culture, their primary language spoken at home, their community, and their background experiences. This context informs how readers process text, and the transactional model suggests that teaching is adjusted to consider all of these elements that the child brings with them to the reading experience. This is another example of how research continues to inform practice, as well as an example of its cyclical nature, which is discussed in the next section.

RESEARCH METHODS IN THE FIELD OF EDUCATION

All educational research, whether qualitative or quantitative, engages specific steps of inquiry to answer a specific research question. Creswell defines educational research as

> a cyclical process of steps that typically begins with identifying a research problem or issue of study. It then involves reviewing the literature, specifying a purpose for the study, collecting and analyzing data, and forming an interpretation of the information. This process culminates in a report, disseminated to audiences, that is evaluated and used in the educational community.[16]

It is a cyclical process because as the researcher reviews the literature, the information learned sometimes sharpens the question. As the researcher begins data analysis, sometimes he or she realizes that more data must be collected to clarify some of the analysis. And when the research report is written, the author and the reader often discover that more inquiry is needed to probe more deeply into the original research question. Typically there is a final section within a written research report (such as a published journal article) that discusses the implications of the research. In this section, the researcher often gives suggestion for further research, either calling for new studies to address new questions that were raised with the research or a discussion of the study's limitations along with suggestions to better or more fully answer the question the researcher posed.

Creswell identifies six specific steps in the research process: (1) identify a research problem, (2) review the literature that is relevant to the problem, (3) specify a purpose for conducting the research, (4) collect the data, (5) analyze the data, and (6) report and evaluate the research.[17] These six steps provide a general framework for educational inquiry that helps to make a research study manageable, but also ensure a thorough investigation.[18] As you read a study, you can usually identify these six steps in the various subsections. For example, the author typically identifies a purpose for the research in the introduction and discusses how he or she collected data in the methods section. While this is a general framework, all educational research should employ a systematic method for collecting and analyzing data, which is typically based on the scientific method.

The type of methodology used to conduct an educational inquiry depends entirely on the type of question you want to pose. If you want to know the answer to a narrow, specific question that explains trends or relationships among variables, quantitative methodology will best answer the question. If you are interested in seeking to explore a central phenomenon, then you will want to utilize qualitative methodology. Both of these methods are described below.

Quantitative Methodology

In quantitative research, the purpose of inquiry is to answer a research question by gathering measurable data. First a hypothesis is formulated and then the researcher goes about trying to support or disprove the hypothesis. Data collection involves gathering numeric data (e.g., survey results or scores on educational assessments) from a large number of individuals, usually selected at random, and then analyzing this data with mathematical procedures, typically through statistics. The analysis describes trends or relationships among variables. The interpretation of the results is compared with past research as well as the hypothesis. Researchers take an objective and unbiased role in the research report, removing themselves as completely as possible. The report follows a very specific form: an introduction, literature review, explanation of the methods, the results, and discussion.[19]

Quantitative research employs several different designs, depending on the type of research problem posed. I am going to discuss experimental or quasi-experimental, correlational, or survey designs. Experimental or quasi-experimental designs test the impact of an intervention on an outcome for research participants. This type of design utilizes experimental and control groups, and the outcomes of the two groups are measured. For example, a researcher may implement a specific curriculum (the intervention) in a third-grade class and measure the students' learning through a standardized test. The researcher would choose a control group, likely another third-grade class within the same building, who would not use the curriculum, but would be tested on the same standardized measure. The test results of the two groups would then be compared to determine if the curriculum had any impact on the experimental class.

Correlational design uses a statistical technique that measures the degree of an association between and among variables or sets of data. For example, is there a relationship between length of school day and academic achievement, as measured by a standardized test? Is there a relationship between cooperative learning groups and the number of disciplinary actions in a middle school? A researcher would collect data on these two variables and then apply a statistical test to the data to answer the question. School A had 45% of their students reading at grade level before implementing an extended school day. After implementing the change, 59% of their students were reading at grade level. Researchers compare that data, while statistically controlling for any other change, such as a new teacher, a new curriculum, and increased parental involvement. They isolate specific variables to look for a degree of association.

Survey designs measure trends among the population. Researchers administer a survey to an entire population or a sample of a population to examine trends. For example, a state may conduct a survey of how parents perceive a state-sponsored school initiative.

All of these quantitative designs seek to either describe trends (e.g., standardized test scores over time) or explain relationships among variables (e.g., standardized test scores and socioeconomic status of the children taking the test). You can see how all of the designs examine specific and narrowly defined research questions by gathering and mathematically analyzing measurable data.

Qualitative Methodology

Qualitative research seeks to explore and understand a central phenomenon, typically through participants' experiences. Researchers conduct fieldwork, where they gather data, which consist of collecting artifacts (e.g., samples of student work, school communication) and conducting interviews and observations. These data are recorded as fieldnotes. Data analysis consists of text analysis, where researchers typically describe their data and develop themes from the artifacts and their fieldnotes. Results are interpreted by situating the findings within the larger, more abstract meanings.[20] Research reports are typically more flexible than the format used for quantitative research studies, due to the fact that the qualitative design is constructivist[21] and emergent in nature and the written report is typically told through narrative participant stories. The reports are typically written in first person, and the researcher identifies and discusses his or her role within the context of the research, identifying his or her biases. This is referred to as reflexivity.

While a quantitative study may examine standardized test scores, a qualitative study may examine the experiences of the children, teachers, and administrators in the climate of high stakes testing. The qualitative researcher may be concerned with how the children cope with stress during prolonged testing periods, for example, or how teachers' pedagogical practices affect the children's attitudes toward testing. These questions require a different kind of data collection and a different kind of analysis than quantitative methodology can support. Data consist of observational notes, artifacts, and interviews.

The researcher looks for common themes within the text and categorizes and codes these data. In the research report, raw data (e.g., participant quotes or excerpts of fieldnotes) is included to support a described theme.

Like quantitative methodology, qualitative research has various designs. I am going to briefly discuss grounded theory, ethnography, and narrative. The researcher determines which design will best answer the research question. Grounded theory designs employ systematic procedures that researchers use to generate a broad conceptual theory that explains a process, action, or interaction about a topic that a number of individuals have all experienced.[22] The theory must be grounded in the experiences of the participants. The researcher collects interview data to look for themes and composes a visual figure that represents the theory.

Ethnography, typically associated with anthropology, is the study of a cultural group. A cultural group is not limited to an ethnic or a national culture, but is defined as any group that has a shared set of norms. In educational ethnography, a cultural group may be nontenured teachers, children attending urban schools, or administrators of a school district experiencing significant school reform. All of those groups share a common cultural or social experience. Ethnographers spend prolonged time in the field (sometimes several years) conducting fieldwork in order to provide a portrait of this shared cultural group's norms and behaviors.

Narrative research designs also describe the lives of individuals, but not necessarily group behaviors or collective experiences. Researchers collect data that describe the lives of individuals and tell their stories in narrative form. Qualitative research is grounded in the participants' experiences and contexts. This type of inquiry is complex and is concerned with providing rich data, gathered through naturalistic settings and usually over a prolonged period of time.

Mixed Method Designs

Increasingly, qualitative data, which provide rich contextual stories, and quantitative data, which provide statistical trends and relationships, are combined in ways to provide researchers the opportunity to explore and explain educational problems in a different way. In mixed method studies, the researcher decides a priori the weight or value of each form of data and the sequence in which it will be collected.[23] A common mixed method design used in schools is action research.

Action research combines both quantitative (e.g., students' reading scores) and qualitative (e.g., students' reading behaviors) data to explore a practical classroom problem (e.g., how to engage students in small reading groups in order to improve their reading abilities). The purpose of action research is practical: to improve one's own practice or to solve a local, practical problem, such as the effectiveness of a new district curriculum, for instance. Another important purpose is to empower teachers to make informed decisions about their instructional practices based on a systematic study of their own classrooms. Typically teachers conduct action research projects within their own classrooms to explore their own teaching and their students' learning. They collect data by taking observational notes on student behaviors, their own teaching and the classroom climate. They may interview children to obtain an insider perspective of how the student perceives the curriculum or how the children solved a problem, for example. They may administer an assessment or a survey to collect quantitative data about the students, or may collect standardized test scores. All of these data are analyzed to lead the teacher to make decisions about instructional practices within his or her classroom. These decisions can be described as an action plan. Sometimes the action research project is composed in a formal report for the district or an article for an educational journal, and other times no report is produced. The product is often simply a change the teacher makes to his or her own practice.

Action research empowers teachers to be agents of change. "This vision is not of passive teachers who perpetuate the system as it is, but of teachers who see how the system can be changed through their research."[24] Through conducting classroom research, teachers make curricular and pedagogical decisions that are based on their own naturalistic inquiry.

Educational research—quantitative, qualitative, and mixed methods—follows a specific set of procedures that helps ensure a thorough and manageable investigation into an educational problem. All three of the methodologies I have described support the three main purposes of educational research—to add knowledge about educational issues, to improve practice and to inform policy decisions.

ANNOTATED BIBLIOGRAPHY OF RESOURCES IN THE FIELD

There are numerous publications that reflect the current and historical thoughts in the field. There are publications that reflect the controversies of educating children that have ensued over the years and works that reflect the varying ideologies representing the best thinking and the interdisciplinary nature of the field. These publications are too numerous to list in one chapter. I have chosen books that are important to the profession of education, that are most appropriate to the field of Child and Childhood Studies, and that reflect a wide range of ideas about teaching and learning. While I attempted to include a range of works, I caution you that, just as researchers work through their own perspective, I have crafted this bibliography through my own lens, which is informed by my experience, ideology, and education.

Bennett, Kathleen P., and Margaret D. LeCompte. *The Way Schools Work: A Sociological Analysis of Education*. New York: Longman, 1990.

This text provides a sociological perspective of the processes of schooling. The authors discuss the sociology of schools, defined as the study of groups of people within educational institutions, from contemporary and historical contexts. The book contains an overview of the purposes of schooling, a discussion of the social organization of schools, children and youth culture, teachers and administrators, and the curriculum. It also discusses issues central to sociology—social class, ethnic minorities, and gender and their relation to schools.

Bruner, Jerome. *The Process of Education*. Cambridge: Harvard University Press, 1960.

First published in 1960, Jerome Bruner's work has been seminal in shaping school curriculum. Bruner, a Harvard psychologist, put forth a theory that curriculum should be spiraled, with concepts from science and humanities taught to children at very young ages, which then can later be taught in more abstract and sophisticated ways. This model suggests that knowledge, taught through structured subjects, builds upon previous knowledge that is obtained through readiness, intuition, and motivation of the young learner. Bruner's work was the first argument for a spiral curriculum, which we see evidence of in public schools today.

Connelly, F. Michael, and D. Jean Clandinin. *Teachers as Curriculum Planners: Narratives of Experience*. New York: Teachers College Press, 1988.

Through a longitudinal, qualitative inquiry, Connelly and Clandinin place teachers' experiences with teaching and learning at the heart of our understanding of curriculum. They discuss "personal practical knowledge" of teachers in order to talk about teachers as knowledgeable and knowing. Through this text, teachers' experiences are honored and the field is informed by their stories. At the time of publication, qualitative inquiry was not as commonplace in the field as it is today. This book made important strides to legitimize qualitative, narrative inquiry in educational research.

Dewey, John. *Experience and Education*. New York: Simon & Schuster, 1938.

John Dewey is a paramount educational scholar, and this text is a concise description of his ideas of a democratic, progressive education. This is likely because it is a book written in response to the criticism his theories received, and after he developed his progressive laboratory school. It reflects how his educational philosophy changed over time and through his experience of putting his theory of experience into practice at the laboratory school.

Eisner, Elliot W. *The Educational Imagination: On the Design and Evaluation of School Programs*. New York: MacMillan College, 1994.

This text offers a comprehensive overview of educational reform, curriculum theories and ideologies, teaching, and evaluation in both current educational contexts and from an historical perspective. Eisner challenges educators to critique prevailing practices in education and their underlying assumptions about teaching, learning, and evaluation, and to recognize that there is no one educational practice that will meet the needs of all children in all contexts. He frames his discussions within an artistic paradigm, arguing artistry is inherent in teaching and against the efforts to make it a scientific endeavor. In this text, he discusses his research methodology of educational criticism and connoisseurship, an alternative to the natural science model typically used in educational research and comparable to the work of critics and connoisseurs of art.

Gardner, Howard. *Frames of Mind: The Theory of Multiple Intelligences*. New York: Basic Books, 1983.

This 1983 text challenges the way intelligence is defined. Gardner puts forth his theory that intelligence is not one thing, *g factor*, as described by many psychologists and measured by IQ tests, but instead seven multiple intelligences. His theory greatly influenced classroom instruction, as teachers incorporated his ideas into their curriculum and pedagogy. In response to that influence, ten years later, Gardner wrote *Multiple Intelligences: The Theory in Practice* that discusses the educational implications of his psychological theory.

Hirsch, E. D. *Cultural Literacy: What Every American Needs to Know*. New York: Vintage, 1988.

This text is often at the heart of educational debate about the content of American school curriculum. What should schools teach? Hirsch provides a list that he describes as a descriptive list of what literate Americans should know. He argues that his list will provide a national literacy in order to foster effective national communication, which will equalize our society by teaching the same national content to all Americans. Hirsch developed his traditional approach to education in response to his criticism of a progressive curriculum. Core Knowledge charter schools are established on his manifesto.

Ladson-Billings, Gloria. *The Dreamkeepers: Successful Teachers of African American Children*. San Francisco: Jossey-Bass, 1994.

Ladson-Billings's book is a significant text in the field of multicultural education, in part because it goes beyond looking at multicultural curriculum and describes dedicated, committed, exemplary teachers' pedagogical practice. The achievement gap between African American and white students is an issue in American schools and this book sheds light on the problem and offers solutions through the narratives of eight teachers.

Noddings, Nel. *The Challenge to Care in Schools: An Alternative Approach to Education*. New York: Teachers College Press, 1992.

This book builds on Noddings's work in feminist theory in education, and challenges the academic liberal arts focus of American schools. She suggests that the curriculum should be a moral one, nurturing the growth of caring and loving individuals. Noddings encourages the reader to imagine schools as one large heterogeneous family and poses ways to educate that family in diverse ways, with care at the center of the curriculum. She argues that schools need to care for individual children and to teach children to care about things (themselves, others, animals, the environment—both natural and human-made, and ideas). This book argues for both a moral curriculum and a moral purpose to schools, which she argues is sorely lacking in our current system.

Tyack, David, and Larry Cuban. *Tinkering toward Utopia: A Century of Public School Reform.* Cambridge: Harvard University Press, 1996.

Tyack and Cuban's book provides an historical overview of reform efforts of the past 100 years and an explanation of how the public has viewed American public schools over the same period. It is helpful to put current reform efforts into an historical perspective of what has been expected of and what changes have been made in public schooling. The authors argue that reformers need to remember the democratic purposes of American public schools and that reform efforts may be best if they work from the inside—helping teachers to improve instruction.

NOTES

1. John W. Creswell, *Educational Research: Planning, Conducting, and Evaluating Quantitative and Qualitative Research* (Upper Saddle River, N.J.: Merrill Prentice Hall, 2002); Lee S. Shulman, "Seek Simplicity . . . And Distrust It," *Education Week* 24, no. 39 (2005): 36, 48.

2. Camilla Persson Benbow and Julian C. Stanley, "Inequity in Equity: How 'Equity' Can Lead to Inequity in High Potential Students," *Mensa Research Journal* 40 (1998): 6–52; Karen B. Rogers, "Grouping the Gifted and Talented: Questions and Answers." *Roeper Review* 16 (1993): 8–12.

3. Jeannie Oakes, *Keeping Track: How Schools Structure Inequality* (New Haven, Conn.: Yale University Press, 1985).

4. Schulam, "Seek Simplicity," 6.

5. Creswell, *Educational Research*, 7.

6. Creswell, *Educational Research*.

7. Richard Vacca, "CRA [College Reading Association] and the World of Literacy: Retrospect and Prospect" (paper presented at the annual meeting of the College Reading Association, Boca Raton, Fla., October 2004).

8. William D. Bursuck, Dennis D. Munk, Cynthia Nelson, and Margaret Curran, "Research on the Prevention of Reading Problems: Are Kindergarten and First

Grade Teachers Listening?" *Preventing School Failure* 47, no. 1 (Fall 2002): 4–9. For an argument in support of whole language and a challenge to phonics-first instruction, see Stephen Krashen, "Defending Whole Language: The Limits of Phonics Instruction and the Efficacy of Whole Language Instruction," *Reading Improvement* 39, no. 1 (Spring 2002): 32–42.

9. Larry Cuban, "The Open Classroom," *Education Next* (Spring 2004), www .educationnext.org/20042/68.html (accessed November 14, 2005): 1.

10. Cuban, "Open Classroom."

11. Peggy Dutcher, "Authentic Reading Assessment." *Practical Assessment, Research & Evaluation* 2, no. 6 (1990). PAREonline.net/getvn.asp?v=2&n=6 (accessed November 9, 2005).

12. Stephen Krashen, "Bilingual Education and the Dropout Argument," *Discover* 4 (1998): 1–6.

13. Lisa Delpit, *Other People's Children: Cultural Conflict in the Classroom* (New York: New Press, 1995).

14. Delpit, *Other People's Children.*

15. D. Ray Reutzal and Robert B. Cooter, *Teaching Children to Read: Putting the Pieces Together* (Upper Saddle River, N.J.: Merrill, 2000).

16. Creswell, *Educational Research*, 8.

17. Creswell, *Educational Research.*

18. Creswell, *Educational Research.*

19. Creswell, *Educational Research.*

20. Creswell, *Educational Research.*

21. James H. McMillan and Sally Schumacher, *Research in Education* (New York: Addison, Wesley Longman, 2001).

22. Creswell, *Educational Research.*

23. Creswell, *Educational Research.*

24. Ruth Shagoury Hubbard and Brenda Miller Power, *The Art of Classroom Inquiry: A Handbook for Teacher-Researchers* (Portsmouth, N.H.: Heinemann, 1993).

WORKS CITED

Benbow, Camilla Persson, and Julian C. Stanley. "Inequity in Equity: How 'Equity' Can Lead to Inequity in High Potential Students." *Mensa Research Journal* 40 (1998): 6–52.

Bursuck, William D., Dennis D. Munk, Cynthia Nelson, and Margaret Curran. "Research on the Prevention of Reading Problems: Are Kindergarten and First Grade Teachers Listening?" *Preventing School Failure* 47, no. 1 (Fall 2002): 4–9.

Creswell, John. W. *Educational Research: Planning, Conducting, and Evaluating Quantitative and Qualitative Research.* Upper Saddle River, N.J.: Merrill Prentice Hall, 2002.

———. *Qualitative Inquiry and Research Design: Choosing among Five Traditions.* Thousand Oaks, Calif.: Sage, 1998.

Cuban, Larry. "The Open Classroom." *Education Next* (Spring 2004). www.educationnext.org/20042/68.html (accessed November 14, 2005).

Delpit, Lisa. *Other People's Children: Cultural Conflict in the Classroom.* New York: New Press, 1995.

Dutcher, Peggy. "Authentic Reading Assessment." *Practical Assessment, Research & Evaluation* 2, no. 6 (1990). PAREonline.net/getvn.asp?v=2&n=6 (accessed November 9, 2005).

Hubbard, Ruth Shagoury, and Brenda Miller Power. *The Art of Classroom Inquiry: A Handbook for Teacher-Researchers.* Portsmouth, N.H.: Heinemann, 1993.

Krashen, Stephen. "Bilingual Education and the Dropout Argument." *Discover* 4 (1998): 1–6.

———. "Defending Whole Language: The Limits of Phonics Instruction and the Efficacy of Whole Language Instruction." *Reading Improvement* 39, no. 1 (Spring 2002): 32–42.

McMillan, James H., and Sally Schumacher. *Research in Education.* New York: Addison, Wesley Longman, 2001.

Oakes, Jeannie. *Keeping Track: How Schools Structure Inequality.* New Haven, Conn.: Yale University Press, 1985.

Reutzal, D. Ray, and Robert B. Cooter. *Teaching Children to Read: Putting the Pieces Together.* Upper Saddle River, N.J.: Merrill, 2000.

Rogers, Karen B. (1993). "Grouping the Gifted and Talented: Questions and Answers." *Roeper Review* 16 (1993): 8–12.

Schulman, Lee S. "Seek Simplicity . . . And Distrust It." *Education Week* 24, no. 39 (2005): 36, 48.

Vacca, Richard. "CRA [College Reading Association] and the World of Literacy: Retrospect and Prospect." Paper presented at the annual meeting of the College Reading Association, Boca Raton, Fla., October 2004.

7

ENGLISH

Holly Blackford

"You know that little piece of land across the brook that runs up between our farm and Mr. Barry's. It belongs to Mr. William Bell, and right in the corner there is a little ring of white birch trees—the most romantic spot, Marilla. Diana and I have our playhouse there. We call it Idlewild. Isn't that a poetical name? I assure you it took me some time to think it out. I stayed awake nearly a whole night before I invented it. Then, just as I was dropping off to sleep, it came like an inspiration. Diana was *enraptured* when she heard it. . . . The fairy glass [we have in it] is as lovely as a dream. Diana found it out in the wood behind their chicken house. It's all full of rainbows— just little young rainbows that haven't grown big yet—and Diane's mother told her it was broken off a hanging lamp they once had. But it's nicer to imagine the fairies lost it one night when they had a ball, so we call it the fairy glass."

—Anne, of *Anne of Green Gables*[1]

As the internationally beloved character of Anne demonstrates, and as any fans of *Harry Potter*[2] will tell you, language is a magic wand. Wave it around and it transfigures everything. By mastering a "poetical" command of language, the child can transform her environment and her relationship to it. Readers and writers of imaginative literature have identified with Anne since her inception in 1908. It makes a difference if you call an object fairy glass rather than a broken piece of lamp. Consider *Idlewild*. It is a "poetical" name with an appealing and symmetrical assonance, a balanced repetition of the unusual and leisurely-sounding long "i" sound. "I-dle wi-ld" opens then relaxes the mouth just like the name opens the reader to a vision of being idle (skipping out on chores, e.g.) and wild at the same time. Anne has a talent for transforming her environment with her linguistic imagination, which is what writers of literature do for us all. In fact, classic literature, particularly works written for children, has a way of becoming indistinct from the environment of childhood. Sometimes, people remember the stories that influenced them as children more than the actual environment in which they lived.

Anne's propensity for shaping her environment with discourse symbolizes the object of study for literary critics who engage in childhood studies. They study the way in which language *shapes* children's environments and our understanding of childhood. In chapter 1 Bowman and Spencer use the parable of "The Blind Men and The Elephant" to illustrate the difficulty of description, given the descriptive tools that scholars bring to the study of phenomena. One interpreter of the elephant may compare it to a pot, while another may compare it to a fan. The literary critic would actually say that there is *no* elephant apart from the language used to describe it. The elephant is thus a text that the "reader" interprets through the application of words, sentences, stories, and the cultural meanings attached to them. The literary critic would maintain that language, and the stories we tell with it, constructs and shapes the elephant. We cannot recognize the elephant without language, which is the only means by which we can actually see that there is an elephant standing before us. "Fairy glass" and "broken piece of lamp" denote entirely different objects—though both may be composed of the same atoms—to a scientist.

The study of childhood from the perspective of an English scholar is less concerned with the biological and physical child that exists in the world, and more concerned with the child as a textual construct—as something invented by discourse that positions and denotes what we understand to be a child. The English scholar studies the discourses, languages, and ideologies that inform the way we view children and adolescents. If you are asked to study childhood and literature for or about children from an English perspective, then you are committed to explicating the language through which a particular notion of childhood is born, perpetuated, and challenged. Language and literature are actually sites of contestation, sites that work out the meaning of childhood and adolescence.

For example, Puritan Americans, in sermons and like treatises, often depicted the child as a kind of savage in need of education and redemption into the Godly task of reading the Bible, to be saved. On the other hand, Romantic poets saw in the child a kind of muse, understanding the child as naturally playful, poetic, inspirational, innocent, and closest to the divinity of nature. Scholars of literature and childhood explore these various ways that cultures think and talk about children, ways that presumably shape the lives of children at any given time. Childhood studies scholars from an English perspective might explicate the redemptive value of Little Eva in Harriet Beecher Stowe's 1852 *Uncle Tom's Cabin*, arguing that the sentimental child in that novel is a symbol for the purity of Christ who can redeem the souls of those involved in the sin of slavery.[3] The death of Little Eva, and the death of the character Little Nell in Charles Dickens's popular 1840–1841 serialized novel, *The Old Curiosity Shop*, signify important messages about the meaning of childhood in Victorian America and England.[4] The re-demptive or reform value of the child character becomes a *theme* for the scholar to study, a theme that circulates throughout popular stories that de-fine the character of the child and/or adolescent.

Childhood studies scholars often study the use to which the child is put in discourse—what cultural or political values are constructed "for the good of the child." Jacqueline Rose's book *The Case of Peter Pan: Or the Im-possibility of Children's Fiction*, is an excellent example of such a study.[5] She traces the reception of J. M. Barrie's 1904 play *Peter Pan* and investigates the way adults have used the text, suggesting that the play helped Edwardian culture understand childhood in a particular way.[6] Scholars studying texts in this way are responding to the groundbreaking work of childhood studies by Philippe Ariès, who, in *Centuries of Childhood*, argues that the concept of childhood as a distinct phase of life was gradually invented in the Middle Ages.[7] This does not mean that there have not always been little people called children, but it means that our modern conception of childhood as a special time of life was not always understood in the same way that it is understood now. Childhood is thus an ideological concept, produced at particular points of history by particular historical conditions, practices, and discourses.

Childhood studies scholars with an English background also explicate texts specifically produced for, or addressed to, children and adolescents. These texts are windows into the way a culture and specific authors wish to communicate with children, and what they wish to say. Sometimes a liter-ary text reproduces cultural values, such as in the British empire-building tradition of island narratives like Robert Louis Stevenson's 1883 *Treasure Is-land*;[8] but even though this novel serves as a narrative of empire, it also in-troduces a pirate villain in Long John Silver, who ironically breaks down the distinction between good and evil because he is a kind father figure to the fatherless teen Jim. A children's novel might overtly challenge a culture's values, such as the 1960 American novel *To Kill a Mockingbird*, by Harper

Lee, which challenges racial segregation in the South.[9] But even a text that challenges values, such as Lee's, may participate in other cultural values, such as class segregation. It is up to the scholar of childhood studies and children's literature to recognize the complexities of all texts and the cultural work that they perform.

CHILDREN'S LITERATURE AND CHILDHOOD STUDIES: AN INTERDISCIPLINARY INTERSECTION

Stevenson's *Treasure Island* was specifically produced for children, although enjoyed by adults and children, while Lee's novel was not specifically written for children, although it has become the province of children's literature through canonization and adoption by schools. These two texts illustrate the diversity of ways through which a canon of children's literature is formed. Children's literature can include texts produced for children, texts that adults have deemed appropriate for children (such as fairy tales), or texts that real children read (such as the works of Steven King, enjoyed by many teens and preteens). If most childhood studies scholars have trouble agreeing on the definition of a child, literature critics can also not agree on a definition of children's or adolescent literature. Many works become family fare, and many substantial novels are simplified and condensed for the enjoyment of children. For example, Shakespearean works have been adapted for children, Stowe's *Uncle Tom's Cabin* was enjoyed by Victorian children, and some works originally intended for children such as *Adventures of Huckleberry Finn*, published in 1885 by Mark Twain, have over time been thought of as more adult.[10]

Some critics maintain that the best children's literature is cross-audienced for adults and children. C. S. Lewis is famous for saying that any book that can be enjoyed at ten should also be rich enough to be enjoyed at fifty. Only today is the children's book market segmented by age, the result of the efforts of publishing houses. Any trip to the bookstore will reveal that publishers and today's authors think of children's books by developmental categories such as "early readers," "chapter books," "series for the middle-schoolers," "young adult section," etc. This developmental lens is a fairly recent trend in thinking about children's literature, and is less applicable to classic children's literature and even today's most popular children's books such as the *Harry Potter* series, although scholars such as Roberta Trites have used the latter to explore the difference between children's and adolescent literature.[11] The categorization of books by age is often inconsistent; Brian

Jacques's *Redwall* fantasy series is found in different places in different stores.[12] The student of children's literature should be aware of the diversity of ways such literature is categorized and comes to be called children's literature; the student of childhood studies should be aware of the constructed nature of such categories and should open himself or herself up to studying how various forces and institutions influence our understanding of childhood and children's literature.

Children's literature scholar Richard Flynn summarizes the kind of criticism encouraged by a childhood studies framework, which, he says, "examines the representation of children and childhood throughout literature and culture; analyzes the impact of the concept of 'childhood' on the life and experience of children past and present; investigates childhood as a temporal state that is often experienced more in memory than in actuality; explores childhood as a discursive category whose language may provide a potentially useful perspective from which to describe the human person and to understand subjectivity."[13] Discussing Tom Travisano's paper "The Case of Childhood Studies," presented in 1997, Flynn agrees with Travisano that "childhood studies is, in fact, being done all the time. And nowhere is it done more skillfully than by the scholars of children's literature whose primary concerns have included defining and historicizing representations of childhood and exploring childhood as a notion constructed by politics, rhetoric, and human institutions."[14] In other words, children's literature scholars have been just as interested in Louisa May Alcott's 1868 *Little Women* and Lewis Carroll's 1865 *Alice's Adventures in Wonderland* as they have been in the complex child characters of Nathaniel Hawthorne, D. H. Lawrence, and Henry James.[15] Scholars wish to understand both texts addressed to children and texts about children, to fully understand cultural images of childhood.

The Modern Language Association puts the field of children's literature in the umbrella category of "Interdisciplinary Approaches to Literature," for good reason. Kenneth Kidd, in his article "Children's Culture, Children's Studies, and the Ethnographic Imaginary," comments on the inherently interdisciplinary nature of children's literature scholarship:

> Children's literature, of course, has long been more eclectic and interdisciplinary than other academic specialists, perhaps necessarily so. Children's literature has often meant children's culture, embracing not only a diverse group of written texts but also oral narrative. Scholars in the field have been writing about film and television for quite a while, even if film and media theory is a more recent arrival. Scholars of children's literature already know quite a bit about children's work and children's play.[16]

And while this is true, Kidd says he also feels that the anthropological model of studying children as if they inhabit an "other" culture has its own problems. See his article for further exploration of this problem. Suffice to say here that children's literature is a cultural sharing between adults and children. Childhood studies scholars need to understand the exchange of cultural viewpoints embodied by literary texts and the meanings that different people, of different ages, derive from them.

If you were to actually gather a group of literary critics around the elephant, you would have a diverse range of responses to the question "What is the elephant?" English scholars study a great variety of cultural materials and deploy a great variety of lenses to explicate the meanings of cultural materials such as literature. Taken broadly, the study of English covers all discursive practices of an English-speaking culture. Since the advent of poststructuralism and cultural studies, English critics have regarded the entire terrain of semiotic and textual practices as appropriate areas of inquiry. Even advertisements deploy language to shape reality. For example, advertising the amount of milk in an individual slice of cheese taps into a culture's feelings about milk, nutrition, and mothers. Using a brand name associated with grandmothers to sell cookies taps into our cultural associations between grandmothers and homemade, tasty food. If you take a Childhood Studies course from an English perspective, you will probably encounter traditional scholars of literary study who look at the plots, themes, stylistics, tone, characters, and poetic images of children's literature and poetry. But you might also encounter scholars looking at nonfictional discourses such as diaries, periodicals, essays, religious tracts, political rhetoric, advertisements, and education materials such as primers. You might encounter professors lecturing on adaptations of literature into films, theater, toys, and other items of material culture—such as Disney's adaptation of fairy tales into an industry of materials, or the marketed industry of Anne of Green Gables in Canada.

As such, the range of discursive practices addressed to and deployed by children, and thus studied by English scholars of childhood, include all of the following areas (which may not be an exhaustive list):

- children's literature and historicity, including works written for children and those canonized for or read by children, as well as the ideological construction of childhood by literature and nonfiction texts
- children's folklore and poetry
- children's illustrations and picture books, including artistic contexts and influences

- children's film and animation
- children's theater, drama, and puppetry
- children's media, including radio, television, periodicals
- children's material culture, possibly including play and imagination theory
- creative writing for children, including adaptation (written, graphic, performative) of texts for children
- the publishing industry for children
- language acquisition and linguistics, including narrative development and literacy
- children's art and development
- children's software and gaming
- children's learning and educational methodology
- librarianship

These fields intersect with other disciplines such as psychology, sociology, education, art, theater, and even medicine, as the language of English and the nature of discourse cuts across all disciplines. In some sense, literature itself reflects the multidisciplinary nature of human experience, and language and the imagination infuse every facet of child development.

CRITICAL APPROACHES TO LITERATURE AND MATERIALS FOR RESEARCH

Children's literature and childhood studies critics utilize a great variety of approaches to understanding texts for and about children. Critics might variously focus on authors, historical and cultural contexts, themes and poetics of literary texts, issues of reception, and issues of adaptation. Most keep the study of the primary texts foremost in their writing. You can begin to understand the field by reading the pioneer series of three volumes titled *Touchstones: Reflections on the Best in Children's Literature*, edited by Perry Nodelman, which cover major authors and works.[17] These volumes signify the efforts of many children's literature scholars who sought to reverse the marginalization of children's literature in many English departments. Early children's literature critics sought to apply the tools of literary scholarship to children's literature in a way distinct from the use of children's books in Education departments and settings. Children's literature scholarship is thus distinct from the study of Education, although there is a dynamic relationship between the two since children's literature is used in schools to teach children literary understanding, reading, critical thinking, history, morality, and appreciation of culture. Children's literature scholars explicate the texts themselves while Education scholars and teachers of children may draw from these studies for curriculum development.

Scholars of children's literatures tend to think both aesthetically and historically about the diversity of genres and thematic traditions in the field. There are several excellent reference materials that survey prominent genres and traditions. In addition to general introductory texts such as Peter Hunt's *An Introduction to Children's Literature*, and similar works by Donna Norton and Saundra Norton, David Russell, Kimberley Reynolds, and Maria Nikolajeva, Peter Hunt's *International Companion Encyclopedia of Children's Literature* is a crucial reference material.[18] It contains introductory chapters on fairy and folk tales, myth and legend, playground rhymes and oral tradition, poetry, drama, illustrated texts and picture books, comic books and dime novels, religious writings, animal stories, domestic fantasy, high fantasy, science fiction, adventure, school stories, family stories, pony books, historical fiction, teen realism and problem novels, information books, and children's magazines. The *Encyclopedia* also features chapters on the production of children's literature, national traditions around the world, applications for teaching, and critical approaches to children's literature, including chapters on history and culture, ideology, linguistics and stylistics, reader-response criticism, psychoanalytical criticism, feminist criticism, and comparative intertextuality. These theoretical frameworks are important to the field of literature in general, adding to the complexity of the way in which scholars view the elephant of children's literature.

The student in this field would benefit from purchasing a glossary of literary terms that also includes definitions of major theoretical approaches. M. H. Abrams's *A Glossary of Literary Terms* is one such manual.[19] In it, you can look up traditional terms of literary study such as *symbol, character, genre, meter, stanza, narrator,* and whatnot, but also literary criticism. It is continually updated and is presently in its eighth edition. The sixth edition separates literary criticism from the rest of the glossary but in the seventh edition, you need to look up "literary criticism" in the index to review each major school of criticism, including the ones mentioned above and anxiety of influence, archetypal criticism, art for art's sake, the Chicago school of critics, contextual criticism, critics of consciousness, dialogic criticism, linguistics in modern criticism, New Criticism, new historicism, phenomenology, postcolonial studies, reader-response criticism, reception theory, rhetorical criticism, Russian formalism, semiotics, sociological criticism, speech act theory, structuralist criticism, and stylistics. See the latest edition's index to determine how to find entries on literary criticism.

Scholars' theoretical frameworks are a matter of what they emphasize in their interpretations. For example, if a historical critic were to interpret and write about Lewis Carroll's *Alice's Adventures in Wonderland*, he or she might emphasize the way in which the novel signaled a departure from earlier didactic literature for children, or the state of the British Empire at the time of its publication. A Marxist critic might emphasize the social class of various characters in the novel—the plight of the Mad Hatter, for example. A feminist critic might interrogate the agency of Alice in the fantasy, or the evil quality of the adult women, the Duchess and the Queen. A deconstructionist critic might emphasize the linguistic play in the novel, the philosophical riddles and puns (even chaos) resulting from the semantic fun of Wonderland. A psychoanalytic critic might look at the text as expressive of Lewis Carroll's desire for young girls (such as Alice Liddell), or he or she might interpret the hyperbolic body changes of Alice and Freudian symbols that pepper the novel (Alice's elongated, phallic neck; her growth and entrapment in the rabbit's house as a symbol for pregnancy; her fall into her tears as a descent into the womb for rebirth, etc.). A queer theorist might look at other facets of desire in the novel, such as Alice's desire for the Queen or the way the male characters project their desires for one another onto Alice. A comparative critic might explicate all the poetry that Alice recites, linking them to primers popular at the time. These are just thumbnail sketches of differences in theoretical stance, which result in critics' asking different questions about texts.

When you are researching articles, the titles often indicate what approach the critic is taking. For example, if you see the word *narcissism* in an article about Emily Brontë's *Wuthering Heights*, you can guess that the critic is a psychoanalytic one. With practice, you will come to understand these perspectives and the way in which, in practice, most critics combine them. If you want to understand how critics apply perspectives to a particular text, you could purchase one of the Bedford/St. Martin *Case Studies in Contemporary Criticism*, which feature an edition of a text and various critical approaches to it. For example, the edition of *Wuthering Heights* in this series contains the text of the novel, background materials, and then an exemplary essay from a psychoanalytic critic, a Marxist critic, a feminist critic, a deconstructionist critic, and a cultural theory critic. Each perspective is explained and applied to show you how critics from different schools of criticism interpret texts and make their arguments with textual evidence.

While doing research in children's literature and childhood studies, you might find secondary sources written by critics who do any of a myriad of the following things:

- interpret the lives of authors, as exemplified by critics Humphrey Carpenter and U. C. Knoepflmacher, who explore the reasons why British authors chose to express themselves in children's fantasy during the late Victorian "golden age";[20]
- advance the cultural work of a text, as exemplified by Anita Fellman's argument that the *Little House* series promotes the myth of the independent nuclear family and the self-sufficient pioneer;[21]
- define the power relations of young characters to adult institutions, as exemplified by Roberta Trites's study of adolescent literature;[22]
- explore the meanings of folk and fairy tales in their various permutations, as exemplified by Jerry Griswold's *The Meanings of "Beauty & the Beast*, the many works of Jack Zipes, and the studies of Peter Opie and Iona Opie;[23]
- survey the adaptation of a text through time, as exemplified by Richard Wunderlich and Thomas Morrissey's book on U.S. adaptations of Carlo Collodi's *The Adventures of Pinocchio*, serialized in 1881–1883;[24]
- interpret children's diaries, as exemplified by Lynne Vallone's work on the young and future Queen Victoria and Joan Bromberg's explication of nineteenth-century female diaries that talk about the body;[25]
- critique how the academy has constructed and marginalized children's literature, as exemplified by Beverly Lyon Clark's *Kiddie Lit*;[26]
- argue the meaning of prominent themes, as exemplified by Lois Kuznet's *When Toys Come Alive*;[27]
- articulate the relationship between adult narrator and child reader, as exemplified by Maria Nikolajeva's numerous works on narrative theory in children's literature;
- interrogate the nature of reception and adult exploitation of children's literature, as exemplified by Rose's *The Case of Peter Pan*;
- argue national and historical traditions of children's literature, as exemplified by Gillian Avery's *Behold the Child: American Children and Their Books, 1621–1922*;[28]
- explore ethnic traditions, as exemplified by Michelle Martin's *Brown Gold: Milestones of African-American Children's Picture Books, 1845–2002*;[29]
- explicate the ideology of childhood in various nonfictional discourses, as exemplified by Karin Lesnik-Oberstein in her book *Children's Literature: Criticism and the Fictional Child*, in which she traces the construction of "the child" by early literacy advocates, children's literature critics, psychoanalysts, and other childhood professionals;[30]

- analyze reader response and children's use of narrative and story, as exemplified in the work of Arthur Applebee;
- compare characters across texts, as exemplified by Amy Billone's comparison of Alice, Peter Pan, and Harry Potter, in her article "The Boy Who Lived," which allows her to make assertions about the changing relationship between audiences and fictional child characters.[31]

This by-no-means-exhaustive list of examples is meant to show you major areas of inquiry for literary critics, who may deploy contemporary critical theories such as feminism and Marxism but who keep a primary focus on the elements of traditional literary study. All these methods are open to you in your research and writing.

There are numerous professional journals in the field that allow scholars to exchange their knowledge. Some of these include *The ALAN Review* (published by the National Council of Teachers of English), *Bookbird*, *Canadian Children's Literature*, *Children's Literature* (Yale University Press), *Children's Literature Association Quarterly* (the journal of the MLA-affiliated Children's Literature Association), *Children's Literature in Education*, *Journal of Children's Literature*, *The Lion and the Unicorn* (Johns Hopkins University Press), *Marvels and Tales* (Wayne State University Press), and *Papers* (Australia). There are many others that review and evaluate children's literature, such as *Horn Book Magazine*, *Signal*, *The Bulletin of the Center for Children's Books*, *The Looking Glass*, *Five Owls*, and *School Library Journal*. Other journals in the discipline of English often run special issues on children's literature (like *Style* in 2001) or publish criticisms of cross-audienced texts.

Teachers of children might find useful journals and organizations more geared to the use of literature in the classroom. The National Council of Teachers of English has a comprehensive website of resources for teaching children literature, and certain journals such as *Children's Literature in Education*, *School Library Journal*, and the reading journals of the International Reading Association are oriented toward teaching language arts. Education presses such as Teachers College Press also maintain a leading list of books that combine the orientation of literary critics with educational needs. The recently formed *ALAN Review* is an example of a journal currently bridging the gap between children's literature scholars and educators. It is published by the Assembly on Literature for Adolescents, a division of the National Council of Teachers of English. It offers interpretations of adolescent and young adult literature as well as reviews of current novels and professional materials. The status of adolescent literature in schools is still being negotiated. Some high schools adopt classic adolescent fiction such as *Huckleberry Finn, The Catcher in the Rye, The Pigman, The Outsiders,* or the recent novel *Scream* by Laurie Halse Anderson (or teachers may put such works on recommended summer reading lists), while most sacrifice this material and teach canonical literature such as works by Shakespeare, *The Great Gatsby, The Scarlet Letter,* and *A Raisin in the Sun.*[32] If you define children's literature by age or by what children read, then these works would have to become part of the canon of children's and adolescent literature.

Two leading professional organizations for the study of children's literature include The Children's Literature Association and The International Research Society for the Study of Children's Literature; both feature annual conferences, publications, and websites for resources. There are numerous others that offer students, writers, and other interested parties the opportunity to exchange information and views on children's literature and on writing for children, such as "The Children's Book Guild." Other excellent resources can be found on the following websites:

- Perry Nodelman's extensive bibliography of children's literature criticism, io.uwinnipeg.ca/~nodelman/resources/general.html
- Mike Cadden's extensive list of Internet resources on children's literature, including a complete list of children's literature organizations and centers, staff.missouriwestern.edu/~cadden
- Linnea Hendrickson's online book *Children's Literature: A Guide to the Criticism,* www.unm.edu/~lhendr
- David Brown's children's literature Web guide, www.acs.ucalgary.ca/~dkbrown/index.html
- Homepage of the Child-Lit listserv, which features a directory of children's literature scholars' homepages, all of which have further resource lists, www.rci.rutgers.edu/~mjoseph/childlit/about.html
- ABC-Lit: An Index of Children's Literature Scholarship, www.abc-lit.com
- San Diego State's list of Internet resources, www-rohan.sdsu.edu/~childlit/links/links_general.html
- Maria Nikolajeva's links to Internet resources, www.littide.su.se:16080/littvet/homepages/mnikolaj/links.html
- The National Center for Research in Children's Literature (UK), www.ncrcl.ac.uk/clsites.htm

There is a very active listserv called Child-Lit (see home page above), hosted by Rutgers University, which features the voices of many engaged in the study and selection of children's literature. Scarecrow Press has traditionally been strong in publishing children's literature criticism, and many presses have special series in children's literature or childhood studies. For example, Routledge features a series in children's literature and culture, Ashgate has initiated a series in childhood studies, and Wayne State University Press has initiated a series on childhood studies and another on fairy tales. Rutgers University Press features a series of books on childhood studies, but it does not publish literary criticism.

The amount of materials on children's literature can be overwhelming, particularly since it is a flourishing field and profession, and since new children's books are published every day. If you type in keywords *children's literature* into an academic library database, you will quickly be overwhelmed by the array of materials. You are better off narrowing your focus on a particular author and/or title (of novel, short story, poem, or play) to begin your research. Your main guide to researching a particular novel or author will be the Modern Language Association's International Bibliography Database, to which your academic library should subscribe. When you enter the database, simply type in your title or author and view the articles, books, and chapters indexed by the MLA database. You will then need to find the source in your library. If the index indicates a book you'd like to obtain, you can use guides to finding books in your library. If the database indicates a journal article, you will need to look up the journal title in your library system, then check to see if your library holds the specific volume you need. Because this distinction between article title and journal title, between chapter author and book editor, confuses many of my students, I give two examples of entries in the MLA Bibliography. When I type in the novel title *Charlie and the Chocolate Factory*, two of the entries that appear are as follows, one a chapter in a book and one an article in a journal:

1. An Improper Charlie *By:* Clarke, Roger; Sight and Sound, 2005 Aug; 15(8): 22–25. (journal article) *ISSN:* 0037-4806
2. The Bittersweet Journey from Charlie to Willy Wonka *By:* Seiter, Richard D.; pp. 191–96, *IN:* Street, Douglas (ed); Children's Novels and the Movies. New York: Ungar; 1983. xxiv, 304 pp. (book article)

Often, my students will type "Clarke, Roger" or "Seiter, Richard" into the library guide to books and be puzzled when they cannot locate the articles. These names are the writers of articles and chapters but not of books on *Charlie and the Chocolate Factory*. To access these articles, you need to type

"Sight and Sound" into your library guide to books/periodicals, then check to see if your library holds volume 15.8 of the journal *Sight and Sound*. For entry 2, type "Children's Novels and the Movies" (or editor "Street, Douglas") into your library guide to books. Once you get the book *Children's Novels and the Movies*, you can read the chapter titled "The Bittersweet Journey" by Richard Seiter. Most literary journals are not available electronically, so leave plenty of time to actually obtain your source, at least a few weeks in case you need to use interlibrary loan services. The precise procedure for keyword text changes periodically in the MLA Bibliography. Currently, you need to put quotation marks around novel titles so that the system knows to treat all words in the title as one unit. To look up a particular critic, as opposed to novel author, you need to put the last name first, then type a comma, then type the first name. You can, however, type the full name of a novel author or poet in the correct order to review a list of secondary sources on a particular author.

As the leading professional organization for English departments in North America, the Modern Language Association sets the standards for many English department practices. The MLA citation style is the most commonly used citation system among English scholars. Most literature professors will expect you to learn and deploy MLA style. To assist you with research papers in the discipline of English, the MLA publishes an annually updated *MLA Handbook for Writers of Research Papers*, which covers the basics of doing research in literature and using research in critical essays, including the format that in-text and works-cited pages should take.[33] However, childhood studies professors may or may not choose this style. Be sure to inquire of your professor which citation style to use.

Should you decide that you want to further study children's literature, there are numerous graduate programs available. In the United States, there are master's programs in children's literature at Illinois State University, Simmons College, Hollins University, and San Diego State University. Hollins and Simmons emphasize creative writing for children as well as the study of children's literature. Rutgers University, Camden, has initiated a master's and doctoral program in Childhood Studies, which includes an array of literature, humanities, and social science courses. There are numerous European graduate programs in children's literature and they range from being oriented toward education to cultural studies to creative writing. They include the University of Nottingham, Roehampton University, St. Patrick's College in Dublin, the University of South Africa, the University of Technology in Sydney, and Reading (hosted by the Centre of Research for International Research in Childhood). There are courses in children's literature and minor programs in children's literature/childhood studies at many other universities, many of which have grown in conjunction with children's literature collections owned by libraries such as Western Michigan's and Central Michigan's. This is because children's literature has historically been studied in schools with library science programs, some of which have transformed into literary programs. There are many grants available, in many places of the world, for scholars to study particular library collections in children's literature; they often go unused because few know about them. They offer wonderful opportunities to study archival material and gain exposure to an ever-widening world of different childhoods.

WRITING THE LITERARY PAPER

As a student of childhood studies, studying the topic from an English perspective, you will mostly express your ideas through writing. Excellence in writing is a primary value and means of evaluation in English. Writing may be peripheral in other fields but not in English, where the papers you write will often comprise the majority of your course grade. In general, unless you are asked specifically to write a paper from historical sources, you will be asked to write papers that offer interpretations of literary texts. A literature professor will expect you to do both macro- and micro-level analysis of literary texts. Many guides to writing about literature exist, and I have already referred to the *MLA Handbook for Writers of Research Papers*. You will want to gather secondary sources that offer you background and alternative interpretations of the primary, usually literary, source. But you then need to write your own interpretation of the literary text, developing a thesis and making an argument about the piece of literature. Your thesis statement needs to be controversial rather than obvious to any reader of the primary literature. For example, the statement "In *The Adventures of Pinocchio*, the puppet Pinocchio develops into a real boy by learning not to lie and to respect others," is not a thesis statement because it is merely a restatement of the plot. A true thesis usually has the element of concession, conceding to a common understanding of a text and then asserting your own. For example, Anita Fellman's thesis, in her article about *Little House*, is that *although* we have historically understood the novels to be Laura Ingalls Wilder's autobiographical journey on the frontier, the author *actually* shaped her novels to deemphasize community and exaggerate the family's autonomy. If you can articulate (even orally) your thesis in terms of "*although* this, *actually* that," then you probably have an argumentative thesis statement.

In a paper on literature, you use passages and scenes from the primary text to support your point of view, offering commentary on how you are interpreting your evidence. You will want to comment on the language of passages to nuance your interpretation, should you deploy quotations; if you are not specifically commenting on the language of particular passages and scenes, you do not need to quote them. Keep your voice primary, whenever possible. Use secondary sources to dialogue with your own understandings of the text, offering commentary on secondary sources and smoothly integrating the thoughts of critics with your own. MLA style privileges in-text citations, keyed to a works-cited page, rather than footnotes, particularly discouraging using footnotes for commentary. In general, you want to be careful about "dropping" or "dangling" quotations from sources; rather, you need to foreground your own interpretations of all sources, always properly crediting sources as well. Each paragraph should further your thesis and offer a topic sentence that tells your reader exactly why you are moving to your next point. Your paper needs to have a linear shape that advances your argument, avoiding the listing of scenes or passages that merely replay the same theme. If you find yourself writing "another example of this occurs when . . . ," then your thesis may be too simple. Consider revising throughout the writing process; often, your introductory paragraph is written last, and a truly powerful, original thesis derived after drafting the entire paper.

In the appendix to this book, I include an example of an undergraduate essay written for my introductory-level course "Literature of Childhood." The thesis can be found in the second-to-last sentence of the first paragraph. In her introduction, the writer offers a concession to a dominant understanding of the novel (which is that Pinocchio needs to learn to respect and appreciate Gepetto), then offers her own interpretation (that larger sociocultural forces affect Pinocchio's journey). Throughout the paper she deploys research into Biblical antecedents and the theories of anthropologist Victor Turner (on rites of passage), to explore Pinocchio's relationship to sociocultural forces, including his father and various communities. The writer thus integrates a variety of sources into her argument while keeping her own interpretations in the foreground. Her analysis offers an interdisciplinary approach to the novel and is thus an excellent example of the enlightening nature of literary criticism in a childhood studies context. The Children's Literature Association offers a prestigious prize for the best undergraduate research paper on children's literature. If you are writing such a paper, be sure to ask your professor to enter your work.

CONCLUSION: A YOUNG FIELD WITH
A COMPLEX SET OF ISSUES

Children's literature is a particularly complex field. Most literature is defined by writer rather than reader—women's literature, African American literature, British Literature, Canadian literature. Children's literature is the only body of literature defined by audience, which brings a set of problems. An inevitable fact is that literature is produced by those who are not children; added to this fact is the truth that all writers have once been children, and are thus influenced by memories and mythic revisions of childhood (even contradictory ones, such as "the world was safer and slower-paced when I was young," yet "we had greater hardships such as one pair of shoes," or "children are more precocious today," yet "today's children have fewer skills and cannot make it on their own"). Children's literature is, unfortunately or fortunately, filtered through layers and layers of adults, all of whom bring to the field their cultural and personal biases and myths. Children's literature students should understand the role of adult interests represented by layers of adult mediators: authors, publishers/editors, publishing houses, marketers, bookstores, teachers, librarians, and parents, all of whom influence which works get published for children, and which become part of the children's canon.

While anthropologists tend to think of children as inhabiting a separate culture from adults, this is hardly the case in the field of literature, where adult values and commentaries explicitly and implicitly complexify any claims of what children actually like about particular stories, poems, or plays. As I said earlier, publishing houses and teachers have increasingly defined children's literature by age, but there is a great difference between what children can read themselves and what they can encounter with the help of adults, and there is a great difference between the ages books are designed for and the ages children actually read the books. For example, publishers define the category of young adult variously, some understanding that teens as young as eleven are their real target market. Interpretations of the novels themselves yield wonderful research questions but you may need to dig further into history databases, for example, to fully understand the adults behind a literary work for children. Most scholars at least claim that children's literature focuses on young characters, but the ages of reader and character hardly match in fairy tales, and the species of protagonist and reader does not even match in stories of animals, toys, and aliens. Even toasters can be heroes, and brave ones at that.

The field of children's literature scholarship, like childhood studies, is still young and emergent. Even children's literature itself is young. Although there were earlier works for children, it was not until John Newberry's 1744 publication *A Little Pretty Pocket-Book* that people began to regard books as children's entertainment.[34] Lewis Carroll's *Alice* drove what Newberry began into high gear. The Children's Literature Association, devoted to the serious scholarly study of children's literature, was only founded in 1972. While authors, publishers, librarians, teachers, parents, and reviewers have always exchanged their thoughts about children's books, exercising a great influence on the children's canon, children's literature was increasingly separated from the world of adult publishing only in the early twentieth century, as exemplified by Beverly Lyon Clark's analysis of the career paths of Henry James and his contemporary, Frances Hodgson Burnett (writer of *Little Lord Fauntleroy* (1886), *A Little Princess* (1905), and *The Secret Garden* (1909)).[35] It does not make complete sense to understand children's literature completely apart from adult literature; surely we can best understand the Depression-era politics of *Little House in the Big Woods* if we read it alongside *The Grapes of Wrath*, or analyze its style in relation to modernists and other prairie novels by female local colorists such as Willa Cather.[36] As a student of childhood studies, you have the rare opportunity to place children's literature and texts about children in the context of cultural and aesthetic forces that shape, and are shaped by, texts. How exciting an adventure! One any Alice journeying into such a Wonderland would envy. Even, as Anne might say, poetical.

NOTES

1. L. M. Montgomery, *Anne of Green Gables* (New York: Bantam, 1998), 92–93.

2. J. K. Rowling, *Harry Potter and the Sorcerer's Stone* (New York: Scholastic, 1999).

3. Harriet Beecher Stowe, *Uncle Tom's Cabin* (New York: Bantam, 1983).

4. Charles Dickens, *The Old Curiosity Shop* (New York: Penguin, 2001).

5. Jacqueline Rose, *The Case of Peter Pan: Or the Impossibility of Children's Fiction* (Philadelphia: University of Pennsylvania Press, 1992).

6. J. M. Barrie, *Peter Pan and Other Plays* (New York: Oxford University Press, 1999).

7. Philippe Ariès, *Centuries of Childhood: A Social History of Family Life*, trans. Robert Baldick (New York: Vintage, 1962).

8. Robert Louis Stevenson, *Treasure Island* (New York: Signet, 1998).

9. Harper Lee, *To Kill a Mockingbird* (New York: Warner, 1988).

10. Mark Twain, *Adventures of Huckleberry Finn* (New York: Bantam, 1981).

11. Roberta Trites, "The Harry Potter Novels as a Test Case for Adolescent Literature," *Style* 35, no. 3 (2001): 472–85.

12. Brian Jacques, *Redwall* (New York: Ace, 1998).

13. Richard Flynn, "The Intersection of Children's Literature and Childhood Studies," *Children's Literature Association Quarterly* 22, no. 3 (1997): 144.

14. Flynn, "The Intersection of Children's Literature," 144.

15. Louisa May Alcott, *Little Women* (New York: Signet, 2004); Lewis Carroll, *Alice's Adventures in Wonderland and Through the Looking-Glass* (New York: Signet, 2000).

16. Kenneth Kidd, "Children's Culture, Children's Studies, and the Ethnographic Imaginary," *Children's Literature Association Quarterly* 27, no. 3 (2002): 147.

17. Perry Nodelman, ed., *Touchstones: Reflections on the Best in Children's Literature*, vols. 1–3 (Battle Creek, Mich.: Children's Literature Association Publication, 1986).

18. Peter Hunt, *International Companion Encyclopedia of Children's Literature*, 2nd ed. (New York: Routledge, 2004); Peter Hunt, *An Introduction to Children's Literature* (New York: Oxford University Press, 1996); Maria Nikolajeva, *Aesthetic Approaches to Children's Literature: An Introduction* (Lanham, Md.: Scarecrow Press, 2005); Donna Norton and Saundra Norton, *Through the Eyes of a Child: An Introduction to Children's Literature*, 5th ed. (New York: Prentice Hall, 1998); Kimberley Reynolds, ed., *Modern Children's Literature: An Introduction* (New York: Palgrave Macmillan, 2005); David Russell, *Literature for Children: A Short Introduction*, 5th ed. (New York: Allyn & Bacon, 2004).

19. M. H. Abrams, *A Glossary of Literary Terms*, 8th ed. (New York: Heinle, 2004).

20. Humphrey Carpenter, *Secret Gardens: A Study of the Golden Age of Children's Literature* (Boston: Houghton Mifflin, 1991); U. C. Knoepflmacher, *Ventures into Childhood: Victorians, Fairy Tales, and Femininity* (Chicago: University of Chicago Press, 1998).

21. Anita Fellman, "'Don't Expect to Depend on Anybody Else': The Frontier as Portrayed in the Little House Books," *Children's Literature* 24 (1996): 101–16.

22. Roberta Trites, *Disturbing the Universe: Power and Repression in Adolescent Literature* (Iowa City: University of Iowa Press, 2004).

23. Jerry Griswold, *The Meanings of "Beauty & the Beast": A Handbook* (Guelph: Broadview, 2004).

24. Richard Wunderlich and Thomas Morrissey, *Pinocchio Goes Postmodern: Perils of a Puppet in the United States* (New York: Routledge, 2002).

25. Joan Brumberg, *The Body Project: An Intimate History of American Girls* (New York: Vintage, 1998); Lynne Vallone, *Becoming Victoria* (New Haven: Yale University Press, 2001).

26. Beverly Lyon Clark, *Kiddie Lit: The Cultural Construction of Children's Literature in America* (Baltimore: Johns Hopkins University Press, 2004).

27. Lois Kuznet, *When Toys Come Alive: Narratives of Animation, Metamorphosis, and Development* (New Haven: Yale University Press, 1994).

28. Gillian Avery, *Behold the Child: American Children and Their Books, 1621–1922* (Baltimore: Johns Hopkins University Press, 1995).

29. Michelle Martin, *Brown Gold: Milestones of African-American Children's Picture Books, 1845–2002* (New York: Routledge, 2004).

30. Karin Lesnik-Oberstein, *Children's Literature: Criticism and the Fictional Child* (New York: Oxford University Press, 1994).

31. Amy Billone, "The Boy Who Lived: From Carroll's Alice and Barrie's Peter Pan to Rowling's Harry Potter," *Children's Literature* 32 (2004): 178–202.

32. Laurie Halse Anderson, *Speak* (New York: Puffin, 2001); F. Scott Fitzgerald, *The Great Gatsby* (New York: Scribner, 2004); Nathaniel Hawthorne, *The Scarlet Letter* (New York: Bantam, 1981); Lorraine Hansberry, *A Raisin in the Sun* (New York: Vintage, 1994); S. E. Hinton, *The Outsiders* (New York: Puffin, 1997); J. D. Salinger, *The Catcher in the Rye* (New York: Little, Brown, 1991); Paul Zindel, *Pigman* (New York: Harper Trophy, 2005).

33. Joseph Gibaldi, *MLA Handbook for Writers of Research Papers*, 6th ed. (New York: Modern Language Association, 2003).

34. John Newberry, *A Little Pretty Pocket-Book* (New York: Harcourt, 1967).

35. Frances Hodgson Burnett, *Little Lord Fauntleroy* (New York: Puffin, 1996); Frances Hodgson Burnett, *A Little Princess* (New York: Harper Trophy, 1987); Frances Hodgson Burnett, *The Secret Garden* (New York: Harper Trophy, 1998).

36. John Steinbeck, *The Grapes of Wrath* (New York: Penguin, 1992); Laura Ingalls Wilder, *Little House in the Big Woods* (New York: Harper Trophy, 1953).

WORKS CITED

Abrams, M. H. *A Glossary of Literary Terms*. 8th ed. New York: Heinle, 2004.

Alcott, Louisa May. *Little Women*. New York: Signet, 2004.

Anderson, Laurie Halse. *Speak*. New York: Puffin, 2001.

Ariès, Philippe. *Centuries of Childhood: A Social History of Family Life*. Translated by Robert Baldick. New York: Vintage, 1962.

Avery, Gillian. *Behold the Child: American Children and Their Books, 1621–1922*. Baltimore: Johns Hopkins University Press, 1995.

Barrie, J. M. *Peter Pan and Other Plays*. New York: Oxford University Press, 1999.

Billone, Amy. "The Boy Who Lived: From Carroll's Alice and Barrie's Peter Pan to Rowling's Harry Potter." *Children's Literature* 32 (2004): 178–202.

Brumberg, Joan. *The Body Project: An Intimate History of American Girls*. New York: Vintage, 1998.

Burnett, Frances Hodgson. *Little Lord Fauntleroy*. New York: Puffin, 1996.

———. *A Little Princess*. New York: Harper Trophy, 1987.

———. *The Secret Garden*. New York: Harper Trophy, 1998.

Carpenter, Humphrey. *Secret Gardens: A Study of the Golden Age of Children's Literature*. Boston: Houghton Mifflin, 1991.

Carroll, Lewis. *Alice's Adventures in Wonderland and through the Looking-Glass*. New York: Signet, 2000.

Clark, Beverly Lyon. *Kiddie Lit: The Cultural Construction of Children's Literature in America*. Baltimore: Johns Hopkins University Press, 2004.

Dickens, Charles. *The Old Curiosity Shop*. New York: Penguin, 2001.

Fellman, Anita. "'Don't Expect to Depend on Anybody Else': The Frontier as Portrayed in the Little House Books." *Children's Literature* 24 (1996): 101–16.

Fitzgerald, F. Scott. *The Great Gatsby*. New York: Scribner, 2004.

Flynn, Richard. "The Intersection of Children's Literature and Childhood Studies." *Children's Literature Association Quarterly* 22, no. 3 (1997): 144–45.

Gibaldi, Joseph. *MLA Handbook for Writers of Research Papers*. 6th ed. New York: Modern Language Association, 2003.

Griswold, Jerry. *The Meanings of "Beauty & the Beast": A Handbook*. Guelph: Broadview, 2004.

Hansberry, Lorraine. *A Raisin in the Sun*. New York: Vintage, 1994.

Hawthorne, Nathaniel. *The Scarlet Letter*. New York: Bantam, 1981.

Hinton, S. E. *The Outsiders*. New York: Puffin, 1997.

Hunt, Peter. *International Companion Encyclopedia of Children's Literature*. 2nd ed. New York: Routledge, 2004.

———. *An Introduction to Children's Literature*. New York: Oxford University Press, 1996.

Jacques, Brian. *Redwall*. New York: Ace, 1998.

Kidd, Kenneth. "Children's Culture, Children's Studies, and the Ethnographic Imaginary." *Children's Literature Association Quarterly* 27, no. 3 (2002): 146–55.

Knoepflmacher, U. C. *Ventures into Childhood: Victorians, Fairy Tales, and Femininity*. Chicago: University of Chicago Press, 1998.

Kuznet, Lois. *When Toys Come Alive: Narratives of Animation, Metamorphosis, and Development*. New Haven, Conn.: Yale University Press, 1994.

Lee, Harper. *To Kill a Mockingbird*. New York: Warner, 1988.

Lesnik-Oberstein, Karin. *Children's Literature: Criticism and the Fictional Child*. New York: Oxford University Press, 1994.

Martin, Michelle. *Brown Gold: Milestones of African-American Children's Picture Books, 1845-2002*. New York: Routledge, 2004.

Montgomery, L. M. *Anne of Green Gables*. New York: Bantam, 1998.

Newberry, John. *A Little Pretty Pocket-Book*. New York: Harcourt, 1967.

Nikolajeva, Maria. *Aesthetic Approaches to Children's Literature: An Introduction*. Lanham, Md.: Scarecrow Press, 2005.

Nodelman, Perry, ed. *Touchstones: Reflections on the Best in Children's Literature*, vols. 1–3. Battle Creek, Mich.: Children's Literature Association Publication, 1986.

Norton, Donna, and Saundra Norton. *Through the Eyes of a Child: An Introduction to Children's Literature*. 5th ed. New York: Prentice Hall, 1998.

Reynolds, Kimberley, ed. *Modern Children's Literature: An Introduction*. New York: Palgrave Macmillan, 2005.

Rose, Jacqueline. *The Case of Peter Pan: Or the Impossibility of Children's Fiction*. Philadelphia: University of Pennsylvania Press, 1992.

Rowling, J. K. *Harry Potter and the Sorcerer's Stone*. New York: Scholastic, 1999.

Russell, David. *Literature for Children: A Short Introduction*. 5th ed. New York: Allyn & Bacon, 2004.

Salinger, J. D. *The Catcher in the Rye*. New York: Little, Brown, 1991.

Steinbeck, John. *The Grapes of Wrath*. New York: Penguin, 1992.

Stevenson, Robert Louis. *Treasure Island*. New York: Signet, 1998.

Stowe, Harriet Beecher. *Uncle Tom's Cabin*. New York: Bantam, 1983.

Trites, Roberta. *Disturbing the Universe: Power and Repression in Adolescent Literature*. Iowa City: University of Iowa Press, 2004.

———. "The Harry Potter Novels as a Test Case for Adolescent Literature." *Style* 35, no. 3 (2001): 472–85.

Twain, Mark. *Adventures of Huckleberry Finn*. New York: Bantam, 1981.

Vallone, Lynn. *Becoming Victoria*. New Haven, Conn.: Yale University Press, 2001.

Wilder, Laura Ingalls. *Little House in the Big Woods*. New York: Harper Trophy, 1953.

Wunderlich, Richard, and Thomas Morrissey. *Pinocchio Goes Postmodern: Perils of a Puppet in the United States*. New York: Routledge, 2002.

Zindel, Paul. *Pigman*. New York: Harper Trophy, 2005.

8

HISTORY

Julie M. Still

The phrase *history of childhood* is ironic because all of our histories involve childhood. As yet every single adult human has, at one point, been a child. That having been said, the study of children is a very recent concept. Few people, other than primary and secondary school educators and psychologists, have bothered to study children in an academic sense, although most parents make note of their own children's activities and development. Further muddying the waters, most historical study of children and childhood is made up of the recollections of adults, remembering their own childhoods. Memory can be faulty, especially if it is a long-ago memory. What seems significant to us as adults thinking back may not have seemed significant at the time. Notable lifestyle changes, for example the death of a parent, have always left marks. But how many children who spend many a summer afternoon lying on their backs in a field watching the clouds realize that these simple things, not reckoned as much at the time, may become cherished memories in later life? Likewise, those events considered significant in childhood may seem less so decades later. The slights and fights of adolescence are often meaningless in a few years. The voices of those children who did not live into adulthood are almost completely lost to us. *The Diary of Anne Frank* is a rare exception. Furthermore, it can be argued that Anne was at an age where she might be considered a young adult as opposed to a child.

Historical research generally requires an eye for detail, poring over documents and newspaper articles and diaries and looking at both the big picture and the small particulars. One historian may read accounts of dinner parties to see what political figures were socializing with each other. Another historian will read the same account to see what foods were served, how they were prepared and served, and what utensils were used. A third historian will read it with an eye to the way a skilled hostess formed a part of the power elite. All of them, however, will want to ensure the accuracy and dependability of the source (or to differentiate between accurate and fictionalized accounts) and will use the work of other modern scholars to interpret their findings and either ally their research with current thought or challenge it. A historian's work will find its way into academic journals or popular magazines or museum displays or classroom activities or community celebrations, depending on the venue the historian works within. A list of books on general historical research and the work of historians is at the end of this chapter.

There are other unique aspects of historical research. History students will frequently be required to locate what are called primary sources, materials produced at the time of an event, or written by someone who was an eyewitness, even if the document was written later in their life. Secondary sources are those written later by people who were not directly involved. The Library of Congress has an excellent tutorial on the difference between the two (memory.loc.gov/learn/lessons/psources/source.html). To make matters even more difficult, the materials historians so frequently rely on—autobiographies, printed news sources, household lists, correspondence and government documents—are mostly foreign to children. With some notable exceptions, they seldom write letters or keep diaries. The concept of publications aimed at children may have existed in the past for royalty or the very upper classes but they have filtered down to the middle and working class only recently. There are indexes for periodicals and newspapers going back into the 1700s but the materials indexed will be aimed at adults. Household lists and government documents may provide some information on how children are perceived but very little on how children perceive themselves. So we may find materials that describe what children ate and wore and build on that, but we are less likely to find anything that describes whether the children liked their food and clothing. We may find descriptions of school curriculums and what children were taught, but that is not necessarily an indication of what they learned. The material culture of childhood (games, toys, clothing, and similar objects) has been studied, but usually again as the artifacts of an adult's past, and not necessarily as the artifacts of children themselves. These items are often perishable and there may be little effort to preserve them. One example is the often-told tale of a parent discarding a child's baseball cards or comic books.

The history of childhood is detective work at its most difficult. Like studying the disenfranchised everywhere, the enslaved, the illiterate, the dispossessed, studying childhood beyond our memory is a matter of piecework and, often, guesswork.

Researching childhood in a specific time period is challenging; children who enter into the adult realm and take on adult roles are easier to research, but these are few and far between. The amount of material to be found varies by time period. Depending on the era, there may be diaries or advice books for parents, indexes, periodicals, transcribed oral histories, newspapers, household rolls, court documents, or other types of records.

In short, historical research is a complicated process and is one that requires skill and patience. In this chapter, I walk the reader through the process of researching a topic in preparation for writing a "history-based" paper. I am operating on the assumption that the reader is new to the field of historical research. In order to make the explanation meaningful, I use a sample search to illustrate the various steps and the various kinds of materials that a student would typically draw upon. The following sections reflect the order and the kinds of materials that should be used. The time period under investigation is the 1860s, the United States, in the grip of the Civil War. The topic is, Who were the children who served as the drummer boys for America's bloodiest conflict?

STEP 1: LOCATE BACKGROUND INFORMATION

If you are researching an area unfamiliar to you, reference materials should be your first stopping place. Reference materials will provide you with the key concepts, names, and dates for the period that you are investigating. Reference works will also contain citations to the authors and works. These references will lead you to recommended works on the topics and give you clues as to who are the authorities in the field. As you become more adept at research you may learn to recognize the subheadings in library catalogs that indicate these types of works—words like *encyclopedias, bibliography, chronologies,* and so on.

The American Civil War has seen a resurgence of interest lately and that has resulted in the publication of a number of excellent reference works. Some general titles are listed here and other types of reference books, such as the aforementioned encyclopedias, bibliographies, and chronologies are grouped together below.

Reference Books

Suggested Reference Books for the Civil War

Ireland, Norma Olin. *Index to America: Life and Customs—Nineteenth Century.* Metuchen, N.J.: Scarecrow, 1984.

This is an unusual work in that it indexes a number of books on nineteenth-century America and allows users to look for very specific information. For example, there are six entries under Children's Needlework and over a column devoted to Toys. Readers will have to look carefully to make sure the time period covered is that of the Civil War, but even information not relating exactly to those years may prove useful as general background.

Wright, John D. *The Language of the Civil War*. Westport, Conn.: Oryx, 2001.

When researching any time period outside your own it is important to understand that the words used in documents written then may not mean the same thing they do now. Terminology changes. Words go in and out of style. In this historical dictionary we find out that a *biddy* was the nickname given to Irish servant girls. To *rush* was to court a woman or girl ardently.

Encyclopedias

One of the first types of reference books that librarians often consult are specialized dictionaries and encyclopedias. Here there are several choices. Some will concern the topic of childhood, others the time period in question. There are a number of other encyclopedias available and some would also have relevant material. A number were checked which did not. However, those listed below were selected as being representative of the types of materials a typical undergraduate library might have. Remember to use the index and look under all the relevant terms you can think of, as the terminology will vary from work to work.

Specialized Encyclopedias That Cover the Civil War Era

Current, Richard N. *Encyclopedia of the Confederacy*. New York: Simon & Schuster, 1993.

There are entries on children, slave and free.

Fass, Paula S., ed. *Encyclopedia of Children and Childhood*. New York: Macmillan Reference, 2003.

There is a short article on "Soldier Children: Global Human Rights Issues," that includes a sentence on the American Civil War, providing the name of one boy soldier, John Clem, and provides two potentially useful items (Marten, *Children and War*, and Rosenblatt).

Finkelman, Paul. *Encyclopedia of the United States in the Nineteenth Century*. New York: Scribner, 2001.

This resource does not have entries on children per se but there are index listings for the concept of childhood, custody, child labor, literature, and other topics, as well as references to slave children and ethnic children. There is an entry for "Games and Toys, Children's," that provides some background on this particular aspect of children's lives. It also mentions Marten's book, *The Children's Civil War* within the text and others in entry bibliography.

Harper, Judith E. *Women during the Civil War: An Encyclopedia.* New York: Routledge, 2004.

According to this title not only boys fought in the war but girls also. There is an entry on "Girlhood and Adolescence" and "Military Women." A number of interesting titles show up in the bibliographies of those entries, including King, Forbes, Blanton and McCook, and Leonard.

Heidler, David S., and Jeanne T. Heidler. *Encyclopedia of the American Civil War.* Santa Barbara: ABC-Clio, 2000. 5 vols.

This is normally an excellent resource to go to for information but in this case it falls short. There is nothing under Children, Boys, or Girls.

Sherrow, Victoria. *Encyclopedia of Youth and War: Young People as Participants and Victims.* Phoenix, Ariz.: Oryx, 2000.

Two relevant subject entries, "American Civil War," and "Drummer Boys," as well as entries on two child soldiers, "Clem, John Lincoln," and "Boyd, Isabelle 'Belle,'" (found as cross references under the subject entries), provide a lot of background data as well as some statistics. Entry bibliographies also provide some relevant titles: Marten, *Children's Civil War*, Murphy, Werner, and Wheeler.

Bibliographies

A bibliography is a list of items on a particular topic. Some are annotated, meaning they provide a description or evaluation of each item; others are not. These resources are invaluable in tracking down the types of primary resources that historians need, diaries, statistics, documents, and so on. It is now possible to find full-text databases of some items that may be useful. For example, *North American Women's Letters and Diaries* is a database of letters and diaries that can be searched for relevant items. Ask at your library to see what resources may be available to you. Sometimes a researcher is able to find one or two bibliographies that will tell them everything they need, but not often. Two bibliographies of primary sources specific to the Civil War follow.

Cole, Garold L. *Civil War Eyewitnesses: An Annotated Bibliography of Books and Articles, 1955–1986.* Columbia: University of South Carolina Press, 1988.
———. *Civil War Eyewitnesses: An Annotated Bibliography of Books and Articles, 1986–1996.* Columbia: University of South Carolina Press, 2000.

Like most bibliographies these have multiple access points. The index is by subject, author, title, and regiment. There aren't any subject entries under "children," "boys," "girls," "drummer boys." However some diaries have these words in the title, for example *Drummer-Boys Diary* and *Children of Glencoe.* The entries in both books are divided by North and South and then into military, civilian, and foreign travelers. There is also a section at the back for anthologies and general studies. Simply by browsing through the civilian entries for each side, at least half a dozen diaries by children are found. Some are reminiscences later in life, some are written directly at the time of the war. Both boys and girls are represented. Browsing through the military sections will turn up a few underage soldiers, although it is very much a hit-and-miss effort. The publications include both books and articles.

Recommended Sources for Diaries

Arksey, Laura, Nancy Pries, and Marcia Reed. *American Diaries: An Annotated Bibliography of Published American Diaries and Journals*. Detroit: Gale, 1987.

This is a delightful resource for American diaries from 1492 to 1980. It is arranged chronologically so it is possible to simply browse through entries for the civil war years. There are also name, subject, and geographic indexes. One of the subject listings is "children's diaries."

Briscoe, Mary Louise, ed. *American Autobiography, 1845–1980*. Madison: University of Wisconsin Press, 1982.

While arranged alphabetically, there are subject headings for childhood and civil war that can be cross-referenced to find entries discussing both. It is also possible to browse through looking at dates of birth and then scanning the abstracts. Only monographic publications are included.

Kaplan, Louis. *A Bibliography of American Autobiographies*. Madison: University of Wisconsin Press, 1962.

There is a subject listing for childhood reminiscences, and also for the Civil War, with a variety of subheadings, including "civilians." The entries are arranged alphabetically, and only monographic works are included.

Matthews, Geraldine O. *Black American Writers, 1773–1949: A Bibliography and Union List*. Boston: Hall, 1975.

Arranged by general topic, researchers looking for entries on American Civil War narratives would find "Slavery, Anti-Slavery, Slave Trade, Personal Narratives" most useful. Several accounts of enslaved childhood are listed.

Chronologies

This type of reference book is very useful for placing events in their chronological and cultural context. They will often list significant events by year or by type, for example, popular novels or plays (movies, where relevant), elected officials, recent social unrest or important news stories. This is one example of the genre.

Brown, Thomas J. *Civil War and Reconstruction, 1850–1877*. Detroit: Gale, 1997.

STEP 2: LOCATING BOOKS

While most researchers, even beginners, understand the difference between fiction and nonfiction, there are also other dividing lines. In history one of those is between scholarly history and popular history. In some cases those lines blur, but looking at the credentials of the author, what sort of degrees does he or she have, and what institutions or organizations is he or she affiliated with, one can have a fairly clear idea. There are a number of ways to locate quality book-length treatments of historical subjects. One is to collect titles from bibliographies in reference books. The list below is taken from the bibliographies of encyclopedias mentioned in the "encyclopedias" section of this chapter. Just this list alone would probably provide a good basic overview of the subject from a number of viewpoints and provide the nucleus of a good undergraduate paper.

Blanton, DeAnne, and Lauren McCook. *They Fought Like Demons: Women Soldiers in the American Civil War.* Baton Rouge: Louisiana State University Press, 2002.

Clement, Priscilla Gerguson. *Growing Pains: Children in the Industrial Age, 1850–1890.* New York: Twayne, 1997.

Forbes, Ella. *African American Women during the Civil War.* New York: Garland, 1998.

King, Wilma. *Stolen Childhood: Slave Youth in Nineteenth Century America.* Bloomington: Indiana University Press, 1995.

Leonard, Elizabeth D. *All the Daring of the Soldiers: Women of the Civil War Armies.* New York: Penguin, 2001.

Marten, James, ed. *Children and War: A Historical Anthology.* New York: New York University Press, 2002.

Marten, James. *The Children's Civil War.* Chapel Hill: University of North Carolina Press, 1998.

Murphy, Jim. *The Boy's War: Confederate and Union Soldiers Talk about the Civil War.* New York: Clarion, 1990.

Rosenblatt, Roger. *Children of War.* Garden City, New York: Doubleday, 1983.

Werner, Emmy E. *Reluctant Witnesses.* Boulder, Colo.: Westview, 1988.

West, Elliott, and Paul Petrik, eds. *Small Worlds: Children and Adolescents in America, 1850-1950.* Lawrence: University Press of Kansas, 1992.

Wheeler, Richard. *Voices of the Civil War.* New York: Crowell, 1976.

Finding items beyond this list will usually start with searching the local library catalog. Some of the subject headings that would retrieve the most relevant books are "children," "boys," and "girls." Within these subject headings look for chronological subheadings or search the appropriate subject headings within the primary heading for the Civil War: United States–History–Civil War, 1861–1865. Books focusing entirely on life in the southern states may use the heading "Confederate States of America." Those looking for primary sources should be especially careful to look for the subheadings "sources" and "personal narratives." Those looking for bibliographies should watch for that subheading. If you aren't sure what subject headings to use for a particular search, try looking for the topic as keywords and then seeing what subject headings are used, or ask a reference librarian, or review the printed volumes of the *Library of Congress Subject Headings*. Researchers of the world of children during the 1860s will also find a wealth of information in the oral histories taken of former slaves during the 1930s as part of the WPA works project. Many of those writings are indexed under Slaves' writings, American, or Slaves–United States–Personal Narratives, although a keyword search on slave narratives will retrieve more titles. A number of those interviewed were children during the Civil War and without their accounts no comprehensive history of the period would be complete. One of the most in-depth collections of these interviews is found in this seventeen-volume work.

Federal Writers' Project. *Slave Narratives: A Folk History of Slavery in the United States, from Interviews with Former Slaves*. St. Clair Shores, Mich.: Scholarly Press, 1976.

There are a number of strategies for expanding the list of known books on the topic. One is to look in the bibliographies of known books; this is an especially good way to find relevant primary sources. Another, described above, is to use subject headings. For example, there is an official subject heading for United States—History—Civil War, 1861–1865—Participation, Juvenile. Another is United States—History—Civil War, 1861–1865—Children. Looking up that heading in the Rutgers University Libraries catalog uncovers a total of five titles. Two of these are new to our list:

Clinton, Catherine. *Civil War Stories*. Athens: University of Georgia Press, 1998.

Marten, James. *Children for the Union: The War Spirit on the Northern Home Front*. Chicago: Dee, 2004.

At this point the list includes three titles by James Marten. This leads to another way of locating additional titles. Finding an author who appears to specialize in the topic logically leads to an author search. Indeed, Mr. Marten has at least one more title that could prove useful.

Marten, James. *Civil War America: Voices from the Home Front*. Santa Barbara, Calif.: ABC-Clio, 2003.

In addition to searching your own library's catalog there are a number of other catalogs (known as bibliographic databases if they are online), that may be available to you. Some may only be available to you in paper.

American Library Association. *The National Union Catalog of Pre-1956 Imprints*. 754 vols. London: Mansell, 1968–1981.

New York Public Library. *Dictionary Catalog of the Schomburg Collection of Literature & History*. Boston: Hall, 1962.

RLIN

This is a collection of records from major research libraries; academic, public, corporate, and national libraries; archives and museums; historical societies; and international book vendors. It also includes some archival material.

WorldCat (OCLC)

Similar to RLIN, this catalog represents holdings information from libraries in forty-five countries.

Reviewing one or more of these resources brings up additional titles:

Cohn, Scotti. *Beyond Their Years: Stories of Sixteen Civil War Children.* Guilford, Conn.: Globe Pequot, 2003.

Hull, Susan R. *Boy Soldiers of the Confederacy.* Austin, Tex.: Eakins, 1998. (Originally published in 1905)

Keesee, Dennis M. *Too Young to Die: Boy Soldiers of the Union Army.* Huntington, W. Va.: Blue Acorn, 2001.

STEP 3: PERIODICALS AND SCHOLARLY JOURNALS

There are a variety of indexes to periodicals that can be useful to researchers of the history of childhood. Researchers looking for articles written at the time of the Civil War or shortly afterwards should use the *New York Times Index* to find relevant newspaper articles. Larger libraries may have *Poole's Index to Periodical Literature* (a British publication). Ask at your library for other available resources.

There are a number of indexes available for finding current articles on our topic. One particular problem in researching historical topics is that very few databases allow you to search by time period. Phrases such as "civil war" are used in a variety of places and time periods. Finding information on any one civil war in particular can be tricky. Some of the most common and most useful, whether in print or electronic form, are listed below.

America: History and Life

The primary index to journals in American history as well as some dissertations and book reviews, this excellent resource, in its online form, also allows researchers to limit their search to articles covering a particular decade or century. This is especially useful when researching aspects of childhood that may not have been connected exclusively to the war. For instance, researchers can simply search for articles on childhood in the 1860s by typing childhood or children in the keyword box and 1860d (for the 1860s decade) in the time period box. As of this writing, that search strategy retrieves over 800 articles. Searching for drummer boy in the 1860s decade retrieves three and the more complex strategy of soldier and boy (or girl or underage or teenage) in the 1860s retrieves fourteen. Some examples of the items found here are as follows:

Kemper, Mary Lee, ed. "Civil War Reminiscences at Danville Female Academy," *Missouri Historical Review* 62, no. 3 (1968): 314–20.

Kunkle, Camille. "It Is What It Does to the Souls: Women's Views on the Civil War," *Atlanta History* 33, no. 2 (1989): 56–70.

Marten, James. "I Think It's Just as Mean as It Can Be: Northern Children Respond to Lincoln's Assassination," *Lincoln Herald* 101–3, no. 3 (1999): 117–21.

Marten, James. "Lessons of War: The Civil War in Children's Magazines," *Journal of Southern History* 66, no. 3 (2000): 651–52.

Sutherland, Carl T., and Henry Clay Roney, eds. "Reminiscences of the Experiences of a Boy Soldier in the War Between the States," *Richmond County History* 111, no. 1 (1979): 20–25.

Williams, Ora G. "Muskets and Magnolias: Four Civil War Diaries by Louisiana Girls," *Louisiana Studies* 4, no. 3 (1965): 187–97.

Humanities Index

One of the indexes produced by H. W. Wilson, this venerable resource is a staple, in one form or another, of libraries from the high-school level to research libraries. It covers archaeology and classical studies, art and photography, folklore, history, journalism and communications, language and literature, literary and political criticism, music and performing arts, philosophy, religion and theology, and related subjects.

Haywood, C. M. "Constructing Childhood: The 'Christian Recorder' and Literature for Black Children, 1854–1865," *African American Review* 36, no. 3 (Fall 2002): 417–28.

Marten, James. "For the Good, the True and the Beautiful: Northern Children's Magazines and the Civil War," *Civil War History* 41 (March 1995): 57–75.

Schwartz, M. J. "Stolen Childhood" [book review]. *The Journal of Southern History* 66, no. 2 (May 2000): 405–6.

Sociological Abstracts

The primary index to sociology journals, this index is also a boon to historians whose work involves social history in any way. Its broad international scope can make it difficult to narrow a search down to a specific time period or place.

Woodhouse, Barbara Bennett. "Dred Scott's Daughters: Nineteenth Century Urban Girls at the Intersection of Race and Patriarchy," *Buffalo Law Review* 48, no. 3 (Fall 2000): 669–701.

Education Index (ERIC)

Any topic dealing with children is likely to be covered to some degree in an education database.

Haven, Kendall. *Voices of the American Civil War: Stories of Men, Women, and Children Who Lived through the War between the States.* Greenwood Village, Colo.: Libraries Unlimited, 2002.

Herman, Patricia A. "Southern Blacks: Accounts of Learning to Read before 1861," 1983 ED246394.

Another strategy for locating relevant journal articles is to search for items that cite materials you have already found. The most common citation indexes for history are the *Arts & Humanities Citation Index* and the *Social Sciences Citation Index*, both included in the online Web of Science Database.

Other Commercial Databases

There are a number of other commercial databases available that libraries or research institutions may subscribe to, and which would be useful to someone investigating children in the Civil War. A few are listed here. Researchers are encouraged to talk to their local librarians to see which databases available to them would be helpful, and what might be accessed at neighboring institutions. These types of databases are available for other topics and other time periods also.

American Periodical Series Online, 1740–1900
New York Times Index, 1851–
North American Women's Letters and Diaries, Colonial Times to 1950
Periodicals Index Online

STEP 4: WEB RESOURCES

There are a number of Civil War sites on the Web and many of them will contain some information relevant to the study of children during the war. However, as with all websites, many were produced by interested individuals and are likely to disappear within a relatively short period of time. There are a number of lesson plans for teachers with accompanying resources (one is included in the list, produced by the Library of Congress), historical clothing patterns or toys or other artifacts for sale (none included here), and some scholarly sites affiliated with educational association and likely to be maintained for some years. Three of these are included. Any of these sites are likely to lead researchers to other relevant sites.

American Slave Narratives: An Online Anthology. xroads.virginia.edu/~HY-PER/wpa/wpahome.html.

Ayers, Edward L. "The Valley of the Shadow: Two Communities in the American Civil War." valley.vcdh.virginia.edu.

"Born in Slavery: Slave Narratives from the Federal Writers' Project, 1936–1938," docsouth.unc.edu/index.html.

Caskey, Micki M., and Paul Gregorio. *The Civil War through a Child's Eye.* Washington, D.C.: Library of Congress. hdl.loc.gov/loc.gdc/amlearn.ls1999-03.

  Prepared as a lesson plan for Grades 6–8, these resources are nonetheless useful to anyone researching the topic.

Daley, Ginny. "Civil War Women: Primary Sources on the Internet." scriptorium.lib.duke.edu/women/cwdocs.html.

  This resource links to primary sources written by women during or regarding the Civil War. Some of the authors of these works are children.

"Documenting the American South." docsouth.unc.edu/index.html.

Hoemann, George H. The American Civil War Homepage. sunsite.utk.edu/civil-war/cwarhp.html.

STEP 5: CONSULT INFORMATION EXPERTS

The librarian at your college or university will be of immense help to you in your research. He or she will be able to clue you in on any specialized resources or collections that may be in your geographical region and may be of use to you. In addition, the librarian who serves as your history department's bibliographer may have assembled a resource guide or bibliography for the material available to you through your academic library. There are also a number of well-respected published guides to historical research. A list of a few recommended research guides follows:

Barzun, Jacques, and Henry F. Graff. *The Modern Researcher.* 5th ed. Boston: Houghton Mifflin, 1992.

Camenson, Blythe. *Careers for History Buffs & Others Who Learn from the Past.* 2nd ed. Chicago: VGM Career Books, 2002.

DeGalan, Julie, and Stephen Lambert. *Great Jobs for History Majors.* 2nd ed. Chicago: VGM Career Books, 2001.

Howe, Barbara J. *Careers for Students of History.* Washington, D.C.: American Historical Association, 1989.

McDowell, W. H. *Historical Research: A Guide.* New York: Longman, 2002.

SOME CLOSING THOUGHTS

The example provided in this chapter, that of children and child soldiers in the American Civil War era is only that, an example. These same research steps can be used on any topic for any time period. Researching the history of children and childhood does present some challenges but the standard historical methods remain the same, using reference works, bibliographies, primary sources, books and journal articles. We may never be able to truly understand the lives and thoughts of children in earlier eras, but we can understand the world they lived in and how they were viewed by those around them.

9

PSYCHOLOGY

Sean Duffy[1]

Children and childhood have long been fundamental topics for psycho-logical research. Since psychology aims to understand the mind, the question of how the mind initially emerges and changes with experience and maturation over the course of an individual's development is a central theme in psychological theory. Childhood is a period of enormous changes; infants come into the world with only a limited capacity to think and act, yet ultimately end up as adults like you or I, with extraordinarily complicated mental and behavioral abilities and skills. Understanding the processes of stability and change over the course of childhood, as well as the biological, social, historical, and cultural factors that shape and guide devel-opment, are problems that pose significant conceptual and methodological challenges. Yet the answer to these problems may help solve some of the most fundamental questions about the nature of the mind.

Unfortunately, like any academic discipline, psychology has its own language, vocabulary, techniques, conventions, and culture. Those outside the field, perhaps venturing here for the first time, may feel hopelessly lost navigating through the psychological literature with its rugged landscape of abstruse concepts and technical terms. This chapter aims to provide a short "travel guide" for students of Children and Childhood Studies making their first expedition into the field of psychology. I will provide directions on some useful and interesting places to visit, tips on how to find your way around in case you get lost, and explain some of the local dialect and prac-tices in simplified terms. Hopefully, with this guide, your journey through the terrain of the mind and behavior will go a bit more smoothly. And who knows? You may pick up a few words and phrases, enjoy the local intellec-tual cuisine, and return here again and again.

PSYCHOLOGY: SYSTEMS AND HISTORY

In its broadest definition, *psychology* is the study of mental processes and behavior. Whereas other social science disciplines such as sociology, economics, political science, and anthropology tend to examine the behavior of groups of individuals, psychology generally focuses inquiry at the level of the individual. Psychologists address a diverse set of questions such as how people access, process, store, and retrieve information; how the structures and connections among parts of the brain are related to behavior; how people develop uniquely individual traits such as personality or identity; how individuals understand and think about themselves and others; and how experiential and biological factors influence change over time.

It may be useful to think of psychology as a country divided into states. Each of these states represents one of the many subfields within psychology that have developed over the past 125 years since psychology declared independence from philosophy in the 1870s when William Wundt founded the first psychological laboratory in Leipzig, Germany. In those early days, psychologists were mainly interested in sensory processes and their limitations, such as determining the highest and lowest frequencies detectable by the human ear. However, early pioneers such as William James, Edward Titchener, Sigmund Freud, and Ivan Pavlov explored new territories, vastly expanding the field, developing new approaches toward studying the mind such as structuralism, functionalism, psychoanalysis, and behaviorism. While some used these paradigms to explore 'normal' behavior, others studied 'abnormal' behavior such as psychopathology or antisocial behavior.

Over the past century, certain territories within psychology combined, others divided off and formed new states. The boundaries between subfields were redrawn, gerrymandered, and shifted as new theories, methodologies, and paradigms replaced the old. This disciplinary redistricting has left us today with several common subfields found in many psychology departments: biological, social, developmental, cognitive, personality, organizational/industrial, and clinical psychology. Several other fields exist but are somewhat less common in academic departments: vision and perception, health, community, and educational psychology. In recent decades, some of the most intriguing findings have occurred in new regions that fall near the borders of subfields within psychology, such as social neuroscience or cultural psychology, or fields that represent true interdisciplinary endeavors across the social and biological sciences, such as evolutionary psychology or cognitive science.

The reader of this chapter is likely to be most interested in the area of psychology that is most relevant to the study of children: developmental (or child) psychology. Developmental psychology is concerned with the ontogeny, or origin, of the mind. Developmental psychologists focus upon how processes of stability and change over the course of an individual's development interact to create the mind. Traditionally, developmental psychologists have focused mainly on humans in the first decade or so of their lives, the period in which there is the most obvious and significant growth. In recent years, however, there has been a shift toward viewing development as a lifelong process, and a number of scholars now study developmental processes that occur within the second and third decades of life, a period known as "emerging adulthood." Still others have broadly expanded the concept of development to include the trajectory of one's entire life, a field known as lifespan psychology.

There are a number of specialties within the field of developmental psychology. Cognitive development focuses on the question of the origins of intellectual functioning and thought. Social development examines the emergence of social reasoning such as understanding the self, identity, and mental lives of social others. Developmental neurophysiology addresses brain functioning and behavior, and to a considerable extent concentrates upon the assessment and treatment of neurological disorders. School or educational psychologists address questions concerning how children learn and grow in the context of educational settings. Finally, there is a branch of developmental psychology dealing with clinical issues and mental illnesses in children.

Developmental psychology holds a unique position in the field of childhood studies in that a significant amount of research in childhood studies is in response to, or a reaction against, the traditional perspective of child psychology.[2] Some scholars have charged that developmental psychology fails to account for children's own unique voices or agency and objectifies children as subjects to be evaluated, scrutinized, and measured in studies. Others claim that developmental psychology views childhood as merely a path along the way to maturity rather than a unique stage of life. Whether or not these claims are valid might be a good topic for interdisciplinary debate; however, the work of developmental psychology has provided a strong foundation for childhood studies by providing a language for describing the mental lives of children and numerous concepts, theories, and tools that are essential for understanding childhood.

THEMES IN DEVELOPMENTAL
THEORY AND RESEARCH

Several general themes run through much of the developmental literature. When evaluating different theories and studies, it is useful to keep these themes in mind as they have, in various forms, inspired and motivated most psychological research on children and childhood.

The first, and perhaps most widely known, is the question of whether biological or experiential factors play a larger role in guiding developmental processes or outcomes. Often referred to as the "nature versus nurture" debate, this theme has its roots in antiquity, and a number of scholars fall on both ends of the continuum between biological and experiential explanations for development. Although there is still very little consensus or agreement on this issue in any topic or domain, most discussions on the origins of intelligence, personality, social learning, and cognitive development address the problem in some form.

A second theme concerns the universality of developmental processes; whether all children develop along the same trajectory, or whether there are individual or group differences in development, shaped by differences in biology and experience. This question bears a strong relationship to the question of nature versus nurture in that there is a general assumption that if development is governed by biology rather than experience, there should be significantly less variability in the outcomes of any developmental processes given the fact that all humans share a common biology but certainly not a common set of experiences. However, the history of psychology is littered with studies arguing the opposing view: that innate biological differences between individuals of different races, social classes, and genders give rise to divergent developmental outcomes.

A third theme concerns continuity and discontinuity in development; whether development progresses in a uniform, linear progression, or if there are discrete stages of development that children move through in a particular order to achieve an adult form. Various theories have described development as a series of plateaus. To name a few common theories, Piaget's stages of cognitive development, Kohlberg's stage theory of moral development, and Vygotsky's notion of the zone of proximal development all presume a nonlinear progression of development, in which children lack a particular skill then acquire that skill through maturation, experience, or social interaction. Alternatively, two positions that do not accept that development occurs in stages are the dynamic systems approach and the core knowledge proposal. In brief, the dynamic systems approach views development as a linearly increasing process driven by subtle, ongoing interactions between various internal and external factors, and core knowledge presumes that children are born with an innate understanding of a variety of cognitive and social domains, such as number knowledge or race. Some criticize stage theories on the basis that apparent discontinuities in development may emerge only because the research tools that psychologists use do not capture more subtle progressions in the acquisition of knowledge or skills. The argument is that underlying what appears to be nonlinear stages are more slowly emerging, linear processes that are difficult to detect given the tools that psychologists often use, almost analogous to how astronomers might not observe a distant galaxy in their telescopes because the instruments are simply not strong enough to detect it.

A fourth theme is the degree to which individual psychological processes develop independently or are dependent upon one another as part of a larger emerging general psychological system, a problem known as domain generality versus domain specificity. For example, an important question in cognitive development is how language emerges separately from other cognitive abilities, such as categorization or symbolic understanding. Some argue that language, for instance, is a highly modular system that has very little relationship to general cognitive development, as evident from the fact that individuals exhibiting profound cognitive disabilities in most cases learn language as easily as those with normal cognition.

A final theme is the role of various contexts—family, historical, social, ethnic, educational, socioeconomic or cultural—in shaping development and alternatively determining what role children perform in their own development. There is a vast literature on parenting behaviors and their relationship with child behavior, or the effect of poverty on learning, or how media such as television influence children's understanding of social relationships and aggression. In an increasingly diversified world, this topic has become critical in informing psychologists about the variability of the situations in which children develop, and their resiliency in the face of adversity and various social pressures.

These five themes help organize research and guide the generation of testable hypotheses on the vast majority of questions regarding psychological development. Certainly there are other themes and issues, yet this list contains some of the most common ones you may encounter that cut across the various subfields within developmental psychology. When reading scholarly publications in psychology, it is useful to consider how these themes are incorporated into the arguments and inform a scholar's conclusions.

METHODOLOGICAL ASPECTS OF CHILD RESEARCH

To better understand psychology, it may be useful to consider how psychologists gather data to support or disconfirm their theories. Psychology is largely an empirical science in that researchers rely extensively upon observation of phenomena for developing and testing theories of how the mind works. This section will describe, in broad terms, some of the research methodologies used in psychology more generally, and discuss several specific designs commonly used in studying development in children and infants.

As Amy Masko pointed out in her chapter on education, research in psychology also tends to fall into two broad categories: qualitative and quantitative strategies. Qualitative strategies aim to explain a phenomenon through people's subjective experiences or interpretations. Such strategies generally aim to *describe* and *understand* rather than *measure* and *quantify* a phenomenon. Psychoanalytic theory, for instance, is almost entirely founded on qualitative research, such as the analyst's interpretation of a patient's dream or the determination of a causal link between an individual's early experience and later psychopathology. In ethnographic studies, a psychologist will participate in the customs and traditions of a foreign culture by living in that cultural context and taking extensive field notes, later using these observations to elaborate upon a theoretical issue in psychology. In case studies, a psychologist will write an extensive report about a single individual or group that has some feature that is relevant to broader theories in psychology. Using the hermeneutic approach, a psychologist will identify texts or narratives and determine a strategy for coding and interpreting the data contained in light of some psychological theory.

While qualitative research is useful for describing phenomena, there are a number of limitations of the inferences and conclusions reached using such strategies. Most important, qualitative research rarely allows the researcher to determine the *cause* of a behavior. Most psychological phenomena are so complex that there may be a large number of potential causes that explain why a certain psychological process exists or how it developed. To determine the underlying cause of a behavior, one must systematically and carefully isolate each potential extraneous factor that can influence the behavior in question. Qualitative strategies, being descriptive in nature, rarely allow the researcher to rule out alternative causes. Second, there is almost always a certain subjectivity involved in qualitative research. Just as the example of the "Blind Men and the Elephant" in the opening pages of this book describes how different individuals all describe the proverbial elephant based solely on the part of the animal they touched, different psychologists might interpret the same behavior in children in very different ways based on either their own predispositions and biases, or what aspect of a particular behavior they happen to examine. For this reason, many psychologists begin with a qualitative strategy to identify a phenomenon, and subsequently utilize quantitative strategies to better isolate its cause and effects on development.

In contrast with qualitative research strategies, which seek to describe a phenomenon, quantitative research seeks to *measure* a phenomenon. Most quantitative research rely upon the scientific method in which a researcher first develops theories that explain a certain behavior, generate hypotheses on the mechanism or function underlying the phenomenon, gather data by observing behavior or designing experiments that test the hypothesis, then accept or reject the hypothesis based upon a statistical analysis of the data.

Let us examine a hypothetical example of the process of quantitative research. A psychologist might be interested in a theoretical construct such as "children's vocabulary size" and its relation to another theoretical construct such as the "amount of speech a child hears at home." One might have a theory that there may be a relationship between the two constructs, and hypothesize that the more speech a child hears, the larger their vocabulary size. To test this prediction, one must have some kind of test for measuring the two theoretical constructs. The psychologist operationalizes the two theoretical constructs by developing empirical constructs—some tool that quantitatively measures a certain behavior or characteristic of individuals. So, for vocabulary size, the psychologist might use the results of a commercially available vocabulary test as an empirical construct to measure the theoretical construct of vocabulary size. For "amount of speech a child hears at home," the psychologist might go to a child's home and audiotape five hours of conversation between parents and their children, later measuring the number of words spoken by caregivers in the house. If the hypothesis is correct, then children who are exposed to a significant amount of speech at home should have larger vocabularies than children who are exposed to very little speech. If the hypothesis is incorrect, then there should be no relationship between the two constructs. In fact, research suggests that there indeed is a relationship between vocabulary size and amount of speech a child hears at home, with more parental speech leading to larger vocabulary sizes in children.[3]

Just as there are several general limitations to qualitative strategies, there are a number of limitations of quantitative strategies as well. Foremost, the quality of the conclusions is solely based upon the quality of the measurements. For instance, it is possible that those days when the experimenter measured the amount of speech in the child's home happened to be days that the parent was particularly talkative, or that simply the experimenter's presence in the participant's home influenced the amount of language spoken. Alternatively, given that the psychologist only tests, say, twenty or thirty children in any given study, there is always a concern regarding whether the results obtained from this small sample of children generalizes to all children in all societies. So even when the experimenter does find a relationship between variables, it is not altogether clear whether the conclusions are reliable or whether extraneous factors determined the observed results.

A more philosophical objection to quantitative research is that in measuring something, a significant amount of information is lost because any given phenomenon is far too complex to be adequately measured by a simple test or experiment. For example, a vocabulary test only assesses the comprehension of words; it is possible that other measurements of vocabulary size (i.e., the number of novel words a child produces on any given day) might result in very different conclusions. It is often the case that the limitations of quantitative strategies end up being the strengths of qualitative strategies, and vice versa. Unfortunately, few psychologists have successfully combined both approaches to foster a more comprehensive perspective on development. However, this limitation of psychological research may provide a unique window of opportunity for students of an interdisciplinary approach such as childhood studies. By integrating methods from various fields, childhood studies has the advantage of fostering a unique perspective relying on a diverse set of intellectual resources gathered from the toolboxes of various disciplines to improve our understanding of the mental lives of children.

TWO GENERAL TYPES OF QUANTITATIVE STRATEGIES: TRUE EXPERIMENTS AND QUASI-EXPERIMENTS

Because quantitative strategies are generally more technically complicated than most qualitative strategies, the rest of this section will describe different quantitative strategies in greater detail. There are two main types of quantitative research methods: *true experiments* and *quasi-experiments*. Imagine one is interested in the effects of mood on vocabulary size. In a true experiment, a psychologist identifies a population (i.e., four-year-old children) and selects a sample of this population, such as twenty children from a local kindergarten. The children are divided randomly into two groups, one of which receives one kind of treatment, such as reading a happy children's picture book, and the other half that reads a sad children's book. Mood in this case is considered an *independent variable*; it is the variable that the psychologist manipulates. After each child reads the happy or sad story, they are tested on some measure, such as a vocabulary test. The performance on this test is called the *dependent variable* because its value depends upon the manipulation of the independent variable. The researcher then compares performance measured by the dependent variable for the two groups (happy and sad children). The researcher compares the data from the two groups using statistical tests, and if there is a significant difference between the performance of the happy and sad children, the researcher can conclude that mood affects performance on vocabulary tests.

True experiments are powerful because they rely upon the process of randomization to prevent extraneous factors from influencing behavior. Randomization prevents the groups that are defined (e.g., happy or sad children) from being different in any systematic way that could introduce bias into the results. Unfortunately, randomization in most developmental studies is hard to accomplish, mainly because most developmental psychologists are interested in children's performance at different ages, and it is impossible to randomly assign a group of children into, say, four- or eight-year-old groups. Therefore, the most common research methodology used in developmental psychology is the quasi-experiment. Quasi-experiments are strategies in which participants are not randomly assigned into groups. For example, one could measure individual children's mood using a scale of how happy or sad they feel at the moment, then assess their vocabulary, and determine whether there is a relationship (statistically known as a *correlation*) between the two variables.

The fact that developmental studies generally employ quasi-experimental designs raises a number of concerns about the validity of a study's conclusions. Validity describes the degree to which a study demonstrates that some observed difference is actually due to the specific factor that the psychologist investigates. Let us consider a simple yet ridiculous example. Imagine a psychologist is interested in differences between a newborn baby and an eight-year-old child on their ability to measure the length of a stick. The psychologist places a ruler and pencil in each of their hands, and provides them with a sheet of paper on which to write their answers. It is not surprising that after a minute, the researcher discovers that the baby is merely sucking on the pen while the eight-year-old has written the correct answer. The psychologist concludes that infants cannot measure, but eight-year-olds can.

The problem with this quasi-experiment is that there are multiple alternative explanations that threaten the validity of the conclusion drawn from the data. For instance, the findings could arise because the eight-year-old understood the instructions and the infant did not. It could be due to the fact that eight-year-olds have a certain level of motor skills, such as holding a pen or a ruler, while infants do not. It may also be due to the fact that eight-year-olds can measure, while infants can not. Yet because there are so many potential causes for the difference, it is difficult to determine which offers the best (or most parsimonious) explanation. In fact, I will describe an experiment showing that infants actually *can* measure the length of a stick, but one must design experiments that demonstrate this capacity but do not involve understanding instructions, answering a written test or using a ruler.

QUASI-EXPERIMENTAL DESIGNS FOR STUDYING DEVELOPMENT OVER TIME

The quasi-experimental research designs described above refer to general approaches to studying psychological phenomena. However, because developmental psychologists are generally interested in change over time, there are several more specific research designs common in psychological studies of children. The two most common are *longitudinal* and *cross-sectional* designs. In longitudinal designs, a group of children are tested in a study at age X, and the same children are retested again when they are at age Y. The researcher then compares the performance of the children at age X and age Y. In cross-sectional designs a group of younger children at age X and a group of older children at age Y are tested at the same time, and the performance of the two groups compared. Note that both of these experiments are necessarily quasi-experimental because there is no random assignment into groups. The advantages of longitudinal designs are that they allow one to observe individual growth trajectories over time and that there are no extraneous differences between the children in the two age groups because they are the same children. However, longitudinal designs have the disadvantage of being time consuming, expensive, and, especially for those designs that track children over long periods of time, no guarantee that the children who were originally tested will be available at the second time-period for retesting (i.e., families move to different states, move within the same area and leave no forwarding address). The advantages of cross-sectional designs are that they are fast, cheap, efficient, and have no problems with dropout because children are tested only once. Their disadvantages are that they do not allow one to observe growth trajectories and there are potential differences between the groups in a study other than just age (e.g., children born in 1976 entered a very different world than those born in 2006). Similar to the problem of qualitative and quantitative strategies, note that the advantages of longitudinal designs tend to be the disadvantages of cross-sectional designs, and vice versa. There are several other less commonly used developmental designs that address some of these limitations (cross-sequential, time-lagged, or microgenetic designs); however, these methodologies are only feasible in examining specific kinds of research questions.

SPECIFIC RESEARCH PARADIGMS FOR STUDYING CHILDREN

Experimental procedures used to study older children are similar to those used with adults; however, the complexity of the task and the instructions are often simplified in order for children to understand the task. For instance, in studies that examine mood states using scale measures, instead of using words like "happy" or "sad" researchers may use schematic cartoon faces expressing varying states of happiness and ask the child to point to the face corresponding his or her mood.

Younger children present a number of challenges as participants in research studies. For certain questions, psychologists have developed specific paradigms for acquiring data with infant or toddler participants. For instance, perceptual depth perception has been studied using a visual cliff—a glass tabletop having a fake edge that appears to suddenly drop off in the center of the table. Researchers have used such visual cliffs to determine whether infants will crawl over the apparent edge when prompted by their mothers on the opposite side of the table. Another example is the rouge test, which explores self-perception in infants. A psychologist will surreptitiously place a red rouge dot on the nose of an infant and place him or her before a mirror. While younger infants either laugh or try to touch the nose of the image in the mirror, older children reach for their own nose to wipe off the rouge. Clearly, these methodologies are useless in studying older children and adults, who would perform perfectly in these tasks. However, they are very useful tasks for examining a variety of issues in younger children who have only a limited capacity to verbally respond to questions or understand directions.

Perhaps the greatest challenge for developmental psychologists is studying mental processes in very young infants. Even simplified versions of adult tasks are impossible to use with infants due to their limited understanding of language and motor skills. Developmental psychologists who study infants have developed several clever paradigms for exploring psychological processes that do not require the production or comprehension of language. One such method is known as visual habituation.

The habituation paradigm relies on the fact that organisms pay more attention to novel than familiar stimuli. In habituation studies, infants are shown a stimulus, such as a stick of a certain length on a small puppet stage. An experimenter measures the amount of time the infant watches the stimulus. Once the infants look away in boredom, the experimenter raises a screen that blocks the infants' view of the stimulus. After a short delay, the screen lowers, and the infant sees the same stimulus again. Just as you become bored from listening to the same song on repeat on your stereo, infants tire of seeing the same object over and over again. At some point the infant hardly looks at the habituation stimulus at all. At this point, the screen raises, blocking the infant's view of the stage, and the experimenter switches the habituation stimulus with a new stimulus that differs from the original. In this example, the novel stimulus is a stick that is twice the length of the stick that the infant viewed in the habituation portion of the study. If infants perceive a change in the size of the stick, the amount of time they look at the new object increases relative to the time they look at habituation stimulus. Alternatively, if the infant does not perceive a difference between the two objects, his or her looking time will not differ between the habituation and novel displays. In fact, evidence gathered using the habituation paradigm suggests that under certain conditions, infants *do* notice the difference between two sticks that differ only in length, providing evidence that infants have a primitive ability to measure.[4]

There are a variety of resources that help explain research designs used to study children. For a comprehensive treatment of such designs, there is an exhaustive yet concise chapter by Hartman in *Developmental Psychology: An Advanced Textbook*. There are also a number of textbooks on research methodology in psychology that are not focused exclusively on developmental research, but provide a broader perspective on research in psychology. McBurney and White's *Research Methods* is a simple and readable text, Sarafino's *Research Methods* is a more intermediate-level text, and Kirk's *Experimental Design* is a very advanced text covering many of the statistical aspects of research design.

OVERVIEW OF SCHOLARLY WRITING IN PSYCHOLOGY

After conducting a study, psychologists share their findings with the world by publishing their findings. Scholarly writing in psychology appears in the

form of full-length books and monographs, edited books in which different authors contribute chapters, and in articles that appear in academic
journals. This section will focus mainly on journal articles; however, it is
worth mentioning a few books that are particularly useful in providing a
range of information.

Psychology Books

There are a large number of undergraduate-level introductory textbooks on
psychology, and many focusing upon specific subfields, such as child or developmental psychology. These textbooks serve as a good starting point for
general information about research in psychology, and are typically divided
into thematic section by chapter, allowing one to quickly acquire information. Unfortunately, by their introductory nature, what most textbooks provide in breadth they typically lack in depth. An excellent undergraduate
textbook is Berk's *Child Development*, and a useful textbook for more advanced students is Bornstein and Lamb's *Developmental Psychology*.

Beyond textbooks there are a variety of handbooks that provide detailed information on specific topics related to psychology and childhood.
Handbooks are particularly useful in providing virtually encyclopedic
knowledge about multiple aspects of a single topic. In psychology, Weiner's
Handbook of Psychology is perhaps the most significant. It certainly is the
heaviest: spanning almost 8000 pages in twelve volumes, Volume 6 is devoted exclusively to developmental psychology. Similarly, Damon and col-
leagues' *Handbook of Child Psychology* is a five-volume series covering a wide
variety of topics relevant to children and childhood. Valsiner and Connolly's
Handbook of Developmental Psychology is a useful resource as well. There are
dozens of handbooks on any of a number of more specific topics in psychology, from abnormal psychology to violence prevention. Many of these
handbooks include chapters dealing with issues relevant to CCS.

There are also a large number of edited books and full-length volumes
on any of a number of more specific topics in psychology. Edited volumes
are books containing chapters that revolve around a specific theme. An editor asks various scholars to submit chapters to be collected and printed together as a book. Compared with journal articles, chapters from edited
books are generally easier to read because they review a large number of
findings rather than report data from any single investigation. Full-length
books and monographs, though available, are relatively uncommon in psychology today. Generally, these books tend to summarize a particular point
of view or series of studies conducted by the author(s) of the volume.

Finally, for those new to the discipline, it may be worth referencing a dictionary of psychology terms, such as Hayes and Stratton's *A Student's Dictionary of Psychology*, or for more advanced students, Corsini's *The Dictionary of Psychology*. There are a variety of encyclopedias of psychology that cover important topics in greater detail, such as Gregory's *The Oxford Companion to the Mind*, or Kazdin's *Encyclopedia of Psychology*.

You can search for all of the books described above using your library's catalog, which may be accessible through the Internet. If your library does not have a particular volume, ask your librarian how to search other library catalogs and request the volume through the interlibrary loan service. Your librarian is perhaps your most valuable resource in finding the scholarly sources you require.

Psychology Journals

Because psychology is an evolving field in which theoretical and methodological advancements occur in rapid succession, most psychologists favor journal articles over full-length books as a forum for presenting new ideas and research. However, this fact poses a challenge for students unfamiliar with the process of conducting literature searches in psychology. Psychology journals tend to be difficult to find and locate, articles tend to be densely written using technical terms and statistical analyses, and have the structure and stylized format of a scientific report. This section addresses these issues by explaining how to find journal articles and other resources, and once you find them, how to understand what they say.

Psychology journals are specialized periodicals consisting of a set of articles written by different authors that may or may not be thematically related. Depending on the specific journal, articles can range from a page or two in length to well over fifty pages. There are three major types of articles published in psychology journals: empirical, theoretical, and review articles. Empirical articles present the results of original studies or experiments. Theoretical articles conceptually frame and discuss a particular question. Review articles summarize the most recent findings about a specific problem in the field. Theoretical and review articles are often structured like an essay, while empirical articles tend to follow the general format of articles published in other scientific disciplines.

While there is some variability in structure depending on the specific subfield in psychology and the particular research question examined, most articles begin with an abstract, which is a short (50- to 150-word) summary of the entire paper. Next, the introductory section discusses the problem addressed in the paper by referencing prior studies and discussing the limitations of past research. If the article is an empirical study, the third section presents the method that the researcher used to obtain data and the statistical analysis of the results. Some papers contain a single study; however, many consist of several related experiments. Each experiment presents the methodology of the study. The methodology section typically consists of a section describing the participants of the study, a section describing the study's design, a section outlining the materials and procedures used to gather data, and a section describing the results and statistical analyses of the data, and a section discussing the relevance of the results. After presenting the studies, a final section presenting an overall discussion summarizes the findings of the study, discusses the results in relation to prior research, and provides some directions for future research on the topic. Finally, there is a list of the works cited in the article.

Journal articles generally utilize a highly stylized and technical language that is often difficult to read. However, many students new to the field, reading a journal article for the first time, understand almost everything until encountering the results section of the paper. There they encounter strange and exotic-sounding statistical terms such as ANOVA (short for ANalysis Of VAriance), regression, factor analysis, or partial correlation. Thrown in the mix are strange sequences of letters, numbers and Greek letters, such as $F(2, 34) = 11.16$, $p < .001$, or $\beta = 0.023$, $z = 3.4$, $p < .01$. Many stop reading there; others simply skip over the results to the conclusion section. Both responses are unfortunate because the statistics used in most papers are really quite simple, and they help clarify the conclusions drawn in the article.

While a comprehensive review of statistics is beyond the scope of this chapter, a few points are worth mentioning. The statistics used in the vast majority of psychology articles are covered in most college-level introductory statistics classes. If you are interested in seriously studying psychology, you may want to enroll in such a statistics course; it will help you understand some of the principles underlying research in general. Second, the vast majority of statistics used in journal articles simply do one of two things: describe the relationship among variables (When children get older, do they perform better on math tests?) or assess the degree to which a finding might be due to chance (Is the observed difference in average performance between males and females in a spatial reasoning experiment just random noise or a "real" or "significant" difference?). There are a variety of books that explain statistics in lay terms. Students terrified of statistics might want to invest in one in particular: Jaeger's *Statistics: A Spectator Sport*, which explains statistics in simple terms without using math.

THE PUBLISHING PROCESS IN PSYCHOLOGY

This section describes the process of publishing in psychology. A psychologist will conduct a study, write a research report (manuscript) based on their findings, and send the manuscript to a journal in consideration for publication. In what are known as "peer-reviewed" journals, an editor on the journal's staff reads the manuscript, and determines whether the paper and/or its topic is appropriate for that particular journal. At this point, the editor might reject the paper outright and explain to the author the reason for rejection. Alternatively, if the paper is of relatively good quality and relevant to the topic of the journal, the editor sends the paper to several (usually three) scholars in the field who are knowledgeable about the specific topic addressed in the manuscript. These scholars act as consultants to the editor in the decision-making process of whether to publish, reject, or request that the author(s) modify the paper in some way prior to its publication. The reviewers write a report summarizing the conclusions and provide criticisms of the manuscript for the authors to address in a revision of the paper. The requested modifications and criticisms of the reviewers are then sent to the author who revises the paper and resubmits it to the editor. At this point, the paper is either sent back to the reviewers for a second review, or the editor decides that the author's modifications are sufficient and accepts the paper. Once accepted, the paper is labeled "in press." Often, it takes anywhere from several months to over a year for the article to appear in the journal after it has been accepted.

The peer-review system ensures that the claims in a paper are reasonable and that the authors address obvious problems with the methodology or design of the study. Non–peer-reviewed journals (as well as chapters in edited books and dissertations) do not have the advantage of this review process, and one should evaluate claims in these publications somewhat more skeptically than in articles appearing in peer-reviewed journals.

There are a number of important peer-reviewed general journals in psychology that publish articles on a wide variety of topics that sometimes include children and childhood. Among the best-known are the following: *Annual Review of Psychology, American Psychologist, Cognition, Current Directions in Psychological Science, Journal of Experimental Psychology: General, Journal of Personality and Social Psychology, Psychological Review, Psychological Bulletin,* and *Psychological Science.* There are also a number of peer-reviewed journals that publish articles exclusively on topics related to child psychology. These include the *British Journal of Developmental Psychology, Child Development, Cognitive Development, Developmental Neuropsychology, Developmen-*

tal Psychology, Developmental Review, Developmental Science, Development and Psychopathology, Infancy, Infant Behavior and Development, Journal of Adolescence, Journal of Child Psychology and Psychiatry, Journal of Cognition and Development, Journal of Experimental Child Psychology, Journal of the American Academy of Child and Adolescent Psychiatry, Journal of Child Psychology and Psychiatry and Allied Disciplines, and *Journal of Youth and Adolescence.*

In the last decade, a number of journals have shifted to publishing their journals on the Internet and now issue online articles through a library subscription service in the form of portable document format (pdf) files. Once opened or printed, the file appears exactly like the article in the printed journal, with the correct page numbering and graphics. Usually, your library's online catalog contains detailed information on the availability of electronic versions of journals, and link to the table of contents of each issue. This topic is covered in the next section.

CONDUCTING A LITERATURE SEARCH

To write a paper or conduct a research project it is important to know what information already exists on a particular topic. Thus, you must know how to conduct a literature search and find journal articles, chapters, and books addressing a particular problem or issue. However, there are literally tens of thousands of books, and hundreds of thousands of journal articles published about psychological issues spanning well over a century. The problem is finding the seven that address the specific problem you might be interested in writing a paper about. This section addresses this problem by describing how to conduct a literature search in psychology.

One way of obtaining information is to conduct a haphazard search. For those interested in knowing what range of topics are published in psychology journals, it may be useful to go to the library, go to the section where the psychology books are shelved, and peruse any volumes and the last several issues of a journal that seem to be about a topic that interests you. This strategy may be inefficient, and you may find nothing, but you might stumble upon hidden gems that you might miss otherwise. Alternatively, you might read a textbook or handbook chapter that describes a particular paper or study and you may look up the citation in the reference section of the book and find it using your library's catalog.

Unfortunately, few of us have the luxury of a lazy afternoon to browse around the library. More often, one must find seven to ten articles to use in writing a paper that may be due in a few days (or sometimes even a few hours). To complicate the process, each of these articles may be published in different journals, some of which are bound and available on the shelves of your library, some may be in storage outside the library, others that can only be downloaded electronically, and others that can only be accessed through interlibrary loan service. In this situation, it is useful to use one of the academic search engines that index journal articles published in psychology journals that are available through the Internet. For psychology, the most common index at academic libraries is the database PsycINFO. It indexes a large number of psychology journals and periodicals and is available through your library's website. The online interface that accesses the database varies from library to library; some use a vendor interface, such as OVID or EBESCO, for accessing the database. The interface makes little difference in the resulting search, but there are minor differences in the way the engines work.

The most common approaches to searching the PsycINFO database is by author, title, or keyword. Depending on whether your library uses the OVID or EBESCO interface, there usually is a menu so that you can select one of these options. Imagine you are interested in the research of Lawrence Kohlberg. You select "Author Search" option and type "Kohlberg, Lawrence" in the text box, and click on the search button. A new screen may appear with the names and initials of all authors named Lawrence Kohlberg who have written articles. Select the box next to the name "Lawrence Kohlberg" and click "continue." A list of Kohlberg's article titles will appear with basic bibliographic information such as the authors, journal titles, call numbers, issues, years, etc. If you click on the highlighted title of the article, PsycINFO will provide the abstract of the article and detailed information regarding the journal and volume in which the article appears. In addition, there may be a link that allows you to determine whether the articles are electronically available (although this may vary depending upon the specific way your library accesses PsycINFO). Similarly, you may also conduct a search by article title by selecting the appropriate box. This is a useful tool if you know the title of the article but not the author.

Yet the most powerful feature of PsycINFO is its ability to search for specific terms that are in the title or abstract of the article. To demonstrate the process of finding references, we will go through the steps of a typical literature search. Imagine you are a interested in finding published psychological research on the development of ethnic identity. If you have an Internet connection available, you might want to go to your library's Web page, log into PsycINFO, and conduct the following search for practice, but realize that the numbers you obtain may differ from those reported here, which were accessed in 2006. Go to your library's PsycINFO interface and type in "Ethnic Identity." You will find that there are more than 4500 articles for that topic. It would take a considerable amount of time to read just the titles of all these articles. If you did, you would probably find that very few of them have to do with children at all.

Fortunately, PsycINFO allows searching the database using what are called "Boolean operators." These are terms such as "And," "Or," and "Not" that allow one to efficiently limit and expand the scope of a search by adding additional terms. For example, if you type in "ethnic identity and children," slightly over 600 titles appear, which is still too many to read. At this point you need to use both creativity and thought in narrowing the scope of your research question further. For instance, you may be specifically interested in research on the ethnic identity of children in Latino culture. You type in "ethnic identity and children and Latino" and find twenty-three results. Twenty-three abstracts can be read in a few minutes' time.

You may subsequently need to revise your search or perform multiple searches. For instance, until quite recently, the term *Hispanic* was commonly used to indicate "latino/latina" by a number of researchers. It might be useful to search for articles that use either *Hispanic* or *Latino*. So it is possible to search using the string "ethnic identity and children and (Latino or Hispanic)," which results in sixty articles. Imagine further that you are *not* interested in studies of biracial children. You could use the following search string, "ethnic identity and children and (Latino or Hispanic) not biracial," which results in fifty articles. It is rare that you will use the right search terms on the first try. It is important to gain practice at using PsycINFO as a search tool. An hour or two trying all the options will pay off enormously in reducing the time it will take to conduct literature searches in the future. For further information about the PsycINFO database, please refer to the American Psychological Association website, which contains detailed instructions on its use.[5]

WRITING THE PSYCHOLOGY PAPER

If you are enrolled in a psychology course, you may have to write a term paper or research report. For instance, you may be writing a review paper for an introductory course in psychology, or a theoretical paper for an advanced independent study elective, or writing the results of your own empirical study. The structure and format of the paper will differ depending on the specific course you are taking; however, most professors, and particularly in advanced courses, will assume that you know how to conduct a literature search and use APA citation format. Always ask your professor for specific details.

Regardless of the format, every paper you write should present a thesis. A thesis is simply an argumentative statement that takes a particular stand on an issue of which there is potential for disagreement. Holly Blackford points out in her chapter on literature in this work that a good thesis should be articulated as "Although [this], actually [that]." Two examples of arguments that are not theses are "Recent research demonstrates a strong relationship between watching violent television and aggression" and "Recent research on television violence and aggression fails to account for factors such as parental involvement that might influence aggressive behavior." Both of these are mere statements of fact or opinion, and leave no room for argument. Remember that a thesis must advance an argument that goes beyond the statement of fact and permits an evaluation of a complex position. So a better thesis might be, "While recent research demonstrates a strong relationship between watching violent television and aggression, these studies fail to account for parental involvement which may influence the relationship." At this point you would want to evaluate the claims of the prior literature on violent television and aggression, address the limitations of prior studies using research you have gathered on how parental involvement is implicated in aggression, and state a clear and unequivocal conclusion.

The best writing in psychology is concise and specific: state your point, back it up with evidence, and move on to the next point. Few psychologists value flowery, ornate language or digressions that add little to your thesis. Almost none appreciate personal anecdotes, such as stories about family members or friends whose experiences contradict established findings in the field. However, some felicity or creativity, used judiciously, can greatly reinforce the paper, if used in the proper context. Avoid extensive footnotes or end notes: very few psychologists use footnotes in their writing, and it is better to simply state a point in the text, or eliminate it entirely if it is too nuanced for the main body of your manuscript.

By far, the most important step in the process of writing is proofreading. As a reader, there is nothing quite as disappointing as a set of excellent ideas embedded within a poorly structured, disorganized, and misspelled document. Check your grammar for run-on sentences, fragments, or commonly misspelled words ("weather" for "whether;" "affect" for "effect"). Whenever I finish an article or chapter, I put aside the work for a few days before proofreading it in order to provide some distance between the process of writing and of reading. Then, I read the work from the last sentence to the first sentence, which removes each sentence from its linear context and forces me to examine the grammar without skimming or skipping. Take considerable care with the structure and clarity of your writing, and if you are continually frustrated by your grades or your ability to write, seek the assistance of a writing tutor or composition class.

As noted above, regardless of the particular structure of the paper, a psychology professor will most likely require that you cite and reference scholarly materials using the American Psychological Association (APA) style for citations. Different professors may vary in the degree to which they will enforce adherence to the APA style, nevertheless, it is always a good idea simply to cite in APA format, and to do it correctly the first time. Note that this chapter is not formatted using APA style, and do not use it as a model for APA style. Rather, the details and numerous examples of APA citation style can be found in the *APA Manual of Style*, 5th edition, available at many bookstores and most libraries. The following introductory paragraph to a hypothetical paper provides an example of APA format:

> One of the oldest problems in the social sciences is the relation between culture and thought (Jahoda, 1993). The debate over whether all people think alike regardless of their sociocultural environment, or if people in different cultures think in unique and divergent ways has a number of implications for understanding a diverse set of psychological processes (Kitayama & Duffy, 2003). This paper reviews evidence for the "universalist" and "relativist" positions and argues in favor of Greenfield, Keller, Fuligni, and Maynard's (2003) position that a better understanding of psychological development requires how culture shapes how children experience the social world.

The following is a list of the works cited in APA format:

Greenfield, P., Keller, H., Fuligni, A., & Maynard, A. (2005). Cultural pathways through universal development. *Annual Review of Psychology, 54*, 461–490.

Jahoda, G. (1993). *Crossroads Between Culture and Mind*. Cambridge: Harvard University Press.

Kitayama, S., & Duffy, S. (2003). Cultural competence—tacit, yet fundamental: Self, social relations, and cognition in the US and Japan. In R. Sternberg & E. Grigorenko (Eds.), *Culture and Competence: Contexts of Life Success* (pp. 55–87). Washington, DC: American Psychological Association.

Note that the references differ in structure due to the fact that one (Greenfield, Keller, Fuligni, & Maynard) is an article appearing in a journal, another (Jahoda) is a full-length book, and the last (Kitayama & Duffy) is a chapter in an edited book. Note also that when the citation is within a parenthesis the ampersand sign (&) is used to link the name of authors, while when embedded within a sentence, "in favor of Greenfield, Keller, Fuligni, and Maynard's (2003) position that," the writer must write out the word "and" as a word. In addition, if the writer were to cite Greenfield's article again, he or she would drop all but the first author and simply write (Greenfield et al., 2003), "et al." being an abbreviation for "and others." There are specific citation formats for citing movies, websites, music recordings, and so on. APA citation style can be complex, and generally differs from other citation styles (e.g., MLA, Chicago), so take care to follow the guidelines in the *APA Manual of Style*.

Some professors may require that you conduct an original study on children. Your study may be nonobtrusive (observing children interacting with their mothers at the food court in a local mall) or obtrusive (directly interacting with children by testing them in an experiment such as a Piagetian conservation task). Either way, such projects require both conducting a literature search and collecting data. Before starting such an empirical study, be sure to read the ethical standards for research practice outlined by both the American Psychological Association and the Society for Research in Child Development, both of which are available online.[6] If you hope to eventually publish your findings, you must apply to your University's Institutional Review Board (IRB) *before* collecting data. The IRB is an organization at universities that review projects and determines whether the study potentially violates any ethical standard. Once the IRB has approved your proposal, you may begin to collect data. However, your first step should always be scheduling a discussion with your professor before testing any children; he or she will be able to assist you in clarifying the ethical issues involved in your research, such as obtaining parental consent.

If you do decide to collect original data, it is useful to remember a few practical points. First, children may be extraordinarily fun to play with, but are notoriously uncooperative research participants. Their limited attention span and cognitive and social competencies severely limits their ability to fully cooperate as research participants. Try to design your study to be simple, quick, and fun—much like a game. For instance, in a recent study on kindergartener's ability to measure, I introduced children to a stuffed animal—a dog named Toby—and I presented the task as a game in which the children were helping Toby find a bone he hid the previous day. This allowed children to feel part of a cooperative experience, and helped engage their attention to the task at hand. Second, it is best to conduct your research in a space where there are few external distractions. I conducted the "Toby" experiment in a coat closet in the back of a kindergarten classroom where no other children were allowed to play. Third, if you are collecting data in a classroom or school, try to spend a few hours with the students before running your study so that the children become acquainted with you. This helps reduce the anxiety many children experience around strangers, and it provides you with experience in observing children in a natural context. Some excellent resources containing practical suggestions for conducting developmental research are Christensen's *Conducting Research with Children*, Graue and Walsh's *Studying Children in Context*, and for observational research, Emerson, et al., *Writing Ethnographic Fieldnotes*.

While it is always useful to collect original data, there are a variety of publicly available data sets accessible through the Internet that you may download and analyze yourself. For instance, the *Child Language Data Exchange System* (*CHILDES*) and the *TalkBank* project out of Carnegie Mellon University are databases of hundreds of transcripts of children and adult conversational interactions in English and over a dozen other languages.[7] These databases also store audio and video files of interactions between parents and children. These resources can be used to study language acquisition, or simply to understand what kinds of topics children discuss in everyday life. If you are interested in mathematical reasoning, the *Trends in International Mathematics and Science Study* website provides access to data sets concerning math education in several countries.[8] A wealth of data and information on more general social trends that influence childhood can be found at the National Opinion Research Center's General Social Survey and the United States Census.[9] Finally, one may be both creative and ingenious in finding data. For instance, a number of parents now write online "baby blogs" in which they describe the development of their own children. Such online journals may provide unique insight on a variety of questions regarding the psychology of children and parents alike.

For further reading and tips on the process of writing in psychology, please refer to Robert Sternberg's *The Psychologist's Companion: A Guide to Scientific Writing for Students and Researchers* and for more advanced students who are interested in publishing their work, *Guide to Publishing in Psychology Journals*.

FURTHER RESOURCES ON
PSYCHOLOGY AND CHILDREN

There are a number of professional associations and organizations in psychology that serve as excellent resources for information. Most of these organizations have information and resources for psychologists and the general public, and hold regular meetings that members can attend and give presentations in. Most also publish their own journals, many of which are available through the organization website, or through your university's library.

The major professional organization for psychologists in the United States is the American Psychological Association. The APA publishes a number of important journals and periodicals, maintains the PsycINFO database, and sets the ethical standard for clinical and research practices, and maintains the APA citation style used by almost all journals. Apart from APA, there are a variety of other professional organizations that are geared toward research and practice with children. The largest and most general organization in the United States is the Society for Research on Child Development (SRCD). The SRCD publishes the important journal *Child Development*, provides a set of ethical guidelines specifically for conducting research with children, and holds a large conference every other year. There are a variety of smaller professional organizations that hold annual or biennial meetings on topics relevant to childhood studies. These include the Jean Piaget Society, the Cognitive Development Society, the International Society for Infant Studies, and the Society for Research in Adolescence. There are a number of other professional organizations that are not dedicated exclusively to the study of children or childhood, but may be of interest to some due to their specific disciplinary focus. Some such organizations include the American Psychological Society, the Society of Personality and Social Psychology, the Cognitive Science Society, and the International Association for Cross-Cultural Psychology, among others.

All of the major psychology professional organizations have extensive websites with information on publications, conferences, and e-mail listservs. If you have designed your own study, you should discuss with your professor the possibility of attending a conference sponsored by one of these organizations and presenting a poster or talk. You will gain experience in presenting your ideas to professionals in the field and have the opportunity to discuss your ideas with other scholars and students. Often, professional societies have special travel scholarships specifically to promote undergraduate and graduate student attendance at the conference; you typically can find this information on their websites.

If you are interested in pursuing graduate education in child psychology, there are many master's and doctoral programs in both the United States and abroad. *U.S. News and World Report* issues a yearly evaluation ranking graduate programs in several psychology disciplines, including developmental psychology. While useful as a general guide, it is important to look beyond graduate school rankings and search for departments having faculty that share your particular research interests. There are a variety of teaching and research fellowships available through universities themselves and the Federal government, especially for doctoral programs. Ask your professor or chair of the psychology department at your university for more information about your options.

CONCLUSIONS

The field of psychology is young relative to most other disciplines in the social sciences. However, in little more than a century, psychology has grown enormously, becoming one of the largest disciplines in the social sciences. And while psychology has made great strides toward understanding children and childhood in the past century, there are still vast regions of this field that we have yet to fully explore. Hopefully, like those uncharted regions on the maps drawn by the first explorers, this *terra incognita* will entice you to travel to these unknown lands to search for answers to the mysteries of the developing mind.

And you come at a good time. Now more than ever, psychology requires the perspective of interdisciplinary researchers who are not afraid to transcend the boundaries of traditional theories, methodologies, and paradigms. Psychologists have as much to gain as those in other fields in promoting an interdisciplinary dialogue in order to further our understanding of children and childhood. Such research synergy would enliven discussions, raise new questions, pose new problems, and bring fresh perspectives to some of the stale debates that confine themselves within most academic departments.

So, welcome to psychology! There are countless fascinating lands to explore, and countless ways to get you there. The locals are friendly, so if you ever get lost, feel free to ask for directions, and we'll be happy to explain some of our customs or traditions. I hope you enjoy your stay here, and please come again.

NOTES

1. The author acknowledges Charlene Dunkley, Freddie Renzulli, and Danielle Renzulli for their helpful comments and suggestions on this chapter.

2. See Alison James, "Understanding Childhood from an Interdisciplinary Perspective," in *Rethinking Childhood*, ed. Peter B. Pufall and Richard P. Unsworth (New Brunswick, N.J.: Rutgers University Press, 2004).

3. See J. E. Huttenlocher, W. Haight, A. S. Bryk, and M. Seltzer, "Early Vocabulary Growth: Relating to Language Input and Gender," *Developmental Psychology* 27, no. 2 (1991): 236–49.

4. The details of this study are reported in Sean Duffy, Janellen Huttenlocher, Susan Levine, and Renee Duffy, "How Infants Encode Spatial Extent," *Infancy* 8 (2005): 81–90.

5. The APA website describing the PsycInfo database can be found at www.apa.org/psycinfo. You also may encounter a search engine called PsycArticles, which is an index to articles in APA journals that allows you to access full-text versions of these articles. However, all the journals indexed in PsycArticles are also indexed in PsycINFO, so it is better to use PsycINFO for most literature searches.

6. The APA ethical standards can be found at www.apa.org/ethics. The SRCD ethical standards can be found at www.srcd.org/ethicalstandards.html.

7. The CHILDES database website URL is childes.psy.cmu.edu. The TalkBank project website URL is talkbank.org.

8. The TIMSS website URL is www.timss.org.

9. The General Social Survey's website URL is www.norc.uchicago.edu/projects/gensoc.asp, the U.S. Census website is ww.census.gov.

WORKS CITED

American Psychological Association (APA). *American Psychological Association Publication Manual.* 5th ed. Washington, D.C.: American Psychological Association, 2001.

Berk, Laura. *Child Development.* 7th ed. Boston: Allyn & Bacon, 2006.

Bornstein, Marc H., and Michael E. Lamb, eds. *Developmental Psychology: An Advanced Textbook.* Hillsdale, N.J.: Erlbaum, 1999.

Christensen, Pia, and Alison James. *Conducting Research with Children: Perspectives and Practices.* Oxford: Routledge, 1999.

Corsini, Raymond J. *The Dictionary of Psychology.* Philadelphia, Pa.: Brunner/Mazel, 1999.

Damon, William, and Richard M. Lerner, eds. *Handbook of Child Psychology.* Indianapolis, Ind.: Wiley, 2006.

Duffy, Sean, Janellen Huttenlocher, Susan Levine, and Renee Duffy. "How Infants Encode Spatial Extent." *Infancy* 8 (2005): 81–90.

Emerson, Robert M., Rachel I. Fretz, and Linda L. Shaw. *Writing Ethnographic Fieldnotes.* Chicago: University of Chicago Press, 1995.

Graue, M. Elizabeth, and Daniel J. Walsh. *Studying Children in Context: Theories, Methods, and Ethics.* Thousand Oaks, Calif.: Sage, 1998.

Gregory, Richard L., ed. *The Oxford Companion to the Mind.* New York: Oxford University Press, 2004.

Hayes, Nicky, and Peter Stratton. *A Student's Dictionary of Psychology*. New York: Oxford University Press, 2003.

Huttenlocher, J. E., W. Haight, A. S. Bryk, and M. Seltzer. "Early Vocabulary Growth: Relating to Language Input and Gender." *Developmental Psychology* 27, no. 2 (1991): 236–49.

Jaeger, Richard. *Statistics: A Spectator Sport*. Thousand Oaks, Calif.: Sage, 1993.

James, Alison. "Understanding Childhood from an Interdisciplinary Perspective." In *Rethinking Childhood*, edited by Peter B. Pufall and Richard P. Unsworth, 25–37. New Brunswick, N.J.: Rutgers University Press, 2004.

Kazdin, Alan E., ed. *Encyclopedia of Psychology*. Washington, D.C.: American Psychological Association, 2000.

Kirk, R. E. *Experimental Design: Procedures for the Behavioral Sciences*. Pacific Grove, Calif.: Brooks/Cole, 1995.

McBurney, D. H., and T. L. White. *Research Methods*. 5th ed. Belmont, Calif.: Wadsworth, 2006.

Sarafino, Edward. *Research Methods: Using Processes and Procedures of Science to Understand Behavior*. Upper Saddle River, N.J.: Pearson, 2005.

Sternberg, Robert J., ed. *Guide to Publishing in Psychology Journals*. Cambridge, UK: Cambridge University Press, 2000.

———. *The Psychologist's Companion: A Guide to Scientific Writing for Students and Researchers*. Cambridge, UK: Cambridge University Press, 2003.

Valsiner, Jaan, and Kevin J. Connolly, eds. *Handbook of Developmental Psychology*. Thousand Oaks, Calif.: Sage, 2003.

Weiner, Irving B., ed. *Handbook of Psychology*. Indianapolis, Ind.: Wiley, 2005.

10

SOCIOLOGY

Kimberly Ann Scott and Sarane Spence Boocock

The sociological study of children and childhoods is a relatively new but rapidly developing field that claims its identity as an autonomous subdiscipline on the grounds that: "1) it examines a wider range of children's experiences than other fields of sociology and 2) it challenges the conventional role of children in society."[1] Officially recognized by the American Sociological Association (ASA) only in 1992, the ASA section on the sociology of children is unified by a view of children as active and constructive members of society and childhood as an integral part of the social fabric. What is distinctly *sociological* about this approach is its focus on the following three factors: context, comparisons, and change.

Context refers to the social environments in which children live. These include kids' families, peer groups, schools, and neighborhoods, where they have close, face-to-face interpersonal relationships and learn the routines of everyday social life. These environments are often overlapping; for example, middle-class white families can generally choose to live in suburban communities with good schools, safe neighborhoods, and access to prompt medical and other assistance in emergencies, while low-income families, especially if they are African American or Latino, are more likely to reside in inner-city neighborhoods with higher crime rates, poorer schools, and little or no access to public services of all kinds. Beyond children's immediate environments are political, economic, social, and cultural systems at the municipal, state, regional, national, and international levels. While they may seem far removed from kids' everyday lives, what happens in these external environments can strongly affect their experience of childhood, partly through their effects on families, schools, and neighborhoods. Sociologists have learned that *where* a child is born and grows up is highly predictive of the kind of childhood he or she will experience and his or her subsequent life chances.

Comparisons are used to examine the differences between children and childhoods in various societies and societal subgroups. Through cross-cultural and within-cultural comparisons and by comparing multiple studies on a given topic, sociologists are learning which behaviors and experiences can be generalized across societies and cultures and which are distinct to a particular society, group, or subculture. Equally important, comparative analysis heightens researchers' sensitivity to *ethnocentric bias* (the assumption that the way things are done in one's own society or community is universal or "normal" and that other people's customs are abnormal or inferior); as a well-known anthropologist has put it: "Other cultures teach us that there are other ways to socialize, other ways to play, and other ways for kids to become moral citizens."[2]

Change looks at the transitions in children's lives as they progress through the various stages of childhood and also through historical time. Not only are children constantly growing and developing physically, mentally, and socially, but historical events and trends (e.g., wars, changes of government, economic growth or decline, technological inventions and their dissemination, changes in family structure and functioning, changes in the law relating to children and their families) as well as personal events (e.g., marriage, divorce, school attendance or nonattendance, illness, death) may all enhance or diminish the quality of kids' lives, their social status, and their future opportunities.

How we study social phenomena affects *what* we learn about them, and the new sociological paradigm that defines children as social actors who both shape and are shaped by their social circumstances calls for methodological approaches that avoid the *adult ideological bias* (the tendency to study children from the perspective of nonchildren) by allowing children to speak for themselves. This principle is encapsulated in William Corsaro's often-quoted statement that "children are the best sources for understanding childhood."[3] Corsaro's rule does not, however, imply the need for special techniques for research on children but rather the rigorous application of methodological procedures that "reflect the concrete particularities of the persons being studied" whether they are adults or children.[4] In the following pages we include both quantitative and qualitative studies that utilize a variety of methodologies, including observations, interviews, surveys, and experiments, analysis or reanalysis of statistics gathered by public and private agencies, and analysis of physical materials or artifacts (e.g., photographs, children's clothing, toys and games, child-produced stories and artworks). Our review leads us to conclude that there is seldom a "best" method for any research topic and that there are usually advantages in using multiple methods of data collection and analysis.

We have not attempted to provide an exhaustive set of references in the following bibliography. Rather we have collected examples of conceptual and empirical works relating to various contextual levels, some involving comparisons across time and space, by some of the preeminent pioneers in the field as well as by scholars outside the Western European and North American countries, who have dominated the field until very recently. We have also included examples from the small but growing body of research in which data are gathered directly from children, although it is important to remember that most research on children has been and continues to be designed, executed, and written by adults. Taking kids seriously enough to solicit *their* opinions let alone to include them in the design, execution, analysis, and presentation of a research project, a revolutionary idea only a few decades ago, remains controversial today.

In section 1 of the bibliography, we begin with some general texts and collections of readings that provide an overview of the field, followed, in section 2, by brief descriptions of the journals and other periodicals that publish some of the best research, both qualitative and quantitative, about children's experience of childhood in various times and places. In section 3, which addresses the design of sociological research on children and childhoods, we have given special attention to theoretical and methodological approaches that enable children to speak for themselves and, occasionally, involve them in the research process. Sections 4 and 5, on children's relations with their families and peer groups respectively, focus on the contextual environments that are most significant for kids, where they become social beings through interacting with adults and other kids and learn to function in various social settings. Section 6 contains comparative studies that examine variations in children's social positions and childhood experiences based upon differences in their social backgrounds, in particular, how inequalities of race, ethnicity, gender, and social class produce—or reproduce—social hierarchies and social stereotyping and thus determine how kids are perceived and treated by other kids and by adults. In section 7, we have selected examples from the vast literature on contextual effects at the societal and global levels, documenting the enormous and ever-greater differences in children's status and well-being, across and within nations, and how childhood as a social phenomenon is being transformed by political events and social and economic trends that originate far from their homes and local communities.

We have devoted the final section (section 8) to a few studies from the small but growing body of research in which children are allowed to express their views on subjects ranging from family life and how to deal with the divorce or separation of their parents, to critiques of the adult-controlled schools they attend, to their feelings about being "outsiders" or members of discriminated-against minority groups. We also include accounts of kids engaging in seemingly non-child-like activities, for example, as inventors and social activists. Among the children's voices, that of Craig Kielburger, who as a teenager founded Free the Children, the world's largest and most influential child-initiated social service project, is particularly resonant with the emerging paradigm for the sociology of children and childhoods as well as with empirical findings from a number of the adult-designed projects cited in earlier sections of this bibliography. In his work with fellow children around the world, observes Kielburger,

> I have found two extremes. In many developing countries, children are often asked to work long hours at hazardous jobs with no opportunity to play or to go to school. They are not allowed to develop physically, intellectually, and emotionally. . . . They support entire families. They fight in wars. They are given too much responsibility at too young an age.
>
> On the other hand, in many industrialized countries everything is done for children. They are segregated most of their lives with members of their own age group and are given little opportunity to assume responsibility, to develop a social conscience, or to learn through interaction with adults. Through media they learn to be consumers, to gain their self-image through electronic toys they own and labels they wear. They, too, are exploited. They see violence and suffering on the news every day but are told that they are too young to do anything about it. They are conditioned to become passive bystanders. . . .
>
> We want to help free children from both extremes.
>
> Children are not simply empty vessels to be filled. They are people with ideas, talents, opinions, and dreams.[5]

And like many adult sociologists trying to empower child research subjects by including them in the design, execution, analysis, and presentation of a research project, Kielberger maintains that the most serious obstacle to his work is the reluctance of so many adults to take him—or kids in general—seriously.

BIBLIOGRAPHY

Section 1: Overviews of the Field

Bandelj, Nina., Viviana Zelizer, and Ann Morning. *Materials for the Study of Childhood.* Princeton, N.J.: Department of Sociology, Princeton University, 2001.
    This work is an invaluable guide for the study of children's social worlds assembled by researchers at Princeton University. Part 1 contains a selected bibliography

of social science literature, grouped by the following subjects: general; historical and cross-cultural perspective; households; schools; production and consumption; literature, popular arts and media; child welfare and inequalities among children, children's organization of their lives, including use of time and space; and methods for studying children and childhoods. Part 2, which contains information on data sources, research centers, and other resources for the study of children and childhoods, including listings of Internet websites and of sociologists, in the United States and elsewhere, who conduct research and/or teach courses about childhood, will be helpful to experienced researchers and teachers as well as to those new to the field.

Boocock, Sarane S., and Kimberly A. Scott. *Kids in Context: The Sociological Study of Children and Childhoods.* Lanham, Md.: Rowman & Littlefield, 2005.

Kids in Context gives a comprehensive overview that examines alternative perceptions of children and childhood and empirical evidence about children's social worlds, from their day-to-day experiences in their homes, neighborhoods, and schools to the impact on their lives of political, economic, and social trends at the global level. Variations in childhoods resulting from inequalities of race, ethnicity, gender, and social class are compared. In keeping with the authors' view of children as active participants in society rather than simply as passive recipients of adult care and control, each chapter contains data gathered directly from children, and examples of children's contributions to their families, communities, and societies are noted. The final chapter contains assessment of alternative strategies for enhancing children's status and well-being.

Corsaro, William A. *The Sociology of Childhood.* 2nd ed. Thousand Oaks, Calif.: Pine Forge, 2005.

Originally published in 1997, this is probably the first sociology of childhood textbook in English. Criticizing the developmental and socialization theories that had dominated research on children and childrearing, Corsaro proposes an alternative conceptualization, based upon interactionist and social constructionist perspectives, which he terms *interpretive reproduction*. Rather than simply learning and adapting to the culture surrounding them, children are active agents in their own lives and activities, appropriating and reinterpreting the cultural "routines" available to them in their social environments and, moreover, contributing to cultural reproduction *and* cultural change. Corsaro buttresses his theoretical arguments with many examples from social science research, including his own comparative ethnographical work in Italian and American nursery schools, which yields a rich body of findings on children's peer relationships and the creation of children's culture and strong support for his often-quoted claim that "children are the best sources for understanding childhood."

Hofferth, Sandra L., and Timothy J. Owens, eds. *Children at the Millennium: Where Have We Come From, Where Are We Going?* Oxford: Elsevier Science, 2001.

One of a series of edited volumes based upon the life-course sociological perspective, these ten papers, all but one by scholars at U.S. universities or research organizations, include theoretical analyses, empirical studies, literature reviews, and policy analyses. Particularly noteworthy are: H. B. Johnson's review tracing the development of the sociology of children and childhood in the United States during the twentieth century; J. Zinnecker's comparative analysis of children and childhood in "young" and "aging" societies; D. Alwin's analysis of changing parental values and childrearing behavior over the past century, in the direction of greater emphasis on *autonomy* as opposed to *obedience* in children; and S. H. Hofferth and J. F. Sandberg's analysis of longitudinal data on changes in American children's time use between 1981 and 1997, showing a pattern of increased time in structured activities such as school, day care, sports, and other organized, adult-supervised activities, with reduced leisure time for unstructured play, television viewing, hanging out with friends, and sleep.

James, Allison, and Alan Prout, eds. *Constructing and Reconstructing Childhood*. 2nd ed. London: Falmer, 1997.

A collection of studies, most by European sociologists, whose publication in 1990 marked a major turning point in the field. In the introduction to the volume, the editors proposed a new paradigm that has stimulated and shaped much subsequent research. Childhood is viewed not as natural phenomenon but as a *social construction* that varies from one time and place to another. From this perspective, children are not simply the passive recipients of adult care and control, but active participants in the construction of their own social lives, the lives of those around them, and the societies in which they live. It is suggested that in-depth ethnographic fieldwork is a particularly appropriate methodology for the "new" sociology of childhood, since it allows children a more direct voice in the production of sociological data than is usually possible in survey or experimental research. Chapters by Hendrick and by Woodhead critique the conceptualization of children and childhood in psychological and historical research. Analysis of phenomena as seemingly diverse as sexual abuse of children (chapter by J. Kitzinger) and the dissemination of Disneyland pleasure parks (chapter by P. Hunt and R. Frankenberg) reveal an underlying conception of childhood—an idealized world of innocence and happiness dependent upon adult protection—embedded in both. A cross-cultural comparison of social policy by J. Boyden argues that the consolidation of a universal standard for a "good" childhood based on conditions of life in affluent Western nations and ignoring the hugely unequal distributions of wealth and resources between richer and poorer nations and the traditional values and customary law of the latter can lead to the implementation of measures intended to resolve children's problems that in fact worsen them. The chapters by Jens Qvortrup and by Ann Solberg are discussed in later sections of this bibliography.

Mayall, Berry, ed. *Children's Childhoods: Observed and Experienced*. London: Falmer, 1994.

This is another important collection of studies, most by researchers in the U.K. By comparison to the volumes edited by James and Prout and by Qvortrup et al., this one focuses on the micro level and is particularly rich in material that highlights the nature of children's everyday lives: for example, D. Buckingham's study of children's television-viewing habits, including the ways in which they evade their parents' attempts to regulate them; G. Hallden's analysis of girls' written narratives about how they imagine their future families; and Morrow's analysis of children's perspectives on their employment as part-time wage earners, self-employed workers, or unpaid workers in the home or family business. The extension of children's rights is the subject of two chapters: a conceptual piece by G. Lansdown; and P. Alderson's comparison of the views of children facing orthopedic surgery with their parents' views and the opinions of medical professionals.

Qvortrup, Jens, Marjatta Bardy, Giovanni B. Sgritta, and Helmut Wintersberger, eds. *Childhood Matters: Social Theory, Practice and Politics.* Aldershot, U.K.: Avebury, 1994.

As part of the Childhood as a Social Phenomenon project, begun in 1987 under the auspices of the European Centre for Social Welfare Policy and Research in Vienna, scholars in the sixteen participating countries gathered statistical data on the status of children, assembled a bibliography of sociological literature, and published a number of influential reports and books. *Childhood Matters* might be viewed as the culminating work of the project. Most of the chapters are characterized by an interdisciplinary orientation, drawing upon economic, demographic, and social policy research as well as sociological theories and data, and consideration of trends at the macro level that have affected childhood and intergenerational relations. Commitment to extending children's rights as well as increasing their sociological visibility is a unifying theme of the volume.

Section 2: Journals and Periodic Reports

Child Trends Research Brief

A series of four- to eight-page reports by a Washington, D.C., research organization that is a major center for the development and application of childhood *social indicators* (statistics gathered periodically and systematically that can be used to track patterns or trends over time). Recent briefs have discussed the implications for public policy of shifts in family structure and stability; childhood poverty; child abuse and neglect; teen sexual behavior and pregnancy; and parent and peer influences on children's school performance.

Childhood

An international journal that seeks studies on children's experiences and childhood as a social or cultural construction "from the widest possible variety of geographic, social and cultural settings."

Journal of Marriage and Family

The "Decade in Review" issues of this, the oldest scholarly journal in its field, are particularly valuable. The most recent (Vol. 62, No. 4, 2000), a collection of reviews of research published in the 1990s, documents the decline of the married-parents-with-kids family model and examines the implications of recent changes in family structure, in particular, the growing number of children living with a single parent, unmarried parents, stepparents, same-sex parents, grandparents, and foster parents or other nonrelatives.

Sociological Studies of Children and Youth

Originally titled *Sociological Studies of Child Development* (1986–1992, vols. 1–5), changed to *Sociological Studies of Children* (1994–1995, vols. 6–7), then to its present title (2001–2005, vols. 8–10) and joint publication by Elsevier and JAI, these periodic volumes offer longer works, usually on a designated topic, from an increasingly diverse and international pool of contributors. Most chapters include extensive views of recent research.

UNICEF, State of the World's Children

This title is an annual publication devoted to statistical indicators on the conditions of life for children in all nations for which data are available. Included in each edition are rates of infant and child mortality, malnutrition, poverty, disease and disease prevention, school attendance and literacy. Each edition also contains a report on a particular topic; recent reports have addressed the threat to the world's children of political conflict and violence, poverty, and the HIV/AIDS epidemic, and the vast differences between nations in educational access and quality.

Children's Defense Fund, *The State of America's Children*

The annual report of a pioneering U.S. organization devoted to research and advocacy on behalf of American children, with particular attention to the life conditions and needs of poor and minority children and those with disabilities. Indicators of children's physical and mental health, safety, education, and welfare are updated annually, and each report also contains an agenda for legislation in support of public policy and programs for children and their families. Recent editions of *The State of America's Children* and other CDF publications have documented disturbing increases in the proportions of African American and Latino children living in extreme poverty and have proposed lobbying and other strategies to counter this trend.

Section 3: Design of Sociological Research on Children and Childhoods—Theoretical Perspectives and Methodological Alternatives

Christensen, Pia, and Allison James, eds. *Research with Children: Perspectives and Practices*. London: Falmer, 2000.

In this collection, the authors assume a *reflexive* approach that increases the likelihood of adults' "listening and hearing what children say and paying attention to the ways in which they communicate" and explore a variety of techniques that allow children, sometimes in groups or teams, to participate directly in the design and implementation of research projects and the interpretation of results. In a chapter titled "Entering and Observing in Children's Worlds," Corsaro reveals how he turned his relative incompetence in language and art to his advantage by recasting the Italian preschoolers he was studying as child "experts" to teach him the skills needed to participate in their group activities. Although the editors emphasize that the study of children does not require special techniques distinct from those used in research with adults, Mayall's chapter on generational issues cautions that the power inequalities that permeate relations between adults and children cannot be ignored, and that researchers have ethical and practical responsibility to take them into account. Alderson, a British scholar known for her sensitive studies of issues relating to children's consent to surgery and other invasive medical treatments and who has developed a set of ethical guidelines for research on children, contributes a thoughtful discussion on research methodologies that are compatible with children's participation rights.

Graue, M. Elizabeth, and Daniel Walsh. *Studying Children in Context: Theories, Methods and Ethics*. Thousand Oaks, Calif.: Sage, 1998.

Drawing upon their extensive fieldwork experience with children, the authors make the case for face-to-face and prolonged *qualitative* research, as a means to learning about those aspects of children's lives that cannot be readily measured by more quantitative methods, in particular, the day-to-day interactions through which children learn to construct and interpret their social worlds.

James, Allison, Chris Jenks, and Alan Prout. *Theorizing Childhood*. Cambridge: Polity, 1998.

Like Corsaro, James, Jenks, and Prout challenge taken-for-granted "truths" about children, calling for them to be understood as "social actors shaping as well as shaped by their circumstances," rather than simply as adults-in-the-making. After reviewing what they term *presociological* models that define children as inherently evil (original sin model), innocent (Rousseau's natural man model), immanent (Locke's *tabula rasa* model), naturally developing (Piaget's developmental stages), or driven by unconscious inner forces (Freudian model), the authors present four alternative sociological conceptions: the socially constructed child, the tribal child, the minority group child, and the social structural child, which they then apply to a number of different topical areas. Although they suggest how a theoretical framework might incorporate these four models, they maintain that different ways of thinking about children may be complementary rather than competing, "asking different but equally valid questions."

Mandell, N. "The Least-Adult Role in Studying Children." *Journal of Contemporary Ethnography* 16 (1988): 433–67. Reprinted in F. Waksler, ed., *Studying the Social Worlds of Children.* London: Falmer, 1991, 38–59.

An often-cited paper in which the author urged sociologists to cast off their traditional roles as detached observers and to assume the role of a "fully involved" participant in children's activities, interacting freely with them, closely observing their behavior, and allowing them to teach the researcher their ways. Although the least-adult role turned out to be easier in principle than in practice for most sociologists, and later researchers proposed a middle ground between detachment and total involvement, the least-adult model has remained an important standard against which to assess the extent to which research findings about children reflect or incorporate *their* perspectives.

Qvortrup, Jens. "Introduction to Special Issue on the Sociology of Childhood." *International Journal of Sociology* 17 (1987): 3–37.

———. "A Voice for Children in Statistical and Social Accounting." In *Constructing and Reconstructing Childhood*, edited by Allison James and Alan Prout, 78–98. London: Falmer, 1990.

These works represent two examples from the large body of published work by a Danish sociologist who has made major contributions in all areas of the field. In the first, a conceptual overview, Qvortrup compares children as a group to other subordinate and segregated groups, arguing that, as the "only remaining population group that systematically and generally is denied civil rights," children are "*the* minority group *par excellence.*" This explains why women and racial minority groups seeking to free themselves from the restrictions associated with their subordinate status have objected to being characterized as "children" or "childlike," disassociating themselves from the stigma attached to children.

In the second piece, a chapter in the James and Prout volume annotated in the first section of this bibliography, Qvortrup assesses quantitative measures of children's well-being and calls for greater use of *child-specific statistics.* Arguing that official statistics and social accounting methods that classify children only as part of their families never as a category in themselves reflect and reinforce children's marginality in society and may convey a misleading picture of their status and well-being. For example, child poverty rates and the proportion of children living in substandard housing are generally higher if the calculations are based on *children* than if they are based on *families.*

Thorne, Barrie. "Re-visioning Women and Social Change: Where Are the Children?" *Gender and Society* 1 (1987): 85–109.

While feminists have redefined women as active subjects with agency, diversity, and public as well as private roles, a similar redefinition is needed for children, whose lives and experiences continue to be filtered through adult lenses. Even within feminist and sociological thought, children are seldom of central concern unless they are defined as a social problem—and it is adults who do the defining. Until recently, sociological theories tended to assume an adult–child dualism that viewed children as "other," that ignored the variations in children's lived experiences, and that accepted their subordination as natural. Thorne favors a re-visioning of children that takes into account the diversity of their actual lives and circumstances and challenges their conceptual isolation and subordinate status. By applying to the study of children the same analytical tools that they used to reveal the complex realities of women's lives, feminists will be in a better position to empower and enhance the welfare of both women and children.

Section 4: Children and Their Families

Amato, Paul R. "Children of Divorce in the 1990s: An Update of the Amato and Keith (1991) Meta-analysis." *Journal of Family Psychology* 15 (2001): 355–70.

———. "Children's Adjustment to Divorce: Theories, Hypotheses, and Empirical Support." *Journal of Marriage and the Family* 55 (1993): 23–38.

These citations are two of a series of thorough reviews of data and published research by a highly regarded scholar. Amato has consistently found that children with divorced parents tend to score lower on measures of academic achievement, psychological adjustment, self-concept, and quality of relations with parents and peers, and are more likely to exhibit emotional disorders and behavior problems, *but* that the size of the "divorce effect" was generally small, that the more methodologically sophisticated studies showed weaker effects, and that the effects tended "to diminish over time and to fluctuate over time in response to economic trends and shifts in social values." Amato concludes that divorce is not a panacea, but neither is it inevitably harmful to children.

Ambert, Anne-Marie. *The Effects of Children on Parents*. New York: Haworth, 1992.

Challenging the traditional assumption that socialization is largely a process of children learning and internalizing their parent's values, knowledge, and skills, Ambert presents voluminous evidence of children's influences in multiple areas of parents' lives, from which she concludes that being a parent can affect one's health, income and career trajectory, values, attitudes, and feelings of control over one's life, and the quality of interpersonal relations within and outside the family.

———. *Same-Sex Couples and Same-Sex Parent Families: Relationships, Parenting, and Issues of Marriage*. Ottawa: Vanier Institute of the Family, 2003.

This comprehensive review of evidence on same-sex families contradicts stereotypical beliefs and fears, showing few or no significant differences between children raised by gay or lesbian parents and children raised by straight parents on measures of intelligence, school performance, peer relationships, emotional adjustment, behavior problems, and likelihood of becoming gay or lesbian. Despite their ambiguous legal status in most societies, gay or lesbian couples with children are no more unstable than heterosexual couples with children. Ambert concludes that what differences exist "stem largely from the social stigma attached to homosexuality and consequent social rejection outside the home."

Brannen, Julia, and Margaret O'Brien, eds. *Children in Families: Research and Policy.* London: Falmer, 1996.

This collection of studies by sociologists and anthropologists, most at universities or research institutes in the U.K., offers a broad perspective on children and their relationship to contemporary family life, including theoretical and empirical analyses, examination of micro-level and macro-level effects, and utilization of quantitative and qualitative data. At the micro level, O'Brien, Alldred, and Jones gathered data on children's conceptions of a "proper family" from group discussions in which kids assessed vignettes of hypothetical families and from diaries and drawings produced at home; and M. Song analyzed Chinese-British children's participation in family-run takeaway businesses. Studies at the macro level includes analyses of the effects of demographic trends on children's family situations, a cross-national comparison of public policies and their effects on the economic circumstances of children and their families, and an assessment of the effects of social policies on teenage pregnancy in the United States and several European countries.

Hernandez, Donald J. *America's Children: Resources from Family, Government, and the Economy.* New York: Russell Sage Foundation, 1993.

Authored by the former chief of the Marriage and Family Statistics Branch of the U.S. Census, *America's Children* presents a detailed but coherent profile of the transformations during the past century in family size and composition, parents' education and employment, sibling relationships, modes of child care, and allocation of societal resources to children and their families. Hernandez also charts the increase in poverty among children and inequalities between children since the 1970s. While acknowledging the advantages to children of growing up in an intact two-parent family, he also points out that poverty and un- or underemployment are major impediments to marriage and marital stability—his projections of current demographic trends lead him to predict that even if all single parents married, most of their children would still be poor.

Lareau, Annette. *Unequal Childhoods: Class, Race, and Family Life.* Berkeley: University of California Press, 2003.

An example of ethnographic work at its best, Lareau and her research team observed and interacted with a small but carefully chosen sample of third-grade children and their families, with about equal numbers of girls and boys, blacks and whites, and kids from higher- and lower-status backgrounds. Lareau found that the middle- and upper-middle-class black and white families favored a "concerted cultivation" model of childrearing, in which family life was organized around the children's tightly scheduled school and extracurricular activities; children were given "enormous amounts of individualized attention," but they also "squabbled and fought with their siblings and talked back to their parents." Such behavior was "simply not tolerated in working-class and poor families," where, however, a "natural growth" model of childrearing allowed children longer stretches of unsupervised free time and closer and warmer relationships with kin of all generations. Although all the parents were deeply concerned about their children's education and wanted to see them succeed in school, the accomplishments of the lower-status kids did not translate into advantages in the school and the larger society, while the skills and experiences acquired by the higher-status kids through dialoging with their parents and from their often hectic round of team sports, music lessons, and performances gave them confidence and ease in dealing with adults and social institutions outside the home.

Appendix A of *Unequal Childhoods*, recommended reading for all researchers in this field, is a thorough and candid discussion of how the research team faced such dilemmas as obtaining a diverse sample of children in a society whose educational system is so highly stratified by class and race, obtaining consent from and establishing rapport with the families, recognizing and restraining their own biases, and coping with the stress and exhaustion induced by long hours of intensive observation of intimate and sometimes contentious family life.

Lee, Yun-Suk, Barbara Schneider, and Linda J. Waite. "Children and Housework: Some Unanswered Questions." *Sociological Studies of Children and Youth* 9 (2003): 105–25.

The American research reviewed in this study indicates that when mothers are employed outside the home, kids are more likely than their fathers to take up the slack. The amount and type of housework vary by children's age (older kids do more than younger kids), race and ethnicity (African American and Latino kids do more than European American and Asian American kids), and gender (girls do more and different kinds of domestic chores than boys, and the gender gap is even more pronounced for minority kids), and by the mother's marital status (kids do more housework in single-parent and divorced-parent homes than in two-parent homes). Ironically, the disproportionate amounts of household work performed by girls and the sex typing of chores suggest that as mothers challenge stereotypical sex roles outside the home, they may be reinforcing them at home.

McLanahan, Sara, Irwin Garfinkel, Nanacy E. Reichman, Julien Teitler, Marcia Carlson, and Christina Norland Audigier. *The Fragile Families and Child Wellbeing Study: Baseline National Report.* Princeton, N.J.: Princeton University, Bendheim-Thomas Center for Research on Child Wellbeing, 2003.

The Fragile Families Project is an important longitudinal study that is tracing some 3,700 couples, most of them low-income and unmarried, who had a child in the late 1990s. Although most of the unmarried couples interviewed shortly after the child's birth wanted to marry, were committed to each other and to their child, and had "high hopes for their future together," subsequent interviews

showed very few who hoped to marry had actually done so. The major imped-
iment was not, as originally assumed, the parents' disinclination to marry but
rather their *severe shortage of social capital*. Few had annual earnings above the
poverty level (and the lower the father's income, the less the likelihood of his
marrying the child's mother); few had educational or occupational credentials
that would enable them to better their financial situation. Comparison of married and unmarried couples in the sample revealed a far higher incidence of substance abuse, domestic violence, and mental health problems among the latter;
the unmarried fathers were also much more likely than married fathers to have
been incarcerated for a violent crime. The data so far indicate that increasing the
number of stable, healthy families would require more than persuading single
parents to marry and, moreover, that even if services that address fragile families'
daunting financial, employment, and health problems and their weak relationship
skills were substantially expanded, less than half of the couples in this sample
would be likely to benefit from them.

In addition to reports like this one, the project produces *Fragile Family Research
Briefs* several times a year, each on a specific problem or set of research findings.

Solberg, Anne. "Negotiating Childhood: Changing Constructions of Age for Norwegian Children." In *Constructing and Reconstructing Childhood*, edited by A. James
and A. Prout, 118–37. London: Falmer, 1990.

Though reduced availability of parents and scarcity of older siblings has been
accompanied by recent increases in *self-care* in many developed nations, response
to this trend has varied cross-culturally. In the United States, the hazards facing
"latchkey" or "home-alone" kids have received the most attention, although research that is well designed and relatively free of ideological bias is scarce and the
findings are mixed. In contrast, Solberg's study of Norwegian "home stayers"
found that most used the time between their return from school and their parents' return from work to do their homework, to perform certain household
tasks, and to have fun with friends. They rarely reported feeling lonely or afraid
and generally considered taking on some household responsibilities in return for
having the house to themselves, a satisfactory tradeoff. Solberg argues that while
an adult may view a home without adults as "empty" or even dangerous, from a
kid's perspective such a setting may offer independence and freedom to use the
time and space as they choose. The differences between American and Norwegian research findings undoubtedly reflect societal differences in the actual safety
of homes and neighborhoods as well as cultural differences in beliefs about children's capabilities and needs.

Zelizer, Viviana A. *Pricing the Priceless Child*. New York: Basic Books, 1985.

A classic work on the social value of children based upon American historical
data, the author argues that the economic value of children has diminished but
been replaced by their enhanced emotional value, to the extent that children are
now viewed as "economically worthless but emotionally priceless." Zelizer's hypothesis has been supported by data from other nations showing that happiness,

love, companionship, and self-development take precedence over the more utilitarian values of work power or security in old age. Although some studies found children to be both "a source of joy and a source of burdens" for their parents, more recent research documenting the labor and financial contributions made by children to their families suggests that many children are both emotionally priceless *and* economically useful.

Section 5: Children's Group Life and Peer Culture

Adler, Patricia A., and Peter Adler. *Peer Power: Preadolescent Culture and Identity*. New Brunswick, N.J.: Rutgers University Press, 1998.

The central theme of this ethnographic study of third- to sixth-graders in predominantly white, middle- to upper-middle-class suburban community is the significance of *popularity* and *cliques* in children's social lives. The clique structure is highly stratified, dominated by a top clique with highly competitive entry and high turnover. Other status levels, in descending order: *wannabes*, less popular kids who hoped to be accepted by the most popular kids by running errands for them and closely imitating their clothing, hairstyles, speech, and behavior; *middle rank* kids, even less popular kids who did not aspire to membership in the top clique and often enjoyed greater social security and more satisfying interpersonal relationships than classmates higher up in the social hierarchy; and *social isolates*, who had few or no friends, were excluded from most social activities, and were considered fair game for bullying or scapegoating. Thus peer culture both unified these elementary school children by providing them with a group identity and rules governing social behavior and at the same time "divided them by stratifying and setting them against each other."

Ambert, Anne-Marie. "Toward a Theory of Peer Abuse." *Sociological Studies of Children* 7 (1995): 177–205.

It is the first extensive review of sociological research on the prevalence and long-term consequences of a greatly underreported social phenomenon. Kids themselves report far more physical, verbal, and other aggression by other kids than by adults and with stronger and longer-lasting negative effects. Peer abuse has been largely concealed from or ignored by adults because children are ashamed to report it, fear retaliation if they violate the strong norm against tattle-telling, or simply accept it as a normal part of growing up.

Corsaro, William. "The Underside of the Nursery School: Young Children's Social Representations of Adult Roles." In *Social Representations and the Development of Knowledge*, edited by Gerard Duveen and Barbara Lloyd, 11–26. Cambridge, U.K.: Cambridge University Press, 1990.

Corsaro's classic analysis of nursery school life provides convincing evidence of the multiple ways in which young children challenge adult authority and seek to gain control over their lives through secrecy and subterfuge—smuggling forbidden toys into school to share with classmates; using hands, blocks, and other "make-do's" to simulate weapons for war games prohibited by school rules; and engaging in "swearing routines" filled with explicit references to sexual activity and other "bad" language. Corsaro emphasized the collective nature of underside life; kids not only shared toys, words, and activities, they also shared resistance to adult rules and authority.

————. *We're Friends, Right? Inside Kids' Culture*. Washington, D.C.: Joseph Henry Press, 2003.

Drawing on thirty years of ethnographic research with children, Corsaro provides a wealth of colorful empirical examples demonstrating the complexity of children's peer worlds, the intricacies of their interactions, and the variables that shape the contours of their cultures. With careful attention to the details of gaining access to and acceptance in children's social worlds, Corsaro is able to trace the processes by which children establish and maintain friendships, resolve conflicts, negotiate adult–child interactions, and use play to create their social selves.

Goodwin, Marjorie Harness. *He-Said-She-Said*. Bloomington: Indiana University Press, 1990.

The title of the book refers to an intricate and highly structured form of confrontational dialogue created by working-class African American girls as a means of resolving their disputes. Employed when one girl is accused by another of talking about her behind her back, he-said-she-said exchanges could be brief and often playful or could extend over months and occasionally involve the temporary exclusion of a member of the group. While these verbal confrontations do not address deep-seated concerns and conflict, they provide a means for girls to air complaints about others in the group, to develop their individual identities, and to construct and maintain social order. The variety and complexity of the linguistic routines observed and recorded by Goodwin and the skill with which they were performed also refute common stereotypes about lack of structure or logic in the speech of working-class children in general and black children in particular.

Harris, Judith Rich. "Where Is the Child's Environment? A Group Socialization Theory of Development." *Psychological Review* 102 (1995): 458–89.

This award-winning review of literature, originally published in a prestigious psychological journal and later expanded into a highly controversial book (*The Nurture Assumption*, published in 1998), challenged widely accepted theories that explained children's development and developmental problems as a result of how they were treated by their parents. Harris contends that most research purporting to document the power of parental nurturance fails to establish the direction of empirical causation. Her reinterpretation of the same studies concludes that parenting styles are as likely to be the effect as the cause of a particular child's temperament and that parents' influence on their children is limited at best, especially when compared with the effects of (a) *heredity* and (b) children's *peer groups*. Harris's *group socialization* theory posits that over time and in a number of social settings, kids' attitudes and behavior come to resemble those of their friends more closely than those of their parents. The theory explains, for example, why immigrant children tend to learn the language of their host country more quickly than do their parents, to adopt the language they speak with their peers as their "native language," and to become increasingly reluctant to speak their parents' native language, even at home.

Lee, Valarie E., Robert G. Croninger, Eleanor Linn, and Xianglei Chen. "The Culture of Sexual Harassment in Secondary Schools." *American Educational Research Journal* 33 (1996): 383–417.

Renold, Emma. "Presumed Innocence: (Hetero)sexual, Heterosexist and Homophobic Harassment among Primary School Girls and Boys. *Childhood* 9 (2002): 415–34.

Two empirical studies of sexual harassment by peers, carried out in two different countries, focusing on different age cohorts and utilizing different research methodologies. Both support Ambert's contention (see above) that adult stereotyping of children as incapable of cruel or aggressive behavior may blind them to even the most blatant instances of abuse. From a series of informal, open-ended group interviews in two small-town English primary schools, Renold learned that aggression, both physical and verbal, was ubiquitous and multidirectional, though directed especially at boys and girls who were unpopular or did not meet peer norms of appearance and behavior. In neither school had any of the incidents the kids discussed openly among themselves been reported to members of the teaching staff. The national survey of American eighth- to eleventh-graders analyzed by Lee et al. showed that 83 percent of girls and 60 percent of boys reported receiving unwanted sexual attention, ranging from comments and jokes to forced sexual intercourse. An unexpected finding was that nearly three-quarters of the victims also reported having themselves harassed schoolmates. The authors thus reject a "simple perpetrator-victim model" in favor of a more contextually based explanation: that kids experience more—and more severe—harassment in schools and communities where it is so embedded in the culture that it is ignored or viewed as normal behavior and where the underlying ethical issues are never openly discussed—or even acknowledged.

Opie, Iona, and Peter Opie, *Lore and Language of Schoolchildren*. New York: Oxford University Press, 1987.

Decades before many sociologists began to gather data *about* children directly *from* children, Iona and Peter Opie observed and questioned some 5,000 schoolchildren in various parts of England, Scotland, Wales, and Ireland, obtaining detailed accounts of their favorite games, songs, riddles, and jokes, the pranks they played on each other; and the multitude of ways in which they ridiculed and circumvented teachers, police, and other adult authorities. In *The Lore and Language of Schoolchildren*, originally published in 1959, the Opies claim that children's lore is the world's oldest continuous culture (they were able to trace some of the playground games they observed to as far back as Roman times). Their study has been replicated in many other parts of the world with similar results.

Section 6: Variations in Childhood Experiences Related to Race, Ethnicity, Gender, and Social Class

Books, Sue. *Invisible Children in the Society and Its Schools*. Mahwah, N.J.: Erlbaum, 2003.

The ways in which social class, ethnicity, gender, and sexual orientation marginalize some American children while simultaneously heightening youngsters' understanding of social institutions and inequities is the unifying theme of this edited volume. In this as in the first edition (1998), Books has collected empirical studies in which children are allowed to tell their own stories about their hopes, successes and failures, losses and deprivations. Their insightful accounts provide ample evidence of kids' abilities to understand and articulate how complex social, political, historical, and economic forces impact their lives. They are also aware of how the schools they attend have contributed to their "invisibility." Several of the authors tried to identify the pedagogical approaches that promote or prevent positive educational outcomes for these children.

Connolly, Paul. *Racism, Gender Identities and Young Children*. London: Routledge, 1998.

In this ethnographic study of five- and six-year-olds in a racially diverse English inner-city school, Connolly applies Pierre Bourdieu's concept of *habitus*—the collective habits and social rules that govern everyday life and predict which individuals and groups will succeed and which fail—to explain the racism and sexism that permeate children's interactions. Connolly's data indicated that the kids' play activities and their perceptions of self and others are shaped by the meanings of race, gender, and sexuality learned outside of school. Minority children in particular were stereotyped in ways that affected their peer group positions and relations. Thus girls of South Asian origins were perceived as more passive and alien but also more feminine and sexually attractive than black girls; boys of South Asian origins were perceived as more compliant and less threatening than black boys, who aroused mixed feelings of respect and resentment among the white boys, with whom they were often embroiled in conflicts. Like Bourdieu, Connolly is also interested in explaining why some young children are predisposed to succeed while others seem unable to avoid failure.

Ferguson, Ann Arnett. *Bad Boys: Public Schools in the Making of Black Masculinity*. Ann Arbor: University of Michigan Press, 2000.

In this ethnographic study of a California elementary school, Ferguson recorded how the school system criminalizes African American boys and their behaviors. In a series of heartbreaking examples, she documents the powerfully prophetic intersections of race, gender, self-perception, and school experience. A recurrent theme is the extent to which adult school employees encourage each other and the students to perceive boys of African descent as "bad-bad boys" and to contrast them with their white schoolmates.

Good, Catherine, Joshua Aronson, and Michael Inzlicht. "Improving Adolescents' Standardized Test Performance: An Intervention to Reduce the Effects of Stereotype Threat." *Applied Developmental Psychology* 24 (2003): 645–62.

Building upon Claude Steele's important experimental research on the depressant effects of stereotypes that impugn the intellectual abilities of minority, female, and low-income students, Good, Aronson, and Inzlicht tested methods to help girls and minority and low-income students improve their scores on standardized tests by overcoming the effects of "stereotype threat." Seventh-graders in a Texas school serving a low-income population with high proportions of minority (especially Hispanic) students were randomly assigned to experimental and control groups that received different messages about the causes of academic difficulties. Students in experimental groups that were told that intelligence was not a fixed genetic endowment but could be expanded with mental training and practice, or that the difficulties of adjusting to a new school or community were not due to personal shortcomings and could be overcome, earned significantly higher scores on statewide standardized tests in math and reading than classmates in control groups (who were warned about the dire consequences of drug use). These results are consistent with those of other recent research that used different methodologies but also found improvements in the academic performance of disadvantaged or marginalized students when they are taught how to recognize and resist the pressures associated with negative stereotyping.

Lewis, Amanda E. *Race in the Schoolyard: Negotiating the Color Line in Classrooms and Communities*. New Brunswick, N.J.: Rutgers University Press, 2003.

Like Connolly (see earlier), Lewis uses ethnographic techniques to compare how race affects American elementary-school-age children's interactions in two racially diverse urban schools and one predominantly white suburban school. Like Ferguson (see earlier), she presents disturbing examples of school personnel labeling African American boys as criminals in the making. In all three schools, children's comments about race reveal how the socially constructed elements of racial identity allow misleading interpretations of its significance in social and academic achievement, interpersonal relations, and the quality of everyday school life.

Martin, Karin. "Becoming a Gendered Body: Practices of Preschools." *American Sociological Review* 63 (1998): 494–511.

Through semistructured observations in five preschool classes, Martin identified a *hidden curriculum* that teaches young children how to become girls and boys. Girls' clothing tended to be more restrictive than boys, and teachers were more likely to touch the girls (straightening their clothes, fixing their hair) and to reprimand them for inappropriate posture and behavior. At age three, girls and boys were equally likely to engage in rough-and-tumble play, fighting and arguing, but by age five, girls were much less likely than boys or younger girls to engage in these behaviors. At the same time, conformity to gender norms was not complete; Martin observed instances of both girls and boys resisting the gender rules (boys dressing up in women's clothing, girls being loud and physically assertive when teachers were not paying attention to them), leading her to conclude that gender differences are neither "natural" nor "easily and straightforwardly acquired," but *socially constructed*.

Matthews, Sarah H. "Counterfeit Classrooms: School Life of Inner-city Children."
Sociological Studies of Children and Youth 9 (2003): 209–24.

In this case study of an inner-city middle school attended by low-income and
minority children, a team of researchers recorded numerous incidents of misuse
of their authority by school personnel. Rude, even abusive, treatment of students
was common, and many teachers took advantage of their superior status to
lighten their own workloads (coming to class late or leaving early, collecting and
grading homework sporadically, ignoring widespread cheating on homework and
exams, occasionally going so far as to fabricate grades and test scores). Although
school personnel maintained the fiction that teachers were teaching and students
were learning, so little of either occurred that the researchers declared these settings *counterfeit classrooms*.

Perry, Pamela. *Shades of White: White Kids and Racial Identities in High School.*
Durham, N.C.: Duke University Press, 2002.

One of the few empirical studies in the developing field of White Studies, this
ethnographic study focuses on how whiteness as an invisible, taken-for-granted
identity is manifested in the beliefs and behavior of students in two high schools,
one a predominantly white suburban school, the other a multiracial school in a
metropolitan area. In the first school, Perry found that white students distanced
themselves from African American classmates by referring to them in language
borrowed from rap music and hip-hop culture, for example, as "cool" but "men-
acing," and that black students were largely acquiescent in being so labeled by the
dominant peer culture. In the multiracial school, African American students were
more likely to resist being labeled by white students and to object to whites' su-
perficial appropriation of their language and culture.

Perry's data also show that the notion of whiteness implies more than privilege and that students construct its meaning through their contextualized interactions with students of the same or different color.

Scott, Kimberly A. "In Girls, Out Girls, and Always Black: African-American Girls'
Friendships." *Sociological Studies of Children and Youth* 9 (2003): 179–207.

———. "You Want to Be a Girl and Not My Friend? African-American Girls' Play
Activities with and without Boys." *Childhood* 9: (2002): 397–414.

In a pair of articles that illuminate the school experiences of an understudied
group in the sociology of childhood, Scott draws on her observations, interviews, and videotaping of first-grade African American girls' play patterns in two
different schools—one in a predominantly African American urban setting, the
other in a multiracial suburban one. Scott's data set is distinctive in that she not
only videotaped playground activities but also asked the girls to view and interpret the tapes. Only by consulting the participants did she discover that their interpretation of the video data often differed from hers as well as from what she
was told by teachers and other school personnel. Locating race and gender as primary intersecting variables influencing peer interactions, Scott examines how the
girls and their classmates make sense of their racialized identities and how this

understanding affects child–child and child–adult interactions and emergent peer cultures. She also draws attention to adults' complicity in the creation of a py-ramidal peer structure that incorporates race and gender power inequalities. Comparison of the girls' experiences in the two schools suggested the diversity of black female experiences and self-definitions.

Thorne, Barrie. *Gender Play: Girls and Boys in School.* New Brunswick, N.J.: Rut-gers University Press, 1993.

One of the pioneering studies in the field, both in its challenge to conven-tional theories about sex differences and its reliance upon data gathered directly from children (who also advised the author on terminology and how to interpret what she observed). From her extensive observations of and conversations with elementary school students, Thorne concluded that the extent of gender segre-gation and stereotyping both resulted from and reinforced what she termed a *hegemonic view of gender*, the key components of which are (1) emphasis on gen-der as an oppositional dualism and (2) exaggeration of gender differences and dis-regard for cross-gender commonalities and within-gender variations.

Van Ausdale, Debra, and Joe R. Feagin. *The First R: How Children Learn Race and Racism.* Lanham, Md.: Rowman & Littlefield, 2001.

Many readers of *The First R* will be unpleasantly surprised by its portrayal of pre-school life, in particular, its extensive empirical evidence belying the widespread be-lief that young children have little or no awareness of racial differences and are "in-nocent" of racism until taught otherwise by uneducated or bigoted adults. In a highly regarded day care center that many parents chose because of its diversity and its explicitly multicultural curriculum, Van Ausdale (the principal data gatherer, who defined her role as a combination of playmate and listener for the children and as a kind of aide to the adult staff but who did not interfere with the daily routine or ask the children predetermined questions) recorded a staggering amount of racism in the three- and four-year-olds' verbal comments (e.g., a white girl telling an African American classmate that her skin was the same color as rabbit poop) and be-havior (e.g., a girl of mixed race moving her cot away from that of a black child, explaining, "Niggers are stinky. I can't sleep next to one"). Nearly all racist remarks and behavior were in the direction of minority children being stigmatized or re-jected by white children. When Van Ausdale reported her findings to parents and center staff, the common reaction was disbelief or anger, leading the authors to con-clude that many white Americans remain in denial about race and childhood racism.

Section 7: Childhood in Global Society/Cross-Cultural Comparisons/Children as Consumers and Producers

Bass, Loretta E. "Child Labor and Household Survival Strategies in West Africa." *Sociological Studies of Children and Youth* 9 (2003): 127–48.

From a two-year participant observation study of child workers in urban mar-kets in Senegal, Bass learned that child labor, though illegal, was both "visible and tolerated." About a third of all Senegalese children aged ten to fourteen were working full-time, as sellers in market stalls, apprentices to craftsmen, or as beggars, many learning their parents' trade in the expectation that they will eventually replace them (a pattern Bass termed *duplicating dad–imitating mom*). Similarly high rates of child employment were found throughout sub-Saharan Africa, where as a result of drought, famine, and the free-market economic policies associated with globalization, poor nations hugely indebted to international financial institutions are forced to spend more of their national budgets servicing debt repayment than on education, health, nutrition, and family planning services combined.

Cassell, Justine, and Henry Jenkins. *From Barbie to Mortal Kombat: Gender and Computer Games.* Cambridge: MIT Press, 2000.

In this collection of essays and studies exploring strategies for closing the gender gap in computer use, the editors point out that there are different ways to define and achieve gender equity: through equalizing access to all games, through creating games that are more appealing to girls, and through creating games that "encourage new visions of equity itself." In one of the few well-documented projects in which children were given the skills and opportunities to create their own games, Kafai found gender differences in the direction predicted—those designed by boys were more likely to be structured as contests between good and evil and to incorporate the kinds of violence found in commercial video games. She also found, however, that boys displayed more variability in game preferences and design than has been assumed and that girls became more involved in game design and play when they were offered topics and technology that were congruent with their interests and learning styles.

Dencik, Lars. "Modern Childhood in the Nordic Countries: 'Dual Socialization' and Its Implications." In *Growing Up in Europe: Contemporary Horizons in Childhood and Youth Studies*, edited by Lynne Chisholm, 105–19. New York: De Gruyter, 1995.

In the Nordic countries where a normal childhood is defined as one in which young children routinely experience both home care by parents *and* outside-the-home care by professional caregivers, research shows generally positive results (little evidence of anxiety or behavior problems as a result of being apart from their parents; generally higher scores on a wide range of academic and social skills in elementary and secondary school than schoolmates without extensive preschool experience). When children's views are solicited, most rated being with their friends as the best part of day care. Dencik points out that the success of the *dual socialization* model in Denmark, Finland, Norway, and Sweden depends upon their highly developed social welfare systems, which entitle *all* children to a broad range of health, child care, and educational benefits.

Jing, Jun, ed. *Feeding China's Little Emperors: Food, Children and Social Change.* Stanford, Calif.: Stanford University Press, 2000.

In this collection of anthropological studies conducted in China during the 1990s, one of the chapters (Yuhan) traces the processes by which the introduction of snack foods and fast-food franchising has changed the food preferences of children and increased their influence on family diet and eating habits. As in other countries, Chinese children initiated and maintained friendships through eating together and sharing food, and the consumption of trendy foods was such an important element of peer culture that some kids exaggerated their familiarity with them. In a study of Kentucky Fried Chicken's efforts to tap into the world's largest and fastest-growing kid market, Lozada found that KFC equipped its Beijing restaurants with child-sized furniture, play areas, and space for birthday parties, and replaced Colonel Sanders with Chicky Chicken, a more child-friendly mascot who dresses hip-hop style and gives out small gifts to child customers. Jing suggests that children's birthday parties and other new social occasions created by the globalization of food products and eating habits reflects a profound shift in generational power, replacing "rituals of longevity" with "celebrations of youth."

Livingstone, Sonia, and Moria Bovill. *Children and Their Changing Media Environment: A European Comparative Study*. Mahwah, N.J.: Erlbaum, 2001.

For this cross-national study of children's media access and use, the researchers used a multimethod design that combined a survey of large samples of children in twelve countries, in-depth interviews with a smaller subset of survey participants, and background data on the various countries obtained from government statistics and reports. In these relatively affluent societies, having a room of one's own has become the norm for middle- and upper-class children and is increasing among working-class children as well. Teenagers' bedrooms are likely to be equipped with TVs and cable hookups, phones, personal computers, and video games, producing what Livingstone and Bovill term a *media-rich bedroom culture*. They posit that this extension of personal space via electronic modes of communication, by enabling kids to entertain themselves and each other in virtual as well as in real time and space, is not only affecting family relationships but also producing a new peer culture that can transcend community and even national boundaries.

Mizen, Paul, Christopher Pole, and Angela Bolton, eds. *Hidden Hands: International Perspectives on Children's Work and Labour*. New York: Routledge/Falmer, 2001.

Most of the chapters in this volume begin from the premise that employment for children in most countries is a majority experience, or at least one not confined to a small minority. In the developing countries where the majority of the world's children live, the majority of jobs, for children and adults alike, are in the agricultural sector. Although it is commonly believed that child labor has all but disappeared in the affluent industrial nations, children's employment is more widespread and their contributions (in money, goods, and services) are greater than is generally recognized. What is problematic for kids everywhere is obtaining a *good* job; even in the richest countries, a substantial portion of children's work is undertaken illegally. Studies in the United Kingdom, discussed in the chapter by Mizen, Pole, and Bolton, show that opportunities to use or acquire specific skills were rare, most of the jobs available were temporary unskilled work, and almost half of those working were doing so in violations of laws regarding age, the nature of the work, or hours worked. Two chapters draw attention to work that is unpaid but that nonetheless contributes to household and/or national economies. Becker, Dearben, and Aldridge report on children in affluent European countries who, in a reversal of conventional intergenerational relationships, become the major caretakers of disabled family members, performing work that would otherwise have to be done by adult relatives or paid for by the state. In a comparison of paid work versus schoolwork, the ubiquitous Qvortrup argues that the latter should be defined as socially necessary labor, since "it is through schooling that children add value to future processes of wealth creation."

Rainwater, Lee, and Timothy M. Smeeding. *Poor Kids in a Rich Country: America's Children in Comparative Perspective.* New York: Russell Sage Foundation, 2003.

Using quantitative indicators of children's health and well-being from a transnational study of family income, Rainwater and Smeeding compare the situation of American children in low-income families with their counterparts in fourteen other countries. Their analysis shows that while there are poor children in all of the industrialized nations studied, the proportion is substantially higher in the United States, a discrepancy that can be explained by the fact that the United States alone does *not* support generous and comprehensive social welfare programs to which all children are entitled. Rainwater and Smeeding call for the United States to adopt the kinds of policies and programs (such as universal parental leaves, childcare support, and increased income support for working poor families) that have made it possible for parents in other nations to earn a decent living while raising children.

Rosen, David M. *Armies of the Young: Child Soldiers in War and Terrorism.* New Brunswick, N.J.: Rutgers University Press, 2005.

Although Human Rights Watch estimates that at least 300,000 kids under age eighteen are engaged in armed conflicts in some forty countries, this is the first extensive sociological study of children in the military. Rosen emphasizes that child soldiering is not a new phenomenon. What's new is the current effort to exclude children from the military and to highlight situations where child soldiers are abused and exploited.

Schor, Juliet B. *Born to Buy: The Commercialized Child and the New Consumer Culture.* New York: Scribner, 2004.

A sociological analysis of *age compression* as a marketing tactic that targets products originally designed for adults or adolescents—for example, cosmetics, elaborate hairstyles, high-heeled shoes, low-rise jeans, and other provocative clothing—at younger children. Schor argues that encouraging little girls to buy designer clothing modeled on adult fashions does not, as some marketers have claimed, represent "child power" but exploitation of kids by the fashion industry comparable to that by the fast-food industry. Schor supports her claim with evidence from her own survey of 300 children between the ages of ten and thirteen, in which she found that kids with high scores on a scale of "consumer involvement" (who, e.g., said they cared a lot about money and shopping, having clothes with popular labels and other items valued by their peers, and being cool) were also likely to score low on measures of self-esteem and high on measures of depression, anxiety, and several psychosomatic complaints.

Tapscott, Don. *Growing Up Digital: The Rise of the Net Generation*. New York: Mc-Graw-Hill, 1998.

A survey of children's use of computers, with the data obtained from several hundred children on six continents who communicated with the author and with each other via e-mail and computer conferencing. Overall, the major uses were for entertainment, schoolwork, shopping, and communicating with family, friends, and chat groups, although a few kids ran their own businesses or organized protest movements or fundraisers to provide impoverished communities with better schools and computer technology. Although he does not dismiss the concerns of adults who fear that violent computer games will make children unsociable and aggressive, Tapscott argues that children have always played violent games, that kids whose parents refuse to buy them toy guns and other military paraphernalia are often resourceful at creating them from materials at hand, and that the effects of even the most violent computer games are slight compared to the effects of violent families, neighborhoods, and nations. What is more significant about kids and computers, according to Tapscott, is that for the first time in history, "children are more comfortable, knowledgeable and literate than their parents about an innovation central to society."

Zelizer, Viviana A. "Kids and Commerce." *Childhood* 9 (2002): 375–96.

Although the sharing or exchange of money, toys, and food is an important aspect of children's culture, these transactions are likely to be overlooked by or concealed from adults. Zelizer's review of recent research on children's economic activities uncovers many examples of children's engagement in production, consumption, and distribution of valued items, evidence that belies adults' "cherished images of children as economic innocents." The sheer scope of the "kids' market" is vast and growing—Zelizer cites market research findings showing that at the end of the twentieth century, American children's annual income, from allowances, gifts, and their own earnings, totaled more than $27 billion, of which about $7 billion went for snacks and another $7 billion for toys, games, and sports equipment; and that purchases by kids between the ages of four and twelve tripled during the 1990s. Comparisons of children's economic exchanges with other family members, with other children, and with employers, merchants, and other adult third parties outside the home reveal considerable variation in patterns of organization, meaning, and consequences.

Section 8: Children's Voices/Child Innovators and Activists

Coles, Robert. *Children of Crisis: A Study of Courage and Fear*. Boston: Atlantic Monthly Press, 1964.

————. *Migrants, Sharecroppers, Mountaineers*. Boston: Atlantic/Little Brown, 1967.

Two volumes from a series that was twice awarded the Pulitzer Prize. Coles is not a sociologist but a child psychiatrist who rejects "objective" quantitative modes of social science research, opting instead for informal and unhurried conversations with children and their parents (some of whom he revisited over a period of years) and offering kids crayons, paints, and paper with which they drew pictures of the important people and places in their lives and later explained the drawings to Coles. The 1964 volume contains Coles's clinical evaluations of African American children who participated in civil rights demonstrations or braved hostile mobs in order to enter racially desegregated schools. In contrast to researchers and therapists with an adult ideological perspective that views such children as helpless victims of political violence in need of professional counseling, Coles found no consistent patterns of emotional or other damage and considerable evidence that many child activists developed impressive reserves of psychic strength, especially if they had the support of their families, churches, and communities. The children of migrant workers, one of the subjects of the 1967 volume, were a different story, a poignant mix of strengths and weakness—on the one hand, knowledgeable and resourceful about harvesting various crops, troubleshooting and repairing car engines, and the value of money and the things that could be bought with it; on the other hand, frequently tired, forlorn, and "terribly paralyzed by all sorts of things," from dealing with school officials to keeping track of their few prized possessions. Refusing to assume the role of detached scientific observer, Coles freely expresses his anger at the "unspeakably devastating" conditions of migrant life for children, whom he characterized as permanent refugees in their own country.

Galinsky, Ellen. *Ask the Children: What America's Children Really Think about Working Parents*. New York: Morrow, 1999.

To examine parental employment from a kid's perspective, Galinsky conducted a national survey of third- through twelfth-graders, gathering data via self-administered questionnaires and telephone interviews. The principal finding was a *lack of correlation* between maternal employment and most measures of children's social, emotional, and educational outcomes. Similarly, there was little relationship between parents' employment status and children's attitudes toward their parents, although Galinsky did find that the more kids knew about their parents' jobs and the more they believed that their parents liked and were committed to their work, the more highly they rated them as *parents*. Her survey also revealed that children do a fair amount of *caregiving*; over half said they take care of their mothers "sometimes" or "often" and 43 percent said the same about their fathers. Favored strategies for relieving parental stress and fatigue included listening to their complaints, telling them funny stories, and helping with the housecleaning and cooking.

Hoose, Phillip. *We Were There, Too! Young People in U. S. History*. New York: Farrar, Straus & Giroux, 2001.

Drawing from a rich body of primary sources, Hoose documents the substantial economic, social, and political contributions made by children and youth throughout U.S. history. Included are documents from the earliest colonial settlements, where many European American children were employed as apprentices or indentured laborers. America's first factory workers were boys and girls, most aged twelve or younger, and the book includes children's accounts of their work in textile mills (where some participated in the first strikes for better pay and shorter hours), sweatshops, coal mines, and the military. Particularly moving are the accounts of African American kids who were active in the civil rights movement of the 1950s and 1960s, including: a fifteen-year-old girl whose arrest for refusing to give up her seat on a Montgomery, Alabama, bus to a white women *preceded* Rosa Park's more famous refusal that sparked a year-long bus boycott; a fourteen-year-old girl who recalls being hosed by police and attacked by police dogs during the demonstrations that brought about the end of racial segregation in Birmingham, Alabama, and who lost four friends when their church was bombed; and the nine black students who braved mobs to attend a previously all-white high school in Little Rock, Arkansas.

Kielburger, Craig. *Free the Children.* New York: HarperPerennial, 1998.

Arguably the most ambitious and influential child-initiated social service project, Free the Children is an international movement against exploitative child labor founded by Craig Kielberger, a Canadian boy who began to investigate the problem at age twelve after learning of the murder of a Pakistani youngster who had been sold at age five to work in a rug factory, raised enough money to make a solo trip to Asia to observe children's working conditions firsthand, and failing to elicit support from adult-run political and charitable organizations founded his own. Free the Children now has chapters in some twenty countries, runs leadership courses for kids and helps them plan local projects, raises money to build schools in developing nations, and lobbies for employment that does not abuse or exploit child workers or prevent them from getting an education. While FTC has worked mainly on behalf of children in poorer nations, Kielburger believes that it offers kids in affluent countries opportunities to engage in something more challenging and meaningful than hanging out in shopping malls and playing video games. (A passage from Kielburger's book is included in the introduction to this chapter.)

Pryor, Jan, and Bryan Rodgers. *Children in Changing Families: Life after Parental Separation.* Oxford: Blackwell, 2001.

Smart, Carol, Bren Neale, and Amananda Wade. *The Changing Experience of Childhood: Families and Divorce.* Cambridge: Polity, 2001.

Two of the first in-depth studies of kids' lives after parental separation or divorce in which data were obtained from children themselves and the text contains many direct quotations from interviews and groups discussions. While most kids were initially saddened by their parents' separation and few felt that they had been adequately prepared, their subsequent feelings ranged from anger to ambivalence to relief (especially if the separation enabled them to "escape from the war zone" of parental conflict). Most of the inconveniences that followed family breakups, such as having to commute back and forth from one parent's home to the other, became routine for most kids, and many felt that they had become more independent and competent people. Having learned to handle difficult emotions and situations, some began to question adults' attitudes and expectations and to demand more say in family matters that affected them. At the same time, they expressed strong preferences for keeping family problems in the family and objected to unsolicited counseling and other interventions by outsiders that invaded their privacy and diminished their sense of control over their lives—leading Smart, Neale, and Wade to propose replacing current social services based on a theoretical "common good" for all children and imposed on them in a downward fashion with a more "ground-up, research based process" in which kids' perspectives and preferences are taken into account.

Senghas, Ann, Sotaro Kita, and Asli Ozyurek. "Children Creating Core Properties of Language: Evidence from an Emerging Sign Language in Nicaragua." *Science* 305 (2004): 1779–82.

A longitudinal study of a language developed from scratch by kids. In this case, Nicaraguan deaf children who had been placed in an elementary-school special education class but absorbed little of the classroom instruction by adults created a sign language that enabled them to communicate among themselves and that they subsequently taught to younger children. Though the language has become more complex and nuanced as it has passed on from one generation of deaf children to the next, virtually all children, *but no adults*, have become fluent signers.

Shultz, Jeffrey, and Allison Cook-Sather. *In Our Own Words: Students' Perspectives on School.* Lanham, Md.: Rowman & Littlefield, 2001.

Eight of the ten chapters in this book were coauthored by teams consisting of several students working with an adult researcher or teacher. Some of the student assessments challenge adult "expert" opinion. The generally positive evaluation of bilingual education by four Puerto Rican students, who felt that it helped keep them connected with their families and enabled them to help their parents and other family members communicate with government officials, school personnel, and shopkeepers, is at variance with the claims of educators who believe that immigrant children must abandon their home culture and language in order to succeed in the English-speaking world. In another chapter, students exposed some of the ways in which teachers' assumptions and biases resulted in differential, often unfair, treatment of students (e.g., a male teacher who gave higher grades to female students who dressed in "feminine" outfits than to those who wore baggy sweaters and jeans). Student authors found much to criticize in their adult-controlled schools, leveling their most scathing attacks at the competitive, grade-driven system of evaluating students, and the necessity of "staying sweet and silent and complicit on the surface" in order to gain adult approval and good grades.

NOTES

1. Sarane Boocock and Kimberly Ann Scott, *Kids in Context: The Sociological Study of Children and Childhoods* (Lanham, Md.: Rowman & Littlefield, 2005), 6.

2. Meredith F. Small, *Kids: How Biology and Culture Shape the Way We Raise Our Children* (New York: Doubleday, 2001), 6.

3. William Corsaro, *The Sociology of Childhood* (Thousand Oaks, Calif.: Pine Forge, 1997), 103.

4. Alan Prout, "Preface," in *Research with Children: Perspectives and Practices*, ed. Pia Christensen and Allison James (London: Falmer, 2000), xi.

5. Craig Kielberger, *Free the Children* (New York: HarperPerennial, 1998), 290–91.

11

U.S. GOVERNMENT RESOURCES

Donna Wertheimer

U.S. government resources provide valuable information for both the beginning and advanced researcher in the interdisciplinary field of Children and Childhood Studies (CCS). Locating pertinent U.S. government resources is an important part of the research process for the undergraduate student writing a paper on a hot topic in the news such as school violence as well as the graduate student conducting a comprehensive literature review for a research project on children with attention-deficit/hyperactivity disorder. This chapter serves as an introduction to U.S. government resources for researchers interested in children and childhood. A brief discussion of search strategy techniques for finding federal government resources is followed by a Web guide that lists and describes "too good to miss" U.S. government Web resources.

Using the excellent step-by-step research process outlined in chapter 2 of this book (under the heading "Scholarly Research 101") may help you identify some useful U.S. government resources on your topic. For example, the library catalog at your academic library may list some government publications available in the library and may provide links to some government publications available on the Web. As discussed in chapter 12, a search of the World Wide Web using "Google" may turn up some government resources. However, these steps are just a starting point when it comes to finding government information. To uncover pertinent government Web resources, government publications, government statistical sources and government databases, it is often necessary to go beyond these basic library research steps. The following search strategy techniques will help you find your way to the wealth of government information sources that are available to you.

Search strategy techniques for locating key U.S. government resources on your topic involve using specialized search tools as well as learning more about the federal departments and agencies pertinent to your field. A major search tool that CCS scholars should try is the Catalog of U.S. Government Publications (CGP) available on the Web at catalog.gpo.gov/F. This catalog produced by the U.S. Government Printing Office includes records for print and digital publications from all branches of the U.S. government. Currently, the CGP is updated daily and includes over 500,000 records dating back to 1976. If a government publication is available on the Web, the record includes a direct link to the full text of the digital version. Using the basic search screen, you can search by keyword, title, author, and subject. However, the "advanced search" feature links you to a more powerful but easy-to-use search screen that allows you to combine terms and limit your search. Also, this advanced search screen contains a link to GPOAccess (www.gpoaccess.gov), another tool of the U.S. Government Printing Office aimed at providing free access to specific types of electronic government information.

Besides the government publications in print and digital format that are listed in the Catalog of U.S. Government Publications and at GPOAccess, many federal government departments and agencies provide additional important resources on their individual websites. Free and open electronic access on the Web to an abundance of government information is exciting for researchers. On the other hand, it also presents challenges to researchers. In addition to searching the Catalog of U.S. Government Publications for publications in print and available on the Web, it is important for researchers to get acquainted with the websites of federal departments and agencies that produce and disseminate information in their field.

One way to begin learning more about federal departments and agencies as well as federal information on the Web is to try FirstGov.gov, a product of the U.S. General Services Administration. According to its home page, FirstGov.gov is "The U.S. Government's Official Web Portal." This user-friendly Web resource provides an "Information by Topic" directory and a keyword search engine limited to government websites. The "By Organization" feature provides an A–Z index to all federal government agencies and departments, as well as links to federal executive, federal legislative, and federal judicial branches of the government.

The rest of this chapter is devoted to a Web guide created to provide researchers with a quick and easy way to learn more about the Web resources of federal departments and agencies concerned with children. Although many government entities within the legislative, judicial, and executive branches of the federal government provide information about children on their websites, this Web guide is not intended to be exhaustive; it only includes selected departments and agencies within the executive branch of the federal government. These departments and agencies within the executive branch were selected for inclusion in this Web guide because of their involvement in producing and disseminating general information, research, and statistics relevant to the needs of researchers gathering information on topics concerning children or childhood.

The following Web guide, which is organized by federal departments and agencies, includes descriptive entries for selected federal government websites. Each entry contains brief information about the U.S. government department or agency responsible for the website as well as the Web address. Hands-on tips for using the website are an important feature of each entry and are geared to the needs of researchers concerned with children. Also, descriptions of the website highlight specific government publications, government statistical sources, and government databases produced by the department or agency. In some cases, an entire entry is devoted to a specific government resource such as a significant publication or major database.

Most of the U.S. government resources described in the following Web guide are in digital format and are currently available on the World Wide Web. Please note that the source for any quotations and/or factual information included in each entry is available at the Web address listed for the entry. Whether you use this guide while you are on the Web or read it without the Web at your fingertips, we hope it will entice you to explore government resources on you own.

FEDERAL INTERAGENCY FORUM ON CHILD AND FAMILY STATISTICS (www.childstats.gov)

The mission of the Federal Interagency Forum on Child and Family Statistics is "to foster coordination and collaboration and to enhance and improve consistency in the collection and reporting of Federal data on children and families." The forum's official website, ChildStats.gov, is a gold mine for anyone doing research on children and families.

First, ChildStats.gov provides access on its home page to the digital version of the forum's major publication, *America's Children: Key National Indicators of Well-Being* (www.childstats.gov/pubs.asp). Published annually since 1997, this statistical report is an important reference source for CCS scholars looking for current data, historical data, and trends. Part 1 concerns population and family characteristics. Some of the measures covered are child population, racial and ethnic composition, difficulty speaking English, family structure, and child care. Part 2, "Indicators of Children's Well-Being," provides data for twenty-five different indicators in the following four areas: economic security, health, behavior and social environment, and education. A few of the indicators included in this section are child poverty, access to health care, adolescent births, alcohol use, family reading to young children, early childhood care and education, and mathematics and reading achievement.

Next, ChildStats.gov offers a "Related Resources" tab on its home page. On the "Related Resources Page," you can locate useful related resources using the "Related Sites Categories" section or by performing a keyword search in the "Related Sites Search" section. Also, this page contains direct links to all of the twenty federal agencies that are participating partners in the Federal Interagency Forum on Child and Family Statistics.

Finally, ChildStats.gov provides a way for researchers to talk to the federal data experts. Using the "Topic Contacts" tab, you will find a list by topic of names and contact information for staff members from a variety of federal agencies. You can contact these experts concerning data in their area of specialization.

U.S. CENSUS BUREAU (www.census.gov)

The home page of the U.S. Census Bureau is a good starting point for researchers in search of demographic, social, economic, and housing data for a specific geographic area. The U.S. Census Bureau is responsible for conducting the Census of Population and Housing every ten years. This decennial census provides data at the national, state, and local level. In addition, the Census Bureau's "new" *American Community Survey* collects data from a sample of households on an annual basis in an effort "to provide more up-to-date information throughout the decade about trends in U.S. population at the local community level." If you are studying, teaching, or helping children in a particular geographic area, you can learn more about the characteristics of the community by trying the following search strategy. Using the "American Factfinder" tool on the Census Bureau home page, you can quickly access a fact sheet for your state, county, city, or town. The fact sheet includes basic demographic, social, economic, and housing characteristics for your geographic area. This basic profile can be expanded to show more detailed data by selecting the "show more" feature. Also, if more recent data is available for your geographic area, a tab will appear at the top of the table with the date of the new data. By selecting this tab you can update the 2000 census data with a current basic profile from the on-going annual *American Community Survey*. For researchers interested in focusing on specific areas within a city or town, the Census Bureau provides data for smaller geographic units called census tracts and block groups. The "Address Search" feature will lead you to the data that is available for specific census tracts and block groups.

Besides the decennial *Census of Population and Housing* and the annual *American Community Survey*, the Census Bureau conducts over 100 special surveys and produces detailed reports on social, economic, and demographic issues, which may be of interest to CCS scholars. For example, by selecting the "Publications" feature on the Census Bureau home page, you will find informative Population Reports (www.census.gov/prod/www/abs/popula.html) such as *Who's Minding the Kids? Child Care Arrangements*; *School Enrollment—Social and Economic Characteristics of Students*; and *A Child's Day: 2000 (Selected Indicators of Child Well-Being)*.

If you explore the Census Bureau website, you will discover additional data files, data tools, and methods for retrieving current and historical census information. Remember, for questions concerning census data, you can consult the librarian at your college or university.

Statistical Abstract of the United States (www.census.gov/compendia/statab)

Perhaps the best-known publication of the U.S. Census Bureau is the *Statistical Abstract of the United States*. One of the most popular statistical sources in academic libraries, this compendium is available in print and digital format. Published annually since 1878, the *Statistical Abstract* can be used to find current and historical statistics on a wide variety of topics. You can view the latest *Statistical Abstract* in full-text PDF format by selecting "Print Version" on the home page. Using the index located at the bottom of the first page of the PDF version, you will discover that the category under "Children" points to over 100 data tables covering a broad range of topics related to the study of children and childhood such as child abuse, drug abuse, computer use, school crimes, school enrollment, school readiness, and teen suicide. It provides statistics from many different federal agencies as well as private and international sources. In addition to providing data, the *Statistical Abstract* can be used as a tool to lead you to the primary source for statistics related to your topic. Although most of the data is on a national level, it does include some data for states and for other countries.

U.S. DEPARTMENT OF EDUCATION (www.ed.gov)

With the mission "to ensure equal access to education and to promote educational excellence throughout the nation" the Department of Education is important for children and everyone concerned with children. The official website of the department includes portals geared to the information needs of students, parents, teachers, and administrators as well as a link to information about the status of educational reform under the No Child Left Behind Act of 2002. Researchers may find it useful to explore the resources made available through the department's "research arm," the Institute of Education Sciences.

Institute of Education Sciences (ies.ed.gov)

Established by the Education Sciences Reform Act of 2002, the Institute of Education Science consists of four centers: National Center for Education Research (NCER), National Center for Education Statistics (NCES), the National Center for Education Evaluation and Regional Assistance (NCEE), and the National Center for Special Education Research (NCSER). All of these centers provide useful resources for CCS scholars interested in education. For example, recent publications highlighted on the National Center for Education Evaluation and Regional Assistance home page (ies.ed.gov/ncee) include a guide for evidence-based education and a major evaluation study on the effects of after-school programs. Also, the NCEE sponsors a What Works Clearinghouse (www.whatworks.ed.gov) that reviews all types of educational interventions.

All scholars interested in research and statistics in the field of education and education-related areas such as child and adolescent development should get acquainted with the following key resources, which are currently housed within the Department of Education's Institute of Education Sciences.

ERIC—Educational Resources Information Center (www.eric.ed.gov)

Produced by the Department of Education, ERIC is a standard tool for academic research in the discipline of Education. With over one million citations to journal articles and nonjournal documents, ERIC is also the largest education database. The ERIC database provides scholars with access to bibliographic citations for articles from hundreds of education journals from 1966 to the present. Whether you are looking for a few good journal articles on a topic in education or preparing a comprehensive literature review on a topic in education, the ERIC database is an important resource. After you perform a search and identify citations to journal articles on your topic, you will need to locate the actual articles. Researchers using academic libraries will find that many of the journal articles are available either in digital or print format within the library or through interlibrary loan. In addition to citations to journal articles, ERIC also includes citations to nonjournal documents such as conference proceedings, government reports, and other types of sources. Selected nonjournal documents are available in full-text format within the ERIC database.

National Center for Education Statistics (www.nces.ed.gov)

The National Center for Education Statistics (NCES), located within the U.S. Department of Education and the Institute of Education Sciences, is "the primary federal entity for collecting and analyzing data related to education." The NCES website provides researchers with a vast array of useful resources including annual statistical compendiums, statistical analysis reports, assessments and surveys, data tables, and data tools. By selecting the "Annual Reports" tab, you will find links to the following key compendiums for education statistics: *The Condition of Education*; *Digest of Education Statistics*; *Projections of Education Statistics*; and *Indicators of School Crime and Safety*. These annual reports (www.nces.ed.gov/annuals) are standard reference sources for academic researchers. Also included in this annual reports section is the publication *Education Statistics Quarterly*, which provides information about new NCES publications, products, and activities.

In addition to these important annual reports, NCES publishes many statistical analysis reports on a variety of topics of interest to CCS researchers. There are several ways to find the NCES reports relevant to your topic. A quick and easy way is to highlight the "Publications & Products" tab and select the Subject Index A–Z. You can also search the publications section by keyword. Examples of in-depth statistical analysis reports available in the publications section (www.nces.ed.gov/pubsearch) include titles such as *Child Care and Early Education Arrangements of Infants, Toddlers, and Preschoolers*; *Homeschooling in the United States*; *Students Reports of Bullying*; *Trends in Educational Equity of Girls & Women*; and *Youth Indicators*.

Another way to keep up with NCES research findings in your interest area is to get acquainted with the "Surveys and Programs" section (www.nces.ed.gov/surveys) of the NCES website. This section provides information about the many ongoing NCES surveys organized into categories such as early childhood, elementary/secondary, and international. For example, the NCES survey program for early childhood includes the *Early Childhood Longitudinal Study, Kindergarten Class of 1998–99*, which follows children's school experiences through twelfth grade, and the *Early Childhood Longitudinal Study, Birth Cohort*, which surveys children from birth to kindergarten with a focus on health, development, care, and education. Although these two major Early Childhood Longitudinal Studies (ECLS) are ongoing, publications and data from these studies are already available on the ECLS website (www.nces.ed.gov/ecls). The following list includes a few examples of these publications: *Full-Day and Half-Day Kindergarten in the United States*; *From Kindergarten through Third Grade: Children's Beginning School Experiences*; and *Young Children's Access to Computers in the Home and at School*.

National Assessment of Educational Progress (www.nces.ed.gov/nationsreportcard)

"The National Assessment of Educational Progress (NAEP), also known as the Nation's Report Card, is the only nationally representative and continuing assessment of what America's students know and can do in various subject areas." Subjects covered in these assessments of elementary and secondary students include reading, mathematics, science, writing, U.S. history, civics, geography, and the arts. By selecting an academic subject area listed on the NAEP home page, you will be linked to an information page about NAEP assessments in the selected subject. For example, if you select "reading" you can download a copy of the latest reading assessment, *The Nation's Report Card: Reading 2005*. Also, you will find information on "How the Reading Assessment Works" and "Long Term Trends." In addition to these subject-area student assessments, NAEP conducts informative special studies. By selecting the "special studies" heading on the NAEP home page, you will find reports on hot topics such as charter schools, high school transcripts, and private schools. Researchers interested in finding out more about ways to tap into the actual assessment data will find it useful to explore the "researchers" portal available on the home page.

U.S. DEPARTMENT OF HEALTH AND HUMAN SERVICES (www.hhs.gov)

According to its website, the "Department of Health and Human Services is the United States government's principal agency for protecting the health of all Americans and providing essential human services, especially for those who are least able to help themselves." The following entities within this department are concerned in some way with serving the needs of America's children.

Administration for Children and Families (www.acf.hhs.gov)

The mission statement for the Administration for Children and Families (ACF) states that the ACF is "responsible for federal programs that promote the economic and social well-being of families, children, individuals, and communities." The ACF partners with others, including states, counties, cities, and tribal governments and organizations. CCS researchers should investigate the resources in the "Services for Families" section as well as the "Policy/Planning" section.

In addition, the home page provides a drop-down menu for selecting a topic and a drop-down menu with links to program offices within the ACF. The Office of Head Start, Children's Bureau, and Child Care Bureau were selected from this ACF program menu for further exploration because of their relevance to the information needs of CCS scholars. Highlights of each of these divisions can be found in the entries that follow.

Children's Bureau (www.acf.hhs.gov/programs/cb)

The Children's Bureau "has primary responsibility for administering Federal child welfare programs" and "seeks to provide for the safety, permanency and well being of children." Within the "Statistics & Research Section," you will find useful reports and data on adoption, foster care, child abuse and neglect, and child welfare. CCS scholars will find useful legal information in the "Laws and Policies" section. In addition, the Child Welfare Information Gateway (www.childwelfare.gov) is a service of the Children's Bureau. This newly created information gateway provides access to a vast array of print and digital resources pertinent to the needs of child welfare professionals as well as researchers. Topics covered include child welfare, child abuse and neglect, adoption, and related areas. The following are examples of some of the popular titles available in digital format through the Child Welfare Information Gateway: *Child Abuse and Neglect Fatalities—Statistics and Interventions; Definitions of Child Abuse and Neglect; Recognizing Child Abuse and Neglect—Signs and Symptoms.*

Child Care Bureau (www.acf.hhs.gov/programs/ccb)

The mission of the Child Care Bureau is to "enhance the quality, affordability, and availability of child care for all families." The Child Care Bureau's National Child Care Information Center (nccic.acf.hhs.gov) is a clearinghouse for early care and education information geared to the needs of parents, professional child care providers, policy makers, and researchers. In addition, the Child Care Bureau partners with other organizations at the University of Michigan and Columbia University in sponsoring the Child Care and Early Education Research Connections (childcareresearch.org) database, which provides access to original research, data, and literature reviews from government and nongovernmental sources.

Office of Head Start (www.acf.hhs.gov/programs/hsb)

The website of the Office of Head Start offers a wealth of information for scholars concerned with early childhood. Head Start began in 1964 as a "federally sponsored preschool program to meet the needs of disadvantaged children." At present, Head Start, combined with Early Head Start, "serves children from birth to age 5, pregnant women, and their families" with the aim of "increasing the school readiness of young children." Since its inception over forty years ago, the Head Start Program has also been involved in initiating and supporting research and evaluation activities. The "Research and Statistics" section of the website provides links to "Ongoing Research," "Publications and Reports," and "Bibliographies and Research Resources." Under the "Bibliographies and Research Resources" category, you will find a noteworthy resource entitled *Annotated Bibliography of Head Start Research*. This searchable database covers over forty years of research and includes over 3,400 entries. Although this bibliography is quite impressive, researchers should also note that additional Head Start research is available on the website of another Administration of Families and Children component, the Office of Planning, Research and Evaluation (www .acf.hhs.gov/programs/opre).

Centers for Disease Control and Prevention (www.cdc.gov)

According to the Centers for Disease Control and Prevention (CDC) website, the mission of the CDC is "to promote health and quality of life by preventing and controlling disease, injury, and disability." Access to CDC information is provided through a variety of features on the website, including an "A–Z index," a keyword search screen, and a menu with sections on "Health and Safety Topics," "Publications and Products," and "Data and Statistics." The CDC is an important resource for scholars looking for reliable information and current data on topics related to the health of children and adolescents. For example, under Publications and Products, you will find a listing for *MMWR* (www.cdc.gov/mmwr), the acronym for the CDC's *Morbidity and Mortality Weekly Report*. These *MMWRs* are popular sources with researchers as well as health professionals because they include concise and timely articles on a wide variety of health-related topics. Recent issues include articles on topics such as overweight children and cigarette use among high school students. References to scholarly journal articles and statistical sources are generally included within each *MMWR* article. Also available under the *MMWR* publications section are the more in-depth *MMWR Surveillance Summaries*. The *Youth Risk Behavior Surveillance* published every other year is especially useful for researchers concerned with adolescents.

National Center for Health Statistics (www.cdc.gov/nchs)

As the "Nation's principal health statistics agency," the National Center for Health Statistics (NCHS) "compiles statistical information to guide actions and policies and to improve the health of our people." Data is collected from "birth and death records, medical records, interview surveys, through direct physical exams, and laboratory testing." The NCHS website provides researchers with access to the information, data, and documentation from these important NCHS Surveys and Data Collection Systems. Scholars can download public use data files, perform database searches, and extract data using tools provided on the "Datawarehouse" section of this website. For the beginning researcher the "FASTSTATS A–Z" feature provides quick and easy access to health statistics on a wide variety of topics. By selecting "adolescent health," "child health," and "infant health" researchers will find relevant statistics as well as links to the primary data sources. In addition, the NCHS website provides pertinent tabulated data at the federal and state level and a vast array of useful publications. For example, the NCHS publishes in digital and print format the noteworthy annual *Health, United States* (www.cdc.gov/nchs/hus.htm), a standard source for academic researchers in search of health statistics.

Health Resources and Services Administration, Maternal and Child Health Bureau (www.mchb.hrsa.gov)

"In 1935, the U.S. Congress enacted Title V of the Social Security Act, which authorized the Maternal and Child Health Services programs and provided a foundation and structure for assuring the health of American mothers and children." Since 1989, the MCHB has published *Child Health USA* (www.mchb.hrsa.gov/mchirc/chusa). This annual report covering fifty-five child health indicators provides researchers with statistical tables, accompanied by text, and information on trends. Although the main focus is on national data, it also includes state and city data for selected indicators. Another noteworthy resource featured on the website in the "Data" section is *The Health and Well-Being of Children: A Portrait of States and the Nation, 2005* (www.mchb.hrsa.gov/thechild). This informative chartbook "presents National- and State-level data on the health and well-being of children, their families, and their neighborhoods from the National Survey of Children's Health."

National Institutes of Health (www.nih.gov)

As the "steward of medical and behavioral research for the nation," the National Institutes of Health (NIH) conducts, supports, and disseminates research through its twenty-seven institutes and centers covering all aspects of diseases and disorders, as well as human growth and development. By exploring the NIH website, researchers will discover that many of these components are concerned with research relating to the health and well-being of children. For example, the National Institute of Child Health and Human Development (NICHD, at www.nichd.nih.gov) conducts and sponsors research in an effort to ensure that "all children have a chance to achieve their full potential for healthy and productive lives." The NICHD is currently overseeing the planning of the National Children's Study (www.nationalchildrensstudy.gov), a longitudinal study of 100,000 children from before birth to age twenty-one. According to the planning documents, findings from this massive collaborative effort—involving a consortium of federal agencies along with selected academic and medical institutions located throughout the country—will be made publicly available on an ongoing basis.

Another example of a notable NIH survey pertinent to researchers concerned with adolescents is the one sponsored by the National Institute for Drug Abuse (NIDA, at www.nida.nih.gov). Since 1975, NIDA has sponsored annual surveys of U.S. high school students to learn more about the use of drugs, alcohol, and cigarettes among adolescents. Results of these surveys are published annually. The latest report entitled *Monitoring the Future: National Survey Results on Drug Use, 1975–2005* (monitoringthefuture.org) is useful for researchers looking for current statistics as well as trends in drug use. Another component of the NIH, the National Institute of Mental Health (NIMH, at www.nimh.nih.gov), is involved in conducting and sponsoring research on mental and behavioral disorders. On the NIMH home page, under the heading "Health Information" you will find links to information on disorders affecting children and adolescents such as autism, attention deficit hyperactivity disorder, and depression.

National Library of Medicine (www.nlm.nih.gov)

The National Library of Medicine, "the world's largest medical library," is another one of NIH's components that academic researchers in the interdisciplinary field of CCS should get to know. The NLM collects, organizes, and makes available medical and health information to researchers, scientists, health professionals, and the public. Two major Web resources offered by the National Library of Medicine are PubMed and Medlineplus.

Known around the world as the premier database for scholarly biomedical literature, the National Library of Medicine's PubMed (www.ncbi.nlm.nih.gov/entrez) provides free access to the Medline database of over 14 million citations from about 4,800 journals published worldwide from 1966 to the present as well as additional citations from OldMedline dating back to the 1950s. Whether you are searching for scholarly journal articles on child abuse, autism, or teen pregnancy prevention, you will find relevant citations to scholarly articles in the PubMed/Medline database. For some articles, the PubMed/Medline database links you to the full text of the article. Researchers using academic libraries will have access to the full text for additional articles through their library in digital or print format or through interlibrary loan services. Some academic libraries subscribe to a commercial version of this government database. These versions of the Medline database often provide an added linking feature to help the user locate journal articles within the digital or print collections of their academic library.

Medlineplus (www.medlineplus.gov) is another useful service provided by the National Library of Medicine. This website provides researchers with a quick way to get reliable health information that is available from components within the National Institute of Health as well as other government agencies and nongovernmental health organizations.

U.S. DEPARTMENT OF JUSTICE (www.usdoj.gov)

The mission statement on the Department of Justice's website states that the Department of Justice (DOJ) is involved in enforcing the law as well as ensuring "public safety," and the "fair and impartial administration of justice." The DOJ is also responsible for providing "federal leadership in preventing and controlling crime." This department plays a major role in the lives of America's children and adolescents whether they are victims, offenders, or just want the opportunity to grow up in a safe environment.

Researchers need to get acquainted with agencies within the Department of Justice that are engaged in collecting and disseminating statistics. For over seventy-five years, the Federal Bureau of Investigation (www.fbi .gov) has coordinated the Uniform Crime Reporting Program, a "nationwide cooperative statistical effort" involving gathering data on reported crimes from local, state, and federal law enforcement agencies. The annual report *Crime in the United States* (www.fbi.gov/ucr/ucr.htm), produced by the FBI, uses data from the Uniform Crime Reporting Program to provide researchers, professionals, and the general public with an informative snapshot of criminal offenses on a national, state, and local level.

Another way for researchers to tap into the vast amount of statistics available from the DOJ is to visit the website of the Bureau of Justice Statistics (BJS, at www.ojp.usdoj.gov/bjs). As its name implies, the primary function of the Bureau of Justice Statistics is to "collect, analyze, publish, and disseminate" statistical information. The home page includes a directory-style menu entitled "Statistics about" and a useful "Publications" section. On the BJS home page, you will find a direct link to the *Sourcebook of Criminal Justice Statistics* (www .albany.edu/sourcebook), a major publication funded by the Bureau of Justice Statistics but housed in digital format at the University at Albany. Now in its thirty-first edition, this comprehensive sourcebook is a standard resource for academic research. Also, using the "Data Online" feature on the BJS home page, you can link to "Crime Trends" from the FBI's Uniform Crime Reports and create a twenty-year profile for your local community.

The following entries explore the websites of two additional DOJ agencies especially relevant to the information needs of researchers concerned with juveniles.

Office of Juvenile Justice and Delinquency Prevention (www.ojjdp.ncjrs.org)

The Office of Juvenile Justice and Delinquency Prevention (OJJDP) is responsible for providing "national leadership, coordination, and resources to prevent and respond to juvenile delinquency and victimization." In addition to working with states and local communities to provide programs for juveniles, the OJJDP sponsors research and disseminates information.

The OJJDP home page offers a variety of features to help you find information relevant to your interest area. The "Statistics" feature leads you to a "Statistics Briefing Book" organized by broad categories such as Juveniles as Victims and Juveniles as Offenders. Another way to get acquainted with the many different types of OJJDP sources is to select the "Publications" feature on the home page. For example, if you browse the list of publications you will find a listing for a key OJJDP source entitled *Juvenile Offenders and Victims: 2006 National Report*. This highly recommended comprehensive 260-page report pulls together data and research from many different sources to paint an illuminating portrait of juveniles in the United States. It includes data, trends, and analysis for topics such as juveniles in poverty, births to teens, school dropouts, juveniles in the labor force, juvenile homicide victims, juvenile suicides, school crime, juvenile victimization on the Internet, runaway children, child maltreatment, weapon use, drug and alcohol use, and youth gangs.

National Criminal Justice Reference Service (www.ncjrs.gov)

The major function of the National Criminal Justice Reference Service (NCJRS) is to disseminate justice and substance abuse information. To achieve this goal, the NCJRS offers two searchable databases on its website. Using the "A-Z Publications/Products" feature provides a quick and easy way to gain access to hundreds of reports and products produced by federal agencies within the DOJ. However, researchers interested in resources beyond the Justice Department should try searching the NCJRS Abstracts Database (www.ncjrs.gov/abstractdb). This comprehensive database contains abstracts of over 185,000 documents including books and scholarly journal articles as well as federal, state, and local government reports. The NCJRS Abstracts Database is a standard tool for academic research in the fields of criminology, criminal justice, and related disciplines. Since it covers a wide variety of topics concerning juveniles in crisis, such as child abuse, gangs, bullying, suicide, substance abuse, and juvenile delinquency, it is also an important tool for CCS researchers.

Before concluding this chapter it is necessary to mention just one more resource—the reference librarian at your college or university library. As you navigate your way through U.S. government resources, keep in mind that your librarian can help you in your quest to identify government information to meet your needs.

12

WORLD WIDE WEB RESOURCES

Katie Elson Anderson

The nature of interdisciplinary study creates a challenge to the researcher in the field of Children and Childhood Studies (CCS). An important part of successful research is the knowledge of the appropriate words, phrases, and concepts that will provide the best results. When searching within one's own field of study, this is uncomplicated. The complicated part occurs when one is attempting to retrieve a variety of resources from unfamiliar fields. When searching the Web for the variety of resources that pertain to CCS, it is important to choose the correct search tools, enter the most accurate search terms and have the skills to evaluate the websites that are found. This chapter contains general information on searching for Web resources as well as an annotated bibliography of the resources that were found.

USING THIS CHAPTER

This chapter is divided into five sections. The first three sections contain a general discussion about searching for and evaluating resources on the Web. "Understanding Web Searching Tools" will help you gain a better understanding of the search tools available for searching on the Web. "Choosing Search Engines and Directories" will assist you in deciding which of the search tools are most valuable for your searching. This section includes a discussion of websites that provide information on analysis on all the available search tools to further assist you with your chosen search tools. Once you have found websites using the search tools, "Evaluating Web Sites" will help you determine the accuracy and validity of the resources you find. This section includes descriptions of available tutorials to further assist you in your evaluating skills. The fourth section, "Searching for Resources," discusses search techniques specific to CCS to aid your Web searching. The final section, "Finding Resources," is a list of the resources available on the Web, divided into the categories of Education, Organizations, Networks, and Government. Some of these websites have links to other resources that are not included in the section, so you are encouraged to explore.

UNDERSTANDING WEB SEARCHING TOOLS

The best way to start a search on the World Wide Web is with a basic understanding of the different tools for searching and the standard techniques used with these tools. While it is possible to get results from simple searches in your favorite search engine, a better research strategy would be one that uses more of the tools that are available. Taking the time to understand the tools and methods before you begin your search will save you valuable time and minimize frustration during your search.

There are several books, articles, and websites dedicated to the description and evaluation of the different tools available for doing research on the Internet. These sources range from basic definitions to in-depth discussions of the behind-the-scenes workings of a search engine. An excellent resource for information on web searching is Randolph Hocks's "The Extreme Searcher's Internet Handbook" (CyberAge Books, 2004). For the purposes of this chapter, we touch on some of the basics that will assist in your Web searching. A discussion of the two major tools used in Web searching is important in helping a searcher determine where to start a Web search.

Search Engines

A search engine is a service that allows a user to search a database of websites using words, phrases, or other criteria. A search engine should be used when conducting a search where the words and phrases that describe a specific topic are known. There are a number of search engines available on the Web, some more heavily used than others (such as Google and Yahoo). The variety of search engines available provides a searcher with a choice of interfaces, advanced features, and output display. The variety of search engines also expands the number of results retrieved. Each search engine will have results that are unique from others due to the differences in the way the individual engines search the Web. The advantage to having a variety of search engines for researchers is that one can find a search engine that best meets their technical and visual needs. The disadvantage to the number of search engines is that a researcher cannot rely on just the one best-known engine because each of the different search engines will yield different results. In order to have a more comprehensive search on the Web, more than one search engine should be used.

The ability to search multiple search engines at once does exist in the form of metasearch engines, but these must be used carefully and with an understanding that they are not providing a comprehensive search. A more in-depth knowledge of the drawbacks of these types of engines should be acquired before using a metasearch engine.

Directories

There are two very different types of directories available to a researcher. General directories and specialized directories are both compiled by people, as opposed to the robots or crawlers that produce the results of a search engines.

When a specific topic is not yet known, a general Web directory can be used for searching and browsing within a broad topic. A Web directory is a collection of Web pages that are classified by subject. The classification and subclassification by subject makes it easy to browse the collection. General directories do not include as much of the Web as a search engine does, but they can be a good starting point for a searcher, assisting in determining a more specific topic within a subject area.

Specialized directories are different from the general directories in that they have already been narrowed down to a specific topic by professionals. A specialized directory can be a searchable website or simply a collection of links to websites that share similar themes. Other names for specialized directories include resource guides and metasites.

CHOOSING SEARCH ENGINES AND DIRECTORIES

The success of a Web search is increased by the searcher's knowledge of how to conduct the search on that particular search engine or directory. Most search engine and directory homepages offer tips that will provide the user with information such as how to use the advanced tool, how the search engine will accept Boolean commands, and which character to use as a wildcard.

Fortunately there is help available in the form of tutorials and websites dedicated to the description of search engines and directories. The websites below provide a searcher with quick guides, helpful tips, and easy-to-decipher charts that will assist in searching for information on the Internet.

Search Engine Showdown (www.searchengineshowdown.com)

Montana State University Reference Librarian Greg Notess, who is also a writer and speaker specializing in information resources, maintains Search Engine Showdown. According to the website, he has been covering Internet resources since 1990. Search Engine Showdown provides Web users with reviews, charts, news, and statistics on search engines. The Search Engines Feature Chart is a straightforward and uncomplicated way of comparing the features of seven different search engines. Some of these features include Boolean operators and searchable fields. Also included on this website are search strategies, and information on metasearch engines and a chart on searching subject directories. The website is updated regularly.

SearchEngineWatch (www.searchenginewatch.com)

SearchEngineWatch bills itself as "the source for search engine marketing," but don't be fooled by that label. While the target audience of the site may be website developers and professionals in the industry, the information provided is useful to anyone conducting research on the Web. SearchEngineWatch has been in existence since 1997 and was founded by Danny Sullivan, who is an Internet consultant and journalist. The site is kept up-to-date and offers a daily newsletter to provide the most current information regarding search engines. The amount of information on this site makes it appear a bit intimidating, as it is quite a comprehensive site for all things search engine. The most useful links for basic search engine information are included under the "Departments and Info" sidebar, "Web Searching Tips." "The Web Searching Tips" page provides links to a search engine features chart, further information on features, advanced searching, search engine math, Boolean searching and reviews.

Finding Information on the Internet: A Tutorial: UC Berkeley—Teaching Library Internet Workshops (www.lib.berkeley.edu/TeachingLib/Guides/Internet/FindInfo.html)

"This tutorial presents the substance of the Internet Workshops offered year-round by the Teaching Library at the University of California at

Berkeley." The information is up-to-date and divided into categories, allowing the user to pinpoint only the specific part of the tutorial that is needed. The "Search Engine and Subject Directory" portions of the tutorial provide easily read graphs that compare the features of each entry.

EVALUATING WEBSITES

Once the search engine or directory is chosen and searched the next step is to evaluate the results that are received. The results that are returned during a Web search must be viewed with a critical eye; not everything that appears in the results is going to be useful, relevant, or from a trusted source. It is up to the user to determine if the information is accurate and relevant to the research. There are several resources both in print and on the Web that provide instruction on how to evaluate a website. Most of the instruction on assessing the quality of websites includes discussions of similar criteria: source, authorship, authority, motivation, quality of writing, currency, accuracy, objectivity, sources cited, and coverage. There are different approaches to evaluating websites but they all have the same basic goal, which is to identify and evaluate the criteria in order to determine the accuracy and legitimacy of a website. With the different approaches there are different websites that instruct users on website evaluation; two such websites are listed here.

Evaluating Web Pages: Techniques to Apply & Questions to Ask: UC Berkeley—Teaching Library Internet Workshops (www.lib .berkeley.edu/TeachingLib/Guides/Internet/Evaluate.html)

This is a section of a tutorial on finding information on the Internet, maintained at UC Berkeley. This site offers details on how to determine which results from a search to choose and how to determine the quality of the content of the sites that are chosen. The bulk of the site is a list of questions a user should ask when determining the trustworthiness of the site and the techniques on how to locate the answers to these questions. There is a link to a checklist in PDF format that can be used for website evaluation. The section "More about Evaluating Resources" provides links to other websites, including a link to Johns Hopkins University's library, that provide basic evaluation information along with an interesting section on propaganda, misinformation, and disinformation.

Evaluate Web Pages: Widener University, Wolfgram Memorial Library (www.widener.edu/Tools_Resources/Libraries/ Wolfgram_Memorial_Library/Evaluate_Web_Pages/659)

This website includes a tutorial that runs approximately fifteen minutes and includes specific examples for evaluating authority, accuracy, currency, and objectivity. While the tutorial is informative, what makes this website most valuable are the links under "Original Web Evaluation Materials." This section contains detailed checklists for the different types of websites that will be found when conducting research on the Internet. There are evaluation checklists for advocacy, business/marketing, news, informational, and personal Web pages. The advocacy checklist is particularly valuable for websites on CCS because of the large amount of .org websites pertaining to children.

SEARCHING FOR RESOURCES

Search Engines

When searching for CCS resources using a search engine, it is important to remember that using more than one search engine will increase the number of results. The resources provided in this chapter were found using both Google and Yahoo. Google gave the most direct results, focusing in on education sites with program in the topics. Yahoo was more likely to bring up records that contained information on books, journals, or studies related to CCS. Most of the metasites from educational institutes were found by conducting a search using the words *children childhood studies*. This search brought up many websites for universities and colleges that have some academic programs or classes within the topic. This was a good place to start because many of these websites contained links to other websites on the topic.

When searching for more specific topics within the discipline, simple keyword searches within Google were successful. The top results were accurate and direct the user to many of the organizations that deal with the specific topic. These searches can also be narrowed by country or even state. For example, using the terms *child poverty* results in multiple websites for national and international organizations. Narrowing that search to "Child Poverty—California" brings the searcher directly to the California information of some of the national organizations as well as to sites that are specific to California. It is advantageous that search engines will search not only the main page of a website, but the content within the website.

General Directories

General directories are a bit of a challenge to navigate when researching an interdisciplinary field because the resources do not always fit neatly into one area of the directory. While some interdisciplinary areas such as Women's Studies do appear in directories, at this time locating resources in a directory for CCS is not as straightforward. A directory is useful for browsing because it allows a searcher to start with a broad search and narrow the topic by exploring the categories and subcategories. The disadvantage to using a directory is the fact that the resources exist in different areas and it can be time consuming to search for relevant resources using a directory.

There are several general directories to choose from. Many of them have similar categories, but because they are compiled and edited by different groups, the results will not be the same. It is important that a researcher understand how the directory is created in order to better evaluate the results. A good directory will have this information under "About" or "Directory Help."

The directory used for locating resources for this chapter was Google (www.google.com/dirhp). Google was chosen because it uses the hierarchy of the Open Directory Project (dmoz.org), which calls itself the "largest, most comprehensive human-edited directory of the Web." The combination of Open Directory's hierarchy and Google's page ranking system allow for easy browsing and relevant results. Google provides a "related categories" section that is extremely helpful in browsing a topic because it directs the user to the different categories where more information can be found.

The challenge with using any directory is in having the time to browse the different categories that are available. It is not always clear what resources will occur in which categories and it is more than likely that the resources that are needed will be found in many of the categories.

A good category in a general directory to begin the search for CCS is "Society." Within "Society" choose "Issues," and then narrow that down to "Children, Youth and Family." Within the category "Children, Youth and Family" will be several subcategories that can be browsed. The "Children, Youth and Family" category within "Society" was discovered after browsing "Health/Children's Health and Home/Family." While browsing these categories it was observed that the majority of the resources appeared in the "Related Categories: Society/Issues/Children, Youth and Family." The related category feature is very useful when browsing as it directs you to other categories whose subcategories include topics on children. Another nice feature of Google directory is the ability to search only within the category that has been selected. This is useful when browsing is no longer necessary and a specific search is warranted.

When reviewing the result from directory browsing, it is important to realize that the people compiling the list have compiled the list based on their knowledge and expertise. This knowledge and expertise may not always match your information needs. In the case of general directories, not all of the listed sites will be useful to your research or even valid for the topic. It is up to you to explore these links to determine their usefulness.

Specialized Directories

A specialized directory is a directory that has been narrowed down by professionals within the field of specialty. This is helpful because the use of these directories can eliminate the need to look at all of the results because it is known that the sites have been selected for a specific group of users and their needs. There are some specialized directories that have been created to only include academically valuable and scholarly resources. Infomine and Librarians' Internet Index are examples of such directories. While these directories will provide already screened information, they can be more difficult to browse. They are searchable and a good plan of action may be to use the general directories to get results and then use the specialized directories to confirm the value of these results.

Librarians' Internet Index (lii.org)

Librarians' Internet Index is a publicly funded website that contains websites selected, described, and organized by a team of librarians. The websites are selected based on the criteria of availability, credibility, authorship, external links, and legality. New sites are continuously added and sites that no longer meet the criteria will be removed. The site is divided in a similar way to the general directories with many of the same categories. For example, choosing "Society and Social Science" will allow you to choose "Social Issues," and within these issues are child-related topics similar to the general directories. The child-related sites are not as easily found as in the general directories as there is no specific category for children's social issues. The results include brief descriptions along with links to actual documents as well as websites that will provide more information. The site can also be searched with a simple or advanced search.

Infomine (www.infomine.ucr.edu)

Infomine is a "virtual library of Internet resources relevant to faculty, students, and research staff at the university level." The resources contained in Infomine include databases, electronic journals, electronic books, bulletin boards, mailing lists, online library card catalogs, articles, and directories of researchers. This site is set up more for searching within a category than for browsing, which makes it more difficult to locate resources. After choosing a category, a search form is provided, requiring that a search be conducted using title, author, subject, keyword, and description of full text. This type of specialized directory would be most useful to someone who has already narrowed the topic down enough to conduct a search. The biggest challenge is in knowing which category to search for the specific topic. Besides the basic academic categories ("Science," "Humanities," etc.), Infomine has a "Cultural Diversity" and a "Government" category that may be useful for finding resources within this interdisciplinary subject.

FINDING RESOURCES

The resources that are listed are divided into the following categories: "Education," "Organizations," "Networks," and "Government." The sources were found using search engines, general directories, and metasites. As of the time this chapter was written, all links were valid and all websites currently updated unless otherwise noted. These resources are meant to provide a general starting point for research within the field.

Education

The resources listed below are maintained by educational institutions from around the world. These educational institutions have either a degree program in CCS (or related interdisciplinary program) or have a center affiliated with the institution. All of these resources can be considered metasites because they contain a list of links on similar topics. There are more educational institutions that have programs or centers that are not listed below because they do not provide further information and resources beyond descriptions of the academic program.

Many of these sites include links to valuable resources that are local and regional to the educational institution. While some of the links to general information from these sites are detailed in another section of this chapter, many of the links from these pages are not discussed due to their specificity to location or subject matter and should be explored for further details.

Child & Family Studies Resources: Syracuse University Library: Syracuse University (libwww.syr.edu/research/internet/child/index.html)

Syracuse University Library's resources for Child and Family Studies provides a list of print resources (with local call numbers and locations), links to international statistics and organizations, links to locating statistical and demographic information on the federal, state, and local level, and a list of metasites for Child and Family Studies. Some of the links to the statistical sites are only available to local users, but other links are available to any researcher.

Child and Family Web Guide: Tufts University (www.cfw.tufts.edu)

The Child & Family Web Guide "describes trustworthy websites on topics of interest to parents and professionals . . . the sites have been systematically evaluated by graduate students and faculty in child development." The websites are organized into five categories: "Family/Parenting," "Education/ Learning," "Typical Child Development," "Health/Mental Health," and "Resources/Recreation." The "Resources/Recreation" section does not contain research-based information and is geared more toward parents than researchers. The categories are color coded, making the website easy to navigate and the topics easy to identify. The site can also be searched by age group or by using an index search.

CYFC: Children, Youth and Family Consortium University of Minnesota (www.cyfc.umn.edu)

The Children, Youth and Family Consortium was established in 1991 and is committed to "interdisciplinary work, integrating institutional service and outreach into research and teaching, and providing for University and community engagement around child, youth and family issues." The site has links to local and international information on public policy along with resources for current issues. There are extensive lists of resources for early childhood, school-age children, adolescents, and family relationship and parenting. The resources in each of these subject areas are divided into five categories: "University of Minnesota Resources," "Non University of

Minnesota Resources," "Data Sources," "Community Resources and Programs," and "Policy." Clear descriptions of the sites are provided along with
the links in each of these categories.

Georgetown University Center for Child and Human Development:
Georgetown University Medical Center, Georgetown University
(www.gucchd.georgetown.edu)

The Georgetown University Center for Child and Human Development
was "established over four decades to improve the quality of life for all children and youth, especially those with, or at risk for, special needs and their
families." Along with information regarding the center and its work, there
is a link to online resources that can be selected by topic. Topics that are
available are mental health, early childhood, developmental disabilities, special health needs, cultural competence, research and evaluation, and clinical
and community services.

Information Sources for Childhood and Adolescence Studies: Liverpool John
Moores University (cwis.livjm.ac.uk/lea/info/child)

This U.K.-based site is maintained by John Moores University's learning
resource center by subject information officers in Childhood Studies. An
interesting element to this site is the links to interactive tutorials on searching the Internet in the fields of Education, Social Policy, and Social Statistics. The site includes links to abstracts, indexes, electronic journals, statistical sites, and child-centered organizations. As with many of the resource
sites maintained by individual schools, the target audience is made up of local users. The links (requiring a name and password) to the electronic journal titles, abstracts, and indexes will not be useful to a nonaffiliated user, but
the alphabetical listing of over thirty-five journals can be of great use to
anyone exploring topics in CCS.

National Centre for Research in Children's Literature: University of Surrey
Roehampton (www.ncrcl.ac.uk)

The sources on this website are primarily from the United Kingdom and
they include information on publications by the center and links to useful

websites pertaining to the study of Children's Literature. Links to journals, academic sites, and discussion groups supplement the list of general sites.

Online Resources: Center for Children and Childhood Studies, Rutgers University, Camden Campus (children.camden.rutgers.edu/resources.htm)

This page of online resources is broken into three sections: "Researchers/Scholars," "Families/Community," and "Educators/Students." "Researchers/Scholars" includes a descriptive list of journals in CCS including links to the journal's website when available. A section on statistical information provides links to local, state, U.S., and international websites that provide various statistics. Selected national and international research reports are also available in the "Researchers/Scholars" section, providing links to reports on national and international issues related to children. The "Selected Websites" section under "Researchers/Scholars" is an excellent list of available CCS Web resources. Along with links to the megasites that are detailed in another section of this chapter, the selected websites include links to other centers for Children and Childhood and schools with Children and Childhood degree programs. Other sites are sorted by topics such as "Adoption and Foster Care," "Juvenile Justice," "Advocacy Groups," "Children and Poverty," "Children's Literature," "Child Abuse and Neglect," "Children's Health Risks," and "Children with Disabilities."

Peabody Library Resource Guides: Child and Youth Study Resource Guide: Peabody College, Vanderbilt University (www.library.vanderbilt.edu/peabody/articles/guides/youth.html)

This is a resource guide provided by the library at Peabody College, Vanderbilt University. The site includes suggested resources for research in Child and Youth Studies. The resources include reference books, periodicals, indexes, general texts, and briefly described linked sites. The inclusion of library call numbers and links to periodical articles indicate that the target audience is local users, but the information is useful to anyone researching the field. This website provides a nice overview of the resources available including directories, handbooks, encyclopedias, dictionaries, bibliographies, and guides to literature, periodicals, indexes and abstracts, government documents, and online resources.

Resources for Childhood Studies: University of Edinburgh
(www.childhoodstudies.ed.ac.uk/links.htm)

The Childhood Studies program at University of Edinburgh provides a brief description and links to national children's organizations, International children's organizations, networks, and other information resources. The section with the most links is the national section, which contains organizations in England, Wales, and Scotland. A brief description of each link provided is useful in determining the usefulness of the listed sites.

Organizations

There is a multitude of websites for nonprofit organizations dedicated to children. One of the easiest ways to locate nonprofit organizations is to do an advanced search on Google, limiting the domain name to ".org." When a website has a domain name of ".org," this is a good indication that the website belongs to a U.S. nonprofit, nongovernmental organization. It is advisable to use specific search terms; searches using *child OR children* with domain ".org" resulted in 258,000,000 hits.

While there are a lot of organizations and advocacies dedicated to researching, developing, and improving the lives of children, not all of these organizations can be considered a resource. Many of these organizations provide information only pertaining to the organization and its specialty. A lot of organizations include information on how to make a difference by donating or volunteering. The resources included in this section are for websites that provide extensive information and resources beyond the individual organization. Websites were selected for this section based on the area of focus and the amount and availability of resources.

Child Health: World Health Organisation
(www.who.int/topics/child_health/en)

The World Health Organisation website is broken down by health topics. Choosing "Child Health" will bring up this page, which "provides links to descriptions of activities, reports, news and events, as well as contacts and cooperating partners in the various WHO programmes and offices working on this topic." Links to related websites and topics are also available in this section on "Child Health." The World Health Organisation is the United Nations specialized agency for health and the main website contains extensive information on all health-related topics. It is possible to explore other health-related topics to find more resources on a specific topic. The site is also searchable by keyword. Searching with keywords *child* or *children* brought up many items that are found in the Child Health topic section as well as items from other topic areas.

Children's Defense Fund (www.childrensdefense.org)

Children's Defense Fund is a private, nonprofit organization that is supported by foundation and corporate grants and individual donations. Children's Defense Fund "provides a strong, effective voice for all the children of America who cannot vote, lobby or speak for themselves." The "Data" section of the website provides national, state, and census data provided by the organization. The "Links" section includes links to organizations, networks and publications, government agencies, and sites that provide national data. A brief description of the organization, network, and publication is included with these links. The site is searchable and the search can be narrowed down to a specific topic within the website.

Coalition to Stop the Use of Child Soldiers (www.child-soldiers.org)

The Coalition to Stop the Use of Child Soldiers "works to prevent the recruitment and use of children as soldiers, to secure their demobilisation and to ensure their rehabilitation and reintegration into society." The site provides a variety of resources on the use of child soldiers. The resources are made up of global reports, themed reports, international standards, newsletters and press releases. A "Links" section of the website provides an extensive list of international websites relating to children and armed conflict.

Connect for Kids (www.connectforkids.org)

Connect for Kids is an organization that strives to provide the tools and information needed for individuals to work on behalf of children, youth, and families. The site can be searched by topic and subtopic as well as the type of content. Topics include "Diversity," "Education," "Health," "Youth at Risk," and "History of Childhood." The types of content that can be accessed include articles, field reports, organizations, and Web links.

National Center for Children in Poverty: Columbia University (www.nccp.org)

The National Center for Children in Poverty is a research and policy organization whose mission is "to identify and promote strategies that prevent child poverty in the United States and that improve the lives of low-income children and families." The site offers data wizards on all fifty states for policies and demographics allowing for selection of both state and policy. A link to the Research Forum (www.researchforum.org) at the National Center for Children in Poverty allows for more advanced searching of the available resources. The site also provides access to news releases, fact sheets, and other publications.

National Data Analysis System: Child Welfare League of America (ndas.cwla.org)

The National Data Analysis System is part of the Child Welfare League of America's National Center for Research. The Child Welfare League of America is a member-based child welfare organization that is committed to "engaging people everywhere in promoting the well-being of children, youth, and their families, and protecting every child from harm." According to the website the National Data Analysis System is the most comprehensive collection of child welfare and related data in the country. The data and statistics are accessible by topic and much of the data is presented in tables and graphs that can be customized by state and date range. These customized reports can be downloaded. The topics available are: "Adoption," "Agency Administration," "Child Abuse and Neglect," "Child Abuse and Neglect Fatalities," "Child Care," "Children's Health," "Family Preservation and Support," "Fiscal Data," "Juvenile Justice," "Out-of-Home Care," "Outcomes," and "Population Data." There is also a "Research and Information" section for each of these topics that provides links to statutes, related websites, and data and research. The related websites appear in the data and statistics, but there is an additional brief description of these websites provided in the research and information section.

Save the Children (www.savethechildren.org)

Save the Children is, according to this website, "the leading independent organization creating real and lasting change for children in need in the United States and around the world." The resources on this site are publications by Save the Children and links to other organizations' resources. Links to these PDF documents and some links to other websites are found by going to the "Professional" gateway and choosing "More Information and Technical Resources." A publications link provides access to the latest research, annual reports, fact sheets, issue briefs, and other publications.

UNICEF: United Nations Children's Fund (www.unicef.org)

The mission statement of UNICEF states that this organization, which is mandated by the United Nations General Assembly, works to "advocate for the protection of children's rights, to help meet their basic needs and to expand their opportunities to reach their full potential." This international organization provides detailed information by each country. General information about the country is supplemented by statistics for the following topics: "Basic Indicators," "Nutrition," "Health," "HIV/AIDS," "Education," "Demographics," "Economics," "Women," "Child Protection," and "Rate of Progress." Current news links and information about surrounding countries complete the extensive information on each country. There is a search box on every page, making it easy to search for particular key words and topics. The site has a "Resources" section that provides links for development professionals, teachers and students, publications, and UN links. The resources for development professionals and students and teachers include documents, statistics, and UNICEF publications on a variety of topics. The section for development professionals includes a link to childinfo.org, which is the website that accesses UNICEF's key statistical databases. Childinfo.org is dedicated to statistics compiled by UNICEF and is searchable by keyword and by indicators.

Networks

Network websites are a valuable resource since the mission of network is to provide information via a central location. Various organizations join these networks in order to contribute information while also benefiting from the information provided by the other organizations that are part of the network.

Children's House (child-abuse.com/childhouse)

Children's House is a cooperative initiative by the AIFS, Child Abuse Prevention Network, Children's Rights Centre, Childwatch International, CRIN, Family Life Development Center, IIN, ISCA, UNICEF, UNESCO, World Bank, and WHO. Children's House is dedicated to providing a place for the exchange of information that addresses the needs and concerns of children. The resources are divided into sections: "Child Research," "Early Childhood," "Child Health," and "Children's Rights." There is also information and links to nongovernmental organizations and news and other information resources.

Childwatch International Research Network (www.childwatch.uio.no)

According to the website, the ultimate goal of Childwatch International is "through network activities to promote, initiate and disseminate international, inter-disciplinary research that leads to a real improvement in the well-being of children." This nonprofit organization's website offers resources in research and other child-related matters. The "Child Research Resources" section includes links to institutions and organizations that conduct research on children's rights. There are also links to online research reports and journals, data and ongoing studies. The "Child Related Matters" section includes links to pertinent websites. Topics listed include "Abuse and Neglect Prevention," "Child Health," "Child Labor," "Child Rights and Organizations," "Children and Media," "Children and War," "Children and Youth in Conflict with the Law," "Children with Disabilities," "Early Childhood," "The Girl Child," "Homeless Children and Street Kids," and "Youth and Adolescents." Within each of these topics are descriptive links to the related websites.

CRIN: Child Rights Information Network (www.crin.org)

One of the key objectives of the Child Rights Information Network is to meet the information needs of organizations and individuals working for child rights. The Child Rights Information Network is a global network of organizations committed to the UN Convention on the Rights of the Child and to sharing information on children's rights. The website is part of the network's program for child rights and it contains an extensive amount of information, including resources, news, events, and a directory of child rights organizations. The information on this website can be searched by region, theme, or type of resource. The search forms allows for a choice of language, country, information type, and keywords. The resulting resources are made up of publications and reports on child rights. These publications include books and newsletters, journals, conference reports, and training materials.

CYFERnet: Children, Youth and Families Education and Research Network: Practical Research-based Information from the Nation's Leading Universities (www.cyfernet.org)

The CYFERnet website is maintained by a team of workers at land-grant university extension services across the nation. CYFERnet's website, a central location for the information on children, youth, and family resources, is reviewed by college and university faculty. The site is searchable by title, abstract, full text, and author. Information is broken down into the following categories: "Early Childhood," "School Age (K-8)," "Teens," "Parent/Family," and "Community." Each of these categories is broken down into subcategories within the topic. The resources for each subtopic include general information, links to other resources, programming resources, and research.

Government

Government websites are an excellent place to find research and statistics on a variety of child-related topics. The resources listed below were included because of the general nature of the resource and the amount of information available within the department or agency. Other government websites are discussed in the chapter "U.S. Government Resources." When searching for government websites, do not limit the search to the U.S. government. There are valuable resources on websites for international government agencies as well.

Administration for Children and Families: U.S. Department of Health and Human Services (www.acf.dhhs.gov)

This site is for the Administration for Children and Families, which is part of the U.S. Department of Health and Human Services. The ACF is a federal agency "funding state, territory, local, and tribal organizations to provide family assistance, child support child care, Head Start, child welfare and other programs relating to children and families." The site includes FAQs and links to websites on a number of topics related to children and families. Topics include "Adoption and foster care," "Child Abuse and Neglect," "Childcare," "Child Support," "Disabilities and Children," "Youth and Families." A drop-down box allows for locating the websites of specific programs with the Administration for Children and Families. There is also an area to find information on various topics by navigating a drop-down box and selecting the suggested questions that will meet your information need.

ChildStats.gov: Federal Interagency Forum on Child and Family Statistics (www.childstats.gov)

This is the official website of the Federal Interagency Forum on Child and Family Statistics. This forum is a working group of twenty federal agencies that collect, analyze, and report data on issues related to children and families. The website "offers easy access to statistics and reports on children and families, including population and family characteristics, economic security, health, behavior and social environment, and education." A "Related Resources" section contains links to data sets, tables, databases, and reports provided by related websites on different aspects of child well-being. These aspects are broken down into the following categories: "Child Well-being and Youth Indicators," "Population and Family Characteristics," "Economic Security," "Health," "Behavioral and Social Environment," "Education," "Kids Pages," and "Research on Child Well-being." The site is searchable by keyword.

National Child Protection Clearinghouse:
Australian Institute of Family Studies (www.aifs.gov.au/nch/info.html)

The National Child Protection Clearinghouse is funded by the Australian Department of Family and Community Services. The clearinghouse "collects, produces and distributes information and resources, conducts research, and offers specialist advice on the latest developments in child abuse prevention, child protection and associated violence." A "Resources" section contains different references and information including bibliographies, statistics, and links. The links consist of local, regional, and international sites pertaining to child abuse and child abuse prevention.

APPENDIX: SAMPLE PAPER

Ellen Firth

COLLODI'S PINOCCHIO:
BIBLICAL AND CULTURAL RITES OF PASSAGE

Pinocchio's journey in Carlo Collodi's *The Adventures of Pinocchio* can be interpreted in many ways. This episodic adventure resembles episodic adventures and happenings as told in the Bible, especially that of the *prodigal son*. The parable structure of the narrative allows for the reader to interpret the story of Pinocchio's relationship with his father and provides insight into Pinocchio's individual development. But the story is much more than a parable. It is a story about Pinocchio's relationship to the outside world and his struggle to be included in society—a society that requires its members to experience rites of passage in order for them to successfully attain a place in the community. Although the father–son relationship is a source of struggle, it offers little growth and benefit to Pinocchio in his struggle for acceptance. However, Pinocchio's journey through the stages of cultural development, when viewed under the principles of Victor Turner's theory of the ritual process, allows for the reader to understand the importance of the larger sociocultural influences affecting Pinocchio's metamorphosis. Pinocchio's story is a human one and strikes a familiar chord in anyone who has ever struggled for acceptance.

Biblical themes abound in *The Adventures of Pinocchio*, but none so much as that of the *prodigal son*. In *The Oxford Companion to Children's Literature*, Humphrey Carpenter and Mari Prichard (1984) write of Collodi's novel: "If there is any theme to the story, it is that of the Prodigal Son, and Lorenzini is always stressing the moral that Pinocchio gets into trouble because he is disobedient" (414). Pinocchio's disobedience and poor judgment continually land him in trouble and danger, yet his ever faithful and loving father patiently awaits his return. In the opening pages of Collodi's novel, Pinocchio steals Gepetto's wig and Gepetto responds by saying, "You young rascal! You are not yet complete, and already you are beginning to show lack of respect to your father!" (Collodi 1985, 11). Does this imply that Pinocchio is *born* bad and is disobedient by nature? Or does it allude to the possibility that Pinocchio cannot be a complete person if he does not have the respect of the outside world, of which Gepetto is a representation?

The biblical prodigal son, like Pinocchio, is introduced to the reader as inherently bad. And also like Pinocchio, the biblical prodigal son experiences the world and returns a changed person. The Bible says of the prodigal son after his father has given him his fortune: "And not many days after, the younger son gathered all together, journeyed to a far country, and there wasted his possessions with prodigal living" (Luke 15:13). The Bible tells of the father's reaction when he sees his son returning in the distance: "But when he [the son] was still a great way off, his father saw him and had compassion, and ran and fell on his neck and kissed him" (Luke 15:20). It is here we see that although the son is forgiven by the father, it is the son's exposure to the outside world that effects change.

In yet another parallel between Pinocchio and the prodigal son, Pinocchio's journeys find him lost and found, hopeless and redeemed. He is rescued from death by the Blue Fairy but it is Pinocchio who eventually redeems himself and becomes reborn in body as well as spirit before he returns to Gepetto's forgiving arms. Both Pinocchio and the prodigal son receive joyful receptions from their fathers, but more important, both return changed due to societal influences. The prodigal son's father explains his joy over his lost son's return: "It [is] right that we should make merry and be glad, for your brother was dead and is alive again, and was lost and is found" (Luke 15:32). Pinocchio is lost or *dead* in the literal sense in that he is made of wood, not recognized as flesh and blood, and therefore not humanly alive. More important, he is dead culturally and spiritually until he experiences the rites of passage necessary to validate his existence. Pinocchio is *found* by society because he does what is necessary to become a part of it.

Although Pinocchio is figured as the prodigal son, he is also hung, reminiscent of the creator's son, Jesus, which casts him in a sacrificial light. In chapter 15, the Fox and the Cat, disguised as assassins, hang Pinocchio from a tree much like Jesus is hung on the cross (sometimes referred to as a tree) at Calvary. Jesus hangs between two thieves much like Pinocchio, who hangs *among* two thieves. Both are sacrificed for failure to adapt to the world in which they live. Jesus is born human but without sin and this separates him culturally from society because his sinless nature prevents him from assimilating into society. Pinocchio, like Jesus, has not experienced the rites of passage necessary to obtain societal inclusion and is persecuted for his *otherness* and his failure to assimilate. Pinocchio and Jesus cry out in vain with their last breaths to their creators. Pinocchio says, "Oh papa, papa! If only you were here!" (Collodi 1985, 68). Similarly, Jesus reaches out to his father with his last breath when he says "My God, My God, why have You forsaken Me?" (Matthew 27:46). In an effort to understand a society they are not a part of, both reach out to their creators.

It is in the creation process that Pinocchio and another biblical character, Adam, share a common origin. In the book of Genesis, God makes Adam from the dust of the earth just as Gepetto makes Pinocchio out of a piece of wood. Both are "born" from their father's hands and both change into something else due to their behavior. Adam changes from Divine to human as a punishment and Pinocchio changes from a puppet to a real boy as a reward. They both also inflict pain on their creators and are initially separated from society. Pinocchio, however, seeks reintegration to society.

The importance of community in individual development is explored in Victor Turner's work on the rites of passage. In *The Ritual Process: Structure and Anti-Structure*, Turner articulates his theory pertaining to rites of passage, which can be applied to Collodi's *The Adventures of Pinocchio* by comparing the components of Turner's theory to the rites of passage Pinocchio experiences in his journey from puppet to boy. Although the parable structure in *The Adventures of Pinocchio* functions as a didactic moral guide, it offers little insight into the issues surrounding Pinocchio's transformation. By applying Turner's theory on the rites of passage to Pinocchio's journey, the reader can better understand the larger sociocultural forces affecting Pinocchio's change.

According to Turner, before a rite of passage can be experienced, a person (or nonperson in this case) is separated from society in some way for any number of reasons (such as social rank or human differences), and begins his journey set apart in some way from the rest of society. Pinocchio is set apart in obvious ways because he is not technically human but he also sets himself apart by choosing not to conform to the rules of his father or the larger society as a whole. Pinocchio's initial place in society is as Gepetto's son and he is literally and symbolically set apart from the human race because his body is wooden, as are his thoughts and actions. The Cricket believes as much when he says, "Poor Pinocchio! I really pity you . . . because you are a puppet and, what is worse, because you have a wooden head" (Collodi 1985, 17). The Cricket refers to Pinocchio's body, which in a literal sense sets the puppet apart from the human flesh–and–blood body. The Cricket's reference to Pinocchio's wooden head alludes symbolically to Pinocchio's thoughtless or "wooden" demeanor. Pinocchio is *other* to both his father and the other puppets. His is not quite real but certainly alive. Turner would say he is *liminal*.

According to Turner, "Liminal entities are neither here nor there; they are betwixt and between the positions assigned and arrayed by law, custom, convention, and ceremonial" (Turner 1969, 95). Pinocchio is neither here nor there when it comes to defining his identity. He is almost a real boy and not merely a puppet and so he stands straddling two worlds. Turner calls liminal beings "liminal personae" or "threshold people." Threshold people have no status. In order for Pinocchio to enter into a state of liminality, he must enter a ritual space, which Turner calls *communitas*. Turner argues that in order for a person or entity to experience liminality, he must experience a stripping away of old ways, including the ability to release selfish individualistic motives, and realize that a generic human bond exists and must be recognized in order to enter into the symbolic ritual space (communitas) where one can be brought into society. It is important to note that Turner is not implying that individuality is selfish and that the status quo is more acceptable. He is saying that one cannot exist without the other. He writes, "[Each] individual's life experience contains alternating exposure to structure and communitas, and to states of transition" (Turner 1969, 97). One cannot be an individual unless he measures his singularity against the community. In order to achieve individuality and a sense of community, one must undergo the ritual process.

Pinocchio must experience certain rites of passage in order to supplant himself as a member of the human race. From the first pages of Collodi's tale, Pinocchio is already experiencing a *separateness* from humanity. He is part of a hierarchy in which society sees him as different and perhaps inferior and lower than human beings, but he is also in a hierarchy in which he places himself at the top. He wants to be a real boy at times, but during most of his adventure, he does not conform to societal rules and places his needs and wants at the forefront, carrying on much like a king who is ruler of all that is around him and subservient to no one but himself. Pinocchio sums up his self-indulgent philosophy when he says, "Among all the trades in the world there is only one that really takes my fancy . . . it is to eat, drink, sleep, and amuse myself and to lead a vagabond life from morning to night" (Collodi 1985, 17). Does Pinocchio have a certain power because of his liminiality? Is there pleasure in this status that the reader gets to enjoy? Is that why the liminal space takes up so much of the book?

Turner says that in the liminal stage, along with the stripping away of one's old structure, a person must experience what it is to be low. In other words, Pinocchio must hit rock bottom in order to experience what it is like to be a part of humanity. Adversity and strife are common to all, no matter the social position of the person in society, and Pinocchio must experience and appreciate this adversity so that he can share a commonality with all of society. It is also important to note that in Turner's opinion, value is placed on the weak and downtrodden *if* they accept with humility what others ask of them. The acceptance of what society offers is part of the process of crossing over. Turner writes, "They [*liminals*] have to be shown that in themselves they are clay or dust, mere matter, whose form is impressed upon them by society" (Turner 1969, 103).

In order for Pinocchio to ascend and cross over into the third part of Turner's rite of passage and become a member of a new social structure (*reaggregation*), he must first experience a tearing down of his old ways if he is to be able to reaggregate and return to society as a changed person. Not until nearly the end of Collodi's tale does Pinocchio cross over or reaggregate. It is only after Pinocchio hits rock bottom that he is able to recognize the importance and value of his community, even if that community is composed only of his father and the Blue Fairy. Pinocchio puts the needs of others ahead of himself and sacrifices for the greater good of others. He changes, and with that change he effects change on the larger society that is humanity. By acting humanely, Pinocchio is rewarded by the Blue Fairy. She says, "Boys who minister tenderly to their parents, and assist them in their misery and infirmities, are deserving of great praise and affection" (Collodi 1985, 219). Once Pinocchio is stripped of his old ways, he recognizes a common human bond with society.

In applying Turner's theory, one would have to recognize that Pinocchio's actions represent an evolution in the individual that affects the larger society that in turn changes that society and makes it better. One would also have to recognize that the Blue Fairy herself represents a liminal figure that transforms in order to make Pinocchio complete. Her role as mother figure completes Pinocchio's creation story by including her as the female and spiritual object in the story. In addition, the Blue Fairy's role of Godlike deity is the safety net that helps Pinocchio successfully navigate the rites of passage. And it is in these rites of passage that Collodi's fairytale mirrors the struggle for acceptance experienced by all of humanity.

WORKS CITED

Carpenter, Humphrey, and Mari Prichard. *The Oxford Companion to Children's Literature*. New York: Oxford University Press, 1984.

Collodi, Carlo. *The Adventures of Pinocchio*. New Jersey: Watermill, 1985.

The Holy Bible, New King James Version. Nashville, Tenn.: Thomas Nelson, 1982.

Turner, Victor. *The Ritual Process: Structure and Anti-Structure*. Chicago: Aldine, 1969.

INDEX

ABOUT THE EDITOR
AND CONTRIBUTORS

Katie Elson Anderson is the Supervisor of Access and Collection Services at the Paul Robeson Library, Rutgers University in Camden, New Jersey. She is currently working toward a Master of Library and Information Science (MLIS) at Rutgers University, New Brunswick, New Jersey. Ms. Anderson holds bachelor's degrees in anthropology and German from Washington University, St. Louis, Missouri.

Holly Blackford (PhD, University of California, Berkeley) is assistant professor of English at Rutgers University, Camden, where she also directs the Writing Program. She teaches and publishes literary criticism on American, children's, and adolescent literature. She has recently published articles on Louisa May Alcott's *Little Women*, Emily Brontë's *Wuthering Heights*, J. M. Barrie's *Peter and Wendy*, Carlo Collodi's *Pinocchio*, Anita Diamont's *The Red Tent*, Julia Alvarez's *In the Time of the Butterflies*, Shirley Jackson's *Haunting at Hill House*, and Margaret Atwood's *Alias Grace*. Her book *Out of This World: Why Literature Matters to Girls* (2004) analyzes the empirical reader responses of girls to literature. She currently holds an International Reading Association research award ($9400) for the study of responses to *Huck Finn* and *To Kill a Mockingbird*.

Sarane Spence Boocock is emeritus professor of sociology at Rutgers University, where she taught in the Department of Sociology and the Graduate School of Education. Formerly, she was a research scholar at the Russell Sage Foundation, taught at Yale University, University of Southern California, and the Johns Hopkins University and was a Fulbright Research Scholar in Japan and a visiting professor and Fromer Memorial Lecturer at the Hebrew University of Jerusalem. Her most recent book, coauthored with Kimberly Ann Scott, is *Kids in Context: The Sociological Study of Children and Childhoods* (Rowman & Littlefield, 2005). She is also the author or coauthor of books, chapters, and articles in scholarly journals on the sociology of education, simulation games as learning devices, historical and sociological trends in family structure and family life, cross-cultural comparisons of childrearing, and the long-term effects of early childhood care and education programs. Her research has been supported by grants from the Carnegie Corporation, ESSO Educational Foundation, Russell Sage Foundation, Social Science Research Council, Spencer Foundation, Packard Foundation, and the U.S. Office of Education. She is currently engaged in a cross-national project on the educational experiences of minority children in Japan and the United States.

Vibiana Bowman is reference librarian and Web administrator at the Paul Robeson Library, Rutgers University, in Camden, New Jersey. Her areas of research include bibliographic instruction, community outreach, Web accessibility, educational Web design, and information ethics. Ms. Bowman is the editor of *The Plagiarism Plague: A Resource Guide and CD-ROM Tutorial for Educators and Librarians* (2004). She has published in various refereed journals, including *Library Hi-Tech, Internet Reference Service Quarterly*, and *Urban Library Journal*, and has been a presenter at local, state, and national conferences. Ms. Bowman is active in various national and state professional organizations. She is the president of the American Library Association's Library Instruction Round Table; and a past president of the New Jersey Library Association College and University Section/NJ ACRL and the ACRL Chapters Council. Ms. Bowman is also the Children and Childhood Studies Section Chair for the Mid-Atlantic Popular/American Culture Association. Ms. Bowman was selected by *Library Journal* as one of the "Library Movers and Shakers for 2005," an annual list that profiles "emerging leaders in the library world . . . who are innovative, creative."

Sean Duffy conducts research on a variety of topics including the development of quantitative reasoning and representation in children, category use in reconstructive memory, and cultural variations in psychological processes. Prior to working as an assistant professor at Rutgers-Camden, Dr. Duffy was a research fellow in the Research Center for Group Dynamics at the University of Michigan's Institute for Social Research, a visiting scholar at the Faculty of Integrated Human Studies at Kyoto University in Japan, and a postdoctoral fellow of the International Max Planck Research School on Evolutionary and Ontogenetic Dynamics in Berlin, Germany. Dr. Duffy received his PhD in Developmental Psychology from the University of Chicago in 2003.

Ellen Fennick is assistant professor of special education at Kean University in Union, New Jersey. Her interest in childhood studies developed during many years as a full-time public school teacher before her shift to university teaching and research. Dr. Fennick's extensive publications and presentations address issues concerning collaborative teaching, disability accommodations in multiple environments, and other inclusive practices affecting children and youth with disabilities. The use of assistive technology devices in schools is Dr. Fennick's current research priority.

Ellen Firth holds both a bachelor's degree in English and an elementary education certification from Rutgers University (2004). She currently teaches eighth grade at Woodbury Junior/Senior High School, Woodbury, New Jersey, and is pursuing a liberal studies master's degree at Rutgers University, Camden, New Jersey.

Sara Harrington is art librarian at Rutgers, the State University of New Jersey. Her research interests include nineteenth- and twentieth-century art and material culture, and library support and services for graduate students. She holds a master's degree in library science and a PhD in art history, both from Rutgers.

Theodora T. Haynes is business librarian at the Paul Robeson Library, Rutgers University, Camden, New Jersey. She is instruction coordinator, and her research interests include bibliographic instruction. She has been active in the Business Reference and Services Section (BRASS) and Reference and User Services Association (RUSA) of the American Library Association (ALA) for many years. Her MLS and MBA degrees are both from Rutgers University.

Amy L. Masko is assistant professor of English education at Grand Valley State University in Michigan. Dr. Masko's research interests include urban education, the intersection of race and schooling, school and home languages and literacies, critical race theory, and after-school programs and community-based organizations. Dr. Masko received her doctorate in curriculum and instruction from the University of Denver.

Chip Perkins is a doctoral candidate in the Anthropology Department at Southern Illinois University, Carbondale. His interests include early childhood education, discourse analysis, critical pedagogy, whiteness, autoethnography, and materiality. He is presently completing his dissertation that explores how people learn the culture of schooling in the United States. Chip's dissertation investigates how preschool and kindergarten children as well as the adults that work with them learn the skills to become students and teachers, respectively.

Kimberly Ann Scott was an associate professor in the School of Education and Allied Human Services at Hofstra University in Hempstead, New York, while working on this chapter. Currently, she is an associate professor at Arizona State University in the Educational Leadership and Policy Studies Department. As a sociologist of education and sociologist of childhoods, she is interested in race, class, and gender as intersecting features informing the academic and social developments of children in general and African American girls in particular. Scott's current project is a longitudinal multimethod study documenting the lives of the African American girls over time. This research also concerns how the girls' childhoods unfold given the interplay between their black femaleness and the sociopolitical climate of the district. Scott and Boocock examine children and childhoods through a global lens in *Kids in Context* (Rowman & Littlefield, 2005).

Laura B. Spencer is reference librarian at Paul Robeson Library, Rutgers University, in Camden, New Jersey. "The Onus of Originality," her contribution to *The Plagiarism Plague: A Resource Guide and CD-ROM Tutorial for Educators and Librarians* (2004), compared and contrasted student plagiarism to store brand package design and hip hop recording techniques. Her research and writing interests lead her to appreciate both disciplinary coherence and interdisciplinary flexibility.

Julie M. Still is reference librarian and library liaison for the History and English Departments at the Paul Robeson Library, Rutgers University, in Camden, New Jersey. She is the author or editor of a number of books, including the *Accidental Webmaster* and *Creating Web-Accessible Databases: Case Studies for Libraries, Museums and Other Non-Profits*, as well as chapters in other books. She has also written more than twenty-five articles for publications such as *History Teacher* and *Reference Services Review*. Ms. Still has an MA in history from the University of Richmond and an MA in library science from the University of Missouri. In addition to publishing, she has presented papers at conferences at state, regional, national, and international conferences and been active in professional associations.

Donna Wertheimer is reference librarian at the Paul Robeson Library, Rutgers University, in Camden, New Jersey. Her interest areas include library instruction, information-seeking behavior of college students, community outreach, and government information. Her passion for promoting the use of government information to students and faculty began during her career at Elmira College where she served both as a reference librarian and as the head of a federal depository library collection. She has been a presenter at local and national conferences and has recently coauthored an article with Ms. Bowman in *Urban Library Journal*.